How will Christians of the future sing?
As members of the universal Church, or not at all.

> — comment by a committee member, quoted
> by editor Eric Routley in his introduction,
> *Cantate Domino: An Ecumenical Hymnbook*

I am perpetually searching for meaning, but what in fact *is* meaning? Can I stop people from constructing this big dam as an epitaph for the annihilation of their selves? I can only search for the self of the I who is small and insignificant like a grain of sand. I may as well write a book on the human self without worrying whether it will be published. But then of what consequence is it whether one book more, or one book less, is written? Hasn't enough culture been destroyed? Does humankind need so much culture? And moreover, what *is* culture?

> — Gao Xingjian, *Soul Mountain*, written in despair
> on the news of the damming of the Yangtze River
> and the destruction of centuries of civilization,
> including artifacts from the Han Dynasty

[D]iversity is the engine of the evolution of living things,
including living civilizations.

> — Chinua Achebe, *Home and Exile*

The CALVIN INSTITUTE OF CHRISTIAN WORSHIP LITURGICAL STUDIES Series, edited by John D. Witvliet, is designed to promote reflection on the history, theology, and practice of Christian worship and to stimulate worship renewal in Christian congregations. Contributions include writings by pastoral worship leaders from a wide range of communities and scholars from a wide range of disciplines. The ultimate goal of these contributions is to nurture worship practices that are spiritually vital and theologically rooted.

Available

My Only Comfort: Death, Deliverance, and Discipleship in the Music of Bach
Calvin R. Stapert

Christian Worship in Reformed Churches Past and Present
Lukas Vischer, Editor

Gather into One: Praying and Singing Globally
C. Michael Hawn

GATHER INTO ONE

Praying and Singing Globally

C. MICHAEL HAWN

William B. Eerdmans Publishing Company
Grand Rapids, Michigan / Cambridge, U.K.

© 2003 Wm. B. Eerdmans Publishing Co.

Wm. B. Eerdmans Publishing Co.
2140 Oak Industrial Drive N.E., Grand Rapids, Michigan 49505 /
P.O. Box 163, Cambridge CB3 9PU U.K.

Printed in the United States of America

07 06 05 04 03   7 6 5 4 3 2 1

ISBN 978-0-8028-0983-4

www.eerdmans.com

For Collyn

Contents

Contents

Series Preface

In its evocative description of the coming kingdom of God, Revelation 21 teaches us that the "glory and honor of the nations" will be brought into the Holy City of God (vv. 24, 26). In this place of perfect worship and the immediate experience of God's presence, the culturally particular gifts of nations find a natural home. Attending choir rehearsals in the Holy City promises to be an unequaled multicultural musical feast.

In that light, reading this book should be not only an academic exercise but also an eschatological one. As it takes us on a global musical and liturgical travelogue, this book can train our minds and hearts to anticipate the coming of the kingdom of God.

It can also help us think differently about worship in our own congregations. The singing of global songs in Christian worship is nothing new. Songs have traveled over oceans and seas for centuries. But the global economy and internet communication have made our awareness of the broader world more pervasive and acute. Most denominational hymnals in North America now feature several selections from other cultures. Even more global is a culture of pop music that can now be heard in churches on every continent. Often, however, this global borrowing has degenerated into what Michael Hawn himself has called a "liturgical ethnotourism," in which we sing global songs, but with a patronizing attitude. We borrow memorable melodies and rhythms without looking at the people who make this music. We fail to ask how global songs and the people behind them might teach us to pray more honestly and proclaim the gospel more truthfully.

This book calls us to more. It both models and teaches humility. It challenges us to learn from wise mentors — worship leaders and musicians from four continents who have spent lifetimes honing Spirit-given gifts of discernment and leadership. It reminds us that this side of heaven, we will never have worship completely figured out. Even churches that never sing a song described in this volume can benefit immensely from what Michael Hawn can teach about what virtues we should aspire to in our worship. Speaking of eschatological hopes, I wonder: What would happen if Michael Hawn's approach became contagious? What if worship leaders in Christian churches looked harder for wise mentors than for temporarily contagious songs? What if our first response to other parts of the body of Christ didn't begin with "what can we criticize," but rather with "what can we learn"? What if we learned to assess our own culture's limitations and opportunities in a more balanced way by gaining perspective from global studies? What if we all thought of ourselves more and more as global Christians, in daily solidarity with some of the pastoral leaders described here?

At the very least, perhaps we would see how many of our little worship wars are actually quite primitive and provincial. Perhaps then we could be called once again to focus on the primary actions of worship to proclaim the gospel, offer honest prayer, celebrate the mystery of God's love for us in Christ, and express hospitality to a hurting world. May God's Spirit use Michael Hawn's Revelation 21 vision to renew our praise and revitalize our mission.

JOHN D. WITVLIET
Calvin Institute of Christian Worship
Calvin College and Calvin Theological Seminary
Grand Rapids, Michigan

List of Musical Examples and Figures

Musical Examples

Figures

Preface

Oneness has been a theme of the Judeo-Christian tradition from its beginning. The oneness of God was established in Deuteronomy (6:4). The oneness of Christ with God was established in John (10:30). Jesus prays repeatedly for the oneness of humanity even as he is one with his Father (John 17:11, 21, 22). The Epistles continue to embellish this theme in a variety of ways: "We, who are many, are one body in Christ" (Rom. 12:5);[1] "Because there is one bread, we who are many are one body, for we all partake of the one bread" (1 Cor. 10:17); "There is one body and one Spirit, just as you were called to the one hope of your calling, one Lord, one faith, one baptism, one God and Father of all, who is above all and through all and in all" (Eph. 4:4-6). This plea for oneness was not lost upon the nascent church. By early in the third century the Eucharistic Prayer incorporated a petition for oneness at the point of the *epiclesis:* "Gather into one all who share in these sacred mysteries, filling them with the Holy Spirit and confirming their faith in the truth, that together we may praise you and give you glory through your Servant, Jesus Christ."[2] This book is an effort to respond to the leading of the Holy Spirit to seek unity in the worship of the Christian church.

Make no mistake, however. The unity that has for centuries been the vision of Christ for the church and the petition of Christ's body gathered at the table is not a prayer for uniformity. While ethnic, socioeconomic, and generational diversity exists in every corner of North American society, there are

---

1. Unless otherwise noted, the biblical quotations in this book come from the New Revised Standard Version.

2. The Great Thanksgiving from *The Apostolic Tradition* by Hippolytus, ca. 215 C.E.

those who would seek a solution by gathering groups who are similar in many respects. This happens in all segments of liturgical life. Marketing strategies foster a hyper-atomization of society — "the world revolves around you" — at the expense of our common good and, in the case of worship, our common prayer. The disparate forces of ethnic diversity and the tendency toward personal satisfaction appear to be threatening the formation of Christian community in the United States, especially the sense of *ekklēsia* that binds together those called into the community of Christ. The tendency to worship in homogeneous interest groups aligns the church as a promoter of cultural fragmentation, allowing its members the sense of being with others without having to sacrifice their individuality. This practice leads to what Mark Searle calls "shared celebrations rather than common prayer."[3] Francis Mannion is on the same track when he speaks of the "intimization of society" or "the process by which social complexity is eschewed in favor of a model of human coexistence that puts ultimate value on bonds of intimacy, personal closeness, and radical familiarity."[4] Such an environment, Mannion concludes, fosters not so much a worshiping community but a gathering of politically likeminded persons. Strangers, especially those noticeably different from normative society in terms of race, socioeconomic position, and disability, may be "regarded as threatening."[5] The unity of the Christian community has never been based on ethnic uniformity — "There is no longer Jew or Greek" — social position — "there is no longer slave or free" — or differences in gender — "there is no longer male and female; for all of you are one in Christ Jesus" (Gal. 3:28). Our worship should not exacerbate the differences that divide us, but facilitate the unity that binds us together in Christ.

While music in its myriad cultural manifestations has been a metaphor of Christian unity since the beginning of the church, it is not the universal language that some glibly assume. Sung prayer may function, however, to bring unity out of diversity. This is not a unity forged through uniformity of perspective, but a unity that revels in the diversity of God's creation. Such prayerful song fuses the diverse themes of each community represented in the gathered body into a single melodic community of believers.

The power of singing to unify believers did not escape our apostolic forebears. Even before Hippolytus petitioned the Holy Spirit to gather the church into one, others recognized that the act of singing encouraged unity

---

3. Mark Searle, "Private Religion, Individualistic Society, Common Worship," in *Liturgy and Spirituality in Context: Perspectives on Prayer and Culture,* ed. Eleanor Bernstein, C.S.J. (Collegeville, Minn.: Liturgical Press, 1990), 37.

4. Searle, 37.

5. Searle, 37.

among the singers. Clement of Rome (fl. ca. 96) urged Christians to join their praise with the multitude of angels in praise to God: "Let us, therefore, gathered together in concord by conscience, cry out earnestly to [God] *as if with one voice,* so that we might come to share in his great and glorious promises."[6] Ignatius of Antioch (ca. 35–ca. 107) carried the metaphor further when he said: "*it is that Jesus Christ is sung in your unity of mind and concordant love. And to a man you make up a chorus, so that joined together in harmony and having received the godly strain in unison, you might sing in one voice* through Jesus Christ to the Father, that he might hear you and recognize you through your good deeds as members of his son."[7] Johannes Quasten suggests that the early church went as far as to reject polyphony and heterophony in favor of unison singing because singing a single melody together fostered unity among the believers. He quotes Clement of Alexandria (ca. 160–ca. 215) in support of this thesis: "We want to strive so that we, the many, may be brought together into one love, according to the union of the essential unity. As we do good may we similarly pursue unity. . . . *The union of many, which the divine harmony has called forth out of a medley of sounds and division, becomes one symphony, following the one leader of the choir and teacher, the Word,* resting in that same truth and crying out: 'Abba, Father.'"[8] Sung prayer not only symbolizes the unity of the church gathered, it is per se an act of unity. It is in this manner that it has transforming sacramental potential.

Integral to music's nature to encourage unity is its ability to forge an "enhanced group identity . . . as [people] together sense similar types of affect."[9] John Blacking is more specific about the potential of music as a unifier of disparate groups within a society: "Music can bridge the gulf between the true state of human being and the predicament of particular human beings in a given society, and especially the alienation that springs from the class struggle and human exploitation."[10] Rather than singing only in the style of one culture, raising our voices in sung prayer with the songs of Christians around

6. Clement of Rome, commenting on 1 Cor. 14:5-7, *Patrologia Graeca,* ed. J.-P. Migne (Paris, 1857-66), 1:276-77, trans. James McKinnon, in *Music in Early Christian Literature* (New York: Cambridge University Press, 1987), 18, italics mine.

7. Ignatius of Antioch, commenting on Eph. 4:1-2, *Patrologia Graeca,* 5:733-36, trans. James McKinnon, in *Music in Early Christian Literature,* 19, italics mine.

8. Clement of Alexandria, *Protrepticus* 9, as quoted in *Music in Pagan and Christian Antiquity,* trans. Boniface Ramsey (Washington, D.C.: National Association of Pastoral Musicians, 1983), 67, italics mine.

9. John E. Kaemmer, *Music in Human Life: Anthropological Perspectives on Music* (Austin: University of Texas Press, 1993), 148.

10. *Music, Culture, and Experience: Selected Papers of John Blacking,* ed. Reginald Byron (Chicago: University of Chicago Press, 1995), 171.

the world creates a parable of oneness in Christ. Mark Bangert uses the metaphor of varied cuisine to express the richness of sampling diverse, authentic musical styles in worship. He cautions us that "[g]reat cuisine is not an end in itself. Feasts and everyday meals are occasions for conversation and the building of community. It is across food that we get to know each other."[11] Musical anthropologist John Blacking speaks of living not *"for* culture" but *"beyond* culture."[12] Through a varied diet of sung prayer we may learn to pray *beyond* our provincial cultural experience as we offer intercessions for the world and, at the same time, live more fully *within* our cultures of origin as we feel less threatened. When a congregation engages in the ritual of intercessory prayer for the world, it is performing a priestly act of common prayer "for the sake of others."[13] Participating in sung prayers from other cultures, even the cultures for whom we are praying, may strengthen this act. Praying with forms from beyond our culture of origin broadens our experience of *common* prayer and deepens the sense of solidarity that is to some degree already a natural part of intercessory prayer. Intercessory prayer for the world provides a public ritual for living beyond our cultures of origin, freeing us to live more fully within our own context. It is within such a wholesome community that the strangers among us become welcome.

Chapter 1 sets the stage for this discussion by elaborating on the cultural dimensions of praying and singing globally, specifically in examining how we find meaning in music. Chapters 2–6 investigate in depth persons from around the world who have had a significant influence on global song in the United States and Canada through their musical compositions, hymnal editing, and appearances at workshops and major ecumenical gatherings. These persons include, in order, Pablo Sosa (Argentina), I-to Loh (Taiwan), David Dargie (South Africa), Patrick Matsikenyiri (Zimbabwe), and John Bell (Scotland). Drawing from the analysis of their contributions, chapter 7 explores the nature of musical structures that influence congregational singing from a global perspective, how these structures are brought to life, and how they support various parts of liturgical ritual. Chapter 8 proposes an office of liturgical leadership for the church, the office of the enlivener. In addition to describing the theological and practical dimensions of this office, I propose that it is embodied in Mary Oyer, a Mennonite church musician, missionary in Africa and beyond, and music professor from Goshen, Indiana. This chap-

---

11. Mark Bangert, "Welcoming the Ethnic into Our Church Musical Diet," *Cross Accent: Journal of the Association of Lutheran Church Musicians* 5 (January 1995): 7.

12. John Blacking, *How Musical Is Man?* (Seattle: University of Washington Press, 1973), 7.

13. Paul F. Bradshaw, *Two Ways of Praying* (Nashville: Abingdon, 1995), 64.

ter offers a brief background on her contributions to the field of global song. The final chapter, "Polyrhythmic Worship," employs polyrhythmic drumming, common in many cultures around the world, as a metaphor for the vitality that might be experienced in North American worship if congregations assume openness to a diversity of global worship rituals, prayers, and songs as well as to those represented by these forms.

This book may be read in several ways. Chapter 1 provides an overarching rationale for the study. Some sections of Chapter 1 may be passed over if the reader does not wish to reflect on the methodology of the book. Accordingly, the sections entitled "Purpose, Delimitations, and Methodology" and "Music and Semiology: Asking New Questions" may be omitted from the reading of the first chapter or returned to later if the reader so chooses. For those who may choose to use *Gather into One* as a reference book, Chapters 2-6 may be read independently of each other. While there is a cumulative effect of the presentations on the five major global mentors, these chapters have been written in such a way so as to permit them to be read in any order. In a few instances this approach has necessitated brief repeated sections of material presented earlier in the book. Rather than distract, I hope that this reinforces the ideas and makes the book more useable for those who cannot read it in its entirety. Likewise, Chapters 7, 8, and 9 may stand alone, to some degree, as essays on issues in multicultural music, though the previous five chapters present topics that lead, in my opinion, to the necessity of including these chapters in the book. The final three chapters do allude to the global mentors in Chapters 2-6, in a few places, but not in a way that would detract significantly from their understanding.

Any effort of this nature cannot be done in a vacuum. I am most grateful to the six global mentors — John Bell, David Dargie, I-to Loh, Patrick Matsikenyiri, Mary Oyer, and Pablo Sosa — who have allowed me to visit them on-site in their homes, discuss with me their vocations, and model a vision for the church by embodying a global sung faith. I have received the support of many of my colleagues at Perkins School of Theology for this project both formally and informally, including but not limited to Ed Aponte, Ruben Habito, Robin Lovin, Marjorie Procter-Smith, Ed Sylvest, and others who have been cited within the body of the manuscript for their help at specific points. Former church music students at Perkins, including Swee Hong Lim, Edgardo Macapili, and Arturo González Rivera, have been supportive in ways that they do not know. The international students for whom I serve as academic adviser have offered encouragement and support by responding to my attempts to sing songs from their homelands and integrate them into worship at Perkins. Beyond Perkins, Melva Wilson Costen, Terry MacArthur, Simei

Monteiro, John Thornburg, Paul Westermeyer, John Witvliet, and Carlton Young have been most helpful by example, encouragement, and specific insights at several places in the manuscript. Thanks to Marilyn Houser Hamm, Ken Nafziger, and Rebecca Slough for insight into Mary Oyer's work and witness. The Global Praise Project of the Board of Global Ministries of the United Methodist Church has sponsored events and published helpful resources that have made the research for this project much easier than it might have been. S T Kimbrough, Jr., Carlton Young, and Jorge Lockward have been gracious in inviting my participation in Global Praise events which allowed me to deepen my relationship with three of my global mentors: I-to Loh, Patrick Matsikenyiri, and Pablo Sosa.

Perkins School of Theology and Southern Methodist University have supported much of the travel necessary for conducting the research. Specifically I am grateful to Perkins for granting me a sabbatical leave during the 1998-99 academic year and to Southern Methodist University for two university travel grants for research in Asia and Africa. The Association of Theological Schools assisted in funding an earlier sabbatical in Nigeria and Kenya during the fall of 1989. The Louisville Sabbatical Grant Program, through the Lilly Endowment, provided critical financial assistance during my 1998-99 sabbatical leave that allowed me to visit South America, southern Africa, and eastern Asia. I am also grateful to countless congregations throughout the United States that have invited me into their sacred space to sing the songs of the world church — putting them into their mouths, feeling them in their bodies, and hopefully planting them into their hearts. Finally, I am most grateful to my wife Collyn, whose constant support and patience with my peripatetic schedule has allowed me to conduct this research.

When working with living people and continuously evolving cultural and political situations, an author may have difficulty wrapping up a book. Much of my on-site research took place during 1996-99. By the time of the publishing of this book, many things have changed in each of these countries that cannot be referred to in the body of the text. For example, Argentina has undergone a significant economic depression as the Argentine peso was allowed to float freely from the dollar. This has caused many to lose everything, increasing the marginalized ranks of people who must scavenge from trash bins or collect recyclable materials *(cartoneros)* to survive. There are reports that Argentina may default on its international debt, creating more hardship for a struggling people and further increasing the economic gap between the have-nots and the haves. South Africa has suffered increased economic hardship in the days following the presidency of Nelson Mandela. Since I was there in November of 1998, human suffering due to HIV/AIDS is becoming even more critical, draining the region of scarce economic resources. President Mbeke attempted to spread a false understanding of the disease by questioning the link between HIV and AIDS, adding further to the misinformation that many people have about the virus and its origins. Crime is on the rise as people become more desperate. Zimbabwe is in the throes of great civil upheaval as President Mugabe has permitted the takeover of white-owned farms in order to maintain his own political power. The result may be famine and starvation for thousands of Zimbabweans. Has there ever been a more important time for the Christian church in its myriad manifestations to pray and sing for the problems of the world?

MICHAEL HAWN
Perkins School of Theology
Southern Methodist University

CHAPTER 1

From Center to Spectrum

Praying and Singing Globally

So [Christ] came and proclaimed peace to you who were far off and peace to those who were near; for through him both of us have access in one Spirit to the Father. So then you are no longer strangers and aliens, but you are citizens with the saints and also members of the household of God, built upon the foundation of the apostles and prophets, with Jesus Christ himself as the cornerstone.

EPHESIANS 2:17-20

During the summer of 1996 I attended a conference of Asian Christians in Kuala Lumpur, Malaysia. Approximately fifty Asians from over twenty countries gathered to investigate the topic "Doing Theology with Asian Resources."[1] I was the only non-Asian observer at this event sponsored by the Programme for Theology and Culture in Asia, a theological forum growing out of the Christian Conference of Asia. As we listened to the diverse stories of those assembled, a recurring theme emerged: Can one be both truly Christian and truly Asian? Asian Christians often face a conundrum. While they are grateful to Euro-American Christian missionaries for a legacy of the good news of Jesus Christ, they are frustrated for feeling like cultural aliens in their

---

1. This conference was part of an ongoing program on this topic. A summary of the work of the first ten years can be found in *Doing Theology with Asian Resources: Ten Years in the Formation of Living Theology in Asia,* ed. John C. England and Archie C. C. Lee (Auckland, New Zealand: Programme for Theology and Culture in Asia, 1993).

own land. Euro–North American influences remain stifling, especially in the area of liturgical ritual and congregational song.

At one point in the conference a Malay woman stood and reframed the dilemma this way: "We need to remember that Jesus was born in western Asia and sought refuge in northern Africa." Then she seemed to look at me and concluded, "He never visited the United States." Her statement implies a struggle: Who is at the center of Christian experience and who is on the periphery? While there is gratefully some evidence that things are changing, liturgical practice in the United States rarely reflects the cultures in which the gospel originally took root — Asia and Africa.

Center versus Periphery Dichotomy

During the last thirty years of the twentieth century, a center versus periphery dichotomy has provided one model for viewing Jesus' ministry. The intentions of those who use this model are often noble, especially as they focus on the condition of poor, dispossessed, and marginalized persons at the "periphery" who do not share in the wealth, privilege, and power enjoyed by those at the "center." Similarly, scholars have also indicated that much of Jesus' ministry was with those at the periphery or margins of established authority.[2] While a center/periphery approach may offer some insight, any analogy has its limitations. In matters of liturgy and culture, the use of the center/periphery dichotomy may set up a de facto hegemony. The hope for a centripetal pull of the marginalized toward the economic center may be legitimate, but there are cultural and liturgical consequences that need to be considered if one continues to use this approach as a theological and liturgical model. The Asian Christians with whom I was privileged to meet in Kuala Lumpur found that the price for moving toward the Euro–North American cultural "center" of Christianity was very high, especially in terms of their identity as Asians.

In the letter to the Ephesians cited above, it is interesting that "those who were near" were the circumcised Jews and those "who were far off" were the uncircumcised Gentiles. The circumcised felt they were at the center of Christ's revelation while the uncircumcised were at the periphery. Paul renders the center/periphery dichotomy irrelevant; through Jesus Christ both those near and those far become "citizens with the saints and also members of the household of God." The good news then is a word of humility for those

2. For example, see Orlando E. Costas, *Christ outside the Gate: Mission beyond Christendom* (Maryknoll, N.Y.: Orbis, 1982).

who perceive themselves at the center, and a word of inclusion for those who sense themselves at the periphery.[3]

The center/periphery model subconsciously influences much of the discussion about liturgy in the United States, especially that related to music in worship. Within the normative culture,[4] "worship wars" seem to be raging between two main groups, each claiming to be at the center of worship life. This struggle is often expressed in a dichotomy that pits traditional versus contemporary worship groups against each other. Generally the "traditional" stream finds the source of Christian worship in the historical shape of liturgy, especially as it has been reclaimed in the ecumenical ferment since the Second Vatican Council (1962-65).[5] The "contemporary" stream proposes that worship

3. In Eric H. F. Law, *The Wolf Shall Dwell with the Lamb: A Spirituality for Leadership in a Multicultural Community* (St. Louis: Chalice Press, 1993), the dichotomy is between the powerful and the powerless. Law suggests that the powerful (wolves) should choose the way of the cross while the powerless (lambs) should choose the way of resurrection. See chap. 4, pp. 37-43.

4. I am grateful to David Maldonado, who suggested "normative culture" over other terms when referring to the prevailing cultural expectations of society in the United States as experienced in mainline religious denominations and portrayed more generally through the media. This term also refers broadly to cultural groups, e.g., those of Anglo-Saxon descent, that hold most of the political influence, economic power, and control of the media. It is not used as a synonym for "normal," nor does the dictionary definition of the term "normative" indicate that it is. Neither is this term used in the same sense as liturgical scholars do when they speak of "normative texts." In her book *Teaching to Transgress: Education as the Practice of Freedom* (New York: Routledge, 1994), bell hooks speaks of "whiteness" as a "norm ethnicity" (41). Mark R. Francis, speaking in the context of the Roman influences on the Catholic Mass, correctly notes in "Liturgical Inculturation in the United States and the Call to Justice," in *Living No Longer for Ourselves: Liturgy and Justice in the Nineties*, ed. Kathleen Hughes and Mark R. Francis (Collegeville, Minn.: Liturgical Press, 1991), that "There is no 'superior' or 'normative' culture by which other societies are to be judged 'civilized' or 'barbarian'" (86). For the sake of discussion, however, I find it necessary to use some term that communicates in this situation. I find "normative" preferable to "majority" (versus minority) culture and "dominant" culture.

5. Two representative books that articulate a "traditional" position are Marva L. Dawn, *Reaching Out without Dumbing Down: A Theology of Worship for the Turn-of-the-Century Church* (Grand Rapids: Eerdmans, 1995), and Donald P. Hustad, *True Worship: Reclaiming the Wonder and Majesty* (Wheaton, Ill.: Harold Shaw; Carol Stream, Ill.: Hope Publishing, 1998). Dawn speaks largely out of the mainline church context while Hustad voices concerns about contemporary worship practice as an evangelical. Robert Webber is an evangelical Episcopalian who, among others, encourages "blended" or "convergence" worship, a proposal to bring together the traditional and contemporary camps. Webber's *Blended Worship: Achieving Substance and Relevance in Worship* (Peabody, Mass.: Hendrickson, [1994] 1996), *Planning Blended Worship: The Creative Mixture of Old and New* (Nashville: Abingdon, 1998), and *Renew: Songs and Hymns for Blended Worship* (Carol Stream, Ill.: Hope Publishing, 1995) provide background and musical examples for this approach. See also Andy Langford, *Transitions in Worship: Moving*

should speak (and sing) in a language that reaches today's generation. Old structures are no longer relevant.[6] At times each is guilty of stereotyping the other's position. Important for this discussion, however, is the tendency of both perspectives to ignore or minimize voices beyond the normative "center" of cultural life in the United States. The traditional/contemporary dichotomy perpetuates a colonial mentality that denies the multicultural reality of society in the United States. The voices of minority groups or cocultures[7] within North America are either mute or barely audible on either side of this worship war.[8] I suggest that neither justice will prevail nor true reconciliation be found until all voices are heard at the table of liturgical discourse. Rather than a two-part dichotomy, questions concerning the relationship between the Christian liturgical tradition and contemporary culture need to be addressed within a multicultural conversation. A discussion between two groups that are largely normative in their cultural outlook can only render provincial, partial, and erroneous conclusions. Furthermore, those largely enculturated by normative societal values cannot fully become "citizens with the saints" if others remain "strangers and aliens," even in their own land.

Singing and Praying for the Sake of the World

This book offers an approach to worship where strangers and aliens become full citizens with the saints. It is about one of the most historical actions of

from *Traditional to Contemporary* (Nashville: Abingdon, 1999), and Martin Thielen, *Ancient Modern Worship: A Practical Guide to Blending Worship Styles* (Nashville: Abingdon, 2000).

6. The "contemporary" perspective is represented by the "seeker service" stream such as David L. Olsson, *Church Leaders Handbook: Willow Creek Community Church*, 2nd ed. (South Barrington, Ill.: Willow Creek Community Church, 1991, 1993), and Timothy Wright, *A Community of Joy: How to Create Contemporary Worship* (Nashville: Abingdon, 1994). The "praise and worship" stream is represented by Barry Liesch, *The New Worship* (Grand Rapids: Baker, 1996), and Michael Vegh, ed., *Praise Hymns and Choruses: Classic Songbook*, expanded 4th ed. (Maranatha Music, 1997).

7. I have chosen the term "cocultures" rather than "subcultures" in accordance with Larry A. Samovar, Richard E. Porter, and Lisa A. Stefani, *Communicating between Cultures*, 3rd ed. (Belmont, Calif.: Wadsworth, 1998), 10ff.

8. There are exceptions, such as the work of the Lutheran World Federation. See two volumes edited by S. Anita Stauffer: *Worship and Culture in Dialogue* (Geneva: Lutheran World Federation, 1994) and *Christian Worship: Unity in Cultural Diversity* (Geneva: Lutheran World Federation, 1996). Also Thomas Schattauer, Karen Ward, and Mark Bangert, *What Does "Multicultural" Worship Look Like?* ed. Gordon Lathrop (Minneapolis: Augsburg Fortress, 1996), and Mark R. Francis, *Liturgy in a Multicultural Community* (Collegeville, Minn.: Liturgical Press, 1991), to mention a few.

the gathered church — congregational singing. While music making is a primary symbol system in any given culture and, perhaps, a universal phenomenon of cultures in general,[9] music is not a "universal language" any more than the approximately four thousand discursive language systems worldwide can be understood universally. Music has meaning because of its context. Musical anthropologist John Blacking offers an assertion that is central to this study: "We must recognize that no musical style has 'its own terms': its terms are the terms of its society and culture, and of the bodies of the human beings who listen to it, and create and perform it."[10] Christian liturgy is the principal context for the music and musicians discussed in this book. Liturgy, however, cannot be limited only to the official gatherings of the body of Christ. In its original meaning of public service or work done on behalf of the people, liturgy may break out anywhere, at any time. The solo singing and dancing of a *cueca* in a public plaza in Chile by a spouse whose husband "disappeared" at the hands of an oppressive military regime may be liturgy. Liturgy may break out in a peaceful demonstration in Zimbabwe where friends of a person unjustly "detained" gather outside a government building to sing and speak on his behalf. The spirit of liturgy is present when young people, whose lives had only recently revolved around stealing and selling drugs in the *favelas* (makeshift slums of those without land) of São Paulo, gather in a neighborhood church to learn drumming and dancing to traditional music. When children from the slums of Bangkok meet each afternoon to learn traditional Thai instruments and dance, encouraged by Christian Thai musicians, liturgy is at its best. The Sunday liturgy is enriched when the unjust situations of life become part of the prayers of the people. The sounds and dances of life provide avenues for a "full, conscious and active participation"[11] by all who have gathered.

It is my hope that the reader will experience a cultural reorientation concerning the nature of congregational singing, including a greater diversity of song sources, a richer variety of cultural understandings, and a broader understanding about the way congregational song enriches worship. This may involve a process of learning to see our primary cultural orientation toward congregational singing (whatever that may be) not as the center of the singing universe of liturgical song by which all others are evaluated, but as

9. John Blacking, *How Musical Is Man?* (Seattle: University of Washington Press, 1973), 6-7. Blacking states that "There is so much music in the world that it is reasonable to suppose that music, like language and possibly religion, is a species-specific trait of man" (7).

10. Blacking, *How Musical Is Man?* 25.

11. "Constitution on the Sacred Liturgy," 14, from *The Liturgy Documents: A Parish Resource,* 3rd ed. (Chicago: Liturgy Training Publications, 1991), 12.

part of a spectrum of singing experiences that bear witness to the fresh breath of the Holy Spirit.

When the Western church views its particular heritage of hymnody as the center of congregational singing, we run the risk of setting up a "West versus the rest" dichotomy. Anthropologist Jack Goody suggests that dichotomies as structures for analysis between cultures are essentially ethnocentric.[12] I believe that a major challenge for worshiping communities in general and congregational singing specifically in coming years will be to move beyond an ethnocentric, them-versus-us dichotomy. Let us revisualize our hymnic cultural heritage(s) as part of a spectrum of congregational singing in which our inherited traditions are among many ways to sing and pray. Musical anthropologist John Blacking spoke of living not only "*for* culture" but "*beyond* culture."[13] Blacking expressed the need for musicians to become a bridge between the particular and the universal. The liturgical ramifications of this perspective are pregnant with possibility. Can we worship as fully when we are not aware of the ethnic aliens and strangers among us? Can we engage the diverse ministries of the Holy Spirit when worship reflects only a central cultural perspective and is not open to a wider spectrum of ways of singing and praying?

Gordon Lathrop poses the issue in ecclesiological terms when he notes that the primary "mission [of the church as assembly] may well be to maintain strong and healthy communal symbols of the truth about God and to do so for the sake of the well-being of the world."[14] Congregational singing is one of those primary cultural symbols that allow the Christian assembly to experience the liturgical equivalent of Blacking's "living beyond culture" — sharing in "communal symbols of the truth about God and to do so for the sake of the well-being of the world." Singing and praying for the world may be one way to learn to live beyond our culture of origin.

12. Jack Goody, *The Domestication of the Savage Mind* (New York: Cambridge University Press, 1977), 36.

13. Blacking, *How Musical Is Man?* 7, italics in original. The theme of living beyond culture was very important to Blacking and was reiterated later in *Music, Culture, and Experience: Selected Papers of John Blacking*, ed. Reginald Byron (Chicago: University of Chicago Press, 1995), where he says, "If the artist who expresses personal experience may in the end reach universal experience, it is because he or she has been able to live beyond culture, and not for culture" (240).

14. Gordon Lathrop, *Holy People: A Liturgical Ecclesiology* (Minneapolis: Fortress, 1999), 13.

A Starting Place: Distinguishing between Bias and Prejudice

Stepping outside our culture of origin is impossible. Few people learn to function equally well in two cultural worlds. In most cases those who do are members of cocultures within a normative society. These people are truly bicultural. While liturgy can be greatly enriched through bicultural leadership, this is not the goal of praying and singing globally. Those who live liturgically beyond culture become self-conscious about their bias. Through complex symbol systems, the cultural milieu provides the means for people to participate in society by preserving, transmitting, communicating, perpetuating, and developing knowledge out of all that constitutes meaning.[15] A healthy bias is inclusive of other worldviews and presupposes that there are other cultural ways of making meaning that are equally valid. Bias becomes prejudice when it assumes an exclusive posture toward other cultural perspectives, i.e., what Blacking calls "living for culture."[16]

It is easier to distinguish bias from prejudice when the latter is most blatant. Hilaire Belloc's famous statement made in 1920, "The Faith is Europe's and Europe is the Faith,"[17] could not survive the two world wars that took place before the twentieth century's midpoint. The decline of Christianity's influence within Europe during the second half of the century and continued atrocities in eastern Europe right up to the end of the twentieth century expose the fallacy inherent in this prejudiced assertion.

Musicians and musical theorists have also made bold claims about the superiority of the Western tonal system above all others. Deryck Cooke proposed that the Western tonal system was grounded in a natural harmonic structure. This "natural" system supplants less deserving musical styles: "Wherever Western European civilization has penetrated another culture, and set the people's thoughts along the road to material happiness, the tonal music of Western Europe has begun to oust the music of that culture from the people's affections."[18] While it is true that both classical and popular

15. From a classic definition of culture by Clifford Geertz, *The Interpretation of Cultures* (New York: Basic Books, 1975), 89.

16. The distinction between bias and prejudice is made in Alexander L. Ringer, "One World or None? Untimely Reflections on a Timely Musicological Question," in *Comparative Musicology and Anthropology of Music: Essays on the History of Ethnomusicology,* ed. Bruno Nettl and Philip V. Bohlman (Chicago: University of Chicago Press, 1991), 192-93.

17. Hilaire Belloc, *Europe and the Faith* (New York: Paulist, 1920), 261.

18. Deryck Cooke, *The Language of Music* (London: Oxford University Press, 1959), 55. For a more complete discussion of the assumption of superiority by Western musicians, see Anthony Storr, *Music and the Mind* (New York: Ballantine Books, 1992), 49-64.

styles of Western music have gained prominence throughout much of the world, Cooke falls short on at least two fronts: First of all, popular styles have always been modified and enriched by local musical traditions. Furthermore, the reverse situation is recently becoming quite common. During the last decade of the twentieth century, popular global music, especially from Africa and Latin America, has begun to influence popular music in the West, usually under the guise of "world music."[19] Second, the "material happiness" that Western civilization was to bring to the world at the time of Cooke's assertion in 1959 has turned out to be a combination of neocolonial exploitation and economic ruin, the latter often perpetuated by the indigenous leaders of nascent postcolonial nations. Regardless of one's views on the superiority of Western music, contact with western European civilization and its culture does not guarantee a journey on the "road to material happiness." Vibrant musical traditions are usually the result of cross-fertilization. Music, like the greater culture in which it participates, rarely stands in isolation, but adapts organically.

In the liturgical realm, the continuum between bias and prejudice is blurred by adherence to cultural preferences in liturgy under the name of essentials. Anscar Chupungco, whose theoretical work in liturgical inculturation has proven invaluable in sorting through the complex maze of issues surrounding the interaction of cult and culture,[20] lays a thorough foundation for the importance of language, especially the primacy of Latin, in shaping the thought processes of liturgical rites. The predominance of the Latin language resulted in a ritual ethos of "Roman sobriety" perpetuated through "a language addressed to the intellect rather than to the heart of the listeners . . . , a certain gravity in speech . . . , [and] a simultaneous redundancy and brevity."[21] Furthermore, a highly cultured Latin, compatible with the solemn ethos of the Roman basilica and, later, the Gothic cathedral, became normative for the Roman Church. This form of Latin was exclusive, accessible only to the most edu-

19. Some examples of this trend found in southern Africa are discussed in David B. Coplan, *In Township Tonight! South African's Black City Music and Theatre* (New York: Longman, 1985), and Fred Zindi, *Music Ye Zimbabwe: Zimbabwe versus the World* (Gueru, Zimbabwe: Mambo Press, [1985] 1997).

20. Chupungco's most notable books include *Liturgies of the Future: The Process and Methods of Inculturation* (Mahwah, N.J.: Paulist, 1989); *Liturgical Inculturation: Sacramentals, Religiosity, and Catechesis* (Collegeville, Minn.: Liturgical Press, 1992); *Worship: Progress and Tradition* (Beltsville, Md.: Pastoral Press, 1995).

21. Anscar Chupungco, "Eucharist in the Early Church and Its Cultural Settings," in *Worship and Culture in Dialogue*, 87-93. Essentially the same claims are made in *Worship: Progress and Tradition*, 25-30.

cated worshipers, and "failed to welcome the masses."[22] Roman sobriety, brevity, and directness often run counter to the more florid and sensuous temperaments of Oriental, African, and Iberian languages and the cultures they express. Roman sobriety, for example, may be interpreted by an African Christian worshiper as a lack of spiritual involvement.

An emphasis upon brevity also may stifle a physical response in worship. Movement is an expressive component that necessarily lengthens the liturgy as the assembly responds kinesthetically to repeated cycles of sound and a gradual intensification of the music. In cultural situations where dancing is dominant, an absorption with liturgical brevity curtails a full response to the word and sacrament. Directness, an attribute valued in the normative culture of the United States, may come across as rudeness in many other cultural settings where a measure of hospitality requires taking time to greet and share stories before discussing business. Therefore, many cocultures within North America appreciate longer gathering times of singing at the beginning of the liturgy. Yet vestiges of the Roman ethos dominate many congregations, Catholic and Protestant alike. When the ethos of normative cultural values in the United States becomes associated with the "high culture" of the Western classical tradition, preference for a particular style of worship could become an exclusive prejudice. What is seen as a matter of style by some becomes essential for others.[23]

The attitudes represented by Hilaire Belloc in the relationship between faith and culture, and Deryck Cooke in the area of music, and the liturgical ethos of the Latin rite, highlight the struggle that is always with us — a struggle between bias and prejudice. Moving from a center-based model to a spectrum-oriented understanding of worship practice is much more challenging than naively embracing the new, exotic, or quaint. Welcoming strangers and aliens in worship requires an intentional process.

Liturgical Plurality: Diversity of Songs — Unity of Spirit

In a consumer-driven society, congregations without a firm liturgical footing may fall into either meaningless eclecticism or efficient pragmatism as they plan for worship. There is, however, an evolving ecumenical consensus

---

22. Chupungco, "Eucharist," 93.

23. Mark R. Francis comments on the tendency of the Roman rite to hold on to this earlier ethos in spite of the reforms of the Second Vatican Council in "Liturgical Inculturation," 90-91.

around word and sacrament. This consensus is founded on the recovery of deep historical structures within the context of current cultural awareness. The purpose of this discussion is to explore briefly the cultural processes, theological ramifications, musical-liturgical perspectives, and ultimately new forms of sung prayer that might result from claiming liturgical plurality as an approach for Christian worship in the United States.

Paul Bradshaw posed the thesis that primitive Christian worship was not as uniform as has been assumed by some interpretations of earliest Christian sources.[24] He suggests that the range of worship practices of the early church throughout the world was diverse or "pluriform." Pluriformity extended not only to theological variations within different traditions, but to the very structure of rites and rituals.[25] In spite of moves toward uniformity of rite and ritual within major ecclesiastical traditions over the centuries, the church seems to be returning to liturgical variety once again. This is, however, different from the pluriformity of the first centuries c.e. During the early days of Christianity contact between congregations was minimal, often regional at best. While there is evidence that the liturgical practices of one group may have influenced others, the process of liturgical cohesiveness was very selective and slow.

Since the Second Vatican Council there have been several overarching trends in liturgical practice that are the result of ecumenical consultations. The areas of dialogue between Roman Catholics and many Protestant groups include the development of the lectionary and structural similarity in rites of Christian initiation and Eucharist. While the result of these discussions does not indicate conformity in theology and liturgical practice, many worship traditions have much more in common in the content of the lectionary and the general structure of the sacraments than in the days preceding Vatican II. Simultaneously, liturgical diversity has become more prominent as the process of inculturation has taken root in many areas of the world, especially in Africa, in Latin America, and to a lesser degree in parts of Asia.[26] The

---

24. Bradshaw refers especially to Gregory Dix, who stated in *The Shape of Liturgy* (Westminster: Dacre Press, 1945) that "the outline of the rite — the Shape of the Liturgy — is everywhere most remarkably the same after 300 years of independent existence in the widely scattered churches" (5).

25. Paul Bradshaw, *The Search for the Origins of Christian Worship* (New York: Oxford University Press, 1992), 54.

26. Paul Bradshaw sees the role of inculturation as "a hopeful sign, [but one that] still encounters considerable opposition in some traditions, and that even where it is accepted, it is usually only granted a limited role." "The Homogenization of Christian Liturgy — Ancient and Modern: Presidential Address," *Studia Liturgica* 26, no. 1 (1996): 14.

pluriformity of liturgical practice that was, according to Bradshaw, characteristic of the early Christian church in the first millennium c.e. corresponds in
many ways to a cultural diversity or liturgical plurality that is increasingly a
part of worship in the third millennium.

Aylward Shorter defines inculturation as "the on-going dialogue between faith and culture or cultures. More fully, it is the creative and dynamic
relationship between the Christian message and a culture or cultures."[27]
Anscar Chupungco enlarges on this definition: "[Inculturation is a] process
of reciprocal assimilation between Christianity and culture and the resulting
interior transformation of culture on the one hand and the rooting of Christianity in culture on the other. . . . [This] process of interaction and mutual
assimilation brings progress to both [worship and culture]; it does not cause
mutual extinction."[28] Inculturation has encouraged much more diversity in
style, especially in the areas of the arts — plastic arts, church architecture, liturgical furniture, dance, and music. The pluriformity of liturgical practice
suggested by Bradshaw in the pre-Constantinian church has found a parallel
movement of liturgical plurality in the late twentieth and now the twenty-
first centuries. While pluriformity was the result of relative isolation found in
the centers of early church worship, liturgical plurality — the diversity of
practice and style that exists in worship today — is, in part, the result of a
world that is extremely well connected. It is difficult to imagine a Christian
rite that has not been affected by liturgical plurality. If the Scripture is read,
hymns are sung, or the Lord's Supper and baptism celebrated, it is an experience imbued with cross-cultural understandings. Since this book focuses on
congregational singing, an example from the field of hymnology is relevant.
The Latin hymn "Corde natus ex Parentis" is the work of Spanish monk
Marcus Aurelius Clemens Prudentius in the early fifth century c.e. Prudentius was educated in law before turning to an ascetic spiritual vocation at age
fifty-seven.[29] His devotional poetry was widely read and became influential

27. Aylward Shorter, *Toward a Theology of Inculturation* (Maryknoll, N.Y.: Orbis, 1988),
11.

28. Chupungco, *Liturgical Inculturation*, 29. The term "inculturation" is derived from the
Latin *inculturatio* and is currently used almost exclusively when referring to the relationship between liturgy and culture. "Enculturation" is a term reserved by anthropologists for the social-
ization of individuals. John E. Kaemmer, *Music in Human Life: Anthropological Perspectives on
Music* (Austin: University of Texas Press, 1993), states that "A universal feature of human life is
the replication in every generation of the techniques, values, and symbols that characterize a
particular mode of human life. The instilling of these qualities in the young is called socializa-
tion or enculturation" (75).

29. See *Hymns of Prudentius*, trans. David R. Slavitt (Baltimore: Johns Hopkins University Press, 1996), for an orientation to Prudentius's hymns.

during the Middle Ages. As was the custom, many hymns were derived from much longer Latin poems. Such was the case with "Corde natus ex Parentis." Needless to say, the piety of a Spanish monk in the early fifth century is far removed from a twenty-first-century Christian worshiper. When we attempt to enter the world of Prudentius, there is a significant cross-cultural gap. However, his poetic reflection on the nature of Christ within the Trinity, growing out of the theological controversies of the fourth century, provides a transcultural content — that is, content that has relevance across cultures both in time and space — for the broader Christian community.

The melody that we know, DIVINUM MYSTERIUM, was used as a trope in Italian and German manuscripts from the twelfth through the fifteenth centuries. There is at least a seven-hundred-year gap between the text and the notation of the melody. During this gap, musical notation evolved considerably. Furthermore, the context of the medieval Mass was quite different from the fifth-century rite known to Prudentius. Another cross-cultural component was introduced by pairing the original text with this later tune.

In 1851 John Mason Neale, the guiding light of the Oxford movement in worship, architecture, and hymnody, translated and versified the Latin text into English as "Of the Father's Love Begotten." Translation always modifies the original, especially in hymnody where further restrictions of meter and rhyme must be observed. Even the opening line of the English translation varies significantly from the Latin poem, literally "Born of the Parent's heart." The English text was revised by Henry Williams Baker for inclusion in the first edition of the monumental *Hymns Ancient and Modern* in 1861. A doxological stanza was added to Prudentius's original poem at a later date.

Beyond the context of a fifth-century Spanish monk and a tune found in medieval Italian and German trope collections, the English translation added the imprint of mid-nineteenth-century Great Britain during a time when it was attempting to reclaim the glory of the medieval church, at least as England perceived that glory. England left another cultural imprint on this text by harmonizing the previously monophonic, unaccompanied melody with the organ and encouraging the text to be sung, not by just choirs or monastic gatherings, but by the congregation. This is a significant cultural change. For many of us the hymn comes down to us in our hymnals, more or less in the manner conceived by Neale and Baker in mid-nineteenth-century England.

The story is not over, however, as an increasingly complex cross-cultural situation continues to evolve. Federico Pagura, an Argentine bishop of the Methodist church and a fine poet in his own right, translated the original Latin poem into Spanish, a language descended from the proto-Catalonian native tongue of Prudentius. Though the Spanish of Pagura's Argentina is vastly removed in time and space from Prudentius's original tongue, the Spanish translation, "Fruto del amor divino" (1962), provides Spanish-speaking Christians a way to sing this great classic hymn in their own language. Furthermore, it is a way for contemporary descendants from the Iberian Peninsula to claim through song a sense of unity and identity with the church dating back to the fifth century.[30] The incipit of the Spanish translation, literally "fruit of the divine love," once again is a departure from the original Latin. "Fruto del amor divino" appears in *Mil Voces Para Celebrar* (1996), the United Methodist Spanish-language hymnal, with an organ accompaniment from *Hymnal 1940*, an earlier hymnal of the Episcopal Church in the United States. With Pagura's translation and the new harmonization, this classic hymn is given a thoroughly American (South and North) treatment.

The spirit of Prudentius's original poem pervades the versions we sing today. After several translations and adaptations, however, this is not the same poem as the original. Neither would the musical experience of singing this hymn today be similar to that of Prudentius's day. Depending on the version one sings, "Corde natus ex Parentis" is a cross-cultural mosaic of fifth-century Spain, medieval Italy and Germany, nineteenth-century England, twentieth-century Argentina, and the United States. While perhaps a more complex example than some, suffice it to say that whenever we sing Martin Luther's "A Mighty Fortress," Isaac Watts's "Our God, Our Help in Ages Past," Charles Wesley's "Hark, the Herald Angels Sing," Fanny Crosby's "Blessed Assurance," the anonymous American folk hymn "Wondrous Love," or Charles Tindley's "Stand by Me," we are entering into cross-cultural experiences that have countless permutations depending on translation, textual modifications, and musical arrangement.

While we may not always be aware of it, it would be difficult to worship totally in a monocultural environment. Liturgical plurality is already prevalent, even inherent, in current worship practice. Furthermore, those who attempt to create an environment in which worship is experienced only in the most recent normative monocultural terms, devoid of the influences of history or cross-cultural perspectives, are engaged in a futile effort. To the extent that they succeed, they distort the heart of the gospel they purport to share to contemporary seekers and believers. In attempting to become relevant to a

---

30. Pablo Sosa traces the development of Latin American liturgical music all the way back to Prudentius's hymn in "Spanish American Hymnody: A Global Perspective," in *The Hymnology Annual: An International Forum on the Hymn and Worship*, ed. Vernon Wicker, vol. 3 (Berrien Springs, Mich.: Vande Vere Publishing, 1993), 57-70.

specific cultural or generational group by eliminating all outside or unfamiliar cultural elements, be they historical or current, worship risks losing both liturgical memory and broader global awareness. Exclusion of traditional cultural components from worship in the name of relevancy for a specific group fosters a false Christianity conceived in the sterile environment of amnesia rather than in the abundant climate of *anamnesis*. To attempt to insulate worship from the multicultural environment of society in the United States today in the name of accessibility to a normative cultural group further divides the body of Christ. I propose that we continue to expand the cultural plurality that is already inherent in worship while holding to a central and historical structural core. What do I mean by liturgical plurality?

Liturgical plurality must not disintegrate into meaningless eclecticism and ephemeral experimentalism. There are seven general assertions that frame my understanding of liturgical plurality as a model for worship. First, liturgical plurality is not "ethno-tourism." Madeleine Forell Marshall, commenting on what she calls "Third World/liberation" hymnody, cautions us against this danger. Congregations should not be allowed to think that showing solidarity with others by singing global song is the same as "having fun in the sun in Mexico."[31] Liturgical ethno-tourism leads to the superficial stereotyping of cultures.

Second, liturgical plurality is not denying one's heritage of faith in song, prayer, and ritual. It is a conscious effort to lay one's heritage alongside another's and to critique each, learning from the experience. Bradshaw encourages an openness to "a much greater increase in variety of liturgical practice" balanced with "a greater attentiveness to tradition — to the whole of tradition and not just a selective sampling of it."[32] Margot Fassler and Peter Jeffery note the importance of maintaining traditional musical forms within the contemporary context: "Chant and polyphony will not go away, indeed they are more popular among some of the general public than they have been for centuries. Just as the church, while it must be open to new theological insights from every quarter, can never abandon its biblical and historical Greek and Latin heritage, so the church, while it must penetrate and redeem every culture in the modern world, can never forget its musical heritage."[33]

Third, liturgical plurality does not necessarily imply a synthesis of styles

---

31. Madeleine Forell Marshall, *Common Hymnsense* (Chicago: GIA Publications, 1995), 162.

32. Bradshaw, "Homogenization of Christian Liturgy," 14-15.

33. "From the Bible to the Renaissance," in *Sacred Sound and Social Change: Liturgical Music in Jewish and Christian Experience*, ed. Lawrence A. Hoffman and Janet R. Walton (Notre Dame, Ind.: University of Notre Dame Press, 1992), 115-16.

into one "universal" form. To the contrary, it is an acknowledgment of and participation in a diversity of voices within a liturgical structure. Inevitably a juxtaposition of styles causes them to influence each other.[34] Liturgical plurality implies, however, that we attempt to appreciate sui generis the contribution of each perspective to our understanding of God.

Positive assertions can also be made concerning liturgical plurality. Fourth, liturgical plurality is a *countercultural* expression of faith. As a countercultural stance, it calls into question the infliction of normative cultural values upon vital cocultures. In the case of various expressions of popular North American culture — music, movies, magazines, and video electronics, made available through a powerful and pervasive entertainment industry — liturgical plurality suggests that some components of popular culture may be inappropriate for liturgical use. Specific elements of North American popular culture may undermine or contradict the gospel. When under the intense influences of popular, media/market-driven forms of music and art, liturgy may be in danger of cultural captivity. As a *countercultural* practice, liturgical plurality may stem cultural captivity that would lead to the idolatry of a single cultural perspective.[35]

Fifth, liturgical plurality celebrates the incarnation as a *cross-cultural* manifestation of God's presence among us — *all* of us. This does not deny the validity of each person's culture of origin. The transcultural message of the gospel and the historical shape of Christian liturgy require myriad cultural means to express the reality of *logos* made flesh for all people.[36] Participating

34. Such cross-stylistic influences are manifest in a variety of ways, including the combination of text, melody, accompaniment, instrumentation, and movement from two or more cultures in the performance of a single piece of music. Depending on the social dynamics of these combinations, they may be viewed as liberating or imperialistic. I-to Loh explores some of these dynamics in "Contemporary Issues in Inculturation, Arts and Liturgy: Music," in *The Hymnology Annual*, 3:49-56. At what point these combinations become a synthesis of styles is open to question. In "Toward Contextualization of Church Music in Asia," in *The Hymnology Annual: An International Forum on the Hymn and Worship*, ed. Vernon Wicker, vol. 1 (Berrien Springs, Mich.: Vande Vere Publishing, 1991), I-to Loh prefers the term "syncretism," which he defines as "new compositions in the native style using traditional or contemporary Western harmonic idiom[s which are] skillfully integrated into a new composition. The melody may be native, but the harmony remains Western, thereby elements of both are syncretized" (95).

35. S. Anita Stauffer discusses cultural captivity in "Worship: Ecumenical Core and Cultural Context," in *Christian Worship*, 12, 21. Stauffer uses syncretism to describe this, an inappropriate relationship between culture and liturgy. In this way she differs from I-to Loh's use of this term above.

36. The concepts of transcultural, countercultural, and cross-cultural influences on liturgy are clearly stated in the "Nairobi Statement on Worship and Culture: Contemporary Challenges and Opportunities," in *Christian Worship*, 25-28. In this same volume Gordon W. Lathrop

in the incarnational experiences of others different in worldview from ourselves enables us to place in perspective our localized views of the Other who became one of us. Paradoxically, awareness of the universal may be deepened by experiences of the particular.

Sixth, liturgical plurality raises to our consciousness those who have been invisible to us[37] — listening to, learning from, and sharing in their prayers as we join with them in common intercessory prayer for the world. The "voice of the voiceless"[38] becomes heard in our worship in the embodiment of liturgical plurality in song and prayer. In short, liturgical plurality is making room at Christ's table for all those who have been formed in God's image.

Finally, liturgical plurality is essentially eschatological. It is imbued with hope for things that will be. Regaining a sense of hope that was evident in the early church depends on reclaiming the eschatological nature of the church. Bradshaw reminds us that "there seems to be a general consensus that in the earliest period of the Church's existence it was the eschatological theme which dominated eucharistic practice . . . combined with the remembrance of the death of Christ in the early Palestinian tradition."[39] In the words of the mystical Judaistic tradition of the kabbalah — a messianic spirit of reunion between the male and female that occurs every Sabbath — liturgical plurality is a "taste of the world to come."[40] Perhaps many shaped primarily by normative cultural

---

develops the role of the transcultural core or *ordo* and the countercultural critique in the process of contextualization or localization of liturgy in "Worship: Local Yet Universal," 47-66. The value of cross-cultural critique, though supported generally in multicultural settings, is less explicit in the book.

37. I am indebted to two writers who have opened to me an understanding of those who are invisible to many in church and society. Melva Wilson Costen explores this in the context of the African American church in the United States in chap. 3, "Worship in the Invisible Institution," in *African American Christian Worship* (Nashville: Abingdon, 1993), 36-49. Marjorie Procter-Smith raises this theme in the context of women as invisible throughout liturgical history in her book *In Her Own Rite: Constructing Feminist Liturgical Traditions* (Nashville: Abingdon, 1989), 14ff.

38. From Archbishop Oscar Romero's Fourth Pastoral Letter, "The Church's Mission amid the National Crisis," in *Voice of the Voiceless,* trans. Michael J. Walsh (Maryknoll, N.Y.: Orbis, 1985), delivered August 6, 1979. Archbishop Romero made this statement in his pastoral letter: "The church, then would betray its own love for God and its fidelity to the gospel if it stopped being 'the voice of the voiceless,' a defender of the rights of the poor, a promoter of every just aspiration for liberation, a guide, an empowerer, a humanizer of every legitimate struggle to achieve a more just society, a society that prepares the way for the true kingdom of God in history" (138).

39. Bradshaw, *Search,* 53.

40. Eliyahu Schleifer, "From Bible to Hasidism," in *Sacred Sound and Social Change,* 46. See 44-48 for a more complete description of the messianic influence of the kabbalah on Judaism.

perspectives in the United States have forgotten that the church as we now experience it is, at its best, a penultimate reality. Liturgical plurality, however, emphasizes that our worship is a reflection of a time that was, a mirror in many ways of current cultural reality, and "a taste of the world to come."

The eucharistic acclamations remind us that the choice is not among the past, present, or future, but that we participate in all three: Christ has died, Christ is risen, Christ will come again. Instead of contributing to a diabolical distraction between so-called "traditional and contemporary" musical styles, liturgical plurality calls us to devote our energies to becoming local congregations that pray for and with the world.[41] Rather than living for any one culture, the words of the Eucharistic Prayer invite us beyond the boundaries of any given cultural inheritance. We are called, in the words of the Preface, "*always and everywhere* to give thanks to you, [God] almighty, creator of heaven and earth."[42] We are invited, in the preparation for the Sanctus, "to join . . . our voices with angels and archangels and with *all the faithful of every time and place,* who forever sing to the glory of your name."[43] This book is an invitation to sing with the faithful of every time and place.

Purpose, Delimitations, and Methodology

The purpose of this book is to examine the context and songs of selected persons from around the world who have made major contributions to a worldwide view of congregational singing. Congregational song is one of the greatest areas of liturgical and theological cross-pollination. In the spirit of Vatican II, many denominational hymnals published in the United States after 1978 reflect a broad ecumenical perspective by including songs and hymns from a wide variety of denominational traditions, intentional ecumenical communities, and parachurch groups.[44] A few North American English-

41. This is a theme of Gordon Lathrop in *Holy People,* especially in chap. 2, pp. 49ff.

42. *The United Methodist Hymnal,* ed. Carlton Young (Nashville: United Methodist Publishing House, 1989), 9, italics mine.

43. While similar phrasing can be found in many Eucharistic Prayers, this one is taken from the *Book of Common Worship* (Louisville: Westminster John Knox, 1993), 319, italics mine.

44. Nineteen seventy-eight is the date of publication for the *Lutheran Book of Worship* (ELCA) and is generally considered the starting place for the most recent wave of hymnal revisions in the United States and Canada. The Hymn Society in the United States and Canada celebrated the twentieth anniversary of the publication of this hymnal at its annual convocation in Grand Rapids, Mich., in 1998. See the *Hymn* 49, no. 4 (October 1998) for papers delivered at this conference on this theme.

language hymnals, especially those published since 1987, also reflect liturgical plurality by including in varying degrees congregational songs beyond Euro–North American traditions. These hymnals and hymnal supplements display a growing awareness of and interest in songs from outside the normative culture of North America.[45]

A survey of forty hymnals published in the United States and Canada since 1976 provides data concerning ecumenical trends in congregational songs during the last quarter of the twentieth century.[46] This survey reveals a significant increase in congregational songs from four broad ethnic groups: African songs; African American hymns, spirituals, and gospel songs; Spanish-language songs; and Asian songs.[47] Rather than being monolithic musical traditions, each group contains a wide variety of subgenres and, in most cases, myriad languages, each influencing the style of the music. Carlton Young focused specifically on these groups and their inclusion in hymnals published in the United States in a paper presented to an international hymnological gathering in York, England, in July 1997.[48] General analyses in the increased use of world congregational song, introductory articles on the style of these songs, and possible use in worship are of great value.[49] But there remains a wide

45. U.S. hymnals with significant numbers of global hymns include *The Psalter Hymnal* (1987), *The United Methodist Hymnal* (1989), *The Presbyterian Hymnal* (1990), *Hymnal: A Worship Book* (1992), *Singing the Living Tradition* (1993), *The Chalice Hymnal* (1995), *The New Century Hymnal* (1995), *With One Voice* (1995), a hymnal and worship supplement to the *Lutheran Book of Worship* (1978), and *The Faith We Sing* (2000), a supplement to the *United Methodist Hymnal*. Canadian hymnals include *Voices United* (1996), *The Book of Praise* (1997), and *Common Praise* (1998).

46. See C. Michael Hawn, "The Tie That Binds: A List of Ecumenical Hymns in English Language Hymnals Published in Canada and the United States since 1976," *Hymn* 48, no. 3 (July 1997): 25-37, for data on the impact of world hymns on recent hymnals.

47. These are four groups singled out for a helpful discussion in Mark P. Bangert's article, "Liturgical Music, Culturally Tuned," in *Liturgy and Music: Lifetime Learning*, ed. Robin A. Leaver and Joyce Ann Zimmerman (Collegeville, Minn.: Liturgical Press, 1998), 363-78.

48. See Carlton R. Young, "Ethnic Minority Hymns in United States Mainline Protestant Hymnals 1940-1995: Some Qualitative Considerations," *Hymn* 49, no. 3 (July 1998): 17-27.

49. Mark Bangert has been one of the foremost interpreters of world congregational song to North American audiences. In addition to the article cited in n. 47 above, see Bangert's "Dynamics of Liturgy and World Musics: A Methodology for Evaluation," in *Worship and Culture in Dialogue*, 183-203; "Welcoming the Ethnic into Our Church Musical Diet," *Cross Accent: Journal of the Association of Lutheran Church Musicians* 5 (January 1995): 7; "How Does One Go About Multicultural Worship?" in *What Does "Multicultural" Worship Look Like?* 24-33. I have also made attempts to reflect in general terms about the use of world song in worship. See the following articles by C. Michael Hawn: "A Survey of Trends in Recent Protestant Hymnody: International Hymns," *Hymn* 42, no. 4 (October 1991): 16-25; "*Vox Populi*: Developing Global Song

cross-cultural gap between what appears on the page of hymnals and the perceptions of musicians and pastors who wish to bring these songs to life in local settings. Hymnal companions assist by providing, in varying degrees, background information on the general context of individual songs. In addition, some companions include articles on the context and musical performance practice of congregational songs from broad ethnic groupings.[50] Recent books on hymnology also refer to world song in general terms with some examples.[51] As helpful as these materials are, they rarely address in sufficient detail the kind of information necessary for a fuller understanding of these songs. The areas that need specific attention are (1) the general cultural context of each song, (2) the musical performance practice in the original or sending culture, and (3) the potential liturgical use of each song in the worship of the receiving culture, i.e., the cross-cultural component.[52]

This project examines world song in depth through the specific contributions of persons who arguably have been among those most involved in its composition and practice. I have delimited this book in two major ways. First, I have intentionally chosen not to include persons who represent cocultures within the United States, specifically African Americans, Latino Americans,

---

in the Northern World," *Hymn* 46, no. 4 (1995): 28-37; "Singing with the Faithful of Every Time and Place: A Proposal for Liturgical Plurality," *Reformed Liturgy and Music* 32, no. 1 (1998): 15-21; "Worshiping with *Hospitalidad*: Hispanic Worship Songs from around the World," *Reformed Worship* 50 (1998): 27-33; "The Rhythm of Community: Worship Songs from Africa," *Reformed Worship* 51 (1999): 33-37; "Praying for the World: Exploring Asian Hymnody," *Reformed Worship* 52 (1999): 28-33.

50. For example, the *New Century Hymnal Companion: A Guide to the Hymns,* ed. Kristen Forman (Cleveland: Pilgrim Press, 1998), includes specific articles: "A Brief Survey of Asian Indigenous Hymnody," by Swee Hong Lim; "A Survey of Hispanic Hymnody as Represented in *The New Century Hymnal*," by Raquel Mora Martínez; and "Ecumenical and Global Congregational Song in the Late Twentieth Century," by C. Michael Hawn. *Leading the Church's Song,* ed. Robert Buckley Farlee and Eric Vollen (Minneapolis: Augsburg Fortress, 1998), includes very helpful articles on Latino (José Antonio Marchado), African (Mark Bangert), and Asian (Lorraine Brugh) hymnody and performance practice.

51. See Harry Eskew and Hugh T. McElrath, "Cultural Perspectives," in *Sing with Understanding,* 2nd ed. (Nashville: Church Street Press, 1995), 219-35. Paul Richardson is including a broader range of world song in his forthcoming revision and expansion of Erik Routley's *A Panorama of Christian Hymnody* (Collegeville, Minn.: Liturgical Press, 1979).

52. I have attempted to offer more depth in one project using these three areas as a guide. See C. Michael Hawn, author and compiler, *Halle, Halle: We Sing the World Round* (Garland, Tex.: Choristers Guild, 1999), a global hymnal of thirty-six songs for children, youth, and congregation with a separate teacher's edition containing information for each song on general cultural context, musical performance practice, and liturgical application. A CD based on this collection was released in 2001.

and Native Americans.[53] These are worthy projects in themselves, and there is much work to be done here. In the case of African American contributions to congregational singing and recent hymnals,[54] there are significant studies already available written by African Americans.[55] The publication of Spanish-language hymnals in the United States, often drawing heavily on collections from Central and South America, was unprecedented during the last ten years of the twentieth century.[56] While there are many fine Latino American musicians,[57] Argentine Pablo Sosa has had the most profound impact on Spanish-

53. I have not ignored these groups in other articles and publications, especially African Americans and Latino Americans. In addition to articles cited above, see C. Michael Hawn, "The *Fiesta* of the Faithful: Praising God in Spanish," *Chorister* 49, no. 7 (January 1998): 11-13, 24-25; "A Survey of Trends in Recent Protestant Hymnody: African-American Spirituals, Hymns, and Gospel Songs," *Hymn* 43, no. 1 (January 1992): 21-28; "Worship That Transforms: A Cross-Cultural Proposal," *Journal of the Interdenominational Theological Center* 27, no. 1/2 (fall 1999/spring 2000): 111-33.

54. See Melva Costen, "Published Hymnals in the Afro-American Tradition," *Hymn* 40, no. 1 (January 1989): 7-13, for a general orientation to African American hymnals. Hymnals published most recently include: *Lead Me, Guide Me: The African American Catholic Hymnal,* ed. James P. Lyke (Chicago: GIA Publications, 1987); *Lift Every Voice and Sing II: An African American Hymnal,* ed. Horace Clarence Boyer (New York: Church Pension Fund, 1993); *This Far by Faith: An African American Resource for Worship* (Minneapolis: Augsburg Fortress, 1999).

55. A short list includes: Melva Costen, *African American Christian Worship* (Nashville: Abingdon, 1993); William McClain, *Come Sunday: The Liturgy of Zion* (Nashville: Abingdon, 1990); Jon Michael Spencer, *Black Hymnody: A Hymnological History of the African-American Church* (Knoxville: University of Tennessee Press, 1992); *We'll Understand It Better By and By: Pioneering African American Gospel Composers,* ed. Bernice Johnson Reagon (Washington: Smithsonian Institution Press, 1992); Wyatt Tee Walker, *"Somebody's Calling My Name": Black Sacred Music and Social Change* (Valley Forge, Pa.: Judson, 1979).

56. See the following, for example: *Flor y Canto,* ed. Owen Alstott (Portland, Oreg.: OCP Publications, 1989), a Roman Catholic hymnal; *Cáliz de Bendiciones: Himnario Discipulos de Cristo,* ed. Conchita Delgado (St. Louis: Christian Board of Publications, 1996); *Himnario y Libro de Adoración,* ed. Raquel Gutiérrez-Achón (Geneva Press and Westminster John Knox Press, 1999), a core of hymns published in several editions with worship materials appropriate for Episcopalians, Presbyterians, and members of the United Church of Christ respectively; *Libro de Liturgia y Cántico,* ed. Gerhard Cartford (Minneapolis: Augsburg Fortress, 1998), a hymnal for Lutherans (ELCA); *Himnos de Vida y Luz* (Independence, Mo.: Herald Publishing House, 1990), a hymnal for the Reorganized Church of Latter-Day Saints; *¡Cantad al Señor!,* ed. Otto Hintze and Carlos Puig (St. Louis: Concordia, 1991), a hymnal for the Lutheran Church–Missouri Synod; *Mil Voces para Celebrar: Himnario Metodista,* ed. Raquel Mora Martínez (Nashville: United Methodist Publishing House, 1996); *Celebremos su Gloria,* ed. Juan Rojas (Miami: Libros Internacional, 1994), a hymnal for evangelical Latinos.

57. I am personally aware of the contributions of the following persons to Spanish-language hymnody in the United States: Raquel Gutiérrez-Achón, a Cuban American; Jorge Lockward, a Dominican Republic American; Raquel Martínez, a Mexican American; and Carlos

language hymnody both as a composer, publisher, producer of recordings, and enlivener for global gatherings. Native American songs are the least-represented coculture in recent hymnals. The delicate relationship between the normative culture in the United States and Native Americans requires, I believe, a representative from one of the many Native American communities to pursue this work in order for it to have credibility and validity.[58]

A second delimiting factor has to do with the inclusion of those who have had the most impact on hymnals published in the United States and Canada during the last quarter of the twentieth century, not only through their own compositions, but through the collection of songs, the publication of hymnals in their own regions of the world, the production of recordings, and their participation in international ecumenical venues as enliveners of world song. The persons chosen for this book have made a sustained contribution in these areas for two or more decades. They are John Bell (Scotland), David Dargie (South Africa), I-to Loh (Taiwan), Patrick Matsikenyiri (Zimbabwe), and Pablo Sosa (Argentina). While by no means an all-encompassing list of possibilities,[59] these five people represent four continents and a wide ecumenical sweep. They, among others, have become for me global mentors in congregational singing.

The Road to Meaning in Music: Related Literature

The questions we are asking about music generally, and congregational singing specifically, are changing. Concerns of earlier eras continue to remain of interest, but when the answers begin to be recycled in various forms, it is time to ask new questions. A brief overview of related literature in musical aesthetics, psychology of music, and ethnomusicology reveals common trends. In each case there is a move from analysis of music as an isolated phenomenon or examination of musical artifacts (musical instruments, melodic structures,

---

Rosas, a Mexican American. I also appreciated the contributions of Skinner Chávaz-Melo (1944-92), a Mexican American.

58. See *Voices: Native American Hymns and Worship Resources,* ed. Marilyn M. Hofstra (Nashville: Discipleship Resources, 1992), for an introduction to Native American hymns.

59. For example, one could also include Jaci Maraschin and Simei Monteiro from Brazil, Geonyong Lee from Korea, and Francisco Feliciano from the Philippines. Also absent from this discussion is the flurry of hymnological activity in eastern Europe and Russia since the fall of the Soviet Union. The study of this literature demands special research skills and needs more time to discern trends. This literature has had very little impact on recent hymnals published in the United States and Canada.

musical scores, etc.) to a broader understanding of the cultural context in which the music takes place and, finally, to the question of musical meaning.

Aesthetic issues of the nineteenth and early twentieth centuries focused on defining beauty in music. Beauty was an objective truth to be sought for its intrinsic value without any reference beyond itself.[60] There was no question that the search for objective beauty in music, an overwhelmingly Western endeavor, was defined particularly in Euro–North American terms. The music of other cultures was rarely mentioned. Musical psychology focused upon the nature of sound *qua* sound rather than the context in which the sound appeared.[61] Scientific objectivity and quantitative measurement were the goals of this research. Objectivity was also evident in the nascent field of ethnomusicology, then called comparative musicology. The focus was on objective analysis, e.g., measuring the intervals of musical scales and defining the categories of musical instruments.[62] Western ways of thinking were superimposed on non-Western musical practice, resulting in what Philip Bohlman calls "acts of reformulating the exotic . . . [that] served to some degree as a means of extending the colonizer's power."[63] In spite of limitations, these approaches were necessary and often bore within them seeds for further reflection.

By the mid–twentieth century, however, the human factor became increasingly significant. Musical aesthetics began to link the qualitative analysis of music with the nature of human feeling and the ways in which art induced and objectified feeling. Leonard Meyer and Susanne Langer took the lead in this discourse.[64] Their discussions on the nature of human feeling within the context of music drew heavily from scientific analysis as well as philosophic theory. The comprehensive trilogy by Langer, *Mind: An Essay on Human Feeling*, reads in places more like a biology text than an aesthetic treatise.[65] At the

60. For example, see Eduard Hanslick, *The Beautiful in Music*, trans. J. Cohen (New York: Liberal Arts Press, [1891] 1957).

61. See Carl E. Seashore, *Psychology of Music* (New York: Dover Publications, [1938] 1967), and Hermann Helmholtz, *On the Sensations of Tone* (New York: Dover Publications, [1885] 1954). Vida Chenoweth continues this approach in *Melodic Perception and Analysis* (Ukarumpa, Papua New Guinea: Summer Institute of Linguistics, 1972).

62. For example, see E. M. Hornbostel and Curt Sachs, "Systematik der Musikinstrumente," *Zeitschrift für Ethnologie* 46 (1914): 553-90, and Curt Sachs, *The Wellsprings of Music*, ed. Jaap Kunst (New York: McGraw-Hill, [1961] 1965).

63. Philip V. Bohlman, "Representation and Cultural Critique in the History of Ethnomusicology," in *Comparative Musicology and Anthropology of Music*, 132.

64. See Leonard Meyer, *Emotion and Meaning in Music* (Chicago: University of Chicago Press, 1956), and Susanne Langer, *Feeling and Form* (New York: Scribner, 1953).

65. See Susanne Langer, *Mind: An Essay on Human Feeling*, vol. 1 (Baltimore: Johns Hopkins University Press, 1967), 33-69.

same time, the human dimension of art came to the forefront in John Dewey's *Art as Experience*,[66] in which the author argues that artistic experience is ordered by the same structures that give meaning to ordinary human existence.

Musical psychology took a more human turn with James Mursell's *Psychology of Music*,[67] which applied Gestalt psychology to musical perception and understanding. Leonard Meyer's research was influenced significantly by Mursell. The study of how human perception shapes patterns of sound was also an outgrowth of Mursell's work.[68] More recent publications relate musical experience to intelligence theory rather than the analysis of isolated musical stimuli.[69] The development of the field of music therapy during the last half of the twentieth century further humanized the relationship of music and behavior.[70]

Following the earlier insights of German comparative musicologists Erich von Hornbostel, Kurt Sachs, and Carl Stumpf,[71] Bruno Nettl's *Theory and Method in Ethnomusicology* developed descriptive field techniques and methods for the analysis of instruments.[72] Alan Merriam's *Anthropology of Music*,[73] published the same year as Nettl's text, charted a different course, however. He stressed the social and cultural context of music more than the descriptive analysis of music making. John Blacking's *How Musical Is Man?* followed Merriam's lead and asked new questions about who makes music and the context in which music is made.[74] The collection and analysis of folk

66. John Dewey, *Art as Experience* (New York: Capricorn Books, 1934).

67. James Mursell, *The Psychology of Music* (New York: Norton, 1937).

68. See Edwin E. Gordon, *The Psychology of Music Teaching* (Englewood Cliffs, N.J.: Prentice-Hall, 1971) and *Learning Sequence and Patterns in Music*, rev. ed. (Chicago: GIA Music, [1976] 1977).

69. See Howard Gardner, *Frames of Mind: The Theory of Multiple Intelligences* (New York: Basic Books, 1983), esp. chap. 6, "Musical Intelligence," 99-127, and John A. Sloboda, *The Musical Mind: The Cognitive Psychology of Music* (Oxford: Clarendon, 1985).

70. E. Thayer Gaston, *Music in Therapy* (New York: Macmillan, 1968), is the classic text although the research has moved much beyond Gaston's work today.

71. Dieter Christensen, "Erich M. von Hornbostel, Carl Stumpf, and the Institutionalization of Comparative Musicology," in *Comparative Musicology and Anthropology of Music*, 201-9, offers a brief tribute to these pioneers.

72. Bruno Nettl, *Theory and Method in Ethnomusicology* (New York: Free Press of Glencoe, 1964). Mantle Hood's *The Ethnomusicologist* (New York: McGraw-Hill, 1971) also reflects this interest, though his system of analysis differs from that of Nettl.

73. Alan Merriam, *Anthropology of Music* (Evanston, Ill.: Northwestern University Press, 1964).

74. In addition to *How Musical Is Man?* one can find the essence of Blacking's work in *Music, Culture, and Experience: Selected Papers of John Blacking*.

music within the United States brought the issues of cultural context closer to home. Figures like Cecil Sharp, Pete Seeger, and Alan Lomax developed a strong affinity for the music of common people.[75] Music became a source both for chronicling the struggles of the working class and for protesting the political status quo. More than one folk song collector was linked to socialism because of his or her close identity with the people who sang these songs.[76] The Nettl and Merriam streams of research come together in more recent works such as John E. Kaemmer's *Music in Human Life.*[77] Jacques Attali, in his significant book *Noise: The Political Economy of Music,* sets the stage for a discussion of musical meaning by relating music to class structures, suggesting that music is a predictor of and agent for social and political change.[78]

Hymnology also reflects this movement from objectivity to context and, finally, meaning as well. Following the great translators of Greek, Latin, and German hymns of the nineteenth century such as John Mason Neale and Catherine Winkworth, the century closed with John Julian's monumental *Dictionary of Hymnology,*[79] an amazing compendium of hymn texts and hymn writers. Literary analyses of hymns as poetry, scriptural allusions in hymn texts, placement of hymns within the context of church history, and the examination of hymnal collections provide the bulk of research during much of the century. The quality of a hymn text had to do with a combination of objective criteria including poetic quality, biblical foundations, and theological orthodoxy. John Bailey's *Gospel in Hymns,* still a valuable source, is an example of a book with these priorities. Bailey begins the shift, however, to cultural context, albeit in somewhat romanticized narratives of the original situation, by pro-

75. During their research from 1916 to 1918, Cecil Sharp and Maud Karpeles, e.g., lamented the loss of the "instinctive culture" of the Appalachian region as it came into contact with the "polite society" of modern civilization; see Cecil J. Sharp, *English Folk-Songs from the Southern Appalachians,* ed. Maud Karpeles (New York: Oxford University Press, [1932] 1973), xvi. Pete Seeger's collection and performance of protest songs is legendary. Alan Lomax, with his mid-twentieth-century research, provides extensive cultural background for each song in *The Folksongs of North America* (New York: Dolphin Books, [1960] 1975).

76. For example, James Porter discusses the relationship of Cecil Sharp to Marxism in "Muddying the Crystal Spring: From Idealism and Realism to Marxism in the Study of English and American Folk Song," in *Comparative Musicology and Anthropology of Music,* 113-30. One must mention the significant contributions during this era of Charles Seeger in several articles and Max Weber, *The Rational and Social Foundations of Music* (Carbondale: Southern Illinois University Press, 1958), who provide conceptual structures for understanding the fieldwork being done by others.

77. See n. 28 above.

78. Jacques Attali, *Noise: The Political Economy of Music,* trans. Brian Massumi (Minneapolis: University of Minnesota Press, [1977] 1985).

79. John Julian, *Dictionary of Hymnology* (London: John Murray, 1892).

viding tables of historical events and placing the lives of the hymn writers within the times they lived.[80] While the object and necessary efforts of cataloguing hymn texts and tunes continued right up to the end of the twentieth century,[81] Erik Routley (1917-82) was chief among those who helped to place the study of hymns squarely into the theological and liturgical arenas.[82] The outpouring of English-language congregational songs since 1960 reflects a wide variety of liturgical, theological, social, evangelical, and cultural concerns. More recent texts have attempted to articulate these concerns.[83]

In the United States contextual analysis of sacred folk traditions during the first half of the twentieth century led the way.[84] These studies focused not only on the internal structure of the songs themselves, i.e., poetry, scriptural and apocryphal allusions, melodic forms, etc., but also on the lives of the people who sang them, the spiritual values undergirding these people, the context in which they were sung, and the culture that shaped both the people and their songs. By the conclusion of the twentieth century, hymnological scholarship had begun to pursue contextual issues in more depth. The experience of congregational singing becomes an icon for spiritual formation[85] and understand-

80. John Bailey, *The Gospel in Hymns* (New York: Scribner, 1950). Bailey's narratives on the lives of the early Greek Fathers often read like historical novels. Bernard Braley's more recent series of books on hymn writers past and present, *Hymnwriters I, II, III* (London: Stainer & Bell, 1987, 1989, 1991), offers a significant step in providing contextual information about Western hymn writers.

81. The most notable text project is the Dictionary of American Hymnology (DAH) begun under Henry Wilder Foote in the early 1950s and continued under Leonard Ellinwood from 1955 to 1984. Today it is under the auspices of the Hymn Society in the United States and Canada led by Mary Louise VanDyke (Oberlin College) and Paul Powell (Princeton University). A classic discussion of hymn tunes is Erik Routley's *The Music of Christian Hymns* (Chicago: GIA Publishers, 1981) and a more recent source, *The Hymn Tune Index,* ed. Nicholas Temperley, 4 vols. (New York: Oxford University Press, 1998).

82. See, e.g., Erik Routley, *Hymns and the Faith* (Greenwich, Conn.: Seabury Press, 1956); *Hymns Today and Tomorrow* (Nashville: Abingdon, 1964); *Christian Hymns Observed* (Princeton, N.J.: Prestige Publications, 1982).

83. Harry Eskew and Hugh McElrath, *Sing with Understanding,* 2nd ed. (Nashville: Church Street Press, [1980] 1995).

84. These range from George Pullen Jackson, *Spiritual Folk-Songs of Early America* (New York: Dover Publications, [1937] 1964); Edward Deming Andrews, *The Gift to Be Simple: Songs, Dances, and Rituals of the American Shakers* (New York: Dover Publications, 1940); Ellen Jane Lorenz, *Glory, Hallelujah! The Story of the Campmeeting Spiritual* (Nashville: Abingdon, 1980); and Buell E. Cobb, Jr., *The Sacred Harp: A Tradition and Its Music* (Athens: University of Georgia Press, [1978] 1989), to African American gospel song and spirituals mentioned in nn. 54 and 55.

85. For example, see John D. Witvliet, "The Spirituality of the Psalter: Metrical Psalms in Liturgy and Life in Calvin's Geneva," *Calvin Theological Journal* 32, no. 2 (November 1997): 273-97.

ing sociological as well as theological perspectives in society at large.[86] The role of congregational singing as a ritual phenomenon in liturgy, especially in the spirit of Vatican II reforms, is a part of this contextualization and search for meaning.[87] Congregational song becomes a symbol of the experience of the gathered church, a means of ritual and spiritual formation, and a link between the church's liturgy and the people's common life. From this perspective historical events, political ideologies, human struggles, social organization, and deep cultural structures reflect on the creation and performance of a congregational song as much as its liturgical context, biblical basis, and theological foundation.

Music and Semiology: Asking New Questions

The meaning of a song as an event becomes a semiotic encounter in which an array of signs are taken into consideration in order to understand more completely the song's significance. A textual analysis alone will not reveal hidden "surplus meanings" that allow us to understand more fully what is taking place during a musical event. Mieke Bal refers to the process of using signs or exploring surplus meanings as semiosis. The semiological process has three distinguishable steps: (1) a sign-event takes place when something visible presents itself; (2) a sign-user or the one to whom the sign is addressed recognizes the sign-event; (3) the sign-event is interpreted.[88] The process of semiosis focuses on the activity of signs. "A sign does not exist but *occurs*."[89] Furthermore, signs empower the participants who share them to communicate about something that is physically absent. Singing a song in worship

---

86. This kind of scholarship that includes disciplines related to hymnology such as literature, psychology, history, and sociology can be found in Lionel Adey, *Class and Idol in the English Hymn* (Vancouver: University of British Columbia Press, 1988). A more recent example of a multidisciplinary approach to hymn analysis is June Hadden Hobbs, *"I Sing for I Cannot Be Silent": The Feminization of American Hymnody, 1870-1920* (Pittsburgh: University of Pittsburgh Press, 1997).

87. For a free church perspective on the nature of congregational singing per se, see Rebecca J. Slough, "'Let Every Tongue, by Art Refined, Mingle Its Softest Notes with Mine': An Exploration of Hymn-Singing Events and Dimensions of Knowing," in *Religious and Social Ritual: Interdisciplinary Explorations,* ed. Michael B. Aune and Valerie DeMarinis (Albany: State University of New York Press, 1996), 175-206. Edward Foley presents a complementary view of music in liturgy from an ecumenical Roman Catholic viewpoint in *Ritual Music: Studies in Liturgical Musicology* (Beltsville, Md.: Pastoral Press, 1995).

88. Mieke Bal, *On Meaning-Making: Essays in Semiotics* (Sonoma, Calif.: Polebridge Press, 1994), 9-10.

89. Bal, 9, italics in original.

from a cultural context beyond one's own provides a musical/liturgical *occurrence* even in the absence of those represented culturally by the song. A semiological approach allows us to examine the sung symbols of others separated from us in time and/or space. The sung prayers of the world church may become a source for understanding the worldview of others to some degree.[90] It may be possible to interact with them, though absent physically from the liturgical event, through their sung prayers and, in doing so, intercede more completely on behalf of the needs of the world. In moving toward this model, liturgy becomes more than meeting the immediate parochial needs of a gathering of believers. Personal petitions are addressed within the spectrum of human need. Rather than being centered on ourselves, our worship of God is grounded in the spectrum of human pain and joy, suffering and hope.

Musical semiology may shed meaning on the liturgical plurality that is inherent in Christian worship. Whether plurality is the result of musical occurrences on the time spectrum of human history or the space spectrum of contemporary cross-cultural musical confluences, meaning begins with experiencing and interpreting signs.[91] When approaching liturgical plurality from an understanding of musical meaning, one soon realizes that there is no universally meaningful musical experience.[92] Perhaps we may be advised to

90. I am grateful for Alyce McKenzie's insight at this point. She sees a complementary connection between Mieke Bal's approach and Paul Ricoeur's understanding of the reciprocal relationship between a reader and the text in the process of interpretation. Ricoeur moves beyond a mere interest in the original context to the "non-situational references which outlive the effacement of the first [original context] and which henceforth are offered as possible modes of being, as symbolic dimensions of our being-in-the-world." See Paul Ricoeur, "The Model of the Text: Meaningful Action Considered as a Text," *Social Research* 38 (autumn 1971): 536. Similarly, Bal understands that a sign-event or occurrence in its original situation may have meaning in a new situation through a process of interpretation. While original context is relevant, a sign-act may transcend time and space and bear a meaningful witness in a new situation.

91. Albert L. Blackwell presents a holistic view of the sacred in music that brings together transhistorical (time) and transcultural (space) dimensions along with a grounding in acoustical musical principles. His "reconstructive" approach in the recent study, *The Sacred in Music* (Louisville: Westminster John Knox, 1999), represents a grounding in semiotic thought (109ff.). Though grounded in Western musical traditions, his approach draws from a broader cultural awareness than earlier Western aesthetic approaches.

92. The ongoing struggle to find musical universality is one of continuing interest, especially to ethnomusicologists. David P. McAllester expresses the ambiguity of attempting such a task: "Let me venture the opinion, first, that there are probably no absolute 'universals' in music. I say this simply on the grounds of human variability and complexity. Any student of man must know that somewhere, someone is doing something that he calls music but nobody else would give it that name. . . . But I think there are plenty of near-universals and, even though such a term contradicts itself, a near-universal is enough for our purposes. I will be satisfied if nearly

speak of music as a language or experience founded on universal acoustical laws but given sonic presence (occurrence) in myriad cultural dialects.[93] These dialects become for the church ways in which the Word *(Logos)* has become flesh throughout the world. The more we become aware and attempt to enter into the worldviews they represent, the more distinctly we are hearing the voice of God and the more clearly we are seeing the face of Christ as the musical mosaic of the world's cultures reflects his face.

Sharing the musics of the world across cultures requires that one be aware of the dynamic between an "etic" approach — using only the methodology and analytical tools inherent in the culture of the researcher — and an "emic" approach — a process that takes into account the understanding of informants indigenous to the originating culture of the musical experience.[94] While hypothetically clear, the dynamic between the etic and emic becomes nebulous when one attempts to speak *on behalf of* another group *to* a group closer to one's own culture. What does this musical experience really mean in its original setting? Am I translating the experience accurately into my own terms or have I compromised the meaning of the original situation? How can I present the music in such a way as to maintain the integrity and authenticity of its original context, at least to some degree, while making the experience accessible to outsiders? This is a daunting task even for a veteran anthropologist such as Clifford Geertz:

> The besetting sin of interpretive approaches to anything — literature, dreams, symptoms, culture — is that they tend to resist, or to be permitted to resist, conceptual articulation and thus to escape systematic modes of assessment. You either grasp an interpretation or you do not, see the point of it or you do not, accept it or you do not. Imprisoned in the immediacy of its own detail, it is presented as self-validating, or, worse, as validated by the supposedly developed sensitivities of the person who presents it; any attempt to cast what it says in terms other than its own is regarded as a travesty — an anthropologist's severest term of moral abuse, ethnocentric.[95]

---

everybody does it." See "Some Thoughts on 'Universals' in Music," *Ethnomusicology* 15, no. 3 (September 1971): 379.

93. In taking this view I am influenced by Blackwell, 72, and ethnomusicologist George Herzog, who was quoted on this topic in Bruno Nettl, *The Study of Ethnomusicology* (Chicago: University of Illinois Press, 1983), 43.

94. The distinction between etic and emic is discussed in depth in Jean-Jacques Nattiez, *Music and Discourse: Toward a Semiology of Music*, trans. Carolyn Abbate (Princeton: Princeton University Press, [1987] 1990), 61ff.

95. Geertz, 24.

Given the dangers endemic to this research, the scholar must avoid romanticizing the cultures one studies and maintain humility in the knowledge that one's perceptions will always be modified by future encounters with the culture. The ethnocentrism inherent in cultural arrogance and romanticization of another's culture can be assuaged somewhat by participant-observer practices in liturgy and music. By entering into the worship of others and by learning songs, dances, and instruments from mentors in different cultural contexts as a participant-observer, one may employ signs that bypass verbal discourse and communicate the essence and meaning of the musical/liturgical occurrence in a more direct manner.[96]

For many readers, the analyses of the five mentors I have selected include more contextual material than is necessary or, for sure, customary for Western hymnological scholarship. I assure the reader that these analyses have been greatly reduced. They provide what I believe is the bare minimum to begin to understand what the musical experience of congregational singing means for each mentor and those they represent. Furthermore, the written sources cited may run far afield from the kinds of materials used in Western hymnological research, ranging from novels, poetry, historical documentation, political chronicles, and sociological accounts to liturgical and theological texts, ethnomusicological and anthropological descriptions, ritual studies, sound recordings, video recordings, interviews, personal narratives, and transcriptions of songs themselves.

There are two major reasons that such broad contextual background and wide variety of materials are brought to bear on these analyses. The first is that meaning making is a complex experience; the interpretation of meaning is interdisciplinary at its core. Mieke Bal reminds us that "as a field, semiotics constantly crosses the boundaries of other fields. As a discipline semiotics needs more fluid academic boundaries than those currently in place and reflecting the structure of departments established before semiotics gained credibility."[97] This kind of research demands the constant expertise of others in related fields. I am fortunate to have had the advantage of many col-

---

96. According to Kaemmer, *Music in Human Life,* observation alone is primarily an etic or outsider perspective and is usually more objective. The emic point of view is that of the participant (sometimes called commonsense perspective) in the culture and is thought to be more subjective. A participant-observer attempts to bridge the etic and emic continuum. There is always the danger that an outsider may change a situation either by observation or participation (14-15) As Nattiez states in *Music and Discourse,* "Even if we eschew the merely 'etic' approach, there is no longer any purely 'emic' approach; we are condemned to *dialogue* between the foreign culture and the culture of the investigator" (61, italics in original).

97. Bal, 5.

laborators with expertise beyond my primary areas of music and hymnology in order to conduct this study. New collaborations lead to new questions.

The second rationale for this approach is the need for what Clifford Geertz calls "thick description." Geertz reminds us that "cultural theory . . . is not its own master."[98] Thick description permits the interpretation of a sign whose meaning may be assumed in the original culture but whose occurrence may not have been perceived by an outsider. This description is an interpretation that may shed light on a ritual, dance, song, action, or combination of these for those who are outside the cultural realm from which these occurrences originate. Thick description in this book includes biography, historical summary, cultural analysis, political context, and liturgical perspective as well as musical description. It is also hermeneutical, asking four basic questions.

1. The personal question: What does this song mean for me?
2. The theological question: What does this song tell me about the God who became human?
3. The liturgical question: How does this song help me intercede before God on behalf of the world?
4. The ecclesiological question: How does this song help me welcome the stranger and make more room at the table?

These questions are informed by multiple interactions with the five mentors who are the subjects of this book, both within the United States and in their respective countries abroad. I am grateful for the hospitality they have afforded me, for the unselfish giving of their time, and for the analysis of my manuscripts, making corrections and suggesting clearer interpretations. The final product is my responsibility. I have attempted with much trepidation to find meaning in what they do and interpret this meaning for academic and liturgical communities in the United States. More than the collection of information and the verification of facts, it is this hermeneutical task of providing a structure for cross-cultural understanding that gives me the most pause.

A Liturgical Trilemma

Admittedly, I am asking the reader of this book — the person in the pew and chancel, the presider at worship, the church musician, the seminary student, or the pastor — to take on a heavy burden. I am asking all to examine congre-

---

98. Geertz, 25. The term "thick description" is borrowed from Gilbert Ryle.

gational singing and look inside it to see what it might mean in the liturgical and common life of a congregation. This request is the liturgical equivalent of the "trilemmic tension" that characterizes Mark Kline Taylor's view of the postmodern world. Taylor would have us simultaneously "acknowledge some sense of tradition, . . . celebrate plurality, and . . . resist domination."[99] While this is a difficult balancing act theologically, it is no easier liturgically. I would have us enter correspondingly into a challenging "liturgical trilemma": (1) evaluate and embrace the best of the liturgical traditions that have taught us to pray; (2) celebrate liturgical plurality — the manifestations of the incarnate One around the world — by sharing in the sung prayers of those who are outside our cultural context; and (3) resist liturgical centrism by placing our personal concerns within the spectrum of prayer on behalf of the world.

It is perhaps the recovery of a sense of eschatology in worship that is at the heart of this book. Worship that attempts to reflect a community where there are no "aliens or strangers" and all are "citizens with the saints" and "members of the household of God" may be glimpsed rarely. If we will listen to and sing with Christian communities around the world, the excitement of eschatology may once again capture the Western church as it did the early church. The liturgical relationship of the Euro-American church with the world church is no longer one-way — north to south or west to east — but reciprocal. Shared sung prayer within an environment characterized by liturgical plurality may be one of the most powerful symbols of our common future in mission and worship.

---

99. Mark Kline Taylor, *Remembering Esperanza: A Cultural-Political Theology for North American Praxis* (Maryknoll, N.Y.: Orbis, 1990), 20.

CHAPTER 2

The Fiesta of the Faithful

Pablo Sosa and the Contextualization of Latin American Hymnody

The Gospel is like a seed and you have to sow it. When you sow the seed of the Gospel in Palestine, a plant that can be called Palestinian Christianity grows. When you sow it in Rome, a plant of Roman Christianity grows. You sow the Gospel in Great Britain and you get British Christianity. The seed of the Gospel is later brought to America and a plant grows of American Christianity. Now when missionaries came to our lands they brought not only the seed of the Gospel, but their own plant of Christianity, flower pot included! So, what we have to do is to break the flower pot, take out the seed of the Gospel, sow it in our own cultural soil, and let our own version of Christianity grow.

D. T. NILES[1]

1. Quoted in Paul-Gordon Chandler, *God's Global Mosaic: What We Can Learn from Christians around the World* (Downers Grove, Ill.: InterVarsity, 1997), 16. The information for this article comes in large part from conversations between the author and Pablo Sosa in Buenos Aires, Argentina, August 17-31, 1998.

A briefer version of this chapter appeared under the same title in the *Hymn* 50, no. 4 (October 1999): 32-45. In addition to Pablo Sosa, I am grateful for the assistance of the following persons for their suggestions concerning this manuscript: Alan P. Neely and Arturo González Rivera for Latin American cultural background and refinement of translations, Per Harling for comments based on his long-standing friendship with Sosa, and M. Aaron Hawn for translation assistance. Their contributions have only served to improve this chapter. I alone remain responsible for any of its deficiencies.

D. T. Niles, the great Sri Lankan churchman and ecumenist, visited Buenos Aires in 1954 and made this statement in the Carnahan Lectures hosted by the ecumenical seminary now called Instituto Superior Evangelico de Estudios Teologicos (ISEDET). Pablo David Sosa was a student at ISEDET and recalls the tremendous impact that Niles made on the students and faculty. "He was the first Asian of renown that we had ever met. We were charmed by his stories and the folks songs that he sang to us from his native Sri Lanka." Niles, a major figure in the ecumenical movement of the World Council of Churches and a hymn writer in his own right,[2] asked the Argentine seminarians if they had any folk songs from their country that might be used as a basis for congregational song. Sosa said there were none worthy of the church. When Niles asked Sosa to sing one, he did. "You are fools for not using this music in the church," Niles responded upon hearing the song.

At that moment a seed was planted in Sosa which has led to a life devoted to cultivating the gospel in the fertile Argentine cultural soil. Sosa left for study in the United States at Westminster Choir College in 1954, and completed the four-year program in three years and one summer. While there he met a student from Brazil, Joâo Wilson Faustini. They talked about using the most popular forms of music from their countries in the church. For Argentina this was the tango; for Brazil it was the samba. Sosa wrote home and asked his father to send him some tangos.

> I tried to set [one tango] to a religious message in English, and I came more or less to the same conclusion as Faustini [my friend]: It can't be done.
>
> Why can't it be done? We said it was because there was a breach between the religious and the secular, and we did not recognize that the breach was rather between the culture with which we had received the Gospel (*el protestantismo*, if you wish) and our popular culture.[3]

But the plant of the gospel was slowly taking root in Sosa's Argentine spirit and would later blossom. This chapter introduces Pablo Sosa's attempt to overcome the "breach" between the culture of the missionaries that brought the gospel to Argentina and Argentine popular culture, and his con-

---

2. See Ion Bria and Dagmar Heller, eds., *Ecumenical Pilgrims: Profiles of Pioneers in Christian Reconciliation* (Geneva: WCC Publications, 1995), 168-71. In addition to writing many hymns, Niles edited the *EACC Hymnal* in 1963 for the East Asian Christian Council, an organization he founded.

3. Pablo Sosa, "Lo Latinoamericano Nuestra Música Liturgica," in *Todas Las Voces*, ed. Pablo Sosa (San José, Costa Rica: CLAI, 1988), 74.

tinuing efforts to sing the gospel in the diverse rhythms and memorable melodies of his homeland. Because his music grows out of an integral relationship with the religious life, ethnic diversity, history, and politics of Argentina, a brief overview of the general cultural milieu should provide a context for a richer appreciation of his contribution to Latin American congregational song.

Growing Up in Argentina

Before recounting the work of Sosa following his return to Argentina in 1957, we need to look more closely at Sosa's early life and the general social, political, and artistic conditions in Argentina during this time. Pablo Sosa (b. 1933) was the son of a Methodist minister. Much of his childhood before his tenth birthday was spent in Rosario del Tala, a small town in the province of Entre Ríos, where east European settlements and the lesser-known Protestant Italian Waldensians gave a distinct personality to the area. Being Methodist in a predominately Roman Catholic country in those pre–Vatican II years was not easy. His father had to teach English classes and his mother had to rent an extra room in the parsonage to make ends meet, further cramping the family into an already limited space. People in the town would at times cross the street to avoid walking in front of the church. Sometimes the disdain for the Methodist congregation was manifested by throwing stones at the church. The Sosa family moved to Buenos Aires when Pablo was ten years of age.

Between 1950 and 1972 Sosa received degrees from the Facultad Evangélica de Teología ([FET] ISEDET's previous name) in Buenos Aires, Westminster Choir College in Princeton, New Jersey, and Union Seminary in New York, and did further studies at the Hochschule für Musik in Berlin. He married Maria Amelia, who accompanied him to Berlin for study in 1960. "Vatican II (1962-1965) changed many of the negative attitudes toward Protestants," Pablo noted. His mother-in-law was Christian Missionary Alliance and his father-in-law was Roman Catholic. The officiating clergy did not approve of this "mixed marriage." Pablo recalls, however, that "following Vatican II my father-in-law started to go to the Methodist church on Sunday morning and my mother-in-law went to mass on Saturday evening. They participated in Bible studies together." The liturgical reconciliation that took place between his mother- and father-in-law in the days following Vatican II contributed to Sosa's ecumenical development.

Several aspects of Sosa's family life influenced his future direction and attitudes, including his devout Methodist home. Having spent many of his formative years outside of Buenos Aires seems to have helped him overcome an attitude of superiority over those who live in the country that is commonly held by the *porteños,* or those who live in Buenos Aires. Argentines born and reared in Buenos Aires commonly think of themselves as "sophisticated, glamorous and cultured," while the provincial folk were considered by the *porteños* to be "unsophisticated, ugly, superstitious and ignorant."

One does not have to talk long with Sosa to appreciate his solidarity with the rural folk of Argentina and the poor everywhere. Many who come from the country to work in Buenos Aires even today try to disguise their regional accents and blend in with the more urbane culture. Persons of color who might have some indigenous or African forebears are often labeled, somewhat derogatorily, *cabecitas negras,* or persons from the interior provinces. As we will see, Sosa draws much of his musical inspiration from the dances, instruments, and musical forms of the folk culture or *folclore* found alive in the provinces of Argentina.

Argentine Ethnic Demographics

The many musical styles of Latin America are often a mixture of the music of specific ethnic groups in a country. Determining a particular region's unique musical and cultural variety should take into account at least three broad considerations. First, what was the nature of the indigenous populations that existed before colonization and the degree to which these populations have been able to survive European domination. Second is the cultural matrix of the specific European colonial power (or powers) that claimed political control of a given country in the New World. While Spain was a major force throughout much of Latin America, Portugal, for example, colonized Brazil, and other European powers held political sway over smaller regions of Latin America and the Caribbean. A third factor was the introduction of slaves, most often though not exclusively African, into the culture and economy of various countries. The cultural matrix that has evolved in each Latin American country manifests the convergence of these broad ethnic, racial, and societal influences.

There may be a tendency for persons in the United States to view all of Latin America as an extension of Mexican culture or, depending on where one lives, Caribbean cultures such as Cuban or Puerto Rican, because of proximity. While Spanish is the dominant language in these three examples, Mexico has a rich indigenous heritage with approximately fifty languages spoken throughout the country. Among its indigenous groups, the Aztec and

Mayan empires were among the most developed in Latin America. The names of many cities and regions in Mexico reflect the influence of indigenous languages. Except for the Gulf Coast, where the Caribbean influence is stronger, the African presence in Mexico is negligible to the extent that a person of African descent would be considered an anomaly throughout most regions of Mexico. The mix of indigenous peoples, Spanish/European immigrants, and African descendants varies in each region. The culture in Cuba is distinct from that of Mexico. In Cuba the indigenous peoples suffered genocide and extinction at the hands of both Spanish conquerors and rival tribes. Africans were brought to live there in great numbers. In Mexico there were stronger tribal empires that made conquest more difficult, and African influence was relatively minimal.[4]

The situation in Argentina differs in many ways from that of Mexico or Cuba. The Spanish did not find a vast, indigenous empire among the original inhabitants of what is now called Argentina. Rather the country was sparsely populated by small, mostly isolated tribes that rarely numbered more than 150 people each. The Spanish colonizers began to arrive in the early sixteenth century both from Spain by sea and, later, overland from Chile, Peru, and what today is Bolivia. The British invaded Buenos Aires in the early nineteenth century but were driven out. Spain realized it could not maintain its hold directly on Buenos Aires and had to surrender authority to the *criollos,* Argentine-born colonists of pure Spanish descent. An autonomous government was set up by the May Revolution movement of 1810, though independence was not declared formally until 1816. José de San Martín led a legendary march across the Andes to Perú where, in 1822, he joined forces with the other great Latin American liberator, Simon Bolívar, who was slowly ridding the northern provinces of Spanish armies.[5]

African slaves came to Argentina with their Spanish owners beginning in the sixteenth century and functioned mostly as domestic laborers and artisans. Although Afro-Argentines constituted almost 30 percent of the population of Buenos Aires between 1778 and 1815, one rarely sees persons of African descent in the city today. One of the unanswered questions of Argentine history is what happened to the Afro-Argentine population. One theory is that they died in the yellow fever epidemic of 1871. A second theory is that they

4. For more general background on this topic, see Thomas Sowell, *Conquests and Cultures: An International History* (New York: Basic Books, 1998). See esp. chap. 5, "Western Hemisphere Indians."

5. See Brian Bell, ed., *Argentina* (Boston: Houghton Mifflin, 1997), 81, for this as well as for general information on the history, politics, and culture of Argentina. The parenthetical page references in the following text are to this work.

could not survive the horrible living conditions. A third is that they perished while serving in the special Afro-Argentine male battalions of the army. Many ascribe the disappearance to miscegenation or the mixing of races.[6] At any rate, it is rare to see persons of African descent in Buenos Aires, unlike, for example, Brazil, Cuba, or eastern Nicaragua. As we will see, however, this does not mean that there are not vestiges of the Afro-Argentines in the music and culture.

Buenos Aires is a city with a distinctly European *ambiente.* It would be difficult for many Argentines to decide if their primary identity lies with Europe or Latin America. One common joke notes that "the Mexicans descended from the Aztecs, the Peruvians descended from the Incas, and the Argentines descended from boats" (79). Although there is a minority population of mulattoes (whites mixed with Africans), Europeans came to this land of opportunity in great numbers between 1857 and 1939. These immigrants were primarily Italian (45 percent) and Spanish (30 percent), with smaller percentages from France, Poland, Russia, Switzerland, Wales, Denmark, Germany, England, and later Syria and Armenia (79). Today the uniquely Argentine demography consists of a total population of around 33 million, 85 percent of whom are of European descent while the remainder can be divided among small groups of Indians, mestizos (Europeans mixed with indigenous people), and non-Europeans (Arabs and Asians). Over 80 percent of the population is urban, with a third of the total population living in Buenos Aires (80). The demographic analysis that interests Pablo Sosa, however, is that the population of Argentina consists of roughly three economic groups: a third of the people have significant wealth, a third make up the Argentine middle class, and a third live in abject poverty.

Argentine Politics

Sosa's demographic analysis leads to a brief discussion of the political context of the country. Argentina is no stranger to despotic military regimes. The following brief overview highlights only a few of the most significant political eras in Argentine history following the revolution of 1829: the Rosas years during the early nineteenth century, the Perón legacy of the mid–twentieth century, and the more recent "dirty war" of the late 1970s and early 1980s. The intent is not to ignore years of civilian democratic rule and relative prosperity

6. These and other theories are discussed in George Reid, *The Afro-Argentines of Buenos Aires: 1800-1900* (Madison: University of Wisconsin Press, 1980).

in Argentina's history but to select representative events that have served as a crucible for shaping the Argentine political conscience.

Soon after the Spanish army was driven from the region, Juan Manuel de Rosas assumed political power in 1829, and "ruled much of Argentina as his personal domain for over 20 years" (43). Rosas was a wealthy landowner from the pampas, the open plains of Argentina, who ran the country as if it were his own *estancia,* or country estate. While he solidified power among the factious Federalists who lived in the provinces and demanded autonomy and equal standing with Buenos Aires, thereby unifying the country, he also institutionalized brutal methods of the rugged caudillos from the provinces. Atrocities included throat cutting, lancing, castration, and carving out the tongues of his enemies. Members of the Unitarian League who opposed Rosas often were subjected to brutal torture and executions. Many people, functioning as vigilantes, were caught up in Rosas's anti-Unitarian tactics (43-44).[7]

In the mid–twentieth century Juan Domingo Perón, whose tenure in power was only eleven years, had a profound impact on the country. Though he died in 1974, his influence is still felt in Argentine politics. His rise to power was engineered by Maria Eva Duarte de Perón, better known as Evita. Born in squalor, she convinced Perón that his real power base could come from the masses who lived in the *villas miserias,* or slums, that ring Buenos Aires. Because of their love for Evita, these *descamisados* (shirtless ones) rallied and demanded that Perón be put into power. They were called "shirtless" because they worked in wretched conditions in meatpacking plants and demonstrated politically in the streets without their shirts. The affection Evita bestowed on the poor and the political attention she drew to them have endeared her to the people to this day, nearly half a century since her early death from cancer in 1952. The passing of time has caused some to romanticize her story.[8]

The most recent difficult era in Argentine political life has been called

---

7. The Unitarians of Rosas's day were not a movement of theological or religious significance. Esteban Echeverría, a contemporary of Rosas, captured the horror of the time in his story "The Slaughterhouse" in Emir Rodríguez Monegal, ed., *The Borzoi Anthology of Latin American Literature from the Time of Columbus to the Twentieth Century,* trans. Angel Flores, vol. 1 (New York: Knopf, 1992), 209-22. In the story Echeverría, an anti-Federalist, describes a frenzied, hungry crowd who, driven by Federalist ideology, spot a suspected Unitarian young man and execute him on the spot in a manner usually reserved for animals in a slaughterhouse.

8. See Bell, 54-55, for a more complete description of Evita's life and influence. The musical *Evita* by Andrew Lloyd Webber and Tim Rice, and later (1996) a film by Alan Parker, brought her back into the international limelight. The film version starring Madonna "provoked outrage among many Argentines, who felt the sacrilegious popstar was sullying the name of their heroine" (Bell, 54).

the *Proceso* (process), a series of four successive military juntas between 1976 and 1983. The name comes from the amended constitution called the Statute for the National Reorganization Process. General Videla led a guerrilla action, now known as the "dirty war," during which the majority of those the government considered to be a threat "disappeared" or vanished without a trace. Anyone suspected of antigovernment activity could become one of *los desaparecidos,* or disappeared ones. Their estimated numbers range from 10,000 to 40,000 people. Reminiscent of the horrors of the Rosas era of the nineteenth century, the tactics institutionalized by the military junta during this time included the disappearance of nuns, priests, schoolchildren, and even entire families, all of whom were subjected to rape, torture, and murder by a nefarious coalition of military troops, civilian police, and right-wing death squads. The memory of these "disappeared ones" is kept alive by the *Madres de Plaza de Mayo* (Mothers of the Plaza de Mayo, a plaza in front of the seat of government in Buenos Aires). These women and their supporters gather every Thursday afternoon in the plaza that celebrates Argentina's independence, in front of the government building, to march in memory of *los desaparecidos* and to demand information from the government as to the whereabouts of their lost children and loved ones. They are easily recognized by the distinctive white scarves with blue embroidered lettering they wear. Many others gather in solidarity with them each Thursday and hear the stories of the *Madres,* some of whom have albums of newspaper accounts and personal photos to share.

Pablo Sosa is at the time of this writing the pastor of a Methodist church where, during the dirty war, two young women disappeared. Their only apparent "crime" was their involvement in social work to the poor. In many ways this congregation has never recovered from the loss of these young people; others of their age group have left the church, disillusioned by the loss of the two *desaparecidas* and the congregation's silence in the face of this loss. Although Argentina has returned to a democratic civilian government and has enjoyed relative political peace and stability since 1983, there are many who still refuse to discuss the atrocities of this era.[9]

---

9. See Bell, 51-52, for a brief but helpful description of the dirty war. I was able to observe and participate in a weekly march with the *Madres de Plaza de Mayo* during my visit in August 1998. Many were riveted to the television in the evenings during my visit, when video of the official inquiry into the atrocities of the dirty war was aired for the first time with sound over twenty years later (earlier versions had only pictures without sound).

A Heritage of Popular Argentine Poetry

As a prelude to an analysis of the work of Pablo Sosa, some background about the role of popular poetry in the daily life of Argentines may be helpful. As someone from the United States where the writing and reading of poetry seems largely to be an activity of the elite, I was amazed at what seemed to be the ubiquity of poetry as a means of popular expression. *La Nación,* one of the major newspapers in Buenos Aires, sponsors poetry contests. The works of the winners appear on the walls of the busy *Subte* or subway system that runs beneath the city. Much of the folklore of the gauchos, the Argentine cowboys who lived a life of freedom on the open range, or pampas, of Argentina, especially during the nineteenth century, is contained in poetry. It seems that the gauchos spent their evenings reciting or improvising poetry *(payadas),* as well as telling stories around campfires. One of the most popular poetry books, acclaimed "the national poem of Argentina," *El Gaucho Martín Fierro* (1872) by José Hernández, is available in several editions in virtually every bookstore. Hernández came to the defense of these Argentine cowboys who were often on the wrong side of the law yet were romanticized by the city people.[10] The availability of the lyrics of the famous tangos of Argentina in several editions indicates a broad interest in this popular poetic, musical, and dance form.[11] Even the *Madres de Plaza de Mayo* have expressed their grief through several collections of poetry.[12] While these examples are anecdotal, it seems that the art of poetry is in the air of Buenos Aires and integral to popular culture.

Pablo Sosa: Pastoral Musician

It is difficult to separate the various facets of Sosa's life for discussion, for they are interwoven into a graceful montage, each skill and creative sensibility reflecting on the others. The remainder of this chapter will reflect on Sosa in five perspectives: as pastoral musician, poet, contextual theologian, hymnal editor and recording producer, and ecumenical liturgist.

10. See José Hernández, *El Gaucho Martín Fierro* (Buenos Aires: Distribuidora Basilico S.R.L., 1997), with a special introduction, "Symbolism of Martín Fierro," by Leopoldo Marechal. For an excerpt in English, see Monegal, 1:235-39.

11. Héctor Ángel Benedetti, *Letras de Tangos: Antología de Tangos* (Buenos Aires: Macla, 1997), is an example.

12. For example, Rafel Cedeño, ed., *Cantos de Vida, Amor y Libertad* (Buenos Aires: Madres de Plaza de Mayo, 1985).

Sosa is an ordained Methodist minister and has served as an associate pastor in several parishes in Buenos Aires, including the First Methodist Church of Buenos Aires, one of the first Protestant congregations formed in Latin America. Since 1992 he has served as one of the pastors of Iglesia Evangélica Metodista de Constitución ("La Tercera"). The congregation is located near the Plaza de la Constitución in Buenos Aires, from which it draws its name. It also is referred to more informally as the Third Methodist Church. At the time of this writing he served with Pastora Mariel Pons, an energetic and articulate woman with whom he shares liturgical preparation and preaching responsibilities.

Many of his songs have been written with specific local congregations in mind and grow out of the particular needs of these communities. Let us look at three examples with reference to specific aspects of the Argentine contextual information presented above.

"El cielo canta alegría" was written in 1958 for a picnic of theological students. The *carnavalito* style used in this song is derived from the *huayño*, a kind of Argentine folk jazz. The pentatonic melody is derivative of an older, simple folk style. Note the arpeggiated bass line of an eighth note followed by two sixteenths and the use of percussion.[13]

Example 2.1. A basic *carnavalito* accompaniment pattern

13. For a helpful general introduction to the folk music of Argentina, see Isabel Aretz, "Argentina," in vol. 1 of *The New Grove Dictionary of Music and Musicians*, ed. Stanley Sadie (New York: Macmillan, 1980), 566-71. The rhythmic example provided is taken from *Libro de Liturgía y Cántico* (Minneapolis: Augsburg Fortress, 1998), 637. This hymnal includes thirty-five Latin American and Caribbean rhythm patterns in the "Apéndice de ritmos" (627-39). The index of titles suggests patterns that might be appropriate to use with specific songs. The *bombo legüero* indicated in the example is a tall tubular drum just under two feet in length and approximately seven inches in diameter, often with a snakeskin head. Cords attached to the head run the length of the drum. By sliding leather straps around the cords up or down, the pitch of the

After this initial effort, Sosa left this style for some time. Then, after completing his education at FET, he discovered that this song took on new meaning within the context of the political upheaval in Argentina during the 1970s. It was at this time that Sosa decided to change his political support to Perón, a move that he saw as showing solidarity with the suffering of the poor. Sosa's newfound social awareness was a kind of conversion for him in which singing the folk styles of his country became more than an exercise in cultural diversity. Singing the music of his native Argentina became a way of living out his faith. Thus teaching this *carnavalito* became not only a means of sharing a song of joy within the Christian context but a musical symbol for honoring the dignity of those suffering in poverty. The three stanzas demonstrate a progression from the glory of God to humanity (revelation), to the love of God for humanity (communion), and finally proclamation of this reality (proclamation). The joyful alleluias of the refrain contain exuberant ascending leaps and a wide range. The pitch reaches its apex on the final alleluia where it should be sung with energy and a brighter, more open-throated sound. Euro–North American styles of vocal production tend to use a more covered tonal quality which may diminish the song's climax. It is a song that demands the involvement of the whole body and a commitment to the spirit of the text.

"Miren qué bueno," based on Psalm 133, was written for the Flores Methodist Church in 1970, just before Sosa left for study at Union Seminary in New York. He uses the *chamarrita* dance-song form from the province of his early childhood, Entre Ríos. Influenced by that tranquil area, the dance uses simple, graceful steps. While the rhythm is similar to Caribbean styles, the *chamarrita* is a lighter, more peaceful form. Since it is a dance/song, those who know the style are inclined to move as they sing.

Sosa had been asked by the pastor of the Flores church to write a song for a fellowship occasion following the worship service. The pastor wanted to encourage a sense of communion among the members of the congregation, celebrating the joy of being together, both young and old. After choosing Psalm 133 as the text, Sosa inquired among his biblical colleagues at ISEDET about the meaning of oil running down Aaron's beard. He was told that it was an image

---

head can be adjusted. A drum ensemble may include two or more *bombos legüeros*. While the resonance differs, a set of bongos tuned to two different pitches can simulate the sound of the *bombo legüero*. *Cascabeles* are ball-shaped bronze bells two to three inches in circumference. They are used especially during the feast of the Virgin of Rosario on the first Sunday in October, where they are placed around the neck of a horse puppet carried over the body of a dancer during the procession. Information on these instruments is from Rubén Pérez Bugallo, *Catálogo Ilustrado de Instrumentos Musicales Argentinos* (Buenos Aires: Biblioteca de Cultura Popular, Ediciones del Sol, 1993), 39-41, 27-28.

Example 2.2. "El Cielo Canta Alegria," from *Cancionero Abierto,* Primera edición (Buenos Aires: ISEDET, 1994), 6

2. El cielo canta alegría, ¡Aleluya!
porque tu vida y la mía los une el amor de Dios. Aleluya . . .

3. El cielo canta alegría, ¡Aleluya!
porque tu vida y la mía proclamarán al Señor. Aleluya . . .

Words and music copyright © 1991 Pablo Sosa. Used by permission.

A singing translation by Sosa is as follows:

1. Heaven is singing for joy, alleluia!
for in your life and in mine is shining the glory of God. Alleluia . . .

2. Heaven is singing for joy, alleluia!
for your life and mine unite in the love of the Lord. Alleluia . . .

3. Heaven is singing for joy, alleluia!
for your life and mine will always bear witness to God. Alleluia . . .

Example 2.3. "¡Miren qué bueno!" from *Cancionero Abierto*, Primera edición (Buenos Aires: ISEDET, 1994), 4

2. Miren qué bueno es cuando los hermanos están juntos:
   se parece al rocío sobre los montes de Sión.

3. Miren qué bueno es cuando los hermanos están juntos:
   porque el Señor ahí manda vida eterna y bendición.

Words and music copyright © 1974 Pablo Sosa. Used by permission.

A singing translation follows:

Refrain: Behold, how pleasant, how good it is!

1. How pleasant and harmonious when God's people are together:
   fragrant as precious oil when running fresh on Aaron's beard.

2. How pleasant and harmonious when God's people are together:
   fresh like the morning dew that falls on Zion's holy hill.

3. How pleasant and harmonious when God's people are together:
   there is where God bestows the blessing, life for evermore.

of extravagance and joy. At the church social Sosa invited the people to think of other delightful images of extravagance. These were inserted into the song. Among those ideas offered was one by a child who said the joy of being together was like tasting the first ice cream of the hot summer, especially in January, the middle of the summer in the Southern Hemisphere. At the time this song was written, Sosa considered it more of a Sunday school song than something to be used within a formal worship structure. He was surprised when a colleague from ISEDET who had been present at the Flores church asked him to teach the "Miren qué bueno" to the faculty at the conclusion of a faculty meeting. It was this song that helped to launch Sosa's global career in 1978, when he used it at a Methodist Missionary Conference in Dublin, Ireland, at the invitation of Argentine Methodist bishop Carlos T. Gattinoni.

At this early stage (1970) of Sosa's understanding of the role of music in worship, he was only beginning to consider the possibility of using songs like "El cielo canta alegría" or "Miren qué bueno" within the regular liturgy. "Popular" songs were relegated to extraliturgical events only. As I witnessed in Buenos Aires, this reluctance is no longer the case because the congregation at Third Methodist Church sings them often on Sunday morning, sometimes more often than Pablo would like.

"Gloria" (Luke 2:14) was written in 1979 for a Christmas pageant. It was designed so that the entire congregation could join in the nativity drama at the time of the song of the angels. He chose the *cueca,* a lively partner dance/song between a man and a woman, as the stylistic basis for this song. The *cueca* is the national dance of Chile, which is also popular in Bolivia and parts of Argentina. The musical characteristics include a lively three-fourths versus six-eighths cross-rhythm.[14]

Example 2.4. A basic *cueca* accompaniment pattern

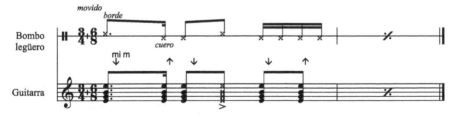

14. *Libro de Liturgia y Cántico,* 2. Sosa discusses how to teach the "Gloria" in "On Singing 'Gloria' (World Premiere in Heaven)," in *Global Praise 1: Program and Resource Book,* ed. S T Kimbrough, Jr. (New York: GBGMusik, 1997), 81-84.

"Gloria" was written during the Pinochet regime in Chile when, as in Argentina, the government institutionalized violence against its own people, resulting in *los desaparecidos*. As a form of protest, Chilean women whose husbands or sons had disappeared would gather in a public plaza and dance this seemingly joyful dance alone, with their missing partner only in their imagination. Sosa has composed a piano accompaniment that captures more fully the fiesta flavor of the *cueca*.[15]

Example 2.5. "Gloria, gloria, gloria," from C. Michael Hawn, *Halle, Halle: We Sing the World Round* (Garland, Tex.: Choristers Guild, 1999), 25

Words: Traditional. Music copyright © 1989 Pablo Sosa. Used by permission.

Orality and Community

"El cielo canta alegría," "Miren qué bueno," and Sosa's setting of the "Gloria" reflect characteristics of songs from predominately oral musical cultures through the use of repetitive forms such as refrain *(estribillo)* and repetition in each stanza, both of which make it easy to learn without written music. Oral tradition, or "orality" as Walter Ong calls it in his groundbreaking book

---

15. See S T Kimbrough, Jr., and Carlton R. Young, eds., *Global Praise 1* (New York: GBGMusik, 1996, rev. 1997), 27(a), for accompaniment. Sting based the song "They Dance Alone" on the experience of the women who danced without partners.

Orality and Literacy: The Technologizing of the Word,[16] assumes several characteristics. An understanding of some of these sheds light on how we can analyze these songs poetically, theologically, and liturgically. Issues of quality, however, cannot be discussed within the rather narrow parameters of traditional Euro–North American written poetry and music.

Oral cultures think "memorable thoughts . . . in mnemonic patterns, shaped for ready oral occurrence" (34). Mnemonic patterns are devices (such as a formula, rhyme, or repetition) used as an aid for remembering. In the three songs discussed above, two make use of words that are familiar to the Spanish-speaking liturgical community, "Alleluia" and "¡Gloria en las alturas a Dios!" Sosa repeats the word "Gloria" two additional times to increase its oral effectiveness. Even the refrain "¡Miren qué bueno, qué bueno es!" (literally "Look how good, how good it is") creates a mnemonic effect by the repetition of "qué bueno." In this case the repetition not only aids the oral learner but doubles the strength of "bueno," making the experience literally "twice as good." The repetition of the first two lines in each stanza strengthens the mnemonic character of the experience, especially since the text "Miren qué bueno" is repeated each time. Sosa uses this same approach in the stanzas of "El cielo canta alegría." Such formulaic expressions are part of the substance of orality as they "help implement rhythmic discourse and also act as mnemonic aids in their own right, as set expressions circulating through the mouths and ears of all" (35).

Ong suggests two other elements related to the repetitive nature of orality and how they affect content. Orality is "aggregative rather than analytic" (38) and "redundant or 'copious'" (39). In the case of the aggregative nature of orality, parallel terms, phrases, clauses, epithets, and other repetitive devices are essential to oral transmission; yet they often come across as clichés in written discourse. Sequential Hegelian-style analysis does not work well in the oral process. The copious nature of orality recognizes that the oral process establishes a totality of experience or oral gestalt better than a linear continuity, the latter being the domain of the print medium. New ideas are introduced in the stanzas of "El cielo canta alegría" and "Miren qué bueno," but only after significant repetition and with as few words as possible. There is a limited sequential growth of an idea, but the overwhelming experience is one of the totality of joy in both cases. The words and music are crafted to give shape and structure to ecstatic communal experience.

16. Walter J. Ong, *Orality and Literacy: The Technologizing of the Word* (New York: Routledge, 1982, 1988). Page numbers in the body of the text throughout this section refer to this book.

The communal implications of orality are many. In discussing the "conservative or traditionalist" nature of orality, Ong notes that "in a primary oral culture conceptualized knowledge that is not repeated aloud soon vanishes . . . oral societies must invest great energy in saying over and over again what has been learned through the ages" (41). Originality, an important feature of written discourse, is expressed differently in oral cultures. Rather than creating new stories, the creativity comes in relating old stories to new contexts. The audience has to be brought into the story so that they can participate energetically (42). The contextual comments behind the songs discussed above indicate Sosa's keen awareness of relating familiar Scripture to the lives of the people. When singing by means of oral tradition, this awareness happens on several levels at once. The text is chosen to fit specific social or liturgical situations, and the music (dance/songs) recalls the communal actions familiar to the participating group. Evaluation of the experience resides not in the composer's or poet's ability to relate new information or original ideas, but to transmit time-honored truths to a particular community in such a manner that it allows them to participate fully in its meaning. In this sense the hermeneutical nature of the experience far outweighs the individual cleverness of the author or the originality of the composer. The degree to which the identity of the composer/author is subsumed and embodied by the particular gathered community without the assistance of written aids determines to a large extent the validity and quality of the experience.

A related feature of orality is that it is "close to the human lifeworld" (42). It is common for songs from Latin American sources to mention animals or fauna specific to a locale or the names of places known to all the singers.[17] The musical dimension of the songs discussed above functions to bring these songs close to the "human lifeworld" of the singer without saying a word. By using musical/dance forms drawn from the "soil" of provincial *folklórico*, there is an underlying incarnational dimension to the experience. Sosa also demonstrated this when he introduced "Miren qué bueno" to those gathered at a picnic and asked them to suggest metaphors for community that could be inserted into the body of the song.

---

17. For example, see the song "Alabanza" (Praise) that cites plants and birds typical to Puerto Rico. It can be found in several sources, including the United Methodist Spanish-language hymnal, *Mil Voces Para Celebrar* (51), and the ELCA Spanish-language hymnal, *Libro de Liturgia y Cántico* (496). Another example is Guillermo Cuéllar's entrance song, "Vamos todos al banquete" (Let us all go to the banquet), from his *Misa salvadoreña*. The second stanza lists the names of *barrios* (neighborhoods) in San Salvador from which people would be traveling to Mass. See *Libro de Liturgia y Cántico* (410). Texts do not need to be this explicit, however, to be related to the life circumstances of the people.

One of the most interesting features of orality uncovered by Ong is that the products of oral experience are often "agonistically toned" (43). "Writing fosters abstractions that disengage knowledge from the arena where human beings struggle with one another. It separates the knower from the known. By keeping knowledge embedded in the human lifeworld, orality situates knowledge within a context of struggle" (43-44). The texts of the dance/songs are ostensibly about joy, but their musical and kinesthetic substance links the participants to the struggle of those represented by the music. The portability of oral forms allows them to be more easily taken to the places where and when similar struggles transpire. Sosa's setting of the song of the angels, "Gloria," with its subtext of the *cueca* danced without a requisite partner *(el desaparecido)* due to political malevolence, is perhaps the most dramatic example of the agonistic nature of orality. It raises the paradox of joy in the midst of struggle, the essence of fiesta, a sacred/secular celebration of food, dancing, and fellowship.

The Fiesta of the Faithful

Sosa's congregational forms explored thus far are dance/songs rather than hymns in the more traditional Euro–North American sense. Those who understand the original context of the musical style will often want to move and clap the rhythm of the particular dance. These three examples embody the spirit of fiesta. Those in the United States may be tempted to trivialize the fiesta as a kind of cultural party, but, as Sosa explains, it is much more in Spanish tradition. "Out of oppression, men and women rise up to celebrate, not forgetting their struggle, to be nurtured by the sweet foretastes of the great fiesta of victory and liberation. It is not ordinary fiesta, intended to have people forget about their worries, to alienate them. It is the fiesta which liberates. For this reason it is said: 'People who have no strength to celebrate, have no strength to liberate themselves.'"[18]

Much of Sosa's music contributes to the fiesta of the faithful as they gather to celebrate in the face of oppression and struggle. By using musical forms associated with various provincial cocultures,[19] Sosa evokes less obvious

18. Pablo Sosa, "Spanish American Hymnody: A Global Perspective," in *Hymnology Annual,* ed. Vernon Wicker, vol. 3 (Berrien Springs, Mich.: Vande Vere Publishing, 1993), 68. In addition to the discussion on fiesta here, I refer the reader to an effective presentation on this topic by Pedrito U. Maynard-Reid, in *Diverse Worship: African-American, Caribbean, and Hispanic Perspectives* (Downers Grove, Ill.: InterVarsity, 2000), 162-86.

19. I have chosen the term "cocultures" rather than "subcultures" in accordance with

layers of meaning embedded in the music of the dance/songs. These meanings interplay freely with the text he has chosen. There is much more going on than the literal communication of a text. There is the paradox of a simultaneous identification with pain, struggle, and oppression on the one hand and the celebration of liberation on the other. The use of musical/textual structures that allow for quick transmission without written music, i.e., oral tradition, frees the singers/dancers to participate completely in the experience themselves and also to join others in the community of the faithful who are present. The kinesthetic dimension of the experience provides both a personal catharsis and the means for a community expression of hope and liberation. Because Christian community *(ecclesia)* extends beyond those physically present to the saints who have passed before and those faithful who exist in our time but in different places, kinesthetic participation strengthens the ritual. Physical participation provides a semblance of wholeness even when the community has been separated by time, location, or even death. Such is the experience of "Gloria" in the form of the *cueca* which allows a spouse to "dance with" her beloved *desaparecido* in a concomitant experience of protest and joy.

Pablo Sosa: Poet

The songs discussed above provide only a partial perspective of Pablo Sosa's work. When the occasion demands, he can also provide poetry that displays ingenuity and creativity within the literate tradition. I sensed Sosa's love for Spanish poetry when he recited by memory a favorite sixteenth-century anonymous devotional poem, "Soneto a Jesús Crucificado," that he had learned in high school. English speakers may know this hymn from Edward Caswall's translation from the Latin, "My God, I Love Thee." It is a product peculiar to Spanish mysticism of the sixteenth century in the province of Castille. This poem was written during the era of the nun Saint Teresa de Jesús de Ávila, the painter El Greco from Toledo, and the composer Tomás Luis de Victoria from Madrid who later resided in Rome. Sosa notes that the "spirit of Spanish mysticism . . . balance[s] both the subjectivity of the experience of the inner presence of God and a very practical attitude in relation to the appropriate strategies for Christian witness."[20] I have provided a literal translation of stanzas one

---

Larry A. Samovar, Richard E. Porter, and Lisa A. Stefani, *Communicating between Cultures,* 3rd ed. (Belmont, Calif.: Wadsworth, 1998), 10ff.

20. Sosa, "Spanish American Hymnody," 63-65. The complete text of the "Soneto a Jesús Crucificado" is on p. 65.

and two beside the Spanish text along with an analysis of the metrical form (number of syllables per line of poetry) and rhyme scheme *(abba)*. When a Spanish word ends in a vowel and the next word begins with a vowel, they are often elided together as one sound. Elisions are indicated below with a lower line (_). Caswall's corresponding stanzas appear below:

> *No me mueve, mi Dios, para quererte,* (11) A
> *el cielo que me tienes prometido,* (11) B
> *ni me mueve_el infierno tan temido* (11) B
> *para dejar por eso de_ofenderte.* (11) A

> Literal Translation:
> I am not moved, my God, to love you,
> because of the heaven you have promised me,
> neither am I moved by Hell so fearful
> that I would keep for this [reason] from offending you.

> *Tú me mueves, Señor, muéveme_el verte* (11) A
> *clavado_en una cruz y_escarnecido,* (11) B
> *muéveme ver tu cuerpo tan_herido,* (11) B
> *muévenme tus afrentas y tu muerte.* (11) A

> Literal Translation:
> You move me Lord, I am moved to see you
> nailed to a cross and mocked,
> I am moved to see your body so wounded,
> your shame and your death move me.

Caswall's versification (1849):
My God, I love thee, not because (8) A
I hope for heaven thereby, (6) B
nor yet because, if I love not, (8) C
I must forever die. (6) B

Thou, O my Jesus, thou didst me
upon the cross embrace;
for me didst bear the nails and spear
and manifold disgrace.

Caswall's translation is a masterpiece in its own right, but it loses some of the qualities that are idiosyncratic to Spanish ways of expression. Note the long lines of the Spanish stanzas (11.11.11.11). This feature, a regular occurrence in

Spanish poetry, is less usual in English-language hymnody. The mood is totally different in Spanish than in Caswall's translation. The longer poetic lines combine with the softer, more liquid consonants of Spanish and one is aware of the alliteration of the sound (m) *(mueveme)* throughout. The effect of anaphora through the repetition of *mueveme* and variants and the feminine accent on the penultimate syllable that concludes each line (so natural to Spanish, and more awkward in English) is impossible to reproduce in the English language. Even the more open rhyme scheme *(abba)* produces a different effect than the tighter *abcb* pattern common in so many hymns of this era. Caswall does manage to achieve longer lines through the technique of enjambment rather than succumbing to the usual short phrases of common meter, but he cannot match the alliterative flow of the Spanish nor the gentle feminine endings of each line. The traditional common meter rhyming pattern of *abcb* is used well by Caswall because it softens the shorter lines of this meter so that the ear hears 14.14 rather than the more choppy 8.6.8.6. Of course, it is very difficult to cover the same content in each stanza when translating from one language to another while maintaining the rigors of classical poetry.

My intention is not to examine in depth the technicalities and difficulties of translating hymns from Spanish to English, but to highlight specific aspects of Spanish classical poetry that have had an influence to some degree on Sosa and other Argentine hymn writers who compose texts within the literate tradition. One of Sosa's favorite places at the seminary is the rare-book room that contains an unusually fine collection of Spanish-language Bibles, theological texts, and devotional books dating back to the sixteenth, seventeenth, and eighteenth centuries. On the one hand Sosa draws from the rich provincial soil of Argentina; on the other, the mysticism of Spain permeates his spiritual roots. In this way he personally reflects the ambiguity of the Argentine identity described earlier.

One of Sosa's early hymn tunes was composed in 1960 for a Spanish text that paradoxically was translated from an English-language hymn by C. Maud Battersby (nineteenth-twentieth centuries), "If I have wounded any soul today." Sara Menéndez de Hall provided the Spanish translation, "Si fui motivo de dolor." Janet May recently provided an English-language translation from the Spanish, "If I have been the source of pain."[21] When Sosa was preparing

---

21. See the Presbyterian Church in Canada's hymnal, *The Book of Praise,* 1997 (199), for the complete English text by Janet May. See *Libro de Liturgia y Cántico* (441) for the complete Spanish version by Sara Menéndez de Hall. *The New Century Hymnal,* 1995, has included both the English translation by May and the Spanish translation by Menéndez de Hall (544). See *The New Century Hymnal Companion,* ed. Kristen L. Forman (Cleveland: Pilgrim Press, 1998), 483, for more information on the origins of this hymn.

Example 2.6. "Si fui motivo de dolor,"
from *The New Century Hymnal,* 544

English translation © 1992 The Pilgrim Press. Used by permission.
Music copyright © 1988 Pablo Sosa. Used by permission.

the Argentine hymnal *Cántico Nuevo* (New Song) in 1960, he wished to include the words of "Si fui motivo de dolor." The committee agreed with him. They were drawn to the poem's longer lines (10.10.10.4), its confessional quality, and its quixotic nature reminiscent of Spanish mystical poetry. Having rejected the original melody, however, and not being able to find an acceptable tune to match this uncommon meter, just the day before the deadline Sosa was told by the committee that unless he wrote a new tune, the text would have to be abandoned. The tune CAMACUÁ, named for the street on which ISEDET is located in Buenos Aires, was the result. Sosa had returned from Westminster Choir College by this time and was influenced by the music of North American composer Vincent Persichetti. The result was a plainsong style modified by a soft bolero rhythm (not the rhythmic style of Ravel's *Bolero*) and supported by open parallel fifths after Persichetti. The committee responded very favorably to the tune, and it has been associated with this text since that time.

Sosa was also attracted to the pensive, interrogative poem by the Uruguayan pastor Juan Damián, "¿Por qué te nombro con miedo, como si fueras viento?" (Why do I name you with fear as if you were the wind?), for similar reasons.[22] In this setting Sosa combines his love for enigmatic texts reminiscent of Spanish mysticism with an Argentine folk form. The gentle syncopations of the rural *milonga*, a form that is often half sung and half spoken, fit the poem perfectly. The *milonga* has a dialogical structure using questions. Damián's text asks the persistent questions of a searching faith, each beginning with "¿Por qué?" (Why?). The response to the questions is provided in the refrain:

> *Yo sé que sé, pere no entiendo,*
> *Yo sé que busco, y sin embargo*
> *estoy desnudo en medio de un misterio.*
> *¡Sí, Señor! ¡Sí, Señor!*
> *Quisiera no preguntar*
> *pero hoy no puedo.*

> I know that I know, but I do not understand,
> I know what I am looking for, and nevertheless,
> I am naked in the middle of a mystery.
> Yes Lord, Yes Lord!
> I would like not to question
> but today I cannot.

© Juan Damián. Used by permission.

An example of a text written by Sosa in the more literate tradition is a poem for a song written for a Christmas program for his community chorus Música Para Todos in 1997. Sosa wanted a song that would identify with the common people who struggle to make a living during the difficult economic times of the current government's (IMF) imposed *ajuste* (tightening), a situa-

---

22. This hymn is available in *Libro de Liturgia y Cántico* (449).

tion of increased unemployment. The result was the "Villancico del Cartonero." A *cartonero* is a person who collects any kind of boxes, cartons, and plastic for recycling. He pushes or pulls a large cart through the streets of the city, often throughout the entire night. In some cases an entire family works together, moving from business to business to see if there is anything they can pick up for recycling. At the end of the night the cartons are taken to a central recycling area and weighed, and the *cartonero* receives a meager amount of money that he can use to barely sustain his family for another day. Sosa celebrates the work of the *cartonero* through the music of a lively *villancico*. It begins with a refrain of vocables, "Larai, larai . . . ," that expresses the spirit of the song. I first heard this song in Buenos Aires. What started as a choral work became everyone's song before the evening was finished. In addition to the traditional percussion ensemble, members of the chorus added to the rhythms of the *villancico* by playing them on cardboard boxes. Even the cursory analysis of meter and rhyme scheme provided below illustrates Sosa's discipline within the literary tradition. A literal translation of the Spanish (not for singing) follows:

Larai, larai . . .

Ni bien empuja la noche_al día	(10)	A
saca_el carrito_y entra_a yirar,*	(9)	B
es cartonero_y con su familia	(10)	A
consecha cajas por la ciudad.	(9)	B
Es cartonero porque no quiere	(10)	C
pedir limosna para comer,	(9)	D
y_aunque quisiera robar no puede	(10)	C
porque se_acuerda de su querer.	(9)	D

> As soon as night pushes away day,
> he takes his cart and makes his rounds;
> he is the carton man who with his family
> harvests boxes around the city.
> He is a carton man because he does not want
> to beg for alms in order to eat,
> and though he could steal, he can not
> because he remembers his loved one(s).

Cartonero, buen obrero,	(8)	A
que te bancas lo peor;	(7)	B
de la noche compañero,	(8)	A
de la calle Gran Señor.	(7)	B

Carton man, good worker,
you endure in spite of the worst;
accompanied through the night,
by the Great Lord of the street.

Larai, larai . . .

Aquella noche, volviendo_al barrio,	(10)	A
se_oye_un llantito_en el callejón,	(9)	B
medio desnudo, casi_en el barro,	(10)	A
hay un bebito_en el corralón.	(9)	B
La cartonera_elige_una caja	(10)	C
linda_y limpita, made in Taiwán,	(9)	D
el cartonero le_arma_una cuna	(10)	C
y los changuitos* le_ofrecen pan.	(9)	D

That night, returning to his neighborhood,
he hears a small cry in the alley,
half naked, almost in the mud,
he finds a baby boy in the storage bin.
The carton woman chooses a box
nice and clean, made in Taiwan,
the carton man prepares him a cradle
and the children offer him bread.

Cartonero, buen obrero,	(8)	A
que_soñás* algo mejor,	(7)	B
te_hacen guiños desde_el cielo	(8)	A
las estrellas del Señor.	(7)	B

Carton man, good worker,
you dream for something better,
the [stars] in the heavens winking at you
are the stars of the Lord.

© Pablo Sosa. Used by permission.

*Words with special forms or meanings in Argentina. Sosa uses the colloquial *soñás* rather than the usual familiar form *tu sueñas* (you hope) to identify with the idioms of the poor people.

As a pastoral musician, Sosa uses elements that facilitate orality in his more literary writing. The four-line strophes function as a brief refrain, each beginning with the same text, "Cartonero, buen obrero." The inner rhyme of this line, "Cartonero" and "obrero," further strengthens the oral nature of the text. The vocables "Larai, larai . . ." actually function as an additional refrain and are sung to a variation of the melody used with the texts. This allows people to participate easily on sections of the song with minimal introduction.

A final example of Sosa's compositions is "Hosanna," a Palm Sunday text that places Christ's entry into Jerusalem into a contemporary context of a media account.

Example 2.7. "Hosanna" (refrain only), by Pablo Sosa, from *Cancionero Abierto*, Primera edición (Buenos Aires: ISEDET, 1994), 36

Words and music copyright © 1994 Pablo Sosa. Used by permission.

The *estribillo* sets the tone and the stanzas alternate between a description of the scene and an account by a television announcer, bringing the events of Palm Sunday "close to the human lifeworld," as Ong says. The refrain has that easily learned quality of orality.

> Estribillo: *Hoy todos gritan ¡Hosanna!*
> *¿Qué gritarán mañana?*
>
> Today everyone shouts, "Hosanna!"
> What will they cry tomorrow?

El abuelo se pone los anteojos,
el nieto se sube sobre_un cajón,
un muchacho pregunta si ya lo vieron,
la madre se_estira_un poco_el batón.
"En vivo y_en directo para ustedes"
dicen la radio_y la televisión,
"traemos los detalles del arribo
y la_entrada triunfal del Salvador."

     The grandfather puts on his glasses,
     the grandson climbs up on a big box,
     a boy asks if they see him yet,
     the mother straightens her housecoat a little.
     "Coming live and direct to you,"
     says the radio and television,
     "we bring you the details of the arrival
     and triumphal entrance of the Savior."

Estribillo.

El trabajo del día se suspendió
y la gente_al camino se dirigió;
la consigna: "Hosanna, Hijo de David,"
y "Bendito_el que viene_en nombre de Dios."
"No_ha formulado_aún declaraciones,
pero_en algunas fuentes se_informó
que_el cumplimiento de_una profecía
es el propósito de su misión."

     The people stopped their day's work
     and went to the streets and shouted
     the watchword: "Hosanna, Son of David,"
     and "Blessed is he who comes in God's name."
     "He has not formulated any declarations yet,
     but we are informed by some sources
     that the fulfillment of a prophecy
     is the purpose of his mission."

Estribillo.

En el templo se_escucha la_aclamación,
y_el pastor ya termina con su sermón;

nos unimos al pueblo_en la ovación,
recibimos a Cristo de corazón.
"Ya se_aproxima_aquí la comitiva,
un tanto_insólita,_a decir verdad;
la gente tira ramas y vestidos
al paso de_un burrito_en el que va."

> In the temple one hears the acclamation,
> and the pastor now ends his sermon;
> we join the people in the ovation
> and receive Christ in our hearts.
> "Already the retinue approaches us,
> [it is] so unusual, to tell the truth, [that]
> the people throw branches and clothing
> in the path of the little donkey as he goes by."

Final Estribillo: *Todos cantamos ¡Hosanna!*
¡Ayúdamos mañana!

> We all sing Hosanna!
> Help us (save us) tomorrow!

Pablo Sosa: The Contextual Theologian

Pablo Sosa has been a part of the community of what has been called Instituto Superior Evangelico de Estudios Teologicos (ISEDET) since early in the 1950s, first as a student and for over forty years as a professor. He studied in the United States at Westminster Choir College from 1954 to 1957, at Union Seminary in New York from 1970 to 1972, and in Berlin at the Hochschule für Musik from 1962 to 1963.

ISEDET was founded in 1884 and assumed its current name in 1970. It is a theological school on several levels, from the bachelor's through the doctoral levels, and is one of the few Latin American theological institutions to offer doctoral level study. It always had an ecumenical reputation and now enrolls students from nine traditions and/or denominations: the Evangelical Church of Rio de la Plata, Methodist, Disciples of Christ, the Anglican Diocese of Argentina, United Evangelical Lutheran Church, Reformed Church of Argentina, Presbyterian Church, Danish Church, and the Waldensian Church from Italy.

Sosa's role has changed as the institution has evolved. In 1962 ISEDET began a school of music which provided a religious context where musicians could study. It was in this capacity that he began work on *Cancionero Abierto* (Open Songbook) in 1974. In 1976 he moved to the department of communications where he started his career as a radio broadcaster in charge of the production of the international religious program *Cristo Vive* (Christ Is Living). This program had originated after World War II as *Christus Lebt* and was exported throughout all of Latin America. At the same time, he began producing church music recordings. Over twenty cassettes and CDs have been produced to date. This is an important medium for dispensing music in a country where many learn through oral tradition.

In 1989 Sosa established the Fondo por Música y Liturgia (Music and Liturgy Fund) within ISEDET with a separate administrative structure. This allowed him to accept contributions directly for the purpose of producing audio materials and presenting special programs. In 1992 ISEDET closed both the School of Music and the department of communications because of *el ajuste,* the difficult period of economic restraint. ISEDET now rents out much of its space for extra income and has consolidated its operations to a single cramped building. Sosa continues to produce recordings through the Fondo and teaches liturgy at ISEDET. He has also been teaching choral conducting "for fun" for over twenty years at the Conservatorio Nacional Superior de Música, the highest-ranking state music school in Argentina. Through all this Sosa continues to be a copastor at Third Methodist Church in Buenos Aires.

The ecumenical theological environment of ISEDET has provided him a setting in which to develop a contextual process that gives structure to D. T. Niles' challenge to plant the gospel in your own soil. The three-part process has been honed throughout the years as he has gradually sought to move the *folklorico* traditions of the provinces inside the church.

1. **The first stage is contextualization.** Questions related to contextualization are:

   – What did the gospel mean at the time it was received and in the culture of the early church? For example, questions about early eucharistic practice, its relationship to Jewish table rituals, etc., could lead to discussion on this topic.

   When discussing a work of art such as a hymn, the questions might be:
   – Who was the original singer?
   – To whom was the author of the text talking?
   – How does this hymn relate to the culture in which it was conceived?

2. **The second stage is de-contextualization.** Sosa refers to this as a stage of *significado* (meaning). Questions might include:

   – What is the essence of or basic idea of the topic or artwork?
   – What is its essential meaning?

3. **The third stage is recontextualization.** Sosa refers to this stage as one in which the *significado* (meaning) is given a new "code" or takes on a new *significante* (significance) because of the current situation. The questions include:

   – What current social/cultural circumstances modify the original meaning *(significado)?*
   – What is the significance *(significante)* for our lives today?
   – What does this teach us now?
   – How does it fit into our current liturgical context?

Assigning a new code to an earlier practice is a potentially powerful procedure because it moves people out of their comfortable structures and into a context where they can be affected and transformed. Bringing the dance/song forms of the *cueca, chamarrita,* and *carnavalito* from their rural settings into the liturgy of the church is what Sosa calls "code switching." Another example would be the Eucharist. In what way do ancient practices of eating together affect the way the church gathers to share in this sacred meal today? In many ways the ecumenical dialogue since Vatican II has contributed to rethinking the earlier "codes" for baptismal and eucharistic practice.

This process is Pablo Sosa's way of responding to D. T. Niles' plea to take the potted plant of the gospel (contextualization), break the pot (de-contextualization), and set the plant in your own soil (recontextualization).

Pablo Sosa: Hymnal Editor and Recording Producer

Editing hymnals and producing recordings of Latin American song have been Sosa's ways of recontextualizing the gospel in Latin America. Following his years at Westminster Choir College, Sosa became the editor for *Cantico Nuevo* in 1960,[23] a hymnal designed to replace *Himnario Evangelico* (1943). *Himnario Evangelico* was an ecumenical hymnal rooted in the Euro–North American tradition and consisted almost entirely of hymns translated into Spanish from other languages. To continue the paradigm introduced by D. T.

---

23. *Cantico Nuevo,* ed. Pablo Sosa (Buenos Aires: Methopress Editorial y Grafica, 1962).

Niles, the gospel plant had come to Argentina in the pot of an alien culture. The process of contextualization had not yet begun.

Cantico Nuevo (New Song), however, did not break the pot either. Sosa noted the absence of folk music and the presence of very little original music from Latin American sources in the preface of this pre–Vatican II collaboration.[24] Sosa's settings of "Si fui motivo de dolor" (CAMACUÁ) and Nicolás Martínez's Easter text "Cristo Vive" (CENTRAL, named after Central Methodist Church in Buenos Aires) are present.[25] But these are anomalies. At this time Sosa did not feel that folk music could be used in the church. Both are fine tunes, but they are derived from Euro–North American models. Sosa sees this hymnal as a scholarly, academic hymnbook using mostly European and North American materials. It included rhythmic versions of German chorales, Gelineau psalm settings, and other Reformation materials. Its contents were molded by people associated at one time or another with ISEDET's predecessor, the Facultad Evangélica de Teología (FET). These include B. Foster Stockwell, president of ISEDET for many years and a Methodist from the northern part of the United States who became the Methodist bishop of several South American countries and was a well-known theologian in international circles; his wife Vera Londen, teacher of hymnology and president of the Hymnal Committee for *Cantico Nuevo*; Rodolfo Obermüller, a German Lutheran, New Testament scholar, and Rembrandt specialist; Eduardo Carámbula, a graduate of Westminster Choir College, music teacher at FET, and choral conductor of renown; and Manuel Gutiérrez Marín, a professor from the Reformed Church of Spain. Their influence shaped a hymnal that was orderly (structured around systematic theology), lectionary based, and historically liturgical. One of the significant aspects of *Cantico Nuevo* was the four hymns by Federico Pagura.

During the Vatican II years (1962-65) the atmosphere at FET began to change. Pagura became its chaplain and started to work with Homero Perera, a talented young musician who had come from Uruguay in 1958. Perera was a tango musician who studied organ and composition at the school. After

24. In Pablo Sosa, "Pagura . . . El Cantor," in *Por Eso Es Que Tenemos Esperanza: Homenaje al Obispo Federico J. Pagura* (Quito: CLAI, 1995), 70. Sosa notes thirty-five years later rather ironically: "We were looking for pearls [from the United States and Europe] to include in our collection [*Cantico Nuevo*], but without having written yet even one note of which we would be able to say, 'This is mine' or better yet 'ours' and that besides would be 'worthy' of placing next to the 'great hymns' of our faith [from the West]." Trans. M. Aaron Hawn.

25. Martínez's "Cristo Vive" was translated into English by Fred Kaan in 1972. It appears in several hymnals in both versions, including *The United Methodist Hymnal*, 1989 (313), *The Presbyterian Hymnal*, 1990 (109), and *The New Century Hymnal*, 1995 (235).

Cantico Nuevo was edited, Pagura offered a fresh challenge to the students and faculty of the theology school in November 1961: "The times are ripe that the bosom of the church, in our America, produce a liturgical and musical renovation to make of worship an act of pleasurable and solemn adoration. The times are ripe for our young churches not only to familiarize themselves with the richest of the Christian musical heritage that has come to us, but also to encourage our new musicians and Christian poets to put wings to the gospel, in agreement with our own methods and talents."[26]

Pagura had written his first important religious poem as a seminary student, in 1943, for the inauguration of FET's chapel. It was entitled "¿Señor, qué es nuestro templo si tu no estas presente?" (Lord, what is our temple if you are not present?). Its provocative, prophetic tone was a portent of Pagura's future as a hymn writer and translator. Pagura and Perera collaborated on the *Cantata Folklorico para Pascua de Resurrección* during this time. This work included three provincial folk forms, the *baguala*, *zamba* (not to be confused with the Brazilian samba), and *chacarera*, as it traced the events of Holy Week. Pagura notes: "This Cantata grew from the search for elements of expression and communication of the gospel intimately connected to everyday life, particularly in this region of the world. It is an attempt to worship our Lord through music; the music that God gave to our people."[27] During the mid-1960s, in the midst of the fervor of Vatican II, choral music by Argentine Ariel Ramírez also added momentum. It was his music that influenced Perera in his composition of *Cantata Folklorico*. Ramírez's *Misa Criolla* (*criollos* are the Argentine-born descendants of Spanish parents), the first vernacular Spanish-language Mass based on folk forms, and *Navidad Nuestra*, a Christmas cantata based on various Argentine provincial forms, brought the issues of recontextualization to a larger public.[28]

However, it was the collaboration between Pagura and Perera on "Soli-

26. Sosa, "Pagura . . . El Cantor," 73-74, trans. M. Aaron Hawn.

27. Sosa, "Pagura . . . El Cantor," 79, trans. M. Aaron Hawn. The *baguala*, "Todo acabó en una tumba," is available in *Libro de Liturgia y Cántico* (346). This is a Good Friday text that uses a slower *vidala* or expanded *baguala* form. Perera wrote the melody first; the text by Pagura followed.

28. Other Central American folk masses came over a decade later and were not part of the Argentine efforts at recontextualizing church music. These would include the collaborations between Archbishop Oscar Romero and composer Guillermo Cuéllar in El Salvador such as *La Nueva Misa Mesoamericana* and *Misa Popular Salvadoreña*. Folk masses from Nicaragua include *Misa Popular Nicaragüense* and Carlos Godoy's *Misa Campesina Nicaragüense*. These are discussed in José María Vigil and Angel Torrellas, eds., *Misas Centro Americana* (Managua: CAV-CEBES, 1988), with cassette. It contains the music of three Central American Masses: *Misa Popular Nicaragüense*, *Misa Campesina Nicaragüense*, and *Misa Popular Salvadoreña*.

tario" in 1963, the first evangelical tango, that set a new course. The tango is in many ways the essence of popular music and dance in the varied cultural milieu of Buenos Aires, where the sounds and sights of the tango are ubiquitous. There are live tango shows, tango bars, tango movies and TV channels, tango books and recordings, and tango street musicians. At first one is tempted to think of the tango as a tourist attraction, as well it is. But it is much more than that. The tango is a product of the unique blend of European immigrants and African slaves that constituted life in Argentina, especially Buenos Aires, in the second half of the nineteenth century. Although I stated earlier that Afro-Argentines virtually disappeared from the country during the nineteenth century, traces of African culture, including music, persist. While many who love the tango are senior citizens, there appears to be a resurgence of interest in the form among younger people as well.

The tango is a melding of the pulsing rhythms of the *candombe* that came to Argentina with the African slaves, the haunting melodies of Andalusia and southern Italy, as well as the Argentine provincial dance/song, the *milonga*. It represents an earthiness and sensuality that is unmistakable, regardless of one's cultural perspective.[29] Sosa notes: "The tango, that hybrid birth of nostalgia, the letting go of everything you love, and male ownership, is the essence and explanation of the Argentine way of being, or at least of a *porteño* . . . way of being. And, so, it was a good day that Federico would write a tango."[30] "Solitario," the first evangelical tango, "didn't win any prizes" according to Sosa, but it did help establish a bond between Pagura and Perera that proved fruitful for the future. Pagura returned to the form in the 1970s when he and Perera wrote a trilogy of "Porque" (Because) hymns: "Porque él venció" (also called "Sursum Corda"), "Porque hay un mundo" (also called "Alegría," or "Joy"), and "Porque él entró en el mundo" (also known as "Tenemos Esperanza," or "we have hope").[31] The first is in the *carnavalito* style of Sosa's "El cielo canta alegría" discussed above, while the latter two are tangos.[32] By

---

29. See Gerard Béhague, "Tango," in *The New Grove Dictionary of Music and Musicians,* ed. Stanley Sadie, vol. 18 (New York: Macmillan, 1980), 563-65, for an introduction to the tango. Béhague distinguishes three kinds of tangos: *tango-milonga* (strictly instrumental), *tango-romanza* (either instrumental or vocal with romantic text), and *tango-canción* (vocal with instrumental accompaniment). The "tango-song," according to Béhague, expresses "views of love and life in highly pessimistic, fatalistic and often pathologically dramatic terms" (563). The tango-songs of Pagura offering hope need to be seen in the paradoxical light of this assertion.

30. Sosa, "Pagura . . . El Cantor," 75, trans. M. Aaron Hawn.

31. All three hymns can be found in *Libro de Liturgia y Cántico* as numbers 478, 579, 458 respectively.

32. Sosa discusses the "Porque" hymns in "Pagura . . . El Cantor," 81-85.

1969 Pagura had been elected Methodist bishop of Costa Rica and Panama. In 1977 he was elected bishop of Argentina, and then president of Consejo Latinoamericano de Iglesias (Counsel of Latin American Churches) (CLAI). The visibility of his positions as bishop and president of CLAI provided him the podium from which to address *derechos humanos* (human rights) throughout Latin America. There are many who say Pagura has been one of the leading Protestant voices against political oppression in Latin America for the last twenty years.

For many within the church, "Tenemos Esperanza" became their "Ein' feste Burg" during the epidemic of political turmoil and oppression of the 1970s throughout South America. After overthrowing Salvador Allende, the first elected socialist president in Latin America, the military regime of Pinochet in Chile (1973-89) was especially vicious. As a result of the struggles in Chile, Argentina's neighbor, as well as Argentina's own "dirty war," people were asking "¿Por qué?" or "Why?" Why is this happening to us? Why has God abandoned us? Pagura's hymns play on the Spanish interrogative "¿Por qué?" and respond by using anaphora, beginning many of the lines with "Porque" (because). In "Tenemos Esperanza" Pagura states that we can have hope *because* Christ came to live among us and suffered with us. Sosa expresses the relationship between the political events of the times and Pagura's hymn this way:

> [In] a time of military dictatorship, the death, the disappearance, the injustice, the horror. . . . How is it possible to have hope? Someone has to raise up our faith before everything is emptied out. It was Federico's turn. He completed the mission of the poet, as he intuited it, to put wings to the gospel. To lift up hope with a song. And Perera accompanied him with a tango, because he needed the male determination (or, perhaps, that determination which many women have, and not all men) to have hope, even in Christ, and especially in Christ in those terrible times.[33]

By using the tango to embody Christ's ministry and hope in a difficult time of persecution and oppression, Pagura had planted the gospel of the incarnation deeply in Latin American soil.

---

33. Sosa, "Pagura . . . El Cantor," 82, trans. M. Aaron Hawn. I first learned Pagura's hymn of hope, "Tenemos Esperanza," in Cuba in 1990 just as communism was on the wane in the former Soviet Union and financial aid was being withdrawn from the island and Fidel Castro's government. The hope expressed by "Tenemos Esperanza" provided a voice of solidarity with the gospel of Christ and with other Latin American churches as people suffered (and continue to suffer) in Cuba. Among many in Latin America, especially those drawn to liberation theology, Pagura could be called the Oscar Romero of the Latin American Protestant church.

Sosa's next editorial project might not have taken hold as well as it did without the theological nurture and poetic skill of Bishop Pagura. In 1961 Pagura had encouraged the Latin American church to "put wings to the gospel." His statement was a challenge to the church to examine its soil and firmly plant the gospel in the hopes, struggles, and culture of Latin American life. *Cancionero Abierto* was the project that began to till the artistic soil of Latin American Christian culture. Begun in 1974, *Cancionero Abierto* was unlike the previous Protestant or evangelical hymnals. Sosa's philosophy was simple: "If you have a song of praise, we will include it and see if people want to use it." Songs were submitted by individuals, were adaptations from choral works, and even were creative group compositions conducted by Sosa with young people and congregations. Six volumes have been published, the most recent, an accompaniment edition, in 1994. Early volumes were prepared by Sosa at his kitchen table using a manual music typewriter. *Cancionero Abierto* has been a primary source for dispensing Latin American hymnody around the world. Several of the recent Spanish-language hymnals published in the United States have used its resources.

Over 150 songs have been published in the six volumes thus far. Volumes 1-5 have been collected together in melody-only and accompaniment editions. The authors and composers, while mostly Argentine, also come from countries throughout Latin America, including Bolivia, Brazil, Costa Rica, Chile, Ecuador, Nicaragua, Peru, and Uruguay. There are occasional additional selections from outside Latin America, including songs from Cameroon, England, India, Israel, Germany, Spain, Sweden, and the United States. Bishop Pagura is the most-represented author in *Cancionero Abierto* with thirteen contributions, nine original texts and four translations. The translations include a hymn by Swedish author Anders Frostenson, Peter Scholtes' "We are one in the spirit," a text by Brazilian Joâo Dias de Araujo, and Sydney Carter's "Lord of the Dance." Most of Pagura's original texts are set to music by Perera, the Uruguayan tangoist who studied and taught at ISEDET, who contributes over twenty melodies and is occasionally the author of both text and music, for example his "Misa en Jazz." After Sosa left to produce recordings in the communications department of ISEDET in 1976, Perera served as the editor of later editions.

Sosa has eleven specific contributions. In four cases he wrote both text and tune. He also provided melodies for texts from the Bible (one) and by Methodist layman Alberto Giacumbo (three), Uruguayan pastor Juan Damián (one), Pagura (one), and Mexican–Costa Rican Elsa Tamez (one). He also provided several singing translations in Spanish from other languages. Another interesting category of hymns are those composed collectively, often by young people. Approximately ten songs fall into this category. Sosa had a hand in both the creative process and editing the final product. Once the philosophy of *Cancionero Abierto* was set and the project began, Sosa moved from being musical editor to producing audiocassettes for the project.

In 1976 Sosa left the music department and joined the faculty of the communications department within ISEDET. Providing written music was important, but producing audiocassettes was even more important in a culture where oral musical traditions are a major means of transmitting the gospel. Upon his return from Union Seminary (New York) in 1972, Sosa began a community choral ensemble called Música Para Todos (Music for All). This group produced nearly twenty recordings. He found that classical music programs were not reaching audiences in Argentina. Concert events were, according to Sosa, often social occasions that allowed upper-class people the opportunity to wear their finer clothes and mingle with those in a similar class of society. By contrast, Música Para Todos continues to take all kinds of music to the people, from classical European to Latin American choral works, and presents this varied musical fare in a more informal and informative atmosphere. Rather than formal concert attire, the singers wear street clothes. He refers to it as a *conjunto* (a musical group) rather than a formal *coro* (choir). Pablo introduces selections and makes connections between the music and the lives of the people.

Sosa organizes the programs around themes common to all people, using music from English madrigals, Latin motets, operas, Latin American folk traditions — any music that will illustrate the theme. The first program was on the theme of emotions common to all people — *Temor, Amor, Humor* (Fear, Love, Humor). A later program had the theme of *Expensas Comunes,* or the maintenance expenses that apartment dwellers and condominium owners must pay. How can we learn to live together in various kinds of relationships? He chose music that dealt with conflict. It was in this context that he introduced, for example, the Renaissance English motet "When David heard that Absalom was slain" as an expression of conflict between a father and a son. In 1995 a small volume of fifteen songs, *Muchos Resplandores,* was produced along with a cassette by the Conjunto Música para Todos Publicaciones Musicales.

Pablo Sosa: The Ecumenical Liturgist

Per Harling, worship consultant for the Church of Sweden, liturgist for assemblies of the World Council of Churches (WCC), and longtime friend of Sosa, describes him in this way: "Above all else Pablo Sosa is first a liturgical man and then a composer."[34] I believe Harling's assessment is correct. After observing Sosa at work on several occasions in the United States, in his local parish in Buenos Aires, and as the conductor of Música Para Todos, I can say music reaches its primary fulfillment for him within the context of liturgy. Sosa's liturgical experience entails a variety of Protestant gatherings: Pentecostals in Latin America, Methodists in the United States, Roman Catholic base community assemblies, and the ecumenical gatherings of the WCC. He began working with the WCC in 1979 during worship preparations for the Melbourne Conference in 1980. In 1988 he convened a group of global church musicians for CLAI in Costa Rica and edited a volume of articles resulting from the conference, *Todas Las Voces*.[35] He has the rare skill of being able not only to write effective congregational songs in a variety of styles, but also to draw a congregation into the experience as "full, conscious, and active participa[nts]."[36] He exemplifies the ecumenical Vatican II spirit of the *animateur*, one who gives life or animates the liturgy through song. Although Sosa champions song that springs from Latin American soil, he is also an effective leader of styles as diverse as African American spirituals, Indonesian folk songs, Orthodox chant, Bach chorales, Taizé ostinatos, a sung Jewish creed, and African call-response tunes.

In August 1998 Música Para Todos embarked on a different kind of program, an ecumenical/interfaith service that Sosa calls a "Celebration." Among Roman Catholics a "Celebration" is a noneucharistic Service of the Word only. Sosa wanted to present an artistic event within both a liturgical structure and a religious setting. The advertisements were designed without religious symbols and gave the appearance of an artistic event without religious music. The first event featured a Swedish folk mass with a text by Per Harling. This work was sung in Spanish but with careful attention given to the style of Swedish folk music. Several Protestant ministries participated, including Buenos Aires' Swedish community.

On the evening following, a global celebration was presented in the framework of the WCC Lima Liturgy (1982). While not an official liturgy of

---

34. Conversation with Per Harling, August 22, 1998, Buenos Aires, Argentina. Harling also noted that Sosa had experience as an organist in a Swedish Lutheran church in Buenos Aires early in his career. Sosa reflected to Harling that this also contributed to his liturgical formation.

35. Pablo Sosa, ed., *Todas Las Voces: Taller de Música y Liturgia en América Latina* (Costa Rica: Ediciones SEBILA, 1988). In addition to Sosa's, there are articles by Jací Maraschin and Simei Monteiro (Brazil), Ricardo Foulkes (Costa Rica), Brother Roberto (Community of Taizé, France), I-to Loh (Taiwan), and Patrick Matsikenyiri (Zimbabwe).

36. *Constitution on the Sacred Liturgy* (Collegeville, Minn.: Liturgical Press, 1963), 12-13.

the WCC, it often is used with ecumenical gatherings. The event featured musical traditions from around the world. The centerpiece of this *Celebración Ecuménica* was Sosa's musical interpretation of the Nicene Creed. The "Villancico de Cartonero" was placed in conjunction with the section of the creed, "For love and for our salvation, he descended from heaven, and was born of the Virgin Mary by the Holy Spirit, and was made man." Pagura's pacan of hope, "Tenemos Esperanza," was used complete with the *bandoneón*, an Argentine accordion intimately linked with the essence of the tango. "Pagura's tango provided the hermeneutical link with the portion of the Nicene Creed, '[I believe] that he will come again in glory to judge the living and the dead, and that his reign will have no end.'" Various Protestant ministers presided and a Catholic laywoman of the *Madres de Plaza de Mayo* read the Gospel, a prophetic act on Sosa's part given the pain and political context of the struggle of these women. The Eucharist was celebrated with an invitation by Sosa to participate according to one's own conscience. Both events were prepared for with a brief congregational rehearsal and an informal explanation. Both events were well attended and received. It was Sosa at his best as an ecumenical liturgist.

De-contextualizing Pablo Sosa

This chapter has been an attempt to contextualize the work of Sosa according to his many gifts and complex sense of vocation. In the spirit of Sosa's model of contextualism, I will attempt to de-contextualize his work so we might recontextualize his ministry for North Americans who share his concern for the church and its music. I would de-contextualize Sosa's ministry in this way:

- People come first.
- Everyone's life is of value to God.
- Everyone's struggle is important to God.
- Music facilitates the drama of liturgy and brings the sacred story to life.
- People need to understand the context of the music they are singing. (As Sosa reiterates in rehearsals again and again, "¿Comprende?" — Do you understand?)
- People need to participate fully in a liturgy that draws from the soil of their experience.
- We can always pray together with others even if we disagree in many ways.
- People need to learn prayers and songs from other cultural contexts.

Recontextualizing the Work of Pablo Sosa for the United States

Sosa's ministry has much to teach us about the nature of congregational singing and the role of music within liturgy. Recontextualizing will be a different
process for every church as it takes a careful look at its own soil. The process
of recontextualizing Sosa's work among us may cause us to ask additional
questions about music and liturgy: Who among us may be left out of the
songs we sing? Whose voice is silent in our liturgies? Who does not experience hospitality in our presence? What musical resources have taken root in
the North American cultural soil that remain uncultivated in our liturgies?
This is a never ending process of learning, experimenting, and reaching beyond our provincial experience to others different from ourselves — different
in race, worldview, socioeconomic class, and age, to list a few.

As an example, we may ask questions about our relationship to Latino
North Americans, who are an ever growing group in number and influence
among us. What might Anglo congregations gain from developing an awareness of this Spanish heritage among them? Congregational song from various
Spanish-language traditions contributes beautiful melodies and rich texts to
our repertoire. More importantly, the many examples of Spanish-language
hymnody that we find in several recent hymnals embody the incarnation of
Christ to *toda la gente* (all people) in both Americas. As we sing these songs,
we are learning literally and metaphorically to pray in Spanish.

Justo González speaks of "reading the Bible in Spanish." He is not referring to reading a Spanish translation of the Bible, but to "a particular perspective to history and to theology, . . . [and] the interpretation of Scripture"
that those cultures who share the Spanish language bring to an understanding of the Bible based on their varied heritages.[37] As González states in a later
work, *Santa Biblia: The Bible through Hispanic Eyes,* "The Bible has been good
to us!"[38] When Spanish-speaking Christians read the Bible, they find their
story contained within its narratives. When we share in these songs of our
Spanish-speaking neighbors, we are accepting their gift to us. It is an act of
hospitalidad (hospitality) to Spanish-speaking Christian *hermanas y hermanos* (sisters and brothers) who live throughout the United States, often in
the neighborhoods where we attend church.

Hospitality to the stranger is a foundation of Jesus' ministry. Sosa

37. Justo L. González, *Mañana: Christian Theology from a Hispanic Perspective* (Nashville:
Abingdon, 1990), 75.

38. Justo L. González, *Santa Biblia: The Bible through Hispanic Eyes* (Nashville: Abingdon,
1996), 118.

would have us extend our hospitality to the poor, to young people, to anyone whose worldview is different from ours. This extension causes us to reflect critically on our cultural heritage(s). Cross-cultural liturgical experiences are one way of appreciating the distinctiveness and beauty of an inherited tradition. To see areas of exclusion is also, by nature, part of the baggage of any provincial view. So, to the "choir" of North American Christianity, Pablo Sosa, our guest director, would have us look around us and dig deeper into our richly varied North American soil, and would gently inquire of us, *¿Comprende?*

CHAPTER 3

Sounds of Bamboo

I-to Loh and the Development of Asian Hymns

> *When a people sings, its members sing from their hearts. Their melodies flow from their souls and bodies. They sing for a whole world to laugh with them, rejoice with them, sigh with them, weep with them. Their tunes, which plead with God, entreat nature, and appeal to humanity, are played in the inner chamber of their hearts not invaded by religious authorities and doctrinal injunctions. These songs and melodies are primitive, unrefined, unsophisticated. They are powerful, sincere, beautiful. They are true to God and humanity. How can those of us preoccupied with God and humanity, nature, life, and death afford not to listen to the people?*

> C. S. SONG, TAIWANESE THEOLOGIAN[1]

Imagine a Pakistani Christian at prayer, chanting sorrowfully a monophonic melody, *Khudaayaa, raeham kar* (Lord, have mercy). Travel to Bangkok and

1. C. S. Song, *Tell Us Our Names: Story Theology from an Asian Perspective* (Maryknoll, N.Y.: Orbis, 1984), 154.

I am grateful for the willingness of the following people to read and comment on drafts of this chapter: Paul Westermeyer, who attended Union Seminary with I-to Loh, and Mark P. Bangert and Mary Oyer, who, like myself, have been pilgrims to Taiwan and have experienced the hospitality and wisdom of I-to Loh and Hui-chin. They are in no way responsible for the failings of this chapter, but have contributed to any improvements that might be perceived. An earlier version of this chapter appeared under the same title as an article in *Hymn* 49, no. 2 (April 1998): 12-24. Significant modifications, additions, and updating are reflected in this more recent version.

participate with a small house church on Sunday morning as they sing *Saen suksan wan prachum nii* (Day of joy, let us be glad) accompanied by a full traditional Thai instrumental ensemble and classical Thai dance. Join with a small Korean congregation in Seoul as they sing a prayer of petition for the reunification of Korea, *Ososo, pyonghwaui imgum* (Come now, O Prince of Peace, make us one body). Sing *Soaniá chhinchhùi hoe hunniong* (Green the wild fields, blue the sky), a song that celebrates the beauty of creation and our responsibility to maintain earth's resources in an aboriginal Taiwanese congregation outside of Tainan. These songs and many others have been collected, composed, arranged, and adapted by I-to Loh through decades of travel and research throughout Asia.

Loh's life reflects the complexities, ambiguities, and diversity of Asian Christian existence. As an Asian Christian ethnomusicologist, he has devoted his life to giving Asian Christians a liturgical voice that sings in culturally authentic ways of the pain, joy, struggle, conflict, and hope of Asian experience. It is impossible to separate worship from struggle when talking to Loh. He comments on events surrounding the fall of the Marcos regime:

> During the critical event in the history of the Philippines on Feb. 23, 1986, churches held their Sunday morning worship services throughout the city of Manila, while thousands of people, including Roman Catholic sisters, gathered on the main highway EDSA, kneeling down in front of the tanks, praying and begging soldiers not to advance and kill their own people. In some services there was not a single reference to what was happening in the country; they simply followed the translated liturgy as a routine. No wonder some young Christians raised their voices to question their church authorities about the relevance of their Christian faith to the situation they lived in.[2]

At the center of Loh's concern is the desire to feel fully Asian and fully Christian. How can Asian Christians express their faith in ways that bring the reality of Christ's incarnation to the very threshold of the Asian cultural ethos? The purpose of this chapter is to examine this question by providing background on the life, work, and cultural context of I-to Loh, who has devoted himself to the collection, publication, and promotion of the songs of Asian peoples for Christian worship. By doing this I hope to increase aware-

2. I-to Loh, "Contemporary Issues in Inculturation, Arts and Liturgy: Music," in *The Hymnology Annual,* ed. Vernon Wicker, vol. 3 (Berrien Springs, Mich.: Vande Vere Publishing, 1993), 49. The personal information in this article is the result of discussions between the author and Dr. Loh, June 15-21, 1996, and April 1999 in Tainan, Taiwan.

ness of Asian hymnody, raise issues in global song and liturgical contextual-ization, and encourage North Americans to make appropriate use of Asian hymns in the liturgies they prepare. By recognizing Loh's work and the con-tributions of Asian Christians who lift their praise and prayer in song, we are giving voice to over 50 percent of the world's people, many of whom live in our communities.

A Brief Biography

Upon his birth in 1936 he was given the name Loh I-to (surnames appear first in Chinese tradition). I-to means "to maintain the Way," a name with a dou-ble significance, referring both to Jesus Christ as "the Way" and the Taoist re-ligious tradition. I-to Loh's interest in indigenous Asian music began during his childhood when he accompanied his father on trips among the Puyuma, Ami, Paiwan, Rukai, and Yami tribes, aboriginal peoples of Taiwan. During his high school years he taught the tribal children regularly on these mission ventures and learned many songs of the Puyuma, Ami, and Paiwan tribes.[3] He found a way of life among the aboriginal peoples that was relatively unin-fluenced by alien cultures. I-to's lifework was inspired in part by his relation-ship with his father, a revered minister in the Presbyterian Church of Taiwan (PCT).

There were several significant influences on Loh's development as a hymnologist. His interest in hymnology and congregational singing began first of all with his father. Sian-chhun Loh (1905-84) was not only a mission-ary to indigenous tribes in Taiwan but also a hymnal editor. *Sèng-Si* (The Hymnal), the primary congregational song source for the PCT for many years, was published in 1964 and remains in use to this day. Sian-chhun Loh, serving first on the hymnal committee as musical editor and then general edi-tor, has seventeen texts and three musical entries in *Sèng-Si*. Typical of Tai-wanese hymnals is the incorporation of both Chinese characters and romanized (transliterated) texts. Since historically only the most literate could read the complex Chinese characters, this practice promotes inclusivity regardless of level of literacy.[4] This sense of hymn singing for all, an inheri-tance from his father, is paramount for Loh.

---

3. I-to Loh, "Tribal Music of Taiwan: With Special Reference to the Ami and Puyuma Styles" (Ph.D. diss., University of California, Los Angeles, 1982), 5. For more information on the music of Taiwan and general cultural context, see I-to Loh, "Taiwan," in *The New Grove Dictio-nary of Music and Musicians,* ed. Stanley Sadie (London: Macmillan, 1980), 18:529-33.

4. *Sèng-Si,* ed. Sian-chhun Loh (Presbyterian Church of Taiwan, 1964). Edward Band,

A second influence relates to the Japanese occupation of Taiwan (1895-1945), an era that shaped his cultural identity and faith. Thomas Barclay, the first significant Presbyterian missionary to the island, noted in 1895 that the purpose of the Japanese invaders, "according to one of their statements, is TO MAKE THE POPULATION OF THE ISLAND — BODY, SOUL AND SPIRIT — JAPANESE."[5] Just before Loh's birth, his father was jailed after being falsely accused of speaking against the Japanese occupation. Loh's formative years were influenced by years of Japanese tyranny, extending to the end of World War II. The tribal peoples, however, maintained their cultural identity in the face of the Japanese invasion. The migration of the Han immigrants from mainland China, appearing in Taiwan (then Formosa) during the late sixteenth century, further affected the lives of the tribal peoples. Although descended from this group, I-to developed an abiding appreciation for the aboriginal peoples of Taiwan that laid the foundation for his future research and ministry.

A third influence on Loh was the PCT and its theological college founded in 1876. The years following World War II and the end of Japanese rule offered no political relief to the people of Taiwan. When the Chinese Nationalists (KMT) under Chiang Kai-shek were forced to retreat from mainland China to the island of Taiwan, the militarily oppressive and culturally destructive occupation of Japan was replaced by martial law and the corrupt rule of the KMT. The martial law was not lifted until 1987.[6] An event early in the occupation of the KMT, often referred to as the February Incident, set the tone for the forty years that followed. During this incident on February 28, 1947, more than twenty thousand Taiwanese were massacred by the Chinese Nationalists and disappeared without a trace. Commenting in 1986, Taiwanese theologian C. S. Song noted that the Nationalists have "made the island into a bastion of anticommunism and ruled its people with martial law."[7] In

---

Barclay of Formosa (Ginza, Tokyo: Christian Literature Society, 1936), emphasizes the importance of literacy for all. The focus on literacy applied to the hymnal and to the reading of Scripture. Thomas Barclay, the first significant missionary to Taiwan (then Formosa), emphasized "The Bible in the Mother-tongue" (p. 130) and the importance of romanization to achieve this goal for all (67-69). The hymnal is an extension of this commitment. Romanization also provides a distinctive Taiwanese (versus Mandarin) sound to reading the Bible and hymn singing. The PCT is committed to Taiwanese over Mandarin as a way of distinguishing Taiwanese culture from the influence of mainland China.

5. Band, 109, upper case in original.

6. The first free elections in Taiwan were held in March 1996 under the threat of missiles from mainland China, falling in the sea south of Taiwan near Kaohsiung and Tainan. At the time of this writing (September 1999), tensions between mainland China and Taiwan are increasing as the president of Taiwan continues to press for Taiwan's independence.

7. C. S. Song, *Theology from the Womb of Asia* (Maryknoll, N.Y.: Orbis, 1986), 101.

response the PCT, though weakened by the Japanese occupation, increased its mission efforts and spoke prophetically against the corruption of the KMT. After being forced to close during the war, the PCT reopened its seminary, Tainan Theological College, in the south of Taiwan.[8] I-to Loh, as a graduate of this school, was nurtured theologically in an environment where candid and often perilous discussions about the Taiwan political situation took place. After he left for study in the United States for the second time, several persons associated with the seminary were either expelled from Taiwan (in the case of a missionary) or imprisoned.[9] The school's first Taiwanese president, Shoki Coe, lived in exile in England after 1965. During his exile he worked on the staff of the Theological Education Fund of the World Council of Churches.[10]

These events influenced the future direction of Loh's vocation in several ways. As a Taiwanese who had spent most of his life under the repressive political regimes of the Japanese occupation and the KMT, he has struggled alongside his people to discover what it means to be a Taiwanese Christian. Taiwan has been a pawn on the board of world politics, both between the United States and the former Soviet Republic, and within the United Nations.[11] Being part of a Christian minority in a religious environment dominated by Confucianism, Taoism, and Buddhism added further complexity to the struggle for spiritual understanding. Even the issue of language has been a part of the Taiwanese search for identity. Older Taiwanese were forced to learn Japanese, and during the rule of the KMT, Mandarin Chinese took preference over the native Taiwanese dialect. This reality instilled within Loh an intense love for the Taiwanese people and an appreciation for other Asians who searched for a cultural voice following decades of colonial rule. Growing

8. See Shoki Coe, *Recollections and Reflections,* 2nd ed. (New York: The Rev. Dr. Shoki Coe Memorial Fund; Tainan: Formosan Christians for Self-Determination, 1993), 107-17, for a discussion of the transition from the Japanese occupation to martial law under the KMT and the response of the PCT.

9. H. Dan Beeby, "Memories of the College in Memory of Shoki," *Theology and the Church* 21, no. 2 (June 1996): 24.

10. In Coe, *Recollections and Reflections,* 233-62, Shoki Coe explains the nature of his political involvement against the KMT and how his role against the government forced his exile to England, a separation from Taiwan that lasted, except for one brief visit in 1987, until his death in 1988.

11. As a more recent case in point, the midair collision of a United States spy plane with a Chinese fighter plane on April 1, 2001, resulted in the detainment of twenty-four service personnel from the United States for nearly two weeks. Among the many points of discussion was the nature of arms sales to Taiwan by the United States and how this might affect Sino-U.S. relations during the negotiations for the release of the detainees and more generally in the future.

up in a family who appreciated both the Taiwanese and aboriginal cultures of Taiwan, worshiping in the prophetic PCT, and studying in a theological school where the biblical text and the political context were placed in dialogue all have shaped Loh's musical and spiritual vocation.

The figure of Shoki Coe, previously mentioned, stands above others in defining Loh's priorities in theological contextualism and liturgical inculturation. As the first Taiwanese president of Tainan Theological College (1949-65), Coe is one of the most highly regarded figures in the history of the PCT. Not only did he revive the school from ashes in the aftermath of World War II and the Japanese occupation, but he set the theological agenda for the "Christ and culture" discussion that took place in response to the publication of H. Richard Niebuhr's influential book *Christ and Culture*.[12] Coe stressed the interaction between the biblical text and the cultural context.[13] This text-context paradigm eventually led Coe to coin the term "contextualization" in the late 1960s and to publish an article outlining the importance of theological contextualization in seminary education. Coe was among the earliest to use this term. Through his publication, the term was given a venue in the United States.[14] Since that time it has become the nomenclature of preference for most scholars who examine the dynamics between theology and culture.[15]

The dialogue between faith and cultural context and the musical instruction Loh received from a missionary at Tainan Theological College set the stage for his further musical and theological study at Union Theological Seminary. There he was granted the master of sacred music degree in composition in 1966.[16] After an additional year of graduate study there, he returned

12. H. Richard Niebuhr, *Christ and Culture* (New York: Harper and Row, 1951). For a liturgical perspective on Niebuhr's five paradigms, see Geoffrey Wainwright, *Doxology* (New York: Oxford University Press, 1980), 384-86. Another helpful analysis can be found in John D. Witvliet, "Theological and Conceptual Models for Liturgy and Culture," *Liturgy Digest* 3, no. 2 (1996): 5-46.

13. Coe, *Recollections and Reflections*, 233. From the beginning Thomas Barclay nurtured this independence of spirit. Barclay arrived in Formosa in 1875. By 1893 he read a paper to the missionaries, "Self-Government in the Native Church," in which he said that "nothing could be said in favour of the continuance of the present system of a despotic government by a few foreigners meeting in Council" and moved to form a presbytery in which the Taiwanese people would have the primary voice (Band, 112-13).

14. Shoki Coe, "Contextualization as the Way toward Reform," *Theological Education* 9, no. 4 (summer 1973): 233-43.

15. For example, see Robert J. Schreiter, *Constructing Local Theologies* (Maryknoll, N.Y.: Orbis, 1985), and Stephan B. Bevans, *Models of Contextual Theology* (Maryknoll, N.Y.: Orbis, 1992).

16. In a personal conversation in Tainan with Kathleen Moody, Loh's instructor in music

to teach at Tainan. He assumed the leadership of the church music program at Tainan Seminary at the insistence of his former professor, Kathleen Moody, and began a course of research that would take him once again among the tribal peoples of Taiwan. A part-time position as coordinator at the Research Center for the Study of Taiwanese Music at Tunghai University (1972-73) provided him with additional time for investigation into the music of his homeland. In 1973 he became the editor of the *Tunghai Ethnomusicological Journal*, and in 1982 he received a Ph.D. in music with a major in ethnomusicology from the University of California, Los Angeles.

In any conversation with Loh, one becomes immediately aware of the importance of his family and the many sacrifices they have made for his study. His wife Hui-chin is a full partner in all of Loh's activities, as expressed here in his own words:

> Hui-chin is a woman of wisdom, an excellent mother and wife, advisor, educator. She sacrificed her own career as a Christian Education specialist just to accommodate my needs — taking full responsibility for raising our three fine children while I was an old graduate student, and later on, a wandering husband, leaving home for more than half of the time of the year, traveling, collecting materials, researching, conducting workshops, attending conferences and teaching. She is my best critic, always helping me to see things from different angles, always demanding more, better and higher standards. She typed my dissertation twice, helped me with all the clerical work, indexing all my major publications: *New Songs of Asian Cities*, 1972, *Hymns from the Four Winds*, 1983, *Sound the Bamboo*, 1990, etc. She proof read and commented on all my writings, even my compositions. If I have any achievement and contribution, it is because of her help; she deserves more than half of my credit. I sometimes joke that I have passed my Ph.D. examinations, but I cannot graduate from her expectations.[17]

All these influences — family, political context, theological and musical education — led eventually to the research and publication of *Sound the Bamboo*, a trial hymnal published by the Christian Council of Asia in 1990.

---

at Tainan Theological College, she spoke with much affection about his student days and referred to his graduation thesis from the college, "Praise from Jerusalem to Taiwan," as an extension of the PCT, a denomination that has been called "The Singing Church." See Kathleen Moody, "Sing and Make Music in Your Heart to the Lord," *Theology and the Church* 21, no. 2 (June 1966): 68.

17. Correspondence with I-to Loh on November 22, 1996.

Life as a Teacher, Hymnologist, and Ethnomusicologist

Between 1982 and 1994 Dr. Loh taught at the Asian Institute for Liturgy and Music (AILM) in Manila as a missionary to the Philippines under the sponsorship of the General Board of Global Ministries of the United Methodist Church. AILM, under the direction of Francisco Feliciano, is also known as *Samba Likaan* — literally, the place for creative worship, in the Filipino national language Tagalog. During these years he also taught music at Tainan Theological College and Seminary in Taiwan in a part-time capacity. The schools in Manila and Tainan served as venues for the discussion and application of the theology of contextualization with a focus on liturgical inculturation.[18] At AILM he was responsible for setting curriculum, teaching, and assisting in the organization of all international and ecumenical conferences. Students from many countries of Asia and beyond studied church music in an environment that fostered an appreciation for choral and congregational music, including "the best of the West" as well as choral compositions and hymnody from non-Western contexts. Loh's tenure as professor of church music and ethnomusicology ended in 1994, when he decided to return full time to his alma mater in Tainan so that he could "do something for [his] people before it was too late."

Manila was also Dr. Loh's home base for travels to all but a few of the twenty-two countries represented in *Sound the Bamboo*.[19] Much of this travel was made possible through his relationships with the Christian Conference of Asia (CCA, formerly the East Asia Christian Conference) and the World Council of Churches (WCC). He continues to serve both the CCA and the WCC as an adviser in liturgy for their international conferences and assemblies. On his travels he took the approach of an ethnomusicologist: recording songs, discussing their origins, and then returning to transcribe them from

---

18. While the term "contextualization" seems to be preferred by theologians when discussing the relationship between theology and culture (see n. 15 above), liturgists have usually used the term "inculturation" when discussing how liturgy might be responsive to culture, especially non-Western cultures. Loh uses both in his writing. The major spokesperson for inculturation is Anscar Chupungco, a Filipino Roman Catholic priest who resides much of the time in Rome. He writes out of the ferment and documents of Vatican II and their impact on the Roman Catholic liturgy, especially in non-Western contexts. See Chupungco's *Liturgical Inculturation: Sacramentals, Religiosity, and Catechesis* (New York: Paulist, 1992), 13-54, and *Worship: Progress and Tradition* (Beltsville, Md.: Pastoral Press, 1995) for more information.

19. Beginning in 1969 Loh visited almost all the countries represented in *Sound the Bamboo*, ranging from India to Bali and Australia to Korea, as many as four or five times in search of indigenous hymnody and folk song. The only exceptions were Vietnam, Cambodia, Tahiti, and Fiji, most of whose political situations prevented travel at that time.

the recordings, sometimes assisted by AILM students. Classes and worship at AILM then became venues for trying out the music with students from diverse cultural backgrounds.

An Analysis of *Sound the Bamboo* (1990)

Sound the Bamboo, a trial hymnal for the CCA, was the result of these efforts. It replaced the *EACC Hymnal* (1963), published by the East Asian Christian Conference (EACC) through the efforts of D. T. Niles, a Christian leader from Sri Lanka, who cofounded the EACC and is almost legendary among Asian Christians. The *EACC Hymnal* was so popular it went through four printings by 1966. Loh, along with Feliciano from the Philippines and James Minchin from Australia, formed the executive editorial committee for *Sound the Bamboo*, with Loh serving as general editor.[20]

Sound the Bamboo represents arguably the most labor-intensive hymnal publication by one person in the twentieth century.[21] Over three-fourths of the songs were recorded by Dr. Loh "amid the traffic noise of busy streets, beside the village fire at night, in huts and homely settings all over the Asian region."[22] The collection of the songs was followed by hours of transcription, translation, and paraphrasing. It is doubtful that any hymnal published in the twentieth century has included so much material that had not previously appeared in print. Feedback on the hymns was sought from "musicians, theologians, poets and writers, pastors, liturgists, and other representatives of Asian churches, including women and youth."[23] The 1990 publication of *Sound the Bamboo* in a trial edition allowed for further input and for cross-fertilization of these hymns among the peoples of Asia. Following a ten-year correction and revision process, *Sound the Bamboo* was revised in 2000.

The first thing that strikes the user of this hymnal is the distinctive title,

20. The information in this paragraph is a combination of discussions with Loh and material found in the preface of *Sound the Bamboo* (Christian Conference of Asia, 1990), 10.

21. In discussions with Loh about the contents of *Sound the Bamboo,* virtually every hymn served as an impetus for a story about the place and persons associated with the hymn, the variant versions recorded, the selection of the text to accompany the melody, and performance practice suggestions for a more stylistic presentation of the hymn. In the annals of hymnology, Loh's personal efforts in the collection, transcription, and production of *Sound the Bamboo* can be compared favorably with the heroic single-person hymnological publication at the end of the nineteenth century by John Julian, *Dictionary of Hymnology* (1892).

22. Loh, *Sound the Bamboo* (1990), 11.

23. Loh, *Sound the Bamboo* (1990), 11.

Sound the Bamboo. While many are generally aware of the prevalence of bamboo throughout Asia, perhaps only those who have traveled there understand its significance for sustaining the necessities of life. Homes, tools, furniture, crafts, pictures — almost anything one can imagine — are made of bamboo. Bamboo may even be eaten, and is a delicacy in many regions of Asia. It seems that the ubiquitous bamboo shoot is the answer to almost all of life's needs. While functional, bamboo also provides shade and beauty wherever it grows. It is amazing that a tree so useful can also provide material for so many kinds of musical instruments. The *kata batang* (bamboo trumpet) of Indonesia contrasts with the soothing *khlui* (bamboo flute) of Thailand. The Sundanese *angklung* ensemble of Indonesia provides a group musical experience similar to an ensemble of handbell players in the West. The *kulibit* (tube zither) of the Philippines and the *khaen* (sixteen-pipe mouth organ) of Thailand display the versatility and flexibility of bamboo as a source for musical sounds when placed in the hands of creative crafters and performers. Bamboo is a primary resource for sustaining and enriching life. The only parallel might be the use of plastic in the West, but something is lost in the translation, especially from an ecological viewpoint. Bamboo resonates all over Asia in the form of myriad string, wind, and percussion instruments. *Sound the Bamboo* resounds from the soul of Asian life and existence.

There are several distinctive features in *Sound the Bamboo* (1990). Many are obvious when one examines the page:

- Original languages (thirty-eight total) in transliteration are included in the hymnal along with English translations or singing paraphrases.
- Melodies are ornamented in the style of the country or locality of origin, including indications for gliding up or down as one approaches or leaves a note.
- Many songs contain melody only, indicating a monophonic performing preference.
- Other features include instructions for instruments (with special performance suggestions in the editor's notes, pp. 15-18) or specific practices related to a more authentic performance of the material.

One readily observes Loh's ethnomusicological training in many of the decisions he made as hymnal editor. However, underlying theological and cultural premises guided his editorial priorities. His attempts to present the hymns in a notational form that expresses the appropriate musical style of each locality have roots in a desire to represent Christian faith in an Asian ethos. One might characterize the work of this hymnal as an effort to make a shift from a Christian faith transmitted (translated) by missionaries to Asians to a Christian faith embraced by Asians. Loh discusses the problem in this way:

> [F]ascinated by the new Christian faith and associating it with the "advanced" western culture (technology, in particular), Asian converts have probably idealized and absolutized these Christian expressions and values. To the new converts it seemed necessary to denounce their past and to remove the association of pagan practices in order to prove their true conversion to Christ. Unfortunately, it led to a denial of the native culture and values; Christians became alienated from their local culture and their own people. They were eager to learn and adapt the new Christian expression, including liturgies and music. Eventually, they became so attached to these forms that they regarded them as the absolutely authentic way of Christian expression.[24]

Many Asian Christians felt they have had to make a choice between Christianity and Asian culture.[25] The publication of an Asian hymnal, notated as nearly as possible in a manner that encourages an authentic presentation of the songs, is not just the work of an ethnomusicologist who specializes in church music. It is a theological endeavor designed to help Asian Christians find their cultural voice in the context of Christian liturgy. C. S. Song's verbal theological reflection mirrors what Loh has accomplished in musical theological performance. Song notes that "[o]urs is the task of incorporating ourselves and the history of our lands into God's plans."[26] He continues this line of thought when he states that Asian theologians must listen "to the stories of the inhabitants of the vast continent of Asia — listen with our heart, our souls, and our might. . . . Theology is not debate. It is not argumentation. It is not reasoning. It is confession. It is a witness to the truth wherever it manifests itself."[27] Loh's ethnomusicological excursions are part of the listening and confessional storytelling process that Song encourages. *Sound the*

---

24. Loh, "Contemporary Issues," 50.

25. Asian Christians expressed the conflict of having to choose between Christianity and Asian culture many times in a conference sponsored by the Programme for Theology & Culture in Asia (PTCA) that I attended in Kuala Lumpur, Malaysia, June 12-18, 1996. The topic was "Doing Theology with Asian Resources" with a focus on economic realities throughout Asia. The PTCA is a theological discussion forum growing out of the CCA. A recurrent theme of the conference emphasized ways to make use of Western technological resources without "selling one's soul" to the West in the process.

26. Song, *Tell Us Our Names*, 34.

27. Song, *Womb of Asia*, 132.

Bamboo is a musical analogue to Song's theological reflection and search for Asian ways of expressing Christianity.

Theological reflection through congregational song is a complex task. The hymns of *Sound the Bamboo* give witness to the cultural intricacies and diverse influences on Asians from beyond their borders. To this end Loh has divided the songs into four categories:

1. Western hymn styles.
2. Traditional styles: adaptations of old native melodies from grass roots, or new compositions in more recent but still traditional styles, with or without accompaniment.
3. Syncretistic styles: folk tunes or melodies with traditional characteristics but arranged with traditional Western harmony.
4. International and contextual styles: innovative works combining native concepts or idioms with contemporary international techniques of composition, culturally contextual and challenging to modern people.[28]

Three additional musical issues complicated the process of preparing a hymnal using Asian resources: the limitations of Western musical notation for representing non-Western musical styles, the practice of oral tradition, and the nature of setting tonal languages to music. In the case of musical notation, there are five recognized world musical systems with written theories and philosophies. Three are in eastern Asia (India, China, and Indonesia) and a fourth, the Persian system, is from western Asia (Iran and surrounding Middle Eastern countries).[29] While the Western system of notation, the fifth, has become standard in many places around the world, it is difficult for Western notation to transmit the nuance of many Asian melodies to the same degree that a system designed originally for a specific musical culture does.

The practice of oral tradition presents different problems for the collector of indigenous melodies, especially where a single song may have numerous versions.[30] Written notation tends to standardize or "freeze" the process

---

28. Loh, *Sound the Bamboo* (1990), 17.

29. I-to Loh, "Transmitting Cultural Traditions in Hymnody," *Church Music Workshop* 4, no. 3 (September-December 1994): 2.

30. See Bruno Nettl, *Folk and Traditional Music of the Western Continents*, 2nd ed. (Englewood Cliffs, N.J.: Prentice-Hall, 1965), 3-5, for a general description of the process of oral tradition. In *Music Cultures of the Pacific, the Near East and Asia* (Englewood Cliffs, N.J.: Prentice-Hall, 1967), William P. Malm discusses oral tradition as a compositional process throughout various musical cultures in Asia.

of musical composition, eliminating the spawning of alternative versions. Oral tradition also encourages improvisation in some situations. Anthropologist Jack Goody notes in general that oral cultures display considerable diversity in performance of rites and rituals. Written cultures "more easily manage to establish relatively stable norms over large areas that in certain spheres inhibit but do not altogether prevent diversity."[31] Coping with the relative diversity of oral traditions in written musical performance practice creates a challenge for any printed hymnal, but especially for *Sound the Bamboo*. Aspects of these practices are not unknown in the written musical traditions of the West, e.g., during the baroque period when performers explored improvisation or spontaneous composition, or even in modern jazz where performers are less encumbered by musical notation. Improvisation allows a performer to immediately contextualize a social experience in sound.

There is also an issue that does not occur in many Western contexts: the relationship of music to tonal languages. The use of a sequential stanza form where a single melody serves several stanzas of text does not work as well with tonal languages. The important relationship between musical meter and syllabic stress in English is analogous to the integral association between melodic direction and tonal inflection of speech in many Asian languages. The use of what appears to be melodic "ornamentation" from a Western perspective becomes integral to the melody when sung in many of the tonal languages.

Asian Hymns in Western Hymnals

One of the most significant issues that surfaced in my discussions with Loh was the manner in which items from *Sound the Bamboo* appear in hymnals published abroad, especially in the United States and Great Britain. This issue might be addressed more clearly if the concepts of authenticity and accessibility are placed on a continuum.[32] Issues of authenticity emphasize the musical style and the theological context of the sending cultural group. Issues of accessibility stress the receiving cultural group and its need to readily assimi-

31. Jack Goody, *The Power of Written Tradition* (Washington, D.C.: Smithsonian Institution Press, 2000), 41.

32. The placement of authenticity and accessibility on a continuum is my reflection on my discussion with Loh and a model developed out of my own struggle in presenting global materials in the United States. Mark P. Bangert speaks of authenticity and fusion (between two cultures) in a similar way in "Welcoming the Ethnic into Our Church Musical Diet," *Cross Accent: Journal of the Association of Lutheran Church Musicians* 5 (January 1995): 4-7.

late a new musical and theological perspective into a preexisting system. Ideally it could be possible to preserve the musical and theological authenticity of the sending culture and, in spite of the use of different musical instruments and translations of texts, etc., allow the receiving culture to have access to (or experience) an authentic semblance of the hymn.[33] Loh has lived on both coasts of the United States and has traveled widely throughout the world, especially in his work on behalf of the WCC. He understands the complexities of Western thought and liturgical life in the West. He feels, however, that too often Western publications of Asian materials lean too far toward the side of accessibility.[34] In the process of moving from the authenticity of the sending culture to accessibility for the receiving culture, many compromises occur naturally:[35]

1. There may be a change in the notational system or a necessary adaptation from oral improvisation to a "frozen" written form.

2. There may need to be a translation of the original text into English.

3. After translating the original text, it is necessary to provide a versification of the literal translation into a "singing" translation for publication.

4. There is almost always a change of vocal style from that of the sending culture to that of the receiving culture.

5. It is usually necessary for the receiving culture to use different accompanying instruments than those found in the sending culture.

6. The receiving culture may be unfamiliar with the accompanying movements, i.e., dance, used by the sending culture.

7. There is almost always a significant change in group dynamics or social interaction patterns, e.g., solo-response form, which are assumed by the sending culture but uncommon in the receiving culture.

---

33. T. W. Hunt, *Music in Missions: Discipling through Music* (Nashville: Broadman, 1987), 45-59, discusses issues of cross-cultural communication in more depth. My use of an authenticity/accessibility continuum is a variation of a standard communication model presented in many texts on missions.

34. Loh, "Transmitting Cultural Traditions in Hymnody," addresses the difficulties of cross-cultural communication through hymns more completely. While grateful that some selections from *Sound the Bamboo* have appeared in Western collections, Dr. Loh expresses some disappointment with the use of stylistically conflicting accompaniments and the omission of some styles of Asian hymnody altogether from Western publications.

35. I am indebted to Mark P. Bangert's article, "Dynamics of Liturgy and World Musics: A Methodology for Evaluation," in *Worship and Culture in Dialogue*, ed. S. Anita Stauffer (Geneva: Lutheran World Federation, 1994), 198-200, for the general approach and some of the specific ideas in the following list.

The list could be extended, but the point is clear. The possible variance between the authenticity of the sending culture and the receptivity of the receiving culture is considerable. The ethnomusicologist is a natural champion of authenticity; the Western music publisher survives on a product that is accessible to the consumer. It would appear that the sending and receiving cultures are on a collision course. When the pendulum swings too far to the side of accessibility, one might say that "Western musical imperialism" (my words, not Loh's) is the result. The following might be seen as examples of musical imperialism in the name of accessibility to the Western consumer:

- Eliminating all melodic "ornamentation."
- Adapting an Asian melody to a Western diatonic scale instead of maintaining the original scale, e.g., substituting a major scale for an anhemitonic scale (a pentatonic or five-tone scale without semitones, i.e., consisting only of combinations of major seconds and minor thirds).[36]
- Adding standard four-part harmony to an originally monophonic melody.
- Changing the harmony or melody submitted by the composer from another culture without consultation.
- Changing one or two notes of the original indigenous melody and securing a Western copyright as an "arrangement."
- Adapting the content of the translation of the original text without consultation or clear notice of authorship.
- Publishing transcriptions of folk songs from recordings as "arrangements" and securing Western copyright. Transcribing music from a recording and arranging music for publication are two different processes.[37]

While enthusiasm for new material by the consumer sometimes produces a "market" for the progressive or innovative publisher, some practices would appear to be unethical, even though technically legal. Loh asks a signif-

---

36. I am not speaking of the adaptation that must take place to some degree when substitute instruments from the West are used for ones indigenous to the sending culture. Nor am I referring to the substitution of the twelve equidistant half steps common to the West for a scale found in another culture, when singing music from a new environment. As Leonard Meyer has demonstrated in *Emotion and Meaning in Music* (Chicago: University of Chicago Press, 1956), our minds naturally attempt to fit new experiences into old patterns of thought (see esp. chap. 5, "Principles of Pattern Perception: The Weakening of Shape"). I am referring to the deliberate alteration of a melody from another culture in order to make it more Western and therefore "correct" in the ears of the receiving culture.

37. While all these issues were of concern to Loh, the final five practices listed presented the greatest problems to him.

icant question in this regard: "[A]re there any guidelines to preserve and protect the native [musical] heritage [of a culture] from being indiscriminately changed, destroyed, or poorly syncretized?"[38]

Guidelines for the Publication of Cross-Cultural Music in the West

I offer the following suggestions to initiate a discussion on this topic between global musicians and Western music publishers.

Textual considerations:
- Provide the text in the original language as well as English (or a language appropriate to the receiving culture).
- When possible, provide a literal translation of the original text along with a singing versification, especially when the singing version varies considerably from the original in meaning and in the use of metaphor.
- Provide a pronunciation guide for the transliterated (romanized) text in the original language somewhere in the publication, so that the leader may be informed.

Melodic considerations:
- Preserve as much of the original melodic ornamentation as possible, even if there is an indication that it is optional, especially when sung in English.
- Indicate when the usual style of performance in the original culture is monophonic and/or unaccompanied, even if no harmony has been provided. This may discourage overzealous organists and pianists from "improvising" a harmony.

Harmonic and instrumental considerations:
- When guitar chords are added (and appropriate), suggest a performance style in a brief note, e.g., style of strumming, rhythm, etc.
- When percussion instruments are appropriate, indicate the original instrument and a Western substitute (if possible) as well as an appropriate rhythm pattern.

Musical style and movement:
- Provide a broad tempo indication, e.g., half note = 56-72, for the leader.

38. Loh, "Contemporary Issues," 54.

- Indicate songs that are often accompanied by movement or dance and suggest an appropriate step in the preface of the publication.
- When possible, provide an authentic recording of the selection. Musical style is ultimately learned by ear, not from notation. A recording of global music, however, is but a "snapshot" of a given performance. Improvisation is an important feature of many global styles. Therefore a recording should only be an indicator of general style, not a "frozen" selection of music.

Concerning the source of the music and cultural context:
- When available, include a note on the origin and use of the melody and text, along with any information on known composers.

Western musicians are also concerned with issues of stylistic integrity in the performance of music. Those persons who are experienced in performing early Western music (from medieval, Renaissance, baroque periods, etc.) will note that many of the better editions of music from that time contain notes similar to those suggested above. In the area of congregational song, there is a limit to how much material can be placed on the page without confusing the singer. General information can be included in a preface, handbook, or hymnal companion.[39] Loh places the issue in a theological context when he asks, "[D]o we have any right to change [the] music [of other cultures] which is also God's gift to them?"[40]

The Process of Musical Inculturation and *Sound the Bamboo* (1990)

I-to Loh has developed an approach to inculturation for arts, liturgy, and music. The process of liturgical inculturation seeks to bring the established rites and rituals of Christian liturgy into dialogue with aspects of a given culture. The purpose of this dialogue is to make the liturgy more responsive to the people of a specific locality and expressive of their relationship to God through symbols with which they have a cultural intimacy. Within the context of liturgy as a whole, Anscar Chupungco identifies the primary difficulty in the dialogue between a liturgical tradition and culture as "how to distinguish between what is immutable in the liturgy and what is subject to

---

39. See I-to Loh, clinician, *Church Music Workshop: Practical Tools for Effective Music Ministry* 4, no. 3 (September-December 1994): 1-11 (available from Nashville: Abingdon). This resource contains a discussion of the origins and performance practice for several Asian hymns found in *The United Methodist Hymnal* (1989).

40. Loh, "Contemporary Issues," 54.

change."[41] Loh proposes a process for musical inculturation within cultures that the Western church has viewed as "mission fields" for decades and, in some cases, centuries. He suggests that incremental stages of change are necessary for moving from total dependence on the music of an alien culture, transplanted by missionaries, to the nurture of indigenous musical expressions of faith created from the images and resources of the culture.[42] Loh proposes four stages for musical inculturation.[43]

1. Translation and Transplanting

Preservation of the original message and form of the sending culture is paramount in this approach.[44] At this stage the text of the hymns is strictly translated and most of the original music is preserved. While a starting place, this approach is often deemed inadequate when used exclusively.

2. Acculturation[45]

The second stage is adapting existing liturgical rites and rituals from another culture. In the musical sense, this would include changing a Western diatonic melody to a pentatonic tune by modifying the fourth and seventh degrees of the scale.

41. Anscar J. Chupungco, "Liturgy and the Components of Culture," in *Worship and Culture in Dialogue,* 153.

42. For an excellent theological discussion of these issues, see Robin Leaver, "Theological Dimensions of Mission Hymnody: The Counterpoint of Cult and Culture," in *The Hymnology Annual,* ed. Vernon Wicker, vol. 1 (Berrien Springs, Mich.: Vande Vere Publishing, 1991), 38-50. A helpful case study on this subject has been written by Amy Lu'uleialoha Stillman, "Beyond Bibliography: Interpreting Hawaiian-Language Protestant Hymn Imprints," *Ethnomusicology* 40, no. 3 (fall 1996): 469-88. This article examines the interrelationship between the music of Protestant missionaries and the pre-Christian music of the Hawaiian Islands during the nineteenth century, forming what she calls a new "syncretistic" style.

43. The following section draws heavily from Loh, "Contemporary Issues," 49-56.

44. For a thorough discussion of the process of translation of biblical and theological content from one culture to another, see Charles H. Kraft, *Christianity in Culture: A Study in Dynamic Biblical Theologizing in Cross-Cultural Perspective* (Maryknoll, N.Y.: Orbis, 1979). For a broader perspective and critique of the theory of translation, see works cited in n. 15 by Robert J. Schreiter and Stephan B. Bevans.

45. See Anscar J. Chupungco, *Cultural Adaptation of the Liturgy* (New York: Paulist, 1982), 81, for a discussion of liturgical acculturation and inculturation. According to Chupungco, *acculturation* is a process that is the result of liturgical adaptation of an existing rite. *Inculturation* is the process of interpreting and transforming pre- or non-Christian rites (his focus is on Roman rites) in light of the Christian gospel. While this work was a source for Loh's view of acculturation, Chupungco has modified his approach somewhat in later texts cited in n. 18 above.

3. Inculturation

In the third stage the musician adapts existing folk melodies of a culture, writes new ones that reflect the style of the culture, or combines traditional styles with contemporary or Western idioms.

4. Incarnational[46]

"Speaking in our own native language" (Acts 2:8 TEV). Creating new musical and liturgical forms that speak more directly to the heart and mind of the culture characterizes the fourth stage.[47] This would include native music in contemporary styles. The content of *Sound the Bamboo* focuses heavily on levels two and three, with several examples that move toward level four.

I-to Loh's Contributions to *Sound the Bamboo* (1990)

Perhaps one can better understand the process of musical inculturation in light of Loh's specific contributions to *Sound the Bamboo*. In many ways his preparation of this hymnal was similar to the work of any hymnal editor. In other ways his contributions were singular because of the unusual ethnic diversity of the community for whom the hymnal was prepared and the varied musical styles included in this collection. Four categories of contributions have been singled out for discussion.

1. Transcriptions with Added Texts

In discussions of specific items from *Sound the Bamboo* 2000 (SB2000), Loh takes special delight in talking about the music that was indigenous to the Taiwanese aboriginal tribes he came to know as a child while on mission trips with his father, and later studied during his doctoral work at UCLA. Two are of special note.

---

46. Loh referred in discussions to the work of fellow Taiwanese C. S. Song, who also served for a time as president of Tainan Theological College and Seminary. Incarnational theology is a recurring theme in the work of Song. See especially *Tell Us Our Names* and *Theology from the Womb of Asia*.

47. See I-to Loh, "Asian Worship," in *The Complete Library of Christian Worship*, vol. 7, *The Ministries of Christian Worship*, ed. Robert Webber (Nashville: Star Song Publishing Group, 1994), 217-21, for examples of incarnational approaches to liturgy within the Asian context.

"O Give Thanks to the Lord" (SB2000: 99) is a version of Psalm 136 with a traditional solo-response form used by the Amis tribe. Loh transcribed the music and added the text because it matched the spirit of the song so well. The Ami people have used this song successfully. The hymn follows:

Example 3.1. "O Give Thanks to the Lord."
Words: Psalm 136, adapted by I-to Loh (altered).
Music: MIHAMEK; Amis song, Taiwan.

Another selection, "Let All Nations Come, Praise the Lord" (SB2000: 96), is what Loh calls a sectional canon. He recalls that his father taught this song in Sunday school in 1948. In 1972 Loh returned to the composer's home to transcribe the music. It was easy to add a text because much Taiwanese tribal singing is vocalized (without a specific text).

"May the Lord, Mighty God" (SB2000: 80) is perhaps the most widely known selection, and according to Loh, one of the most popular hymns in

Example 3.2. "Let All Nations Come, Praise the Lord."
Words: Psalm 117; adapted by I-to Loh, Taiwan;
Music: KATIPOL; Puyuma song, Chen Shih, Taiwan.

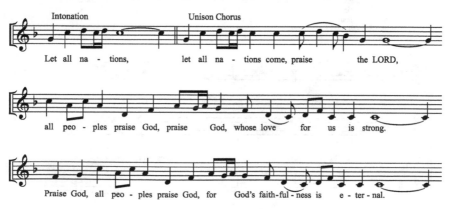

Sound the Bamboo. In this case he noted a melody attributed to Pao-chen Li, matched a text based on Numbers 6:24-26 and Psalm 29:11 to the tune, and translated it into Chinese. This hymn appears in at least three recent American hymnals.[48]

2. Harmonizations

In some cases Loh added a harmonization to an existing melody in an "international style." An example is "Winter Has Passed, the Rain Is O'er" (SB2000: 71), a very popular hymn in the Chinese church since 1975. The accompaniment has a theological significance in that it "follows" the melody in a freely imitative manner. The melody signifies Christ walking ahead, while the accompaniment is symbolic of the Christian who follows Christ. In addition, Loh (under his pen name Pen-li Chen) provided a contrapuntal accompaniment because he knew there would be a tendency for organists to "improvise"

48. See *Hymnal: A Worship Book* (435), *The Presbyterian Hymnal* (596), and *The Worshiping Church* (843).

their own standard Western four-part version. "Holy Night, Blessed Night" (SB2000: 140)[49] is another example of a modestly contrapuntal accompaniment added by Loh (also under the pen name Pen-li Chen) to a Chinese tune and text. A portion of "Winter Has Passed, the Rain Is O'er" follows:

Example 3.3. "Winter Has Passed, the Rain Is O'er." Words: Weifan Wang, China; trans. Ewing W. Carroll, Jr.; Music: JIA-OU, Shengben Kin, China; arr. Pen-li Chen (I-to Loh).

Translation copyright © Ewing W. Carroll, Jr. Melody copyright © Shengben Lin. Musical arrangement copyright © I-toh Loh. Used by permission.

49. Also found in *The Presbyterian Hymnal* (33).

3. Original Music

Perhaps the best examples of original music by Loh in *Sound the Bamboo* are hymns in which he set a text by New Zealander Shirley Erena Murray. Loh particularly enjoyed working with her texts. Although his musical settings were not always understood initially by the author, she was open and often was willing to be convinced. Of particular note is "The Hunger Carol" (SB2000: 144). His compositional style retains the Indonesian *gamelan* flavor of the *bonang* (kettle gong), with the accompaniment anticipating, decorating, and doubling the melody. The tune name, SMOKEY MOUNTAIN, refers to a trash heap in Manila, Philippines, where people lived and searched for food through the refuse. Loh remarked in one conversation with the author: "If all my hymns are forgotten but this one, I'll be happy."[50] The opening of "Hunger Carol" follows:[51]

Example 3.4. "Hunger Carol."
Words: Shirley Erena Murray, New Zealand;
Music: SMOKEY MOUNTAIN, I-to Loh, Taiwan

50. A fuller description of the background of this hymn can be found in *Church Music Workshop* 4, no. 3 (September-December 1994): 12. A choral version of the "Hunger Carol," arranged by I-to Loh, is available through Abingdon Press.
51. The complete text of "Hunger Carol" ("Child of joy and peace") may be found in *In Every Corner Sing: The Hymns of Shirley Erena Murray* (Carol Stream, Ill.: Hope Publishing, 1992), 5, with a musical setting by fellow New Zealander Douglas Mews.

HUNGER CAROL (Child of Joy and Peace) Text © Hope Publishing Co., Carol Stream, IL 60188. All rights reserved. Used by permission. Music copyright © 1996 General Board of Global Ministries, GBGMusik, 475 Riverside Drive, Room 350, New York, N.Y. 10115. All rights reserved. Used by permission.

"Loving Spirit" is another text by Shirley Erena Murray (SB2000: 220) with original music by Loh. In this case he set the text with an Indian scale (similar to the "gypsy" minor in the West) and added an appropriate drum part. The meter (3 + 4 over 8) symbolizes the mystery of the Spirit.

Example 3.5. "Loving Spirit." Words: Shirley Erena Murray, New Zealand; Music: CHHUN-BÍN, I-to Loh, Taiwan

4. Adaptations of Existing Melodies

Additional contributions to the hymnal include variations of the three categories already mentioned. In "Living in Christ with People" (SB2000: 202), a text by another New Zealander, Ron O'Grady, Loh takes a motive from a Balinese song, expands it, and provides a Javanese arrangement with the *bonang* compositional approach described above. A portion of the hymn follows:

Example 3.6. "Living in Christ with People."
Words: Ron O'Grady, New Zealand; Music: TONDO;
motive from Balinese song "Meon-meon"; I-to Loh, Taiwan.

Words copyright © Ron O'Grady. Music copyright © I-toh Loh. Used by permission.

In "For the Beauty of the Earth" (SB2000: 171) he adapts a Chinese folk song that is very popular and was used by Puccini in his opera *Turandot*. The original text of the folk song describes "a Jasmine flower with fragrance and beauty that all love. Let me come and pick it and give it to someone I love."[52] Loh matches the feeling of love for the beauty of the flower and creation ascribed to this Chinese tune to Folliot S. Pierpoint's familiar hymn text.

While this summary cannot completely describe Loh's contributions to the publication of *Sound the Bamboo*, it gives the reader some indication of the depth of his involvement. The influence of this hymnal already can be seen in other hymnals such as the Hakka Chinese hymnal *Hak-Ngî Sun-Sû* (Hakka Hymnal), published in 1999, a project on which Loh was an adviser. Many selections from *Sound the Bamboo* are in this hymnal, and as much as a third of the hymnal reflects various Asian musical idioms.

Sound the Bamboo (2000)

In spite of a busy administrative schedule, Loh succeeded in making extensive corrections and revisions to *Sound the Bamboo* in a revised edition that was published in 2000. The executive editorial committee remained the same as for the 1990 edition: Feliciano (Philippines), Minchin (Australia), and Loh as general editor. In a beautiful, slightly larger format, twenty-one countries are represented. Forty-seven languages plus English are included. Thirteen hymns were dropped from the original 280 of the 1990 edition. Forty-eight new hymns were added, for a total of 315 in the 2000 edition. Of the 267 hymns found in both editions, efforts have been made when possible to continue the same numbering of these hymns in both hymnals. According to the preface in the 2000 edition, the hymns have been dropped either because they were outside the sphere of influence of the CCA (Pacific and Africa) or because the earlier versions were either "unintelligible or unsingable."[53] New hymns come from countries that were underrepresented in the 1990 edition, especially Cambodia, Indonesia, Laos, Myanmar, Singapore, Pakistan, and Sri Lanka. Romanized texts in languages other than English have been updated according to current practice. English translations have been revised to support the melodic and rhythmic flow of the music. Loh notes that "[o]ut of respect to our Jewish brothers and sisters, we are not using the vocalized form

---

52. Conversation with I-to Loh, June 20, 1996.

53. *Sound the Bamboo: CCA Hymnal 2000*, ed. I-to Loh (Hong Kong: Christian Conference of Asia, 2000), viii. The 2000 edition may be ordered through the Hymn Society Bookstore (1-800-THE HYMN) or by contacting the Christian Conference of Asia at cca@pacific.net.hk or www.cca.org.hk.

of 'Yahweh' in this edition of *Sound the Bamboo*."[54] Substitutions, e.g., "I AM," "LORD," are inserted depending on the biblical context of the original.[55] Efforts to be sensitive to masculine language in English in relation to humanity and deity have been attempted, though "our collective wit has not been able to devise a better way forward" than others. The preface of the 2000 edition concludes with a plea: "Is there someone in the Asian Churches burning with zeal to effect a permanent improvement to the gender weighting of liturgical and theological language?"[56]

I-to Loh's Work Today

Loh works in several spheres of activity and influence. First, there are the former students from AILM and Tainan who have caught his vision of musical and liturgical contextualization. They apply this vision in various churches throughout Asia, bringing an Asian balance and perspective to the Western heritage inherited from missionaries and to the continuing Western influences that flood Asia through popular North American culture.[57] As Loh approaches retirement, he channels as much time as possible toward the training of students who will assume leadership in developing, spreading, and encouraging indigenous Asian song in the future.[58]

A second sphere of influence is in the church music community in Taiwan, where Dr. Loh was installed as chair of the Church Music Department and professor of church music and ethnomusicology at Tainan Theological

---

54. Loh, *Sound the Bamboo* (2000), ix.

55. Loh notes that "your editors have fought battles royal within and among themselves over whether to employ 'LORD' or 'Lord' in reference to each distinct Person of the Trinity, viz., Jesus, the Son, the Word; the Father; the Holy Spirit. Apart from the sheer trouble of making a decision and consequent typographical change in every instance, we have almost certainly fallen prey to inconsistency, and seek your indulgence — or, better, your suggestions." Loh, *Sound the Bamboo* (2000), ix.

56. Loh, *Sound the Bamboo* (2000), ix.

57. I have had the privilege of experiencing the ministries of several of Loh's students, including Lim Swee Hong (Singapore), Edgardo Macapili (a Filipino living in Taiwan), and Ruth and Inchai Srisuwan (Bangkok, Thailand).

58. Loh has engaged the services of several church music educators to assist him at the Tainan Seminary in training Asian church musicians who will be proficient and knowledgeable in Western musical styles as well as able to encourage and perform Asian styles. These persons include Mary Oyer (Goshen, Ind.) and Carlton Young (Nashville, Tenn.), who have spent several semesters in Tainan; Terry MacArthur (Geneva, Switzerland) and Pablo Sosa (Buenos Aires, Argentina) have spent shorter terms.

Seminary and College in February 1995. Since returning to Taiwan to teach full time in 1994, he has published a new Taiwanese hymnal, *Ban-bîn Siong-chàn* (literally, Ten Thousand People Praise, or Let All Nations Praise). It contains 157 selections from around the world. While the focus is on hymns indigenous to Taiwan (65), there are hymns from other parts of Asia (32) as well as selections from Africa (24), Latin America (9), Europe (21, with 11 from the Taizé Community), and the USA (6). This publication indicates that his vision for the church in Taiwan includes not only the cultivation of indigenous song but also the inclusion of songs from the global church. As his schedule permits, Loh introduces songs from the hymnal throughout the island.[59] These "praise choruses," as Loh calls them, reflect a broader range of theology and musical style than material under the same name in current use in the United States and other countries.

Loh continues to be a consultant to several religious and denominational bodies, including the Lutheran World Federation, the United Methodist Church Global Praise Project, and ecumenical groups such as the international YMCAs, the CCA, and the WCC. In December 1998 Loh was an *animateur* at the WCC Jubilee Assembly in Harare, Zimbabwe. Participation with these organizations, however, depends upon his schedule in Tainan. In February 1995, just a few days after being installed as chair of the Church Music Department, he was asked by the trustees of Tainan Theological College and Seminary to become its president. The request was one for which Loh and his wife Hui-chin were not prepared. He accepted and began his presidency in August 1995. President Loh regularly conducts the student body in singing. The concept of the seminary community as a choir with Loh as its director is perhaps the best metaphor for his approach to leadership.[60] The first commencement ceremony under Loh's presidency was held in June 1996. His global vision was evident in a processional accompanied by a Taiwanese percussion ensemble, a hymn from Myanmar (Burma), and the official seminary

59. For example, Loh visited twelve congregations in the year previous to my first visit to Taiwan in 1996. I attended a Sunday service in a rural Presbyterian church outside of Tainan during June 1996. The congregation used several selections from the hymnal at the beginning of the service, led capably by an elder from the congregation. While I didn't understand his words, I recognized many of the songs (sung in Taiwanese) from Africa, Latin America, and Taiwan. The people joined in enthusiastically.

60. I am grateful to Mrs. Loh (Hui-chin) for her insight into Dr. Loh's work at the seminary and his vision for the school. Hui-chin is herself a graduate of the Tainan Seminary and Princeton Seminary, where she studied at the same time that Loh attended Union Seminary in New York. She is integral to the completion of the many responsibilities that fall to President Loh on a daily basis.

hymn with music by Loh, as well as a variety of hymns, choral music, and organ selections from the Western Christian tradition. A master's degree in church music has been instituted, with students from around Asia participating in the program. He plans to conclude his tenure as president in 2002.

As Loh concludes his presidency, he is also working on a new hymnal for the PCT. *Seng-si* (Holy Poems or Hymns) is scheduled for publication in 2005 with a maximum of 700 hymns. A sampler of 100 hymns is in process for distribution to the churches and General Assembly in April 2002. "We had planned to have roughly 30% from Taiwan, 30% from the third world and 40% from the West. But I am afraid that it is too optimistic. It may end up with over 50% Western. This will probably be the only way for our church to accept the new hymnal. . . . Sad!"[61] Loh has been developing criteria for the hymnal that relate to the "public statements" of the PCT.[62] "Over four years ago, I had proposed the criteria for editing our hymnal: Historical, Ecumenical, Multicultural, Contemporary, Contextual (Taiwanese), and Liturgical. We are working towards this ideal. I hope we can achieve our goal, but I still have to work very hard on this. We are calling for new hymns written for our present context."[63]

The Impact of I-to Loh's Work in Asia

Contextualization and globalization of the music, liturgy, and mission of the PCT are growing under President Loh's leadership and prophetic witness. While Christianity has a much longer history in Asia than is generally recognized,[64] one must remember that, except for the Philippines, it is a minority faith in this area of the world. While some estimate that 25-30 percent of South Koreans are Christians, fewer than 3 percent of Asians can be numbered among those of the Christian faith. This does not imply that there is a spiritual vacuum in Asia; Asian cultures are highly religious. In the areas of

---

61. Correspondence with I-to Loh, December 19, 2001.

62. *Public Statements*, 3rd ed. (Taipei: General Assembly of the Presbyterian Church in Taiwan, 1995).

63. Correspondence with I-to Loh, December 19, 2001.

64. See John C. England, "The Hidden History of Christianity in Asia: The Churches of the East before 1500 C.E.," in *Doing Theology with Asian Resources: Ten Years in the Formation of Living Theology in Asia*, ed. John C. England and Archie C. C. Lee (Auckland, New Zealand: Programme for Theology and Cultures in Asia, 1993), 129-61. Also see John C. England, "Early Asian Christian Writings, Fifth–Twelfth Centuries: An Appreciation," *Asia Journal of Theology* 11, no. 1 (April 1997): 154-71.

Christian liturgy and music, urban Christians throughout Asia draw very heavily on Western models and materials. While there are small pockets of interest in inculturation, liturgical inculturation is accepted on a very limited basis within the minority Christian church in this part of the world. Increasingly, Westernization of Asian cultures makes efforts toward theological contextualization even more difficult.

At the beginning of this chapter C. S. Song asked the question: "How can those of us preoccupied with God and humanity, nature, life, and death afford not to listen to the people?" I-to Loh has listened to people throughout Asia and has been the midwife to a nascent movement that encourages Asian Christians to raise their voices to God in sung praise and prayer, using the cultural symbols closest to their experience. There is no greater voice throughout Asia for developing indigenous congregational singing than I-to Loh.

CHAPTER 4

Singing Freedom

David Dargie and South African Liberation Song

Unless people have a pride in themselves, how are they to liberate themselves?

DAVID DARGIE[1]

David Dargie has devoted much of his life to the liberation of people through congregational song, especially black South Africans. The purpose of this chapter is to explore the dimensions of sung liberation through Dargie's ministry and teaching. This includes the following: (1) his work as an ethnomusicologist among the Xhosa people, (2) his efforts as a teacher developing group compositional teaching strategies, (3) his role as liturgist serving as a catalyst for using xylophones and other instruments within the Roman Catholic Mass, and (4) his image as a *bawo* or father among the Xhosa people, identifying with the roots of their spirituality and their struggle for political, economic, and spiritual liberation.

Introduction to Recent South African Politics

Since the early 1980s the story of the southern part of the African continent is one of struggle for political liberation. Much of western and eastern sub-

---

1. David Dargie, "African Church Music and Liberation," in *Papers Presented at the Third Symposium on Ethnomusicology,* ed. Andrew Tracey (Durban: University of Natal, September 16-19, 1982), 11.

Saharan Africa had shaken off the yoke of colonial oppression in the 1960s and 1970s. Independence, though, has not been without significant and, at times, seemingly overwhelming complications, especially in the political and economic arenas. Recent events such as civil wars, military coups, and political instability due to tribal conflicts in Nigeria, Liberia, and Sierra Leone in the west and Kenya, Uganda, and Somalia in the eastern part of the continent have been widely publicized.

It was not until 1980 that Rev. Canaan Banana led Zimbabwe, then called Rhodesia, to political liberation. He became its first democratically elected state president, with Robert Mugabe as prime minister. Together they provided the southern part of the African continent a taste of political liberation from colonial oppressors. Ten years later, in 1990, South Africa's other neighbor to the north, Namibia, followed Zimbabwe to independence. And finally, after over forty-five years of apartheid, South Africa broke the grip of oppression in April 1994 by holding its first fully democratic process for all South Africans, electing Nelson Mandela as president. Rarely has the global political community responded with such a unified front against a system of oppression as it did to the atrocities of the apartheid regime in South Africa during the last half of the twentieth century. The drama of the final throes of this struggle was played out on CNN in the early 1990s for all the world to witness. Each day we were able to watch the conflict between the police and black South Africans and hear the singing of the oppressed as they marched for their rights.

On October 29, 1998, former archbishop Desmond Tutu officially presented President Mandela the five volumes of the report of the Truth and Reconciliation Commission (TRC). Tutu, head of the TRC, had heard long hours of personal testimony from the victims of the atrocities committed under the tyranny of apartheid. The first stage of the investigation was complete. When Mandela received the TRC report from Tutu, the South African National Choir broke into jubilant song. Then, before a global audience, Mandela and Tutu danced in celebration, not because the recovery from apartheid was complete — far from it. These two winners of the Nobel Peace Prize danced and sang in solidarity with those who marched and sang before them in the face of unspeakable injustice. They danced in celebration of what had transpired to bring them to this point. They danced in the hope that the songs that had carried them this far along the "long walk to freedom"[2] would sustain them in the difficult days ahead when political change would hopefully lead to transformation in the attitudes and lives of people.

---

2. This is the title of Nelson Mandela's autobiography, *Long Walk to Freedom* (Boston: Little, Brown, 1994).

The ceremony ended with the singing of the greatest of African liberation songs, "Nkosi sikelel' iAfrika" (Lord, bless Africa), written in 1892, over
one hundred years earlier, by Enoch Sontonga, who set the text in Xhosa, the
language of one of the tribal groups in South Africa. Today's version has stanzas in Xhosa, Zulu, Sotho, and Tswana, several of the major tribes of the
Bantu-language group in South Africa. The text in Xhosa with an English
translation follows:

Nkosi sikelel' iAfrika,
Maluphakam' uphondo lwayo,
Yiva imithandazo yethu,
Usisikelele thina lusapho lwakho.

    Lord, bless Africa.
    Lift up the horn (of her power).
    Hear our prayers,
    and bless us your family.

Yihla Moya, yihla Moya,
Yihla Moya oyingcwele,
Usisikelele thina lusapho lwakho.
(Zulu) *Makubenjalo!*
Kude kube ngonaphakade!

    Come Holy Spirit, come Holy Spirit,
    come Holy Spirit,
    and bless your family.
    May it be so
    for ever and ever![3]

The theme song of the African National Congress (ANC), "Nkosi sikelel'
iAfrika," was banned during the apartheid regime. It was not uncommon for
South Africans to be threatened or attacked by police for singing its strains,
especially during the turbulent 1980s.[4] According to Dargie, the final words in

3. See www.polity.org.za/misc/nkosi.html for other translations of this hymn and an audio file, along with a more complete history of its origins.
4. Dargie recalls a specific incident when he attended a political funeral in the 1980s
where a group of Black Sash women (a white women's organization known for their silent, non-
violent protests, although not excluding black membership) were threatened by police for singing this song outside the gate of a black township. It is no wonder that "Nkosi sikelel' iAfrika"
carries the unifying power that it does today. This episode was cited by Dargie in "Thinking
Back to Tiyo Soga," *East London Daily Dispatch*, June 13, 1997.

Zulu were added spontaneously to the Xhosa words during one of the ANC meetings. Other tribes have added their languages to this song since then, making it an ongoing creative process.[5]

This song and the context out of which it comes pose several questions. What is the nature and genesis of liberation song? How does liberation song relate to South African liturgical and political life? What are the theological themes of liberation songs? Now that South African songs are appearing in increasing numbers in hymnals published in North America,[6] a study of the roots of liberation song may inform our liturgy. For South Africans there is a link between singing and liberation. Perhaps an examination of the South African context revealed through the work of David Dargie can shed some light on the synergistic relationship between song and struggle.

Father Dargie: A Vocational Response to Vatican II in Liturgy and Song

At first glance Father David Dargie would not appear to be a likely candidate for nourishing South African indigenous song.[7] Of Scottish descent, Dargie is

---

5. The text provided here and the information about the song is from David Dargie, *Sing an African Song* (Hogsback, South Africa: published by David Dargie, ca. 1995), 15.

6. The collection and cassette, *Freedom Is Coming: Songs of Protest and Praise from South Africa*, ed. Anders Nyberg (Chapel Hill, N.C.: Walton Music Corporation, 1984), first brought these songs to light to a broader audience through the impetus of the Iona Community in Scotland. Selections from this book, originally published by Utryck for the Church of Sweden Mission, have appeared in at least seven North American hymnals since this time. For example, see *United Methodist Hymnal* (1989), "Thuma Mina" (497); *Hymnal: A Worship Book* (1992), "Asithi: Amen" (64), "Thuma Mina" (434); *Chalice Hymnal* (1995), "Masithi" (30), "Siyahamba" (442), "Thuma Mina" (447); *Covenant Hymnal* (1996), "Siyahamba" (424), "Hallelujah! Pelo Tso Rona" (499), "Thuma Mina" (626); *Voices United* (1996), "Sanna Sannanina" (128), "Thuma Mina" (572), "Siyahamba" (646); *The New Century Hymnal* (1995), "Masithi" (760), "Siyahamb'" (626), "Thuma Mina" (360), "We Shall Not Give Up the Fight" (437); *The Book of Praise* (1997), "Thuma Mina" (777), "Siyahamba" (639), "Asithi Amen" (264), "Freedom Is Coming" (725). Recent African American hymnals such as *This Far by Faith* (1999) from the Evangelical Lutheran Church in America (ELCA) make extensive use of South African sources. Current hymnal supplements continue to expand this literature into common usage. See *With One Voice* (1995) from the ELCA; *Wonder, Love, and Praise* (1997), Episcopal Church, USA; and *The Faith We Sing* (2000), United Methodist, for more examples.

7. Information in this section and throughout this chapter comes from personal interviews with David Dargie at his home in Hogsback and at his office at the University of Fort Hare in nearby Alice, South Africa, between November 1 and 8, 1998.

a third-generation South African raised in the coastal town of East London. Following seminary training in Pretoria and ordination in 1964, he served in New Brighton as a priest until 1965. These were the creative days following the Second Vatican Council (1962-65). Two of his colleagues at the Lumko Missiological Institute, Fritz Lobinger and Oswald Hirmer, had come to South Africa in the 1950s and had established work by this time. They began to encourage the local people to create their own music for the Mass in the spirit of Vatican II reforms. The Lumko Institute began as a language institute for missionaries in 1962. Now it promotes the gospel through literature and workshops, developing small Christian communities, Bible study, models for shared ministry between clergy and laity, spiritual growth seminars, and instruction in the Rite of Christian Initiation for Adults (RCIA) leading to baptism in the Roman Catholic Church.

In addition to the experimentation and encouragement of Hirmer and Lobinger, Dargie heard a Mass by Benjamin Peter John Tyamzashe in 1965. Hirmer and Lobinger had commissioned Tyamzashe, the best-known Xhosa composer of his day, to write church music, and he had published the Mass through the Lumko Institute. Dargie notes that before this time Catholic missionaries were content to follow Protestant models of translation of Western hymns into Xhosa. However, totally absurd pairings of text and tune sometimes resulted, such as singing the Latin hymn "Tantum ergo" in Latin to the tune of "My Darling Clementine."[8] Given the tonal nature of African languages, the entire exercise of translating Western texts into Xhosa and joining them to existing Western tunes produced many songs that ranged from humorous to meaningless.

The concept of composing music using traditional Xhosa techniques was new to Tyamzashe. He proceeded, however, using the great hymn of the first Xhosa Christian convert, Ntsikana, a prophet whose Christian witness led to the spread of the Christian faith among the Xhosa people during the early nineteenth century. One of Ntsikana's legacies to the Xhosa people was a great hymn, now commonly divided into four hymns, that has been transmitted through oral tradition to this day.[9] Tyamzashe, born in 1890 as the son of a Congregational minister, was a prolific composer of over two hundred

8. David Dargie, "Xhosa Church Music," in *Music and the Experience of God,* ed. David Power, Mary Collins, and Mellonee Burnim (Edinburgh: T. & T. Clark, 1989), 65.

9. Ntsikana was also a legendary prophet for peace among the Xhosas during the early nineteenth century, a crucial time in their history when they were engaged in a series of wars against the British. See Noël Mostert, *Frontiers: The Epic of South Africa's Creation and the Tragedy of the Xhosa People* (Johannesburg: Pimlico, 1992), 461-66, for an account of Ntsikana's role in this struggle.

works.[10] His "Gloria," commissioned by Hirmer and Lobinger, was part of *Missa I*, now called *Missa Qamata*, named after the old Xhosa name for God.[11]

Tyamzashe mastered tonic sol-fa notation at a young age, following in the footsteps of John Knox Bokwe, a Presbyterian minister, who first adapted the system of John Curwen (a British music educator) to Xhosa music. It was Bokwe's transcriptions of Ntsikana's songs, published in 1878, that conveyed the musical sounds of the oral tradition to print using sol-fa transcription.[12] Both the written version and oral variants live side by side today as they continue the heritage of the prophet Ntsikana's hymn, a song that might be called the "Ein' feste Burg" of the Xhosa people. Vatican II, Hirmer and Lobinger's vision, the discovery of Ntsikana's hymn, and Tyamzashe's Mass, all converging, set Dargie on a prophetic course of his own that would steer his life in unimagined directions in pursuit of Xhosa song and its role in the liturgical and cultural life of the people.

The Making of a Musical Liberator

We will return to Ntsikana, Bokwe, and Tyamzashe. Let us first look at the forces and conditions that shaped Dargie's vocation as a missionary — a missionary I will call a "musical liberator." In order to appreciate Dargie's vision, however, one must gain insight into the cultural, political, and personal obstacles that would seem to make him — a white Roman Catholic priest — an unlikely candidate to champion Xhosa traditional music, learn to perform it, bring it into the church, and foster a vision among black South Africans that their culture could be a significant and legitimate expression of their faith.

While a brief discussion will not do justice to the intricacies of this infamous system of human degradation and political enslavement, it is necessary to lay the stage with a short summary of apartheid and its roots. The events that led to the election of Nelson Mandela in 1994 and the publication of the report by the TRC in 1998 seem all the more amazing in light of the history of black South Africans. There are many sources that describe the initial contact

10. David Dargie, "The Beloved B ka T: Benjamin Peter John Tyamzashe," *East London Daily Dispatch,* May 30, 1997.

11. David Dargie, "African Sunday II Listener's Guide," in *African Sunday II* (Delmenville, South Africa: Lumko Institute, 1988), 3.

12. David Dargie, "Thank God for Music of uMdengentonga," *East London Daily Dispatch,* July 11, 1997. The texts of Ntsikana's hymn were written down in 1822 after the group came to the mission following Ntsikana's death in 1821.

between the Portuguese and the Khoikhoi, the coastal inhabitants of southern Africa, in the late fifteenth century. The later incursion of the Dutch and finally the British into South Africa as trade routes extended is also well documented.[13]

Following over 175 years of war between the colonizers and the Africans (beginning with clashes in 1702 and culminating with the Last Frontier War in 1878), the early twentieth century sets the stage for formal apartheid structures that were instituted by mid-century. Oppression against black South Africans intensified from 1960 until the election of Mandela in 1994. The ANC was formed in 1912 as an organization that would attempt discussion with whites concerning the rights of black South Africans. Consisting at first mostly of Xhosas, it did not become a more militant organization until the conflicts of the 1960s when resolution through peaceful negotiations was deemed impossible.

The Natives' Land Act of 1913 followed immediately on the heels of the formation of the ANC, creating "overnight a floating landless proletariat whose labour could be used and manipulated at will, and ensured that ownership of the land had finally and securely passed into the hands of the ruling white race."[14] It was under this legislation that the solution to the "native problem" was separation of blacks from whites by the control of a black African's right to own land. Thus in 1913 segregation was formally and legally instituted as a way of life, leading to virtual total control over the economic and social destiny of black South Africans in their own country.[15]

After the conclusion of World War II, in 1948, the United Nations adopted the Universal Declaration of Human Rights. South Africa, however, heard the beat of a different drum and elected a slate of National Party leaders driven by Afrikaner nationalism. Jan Christian Smuts was ousted from office and a forty-two-year reign of apartheid began. Segregation of the "natives" into "reserves" was replaced by a tightening of controls that extended into every aspect of life and were enforced by a police state that institutionalized torture, detention without cause, and murder.[16]

---

13. Mostert, *Frontiers* (1992), is the most comprehensive recent volume to detail the beginnings of the European contact with the indigenous tribes of South Africa and the subsequent colonization of the Africans by Holland and Great Britain. While scholarly, it is extremely readable, using extensive narratives from accounts written at the time.

14. Bessie Head, foreword to *Native Life in South Africa*, by Sol T. Plaatje (Randburg, South Africa: Ravan Press, [1916] 1982), ix.

15. The deliberations leading to the adoption of this act as well as arguments against it are eloquently detailed in Plaatje, *Native Life in South Africa*.

16. It is in this context that Alan Paton's famous novel *Cry, the Beloved Country* (New

The Sharpeville massacre of 1960 radicalized the ANC, and the Pan African Conference announced a campaign against the Pass Laws on March 21. This in turn led to the institution of the first emergency by the government on March 30, 1960, when all civil rights of black South Africans were suspended. By 1964 Nelson Mandela was imprisoned on Robbin Island, and then Steve Biko was murdered, both Xhosas. Black South Africans were herded into the "independent homelands" of Transkei (1976) and Ciskei (1981), among others, to live a segregated, impoverished existence. Soweto Day in 1984 was followed by the Mandela March on August 28, 1985. Police brutality intensified, setting the stage for the second emergency, beginning on June 12, 1986.[17]

During these turbulent times, white priests and ministers occasionally would march among the people during funerals. The police forbade the assembly of blacks under most circumstances and sometimes used public funeral processions as an opportunity to open fire on the mourners. Dargie participated in these processions. While their presence tended to mitigate against police violence in these processions, there were no guarantees. Dargie recalled that a young man, Bigboy Mginywa, was shot and killed directly in front of him at one funeral.

It was these tumultuous days of the 1960s and 1970s that shaped Dargie. There is no doubt that as a young priest he was repulsed by the violence and oppression all around him. Moving from outrage to musical liberator, however, was not necessarily as apparent then as it might seem now. While there was a growing interest in African cultures following World War II, in South Africa there were many who found little of value in the indigenous cultures of that region of the world. The earlier attitudes of the Dutch and then the British who colonized South Africa persisted. Noël Mostert captures this sentiment precisely:

> That sub-Saharan Africa really had anything to offer the civilizations which had infiltrated it in modern times, that it might be reevaluated by standards other than those of material and mechanical progress, that it might convey some human sensibility special in its own way, that it had a

---

York: Scribner, 1948) was written. For a graphic description of life in the black townships, see Mark Mathabane, *Kaffir Boy* (New York: Collier, 1986).

17. Two powerful novels by Richard Reve provide a sense of life for "coloured" South Africans during the emergencies in Cape Town, where some of the violence was most confrontive. They are *Emergency* (Cape Town: David Philip, 1964), an account of the emergency in 1960, and *Emergency Continued* (Cape Town: David Philip, 1990), an account of conditions leading to the second emergency in 1986.

history that was as compacted and fascinating as any in the human story, were possibilities not easily entertained in the common perception of the continent between the last quarter of the nineteenth century and the middle of the twentieth. In the minds of many, Africa and its negroid peoples were the only ones unburdened by history.[18]

The notion that Africans were naive folk, who lived without a sense of past and by relatively simple, uncomplicated customs, carried into the colonial perception of their music. Among the more magnanimous appraisals of Xhosa music is that offered by Paravicini di Capelli, a government official for the Dutch, who visited the Xhosa in 1803: "After midday, they entertained us with a dance after the fashion of their country; the men stood, armed, in two rows, one behind the other, repeatedly jumping into the air, giving vent to monotonous noise and muttering; going in time to the muttering song which accompanied them, the women moved around the jumping men, making various turns and bends of the body. The men were stark naked, but the women kept their cloaks on; besides this, the dance was always the same, except when periodically enlivened as the singing grew louder."[19]

Although to many missionaries the music of the Africans was of no value, there were those who recognized the Xhosas as a musical people and saw that singing and composing songs was an important parts of their lives. An account in 1860 by Rev. William Shaw describes hymn singing among Xhosa converts: "I was much pleased with the appearance of the congregation. About one hundred and fifty, chiefly Kaffirs, were present: they sang melodiously a sort of native air, to some expressive words of praise to God, said to be composed by a native Captain."[20] Erich Bigalke speculates that it was likely that the "native Captain" was none other than Ntsikana. He also cites three other sources before 1850 that mention the singing of Ntsikana's hymn.[21]

---

18. Mostert, 43.

19. Paravicini di Capelli, *Reize in de Binnen-Landen van Suid-Africa* (Cape Town: van Riebeeck Society, 1965), 87, as translated by and quoted in Erich Bigalke, "An Historical Overview of Southern Nguni Musical Behaviour," in *Papers Presented at the Fourth Symposium on Ethnomusicology*, ed. Andrew Tracey (Grahamstown, South Africa: ILAM, Rhodes University, October 7-8, 1983), 40-41.

20. William Shaw, *The Story of My Mission in South Eastern Africa* (London: Hamilton Adams, 1860), 329, quoted in Bigalke, 43.

21. These are C. Rose, *Four Years in Southern Africa* (London: Colburn & Bentley, 1829), 135; S. Kay, *Travel and Research in Caffraria* (Oxford: Oxford University Press, 1833), 47; and A. Steedman, *Wanderings and Adventures in the Interior of Southern Africa*, vol. 1 (London: Longman, 1835), 32.

Most historical references to the singing of Africans in the southern region in general, and Xhosas specifically, range from disgust to limited curiosity. When explorers, travelers, and missionaries encountered an alien musical tradition so distinct from their heritage, it was unlikely that they would understand the inherent validity of a musical system that seemed exotic to them. When one considers that few of the early Western observers were musicians, this compounds the problem of finding accurate accounts of musical encounters. J. H. Soga, the second son of Tiyo Soga and a missionary with Xhosa roots, provided some valuable cultural information in his journal, *The Ama-Xosa: Life and Customs,* published in 1931. Even Soga, a Xhosa, did not always find the sounds of his people's music acceptable, as is demonstrated in his comments on *umtshotsho,* a style of rough singing used by boys and girls in some areas. "It is music, of a kind. It is not singing, though songs may be rendered through the *umtshotsho.* It is not a dance though dancing may accompany it. It may be described as a barbaric musical series of sounds, covering the range of the musical octave. . . . The sounds, however, are not produced naturally, as in singing, but quite artificially in the larynx and [b]ack part of the palate."[22] If Soga with his Xhosa background could not provide a sympathetic and somewhat accurate account of traditional Xhosa music, it would appear that the chances of an appreciative understanding by a white South African priest would be negligible.[23] As we will see, Dargie overcame over 150 years of colonial prejudice against the culture and music of the Xhosa. He not only learned about Xhosa music but also performed it, nourished Xhosa traditional musicians, and encouraged the promotion of Xhosa music as a valuable cultural asset. This is but one of the ways he has engaged in cultural liberation — participating in the song of the oppressed culture.

While it is significant that Dargie would become a bimusical Western/ Xhosa musician when few others found value in the Xhosa culture, he had considerable obstacles to overcome as a white Catholic priest in building trust

22. J. H. Soga, *The Ama-Xosa: Life and Customs* (Lovedale: Mission Press, 1931), 314-15, quoted in Bigalke, 44.

23. Bigalke thought Soga was in error and was actually observing *umngqokolo* overtone singing, one of the distinctive styles of Xhosa traditional music among the Thembu Xhosa, rather than the dance-song called *umtshotsho.* Dargie disagrees with Bigalke, being relatively sure that Soga is indeed referring to *umtshotsho* song-dance. (Correspondence to author, May 7, 1999.) As an authority in *umngqokolo,* Dargie may be in the best position to distinguish the difference in this case. I was fortunate to accompany Dargie for field research in the former Transkei area to observe and record several *umngqokolo* singers. Dargie covers this style in more depth in the ethnomusicological works *Xhosa Music: Its Technique and Instruments, with a Collection of Songs* (Claremont, South Africa, 1988) and *Umngokolo* (Hogsback, South Africa, ca. 1993) with cassette tape.

among black South Africans. African literature is replete with accounts of distrust between imported Christianity and the indigenous culture. This culture clash and the apparent insensitivity of many who brought the gospel to Africa are themes of some of the most famous African authors such as Nigerian Chinua Achebe and Kenyan Ngugi wa Thiong'o, to mention just two of the best known.[24] In order to appreciate the dilemma that Dargie faced, I refer to South African author Ezekiel Mphahlele, who discusses in his autobiography, *Down Second Avenue*, the attitudes of submission he encountered with Father Wardle:

> I don't think it's fair for anybody to tell me to expect a change of heart among a bunch of madmen who are determined not to cede an inch, or to listen to reason. It is unfair to ask me to subsist on mission school sermons about Christian conduct and passive resistance in circumstances where it is considered a crime to be decent; where a policeman will run me out of my house at the point of a sten gun when I try to withhold my labour. For years I have been told by white and Black preachers to love my neighbor; love him when there's a bunch of whites who reckon they are Israelites come out of Egypt in obedience to God's order to come and civilize heathens; a bunch of whites who feed on the symbolism of God's race venturing into the desert among the ungodly. For years now I have been thinking it was all right for me to feel spiritually strong after a church service. And now I find it is not the kind of strength that answers the demand of suffering humanity around me. It doesn't even seem to answer the longings of my own heart.[25]

This passionate quotation, poignant with pain and acerbic in tone, points out the potential difficulty of a white South African priest gaining the trust of black South Africans suffering daily at the hands of white police. The bastardized gospel described by Mphahlele promotes the spirituality of love among "neighbors" while ignoring the suffering Christ who is present in human struggle and sorrow and whose realm is one of justice and liberation for the oppressed. The words of the liturgy ring hollow unless the one who delivers them establishes a trust based upon enduring the indignity of the suffering, risking the torment of the tortured, and singing the songs of the sorrowful. It is this relationship that Bawo Dargie established in his quest for liberation song.

---

24. See Chinua Achebe, *Things Fall Apart* (London: Heinemann, 1978), and Ngugi wa Thiong'o, *Petals of Blood* (London: Heinemann Educational Books, 1977).

25. Ezekiel Mphahlele, *Down Second Avenue* (London: Faber and Faber, 1959), 178.

Andrew Tracey and Ethnomusicological Study

In addition to fellow priests Hirmer and Lobinger, Dargie came into contact with Andrew Tracey at Rhodes University in Grahamstown, who directs the International Library of African Music (ILAM). Dargie had pursued a bachelor of music degree from Rhodes, making a total of three bachelor's degrees by 1973. After asking his bishop about the possibility of pursuing African church music as an advanced degree in 1976, he decided to continue his study on the doctoral level with Tracey at Rhodes. This proved to be a wise decision. ILAM had moved its extensive research library of recordings, instruments, and books from Johannesburg to Rhodes upon the death of its founder, Andrew's father, Hugh Tracey, in 1977.[26]

Hugh had a vision that overcame a common cultural prejudice by white South Africans against African indigenous music.[27] In 1929, long before it was considered a reasonable or acceptable activity for a white person, Hugh began studying and collecting African music. In 1930 he began making recordings and in 1954 he published the journal *African Music,* a valuable academic resource that continues under the editorship of his son Andrew. Defying the pre–World War II notion that there was little of value worth preserving in African culture and music, he set about to do just that. Many of his field recordings, ranging from as far as Uganda to the north, Kenya to the east, and Congo in the west, preserve African musical traditions that have since become extinct or nearly so. Hugh maintained his work largely through grants for many years. When the stranglehold of apartheid increased in the 1960s and 1970s, this source of funds dried up, as much of the world boycotted any business activities or cultural exchanges with the white South African regime.

Andrew was able to maintain ILAM and develop it even further under the auspices of Rhodes University. With a new facility on land supplied by the university, it has perhaps the premier research archive of recordings, instruments, scores, and books on African music anywhere on the continent. ILAM also sponsors regular ethnomusicology symposia. In 1999 it added a second

---

26. A very helpful website that introduces ILAM may be found at http://archive.ilam .ru.ac.za/home.asp. Recordings from Hugh Tracey's research archives are available as well as extensive information about ILAM.

27. The information for this section comes from a visit to the home of Andrew and Heather Tracey in Grahamstown, South Africa, on October 31 and November 1, 1998. Andrew introduced me to the International Library of African Music and to the family business, making African musical instruments. In addition to allowing me time to peruse the holdings of the library for several hours, I was treated to an impromptu *mbira* session and, later in the evening, a public program in which he performed *mbira* music and Swahili selections with his son.

full-time ethnomusicologist to the staff. Andrew and his wife Heather also have a family business producing African musical instruments, including versions of the popular *mbira* of the Shona people in Zimbabwe, drums, xylophones, percussion, chimes, and other smaller percussion instruments. Until 1999 Heather administered the instrument-making business, which employs seven others. In addition, Andrew maintains a repair shop at his home for restoring instruments he has collected on his many research trips. He continues his fieldwork, especially among the Shona who play the *mbira*. He is a master *mbira* player himself,[28] but is also conversant in a variety of African musical styles from as far north as the popular urban Swahili music of East Africa.

In addition to introducing Dargie to the many resources of ILAM, guiding his doctoral dissertation on Xhosa music, and nurturing his love of African music as an ethnomusicologist, Tracey introduced him to pulse notation, a way of writing down traditional African music that was at once more efficient, more faithful to the performance process of African music, and more accurate in its visual representation of the African aural experience. Much African traditional music is not based on Western metrical organization but on additive rhythms produced by a sensation of pulse. The music comes in cycles. Once one determines the length of a cycle, one may perceive the structure of the music and understand the nature of additional vocal solos that are improvised over the cycle based on oral tradition and even current circumstances at the time of the performance. Rather than notating a fifteen-minute song on voluminous pages of staff paper, pulse notation allows the transcriber to see on a single page or two the basic cycle, variants used by soloists, dance rhythms, clapping patterns, etc. The researcher can visualize the African musical experience on its own terms and in an efficient manner. Pulse notation involves a process of *perceiving* the structures of the music, *understanding* it through performance and participation, and *crystallizing* what you have perceived and understood into notation. Along with a well-made video recording and an audio reproduction, pulse notation can assist the researcher in several ways: (1) as a reminder of the event recorded, i.e., as a means of preservation; (2) as an aid in teaching; (3) as a way to help the transcriber understand the musical structure of the recorded event better; and (4) as a means for making a comparison of isolated musical factors between or among compositions within a style.[29] Pulse notation and accompanying re-

28. See Andrew Tracey, "The System of the Mbira," in *Seventh Symposium of Ethnomusicology* (Grahamstown: International Library of African Music, 1988), 43-55.

29. Tracey has provided a helpful description of the rationale for and procedures of pulse notation in "Transcribing African Music in Pulse Notation," a monograph published by the International Library of African Music, Rhodes University, Grahamstown, South Africa, 1997.

cordings allow music maintained through oral tradition to speak to the Western researcher while maintaining its integrity as an oral product rather than a literary artifact. This is integral to an African experience of liturgy.

Tracey cooperated with Dargie in the development of marimbas as an accompanying instrument for the song during the Mass. Oswald Hirmer had imported the first marimba xylophones from Zimbabwe. Xhosa traditional music does not use drums but is accompanied by musical bows of various kinds that provide two fundamental tones produced by striking or bowing the string while resonating the sound in the mouth to produce overtones. A simple bow played by scraping the single string is the *umrhubhe*. A bow amplified by a calabash against the chest is an *uhadi*.[30] In another variant from the Sotho, the *inkatari*, the bow rests in a container or can about the size of a canned ham which serves as a resonator. The fundamental pitches of the *inkatari* are played by a small bow.[31] The musical effects of these bowed instruments are, however, relatively intimate. The subtlety of the overtones produced by the player's oral cavity in the case of the *umrhube*, or the calabash in the case of the *uhadi*, would not be heard within the congregational singing context.

The marimbas from Zimbabwe provided a percussive and melodic effect, supplying a lively rhythmic foundation and a full tone that can be heard as a congregation sings. An ensemble of at least four marimbas of varying sizes not only supports congregational singing but enlivens it. Dargie tuned his marimbas to fit the Xhosa scale and trained players to accompany marimba Masses. Well over one hundred parishes use them, especially on festive occasions. Several of Dargie's recordings include marimba Masses. In this way he helped to integrate a new instrumental sound into the Xhosa liturgy, free from traditional musical associations, that is distinctly recognized as a church music sonority.[32]

Tracey gave Dargie the ethnomusicological tools to pursue his vocation in church music. As the quotation at the beginning of this chapter indicates,

30. The *uhadi* bow may be heard on "Ahomna" (no. 9), on the CD *Halle, Halle: We Sing the World Round*, ed. C. Michael Hawn (Garland, Tex.: Choristers Guild, 2001).

31. David Dargie, "Musical Bows in Southern Africa," *Africa Insight* 16, no. 1 (1986), 42-52, describes the construction, variety, and use of musical bows in depth. He also has an instructional cassette with booklet entitled *Make and Play Your Own Musical Bow* (Hogsback, South Africa, 1995).

32. An example of a marimba Mass can be found on the cassette *Africa Sunday II*, no. 126 (Delmenville, South Africa: Lumko Missiological Institute, 1990), complete with listener's guide. The CD *Halle, Halle: We Sing the World Round* has three South African selections that use marimbas: "Amen Siyakudumisa" (no. 7), "Sikulule" (no. 8), and "Nkosi! Nkosi!" (no. 10).

Dargie sees his role as one of helping the Xhosa people and other Africans with whom he works to "have a pride in themselves" so that they can use their music as a means "to liberate themselves." Tracey's approach is that of an ethnomusicologist — collecting music from the people, becoming a skilled performer of African music, notating African music on its own terms rather than borrowing an approach from Western systems, and placing the music in its cultural context. He provided Dargie with a theoretical musical framework for conducting his vocation within the church — a vocation of liturgical, personal, and political liberation through music.

Church Music Composition Workshops

Between 1977 and the completion of his doctorate in ethnomusicology from Rhodes University in 1986, Dargie traveled extensively, conducting church music composition workshops throughout South Africa and in the surrounding countries of Namibia and Botswana. These workshops empowered local musicians to compose music for the liturgy in idioms that spoke from within their cultural context. The first workshop held in 1977 was to encourage the creation of songs for a new Xhosa hymnal to be edited by Hirmer. After observing a similar process in Zimbabwe, Dargie met Hirmer over Easter weekend in Zwelitsha, where he collected fifty-three new songs. Many of these are still being used today.

The success of this event led to the formation of a music department at Lumko in 1979. After conducting over forty workshops and refining the techniques used to facilitate them, the Lumko Institute published a book detailing the process for encouraging the composition of new African church music. *Workshops for Composing Local Church Music* (1983) is a guide accompanied by cassette tapes of actual workshop sessions.[33] This process spread to other regions of South Africa. The Lumko Institute has published over one hundred cassettes of music from these encounters, containing hundreds of new songs for the church.

The organizer of the composition workshops serves as a catalyst for the event rather than a performer. As catalyst, the organizer "inspire[s] and encourage[s] the people, tell[ing] them about the needs of the church, their service to the church, and their own people, the value of offering their own mu-

33. David Dargie, *Workshops for Composing Local Church Music: Methods for Conducting Music Workshops in Local Congregations*, no. 40 (Delmenville, South Africa: Lumko Missiological Institute, 1983).

sic to God, the value of preserving their own musical style which God has especially given to them." The catalyst also provides texts appropriate for the liturgy, enlists local musicians as a source of inspiration, and records the sessions on tape. Following the event the cassettes and texts are made available to those who attended so that they can learn the music and incorporate it into the liturgy.[34]

The suggestion of liturgical texts provided the context for the music to be composed. The use of recordings rather than written scores only[35] ensures that the songs can be learned by those untrained in either sol-fa methodology or Western staff notation. Since most of these musicians learned the music aurally/orally, they were in a better position to transmit their compositions directly to the people without the expense or pretext of needing written music. Music learned at the workshops could be used the next week in the Mass.

The sessions develop songs out of spoken words emphasizing the relationship between the singer and God or Jesus, e.g., "Lord, teach us to praise you," or short acclamations, e.g., "Glory to God in the highest," or psalm responses, e.g., "Blessed is the one who walks with the Lord," from Psalm 1.

The next step is to discover the melody in the words. Since most African languages are tonal, there is an inherent melody in the text. Refining a technique first introduced by Henri Wenan, an authority on African church music, and developed by Oswald Hirmer, Dargie helps the people find this melody by having them speak or shout the text as if they were sending a message across a valley. In such circumstances the receiver of the message can decipher it by the exaggerated tones of the "melody" inherent in the text. In a Zulu composition workshop in 1978 where this technique was used, Dargie noted 100 percent correlation between speech and melody in the songs. This speech-to-song technique was solidified by 1979 in the area of Kavango, in far north Namibia, demonstrating that it is successful across cultural groups and languages.

In composition workshops the group works out a rhythm and a melody that are intrinsic to the spoken language. Through spontaneous suggestions from within the group, all those present recognize when a melody and rhythm appropriate for the text have been discovered. Harmony evolves in a similar way, and percussion and dance follow naturally. A single song may

34. Dargie, *Workshops*, 5.

35. Dargie has made available written scores of the music from many of these sessions both in staff notation and solfège reduction. They include collections of music from the major tribal groups, *Sesotho Church Music Collection* (1978), *Xhosa Church Music Collection* (1978), and *New Church Music in Zulu* (1980), all of which are available from the Lumko Institute. Cassette recordings of the sessions that inspired the notation are also available.

have many composers who participated in the creation process, making songwriting a communal event. Even those songs by an individual composer are modified by the creative inspiration of singers who contextualize them or add variations over recurring cycles of the main theme.[36]

Lest one gain the impression that all the songs are short, simple "choruses," individual composers such as Brother Clement Sithole, a Zulu musician, created elaborate psalm settings in a dramatic recitative style with an extended range accompanied by the *umakhweyane,* a braced calabash-resonated musical bow used by the Zulu.[37] Through the use of the cyclic approach of African composition from this region, other extended compositions result according to the needs of the liturgy and creativity of the leaders.

In summary, the compositional process proposed by Dargie is communal rather than solitary; is inspired by texts appropriate for the liturgy; is based on aural/oral transmission rather than notation; is based on more traditional musical styles; and includes both the musical layperson and the recognized musician. Let us turn our attention to compositions representative of the style.

Church Music from South Africa

A discussion of examples from South African congregational song follows. This sampling includes songs composed in the composition workshops and other settings as well as some which were written by Dargie. Aspects of the musical style and suggestions for making this music more accessible to congregations in the United States will also be addressed.

The first example is "Amen Siyakudumisa" by Stephen Cuthbert Molefe, South Africa (Xhosa). One of the early success stories in the development of indigenous compositions for the liturgy was S. C. Molefe, a Roman Catholic choir leader and composer from Vosloorus, near Johannesburg. Molefe used sol-fa as a basis for composition. His works were typical of the church choir

---

36. Dargie describes this process in several publications, including *Workshops,* 11-17; "Xhosa Music: The Most Natural Music in the World," *The Talking Drum: Southern African Music Educators' Society Newsletter* 7 (May 1997): 10-12; "Group Composition and Church Music," in *Papers Presented at the Symposium on Ethnomusicology* (Grahamstown: Rhodes University, October 10-11, 1980), 10-13.

37. David Dargie, "Woman with the Baby on Her Back," *East London Daily Dispatch,* November 30, 1995, describes an encounter with Sithole. Also "African Sunday Afternoon," tape 154, Lumko Music Department, 1990, contains an extended composition by Sithole with an explanation in the listener's guide.

style used in African Roman Catholic congregations, with little use of rhythmic patterns and organizational forms based on Western styles. Dargie recalls his early experiences with Molefe:

> In 1977 Molefe attended the first music composition workshop held by me at Zwelitsha in the Eastern Cape. At this workshop Molefe entered a new stage in his composition work. For the first time he was encouraged to bring both African cyclic form and body movement (mainly through clapping) into music for use in Catholic liturgy. He gave a new freedom to the performers to assist in designing the harmony and part-singing in the number of new songs he presented at the workshop, and encouraged them to use not only clapping, but also humming. He also now used clear African rhythm, and cyclic call-and-response form. His presentation included his now famous "Great Amen," published first by Lumko and then in the new Xhosa hymn book as "Masithi-Amen!"[38]

The simpler version presented here shows one cycle of the song. The harmony indicates the influence of Western hymns rather than the two-chord pattern of traditional Xhosa music. As is the case among Xhosa singers, the version printed here is but a skeleton of what is actually sung. Lead singers in a group spontaneously tie phrases together so that there are no unsustained, dead places in the music. Movement and clapping are an integral part of the sound. The cycle should be repeated until a leader senses that the congregation has unified behind the song or the song has served its role in the liturgy. The amplified version included here has been notated by Dargie from the oral musical practice of the Xhosas singing across phrase endings, filling in the musical gaps, and embellishing the primary melody.

When presenting this song to Western congregations, prepare the choir in advance and teach the congregation aurally, without music. Sing it with a gentle swaying. Rather than repeating rigidly, think of the repeated cycles as theme and variation. Each cycle (or variation) builds and allows for improvisation and embellishment. In traditional Xhosa singing, one may have as many parts as there are singers present. Don't tell the congregation how many

---

38. From correspondence with the author, May 7, 1999. The transcription with overlapping parts is from *Sing an African Song* (Hogsback, South Africa, 1994), 7. I led a Taizé prayer at a Methodist pastors' retreat in South Africa in October 1998. Members of the group were about 80 percent Xhosa. It was interesting to note how many Xhosa pastors in this gathering naturally "Africanized" several of the Taizé ostinatos with overlapping parts. "Jesus, Remember Me" was a particular favorite and continued in the Xhosa style for many more cycles than when I use it in the United States.

Example 4.1. "Amen Siyakudumisa"
(four-part version), by S. C. Molefe[39]

Words and music © Lumko Institute, South Africa.
Musical transcription © 1983 David Dargie. Used by permission.

39. From *Halle, Halle: We Sing the World Round*, Singer's Edition, ed. C. Michael Hawn (Garland, Tex.: Choristers Guild, 1999), 11. A transcription of a more extensive eight-part version is available in *Halle, Halle*, Teacher's Edition, ed. C. Michael Hawn (Garland, Tex.: Choristers Guild, 1999), 22-25.

times you are going to sing it. Keep the cycles going until people are comfortable and have fully joined into the singing and moving. "Masithi" is the leader's part and is designed to encourage the congregation. The original Xhosa text sung by the leader was "Sive Sithi" (Hear us, we pray) rather than "Masithi."

Originally "Amen Siyakudumisa" was written as the Great Amen to be sung at the conclusion of the Eucharistic Prayer, or Great Thanksgiving, just before the bread and wine are served in the Mass. I also heard this song sung by Xhosa Methodist congregations in South Africa where it served as a refrain for the Te Deum (We praise you, O God), an act of praise chanted regularly in many Xhosa congregations.

"Thuma mina" (Send me, Lord, into the world) is a text that appears in many versions throughout South Africa because it is essential to the worship of many denominations. Commenting on this song, Dargie notes "no traceable origin any more except that it is typical of the women's *manyano* (women's union) meetings. It is a typical procession song, but also a typical collection song: people move around singing it, and each time someone passes the collection plate [or] bag, the person puts in a small coin, until the meeting leader decides that enough has been obtained. Goals can be anything from contributions to some family's funeral expenses to raising tea money [for social occasions at church]."[40]

Example 4.2. "Thuma Mina"
(Send Me, Lord), traditional Xhosa[41]

Musical transcription © 1983 David Dargie.
Administered by Choristers Guild. Used by permission.

40. From correspondence with the author, May 7, 1999. "Thuma Mina" is originally from *Lumko Hymnbook*, ed. David Dargie (Delmenville, South Africa: Lumko Missiological Institute, 1991), 9a.
41. From *Halle, Halle*, Singer's Edition, 44.

"Thuma Mina" is usually sung unaccompanied. Congregations may sing songs such as "Thuma Mina" while beating hymnbooks or other objects close at hand as they do in South Africa to provide an aural foundation and kinesthetic response. The tempo should be sufficient to communicate a joyful sending forth at the conclusion of worship. The musical style is derived from a mixture of traditional Western hymns and the popular township sounds of the South African urban areas. Keep the pulse steady as the cycles are repeated. As long as the cantor sings the overlapping phrase at the conclusion of the cycle, the congregation will continue to sing. Gentle swaying adds to the kinesthetic participation by the people and creates a visual sense of community. Following a spoken blessing, this song may be sung as the choir and/or ministers recess at the conclusion of worship. With very little preparation the congregation can look up and participate in the ritual action of a processional or recessional and, in the case of the latter, continue singing as they depart from worship themselves.

"Nkosi! Nkosi" (Kyrie Eleison) by Mziwamadoda Joseph Singiswa is written in a traditional Xhosa style. It was created in one of the many group composition workshops. Singiswa composed the Kyrie as part of a complete musical setting of the Mass in 1979 while still a schoolboy. His Mass has proven to be very popular in Xhosa churches. Singiswa is now a choirmaster at Zwelitsha. The Mass is often accompanied on the marimbas.

Traditional Xhosa music does not make use of the drums that are so typical of most of Africa. Much of the music is accompanied by the softer sound of the musical bow (uhadi) described above. Two chord structures, usually indicated by F and G major chords in Dargie's transcriptions, are based on the two-note fundamental sounds of the bow. "Nkosi" is a song based on the simple two-chord progression of the Xhosa musical bow. A similar construction can be found in the "Nkosi" setting in the South African collection Freedom Is Coming, made available to a wider audience by Anders Nyberg for the Swedish church.[42] Traditional Xhosa dancers often step on the offbeat after a strong pulse. A cantor might improvise over the dotted half notes in a manner that glues the phrases together and leads into the next cyclic variation of the song.

42. Freedom Is Coming, 29. "Nkosi, Nkosi" is from Lumko Hymnbook, 3. Dargie notes in correspondence with the author on May 7, 1999, that "Nyberg got [this] song and others from me. He never acknowledges his sources, which has not made him very popular. He claims to 'arrange' songs, but with my songs at any rate his 'arranging' consists of adding Swedish texts. (At one church meeting in Sweden I found Molefe's 'Amen' being used as 'African traditional,' with my exact transcription and no mention of Molefe. These things happen, but it is good to set the record straight. Old Molefe's name ought to live forever with his songs!)"

Example 4.3. "Nkosi! Nkosi!"
(Lord, Have Mercy), traditional Xhosa[43]

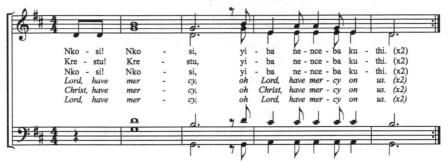

Nko - si!	Nko	-	si,	yi - ba	ne - nce - ba ku - thi. (x2)
Kre - stu!	Kre	-	stu,	yi - ba	ne - nce - ba ku - thi. (x2)
Nko - si!	Nko	-	si,	yi - ba	ne - nce - ba ku - thi. (x2)
Lord, have	*mer*	-	*cy,*	*oh Lord,*	*have mer - cy on us. (x2)*
Christ, have	*mer*	-	*cy,*	*oh Christ,*	*have mer - cy on us. (x2)*
Lord, have	*mer*	-	*cy,*	*oh Lord,*	*have mer - cy on us. (x2)*

Musical transcription © 1983 David Dargie.
Administered by Choristers Guild. Used by permission.

The next example is "Sikhulule" (Liberation Prayer Response), by Thozama Dyani, South Africa (Xhosa). As stated earlier, black South Africans suffered increasing violence and restrictions on their freedom to assemble, receive adequate education, and choose where they could live. In 1960 and 1986 the white apartheid government called two "emergencies" during which the movements of black South Africans were restricted even more severely than usual. It was during these times especially that innocent people could be shot and killed on sight by police without any recourse by the victim or the victim's family.

This song grows out of a personal experience by the composer in 1984 during conditions that led to the second emergency (1986). Dyani's brother was jailed after being shot by police while walking home from a choir rehearsal. In apartheid South Africa the police could declare that a black South African was guilty on the spot. Detainees in jail were without rights and due process. They often died due to the violent conditions of incarceration. Dyani and a group of colleagues from Kwazakhele composed a complete liberation Mass that grew out of this experience and in memory of the events of Soweto Day (June 16, 1984). "Sikhulule" is a part of this Mass. The petition of this simple text (Free us, Lord) undergirds the protest of unwarranted violence against her brother and friends who suffered or died on that day. Singing is a natural response to oppression throughout Africa, serving to unify the prayer of the suffering community, offering healing through the solidarity of singing together, and maintaining hope in the face of seemingly insurmountable odds. As Desmond Tutu has said, "There is no situation that is not transfigur-

43. From *Halle, Halle*, Singer's Edition, 26.

able. There is no situation that is totally devoid of hope."[44] Without song there would be little hope.

The chord structure of "Sikhulule" is typical of the music in the black townships of South Africa during this time. It should be sung with a rhythmic intensity and drive that is indicative of the petition offered in the text. The cantor urges on the people in their prayer. Repeat the cycles of the song several times until its intensity builds.

Example 4.4. "Sikhulule"
(Liberate Us, Lord), by Thozama Dyani[45]

Words and music copyright © 1983 Thozama Dyani and David Dargie. Administered by Choristers Guild. Used by permission.

44. From a conversation between Bill Moyers and Desmond Tutu on the Public Broadcast System (PBS), July 1999. Original transcription of "Sikhulule" by Dargie in *Sing an African Song*, 13.

45. From *Halle, Halle,* Teacher's Edition, 47.

Example 4.5. "Laphalala Igazi"
(Christ Is Risen), by David Dargie[46]

Xhosa words and music copyright © 1983 David Dargie. Administered by Choristers Guild. English translation © 1999 Choristers Guild. Used by permission.

"Laphalala Igazi," David Dargie, South Africa, is in the style of Xhosa traditional music. Not giving in to the myth of the colonial powers who claimed there was little or nothing of value in the African cultures they encountered, Dargie cultivates Xhosa music and brings it to the attention of the broader South Afri-

46. From *Halle, Halle,* Singer's Edition, 37.

can community. He not only encourages others to compose in traditional African styles, but he also has contributed songs for the liturgy in the Xhosa style.

"Laphalala Igazi" is an Easter acclamation. The congregation sings a simple descending pattern based on the two-chord harmony of traditional Xhosa music. The cantor sings Easter acclamations in a typical descending solo line. While no drums are present, note that clapping and stamping may be used for fuller physical involvement. Such offbeat dance is typical of Xhosa traditional music where the step takes place after the primary pulse. Notice that the clapping is two pulses against the three of the music. Dargie often claps quietly as he sings, increasing in intensity as the cycles of the song continue until people respond kinesthetically before they realize what is happening. In traditional Xhosa music the singer-dancers might also have rattles around their ankles that contribute to the sound texture.[47]

The Hymns of Ntsikana

The hymns of the prophet Ntsikana are the prototype of church music in a traditional Xhosa style. One of the primary ways that Dargie has helped Xhosa people find cultural and spiritual liberation is by sharing the story and hymns of Ntsikana, the first Xhosa Christian. The story of this prophet, now nearly two hundred years old, provides Xhosa people a cultural, historical, and musical context for prayer. Furthermore, Ntsikana was a peacemaker among his own people at a very critical time in their history. The sharing of Ntsikana's hymn is integral to Dargie's work as a liberator.

> "The truth will set you free," said the Lord (John 8:32). It is a sad state of affairs when people are prejudiced against their own culture. The missionary must play his part in freeing people from such prejudices, by showing them the truth about themselves in the light of the teachings of the Church. If the people have a healthy pride in their culture and traditions and a sense of respect for their forbears, then not only can they build the church of God in a lasting way, they can also stand with dignity among the families of nations.[48]

Learning, teaching, enabling compositions, and integrating music into the liturgy are crucial methods for helping the Xhosa people find themselves spiritually and culturally within God's realm. Dargie, functioning as what he calls

47. Original composition of "Laphalala Igazi" by Dargie in *Sing an African Song,* 13.
48. Dargie, "A New Kind of Missionary" (unpublished lecture for the South African Council of Priests, 1979), 17.

"a new kind of missionary," cites the mandate of Vatican II as an authorization for his methodology:

> In certain parts of the world, especially in mission lands, people have their own musical traditions and these play a great part in their religious and social life. Thus, . . . due importance is to be attached to their music and a suitable place given to it, not only in forming their attitude toward religion, but also in adapting worship to their native genius.
>
> Therefore, when missionaries are being given training in music, every effort should be made to see that they become competent in promoting the traditional music of the people, both in schools and in sacred services, as far as practicable.[49]

Ntsikana's story and hymns are the starting place for Dargie's efforts in liturgical inculturation, the term assigned to the dynamic interaction between liturgy and culture by Vatican II.[50] His contribution to this discussion focuses on the relationship between liturgical inculturation and liberation. In his experience in apartheid South Africa, liturgical inculturation can lead to political and spiritual liberation.

The area where Dargie has worked most recently is one of the former "independent homelands" (an analogy might be made with a Native American reservation within the borders of the United States) forged by coercion of the Xhosa people by the white apartheid government during the most difficult throes of oppression against the indigenous people. These lands, e.g., Transkei (1976-94) and Ciskei (1981-94), often were not arable, productive agricultural regions. This was also the area of the Xhosa people of Ntsikana's time. Dargie relishes telling the story of Ntsikana.

---

49. "Constitution on the Sacred Liturgy" (1963), in *The Liturgy Documents: A Parish Resource*, 3rd ed. (Chicago: Liturgy Training Publications, 1991), art. 119.

50. There are several important sources for liturgical inculturation. The dynamic relationship between culture and liturgy is evident in Aylward Shorter, *Toward a Theology of Inculturation* (Maryknoll, N.Y.: Orbis, 1988), where he states: "Inculturation implies that the Christian message transforms a culture. It is also the case that Christianity is transformed by culture, not in a way that falsifies the message, but in a way in which the message is formulated and interpreted anew" (14). Anscar Chupungco has interpreted liturgical inculturation for the post–Vatican II church perhaps more than any other person. He has developed several processes for encouraging the dynamic relationship between culture and liturgy. In *Liturgical Inculturation: Sacramentals, Religiosity, and Catechesis* (Collegeville, Minn.: Liturgical Press, 1992), he defines inculturation in this way: "Liturgical inculturation is basically the assimilation by the liturgy of local cultural patterns. It means that liturgy and culture share the same pattern of thinking, speaking, and expressing themselves through rites, symbols, and artistic forms. In short, liturgy is inserted into the culture, history, and tradition of the people among whom the Church dwells" (30). His methods of liturgical inculturation include "Dynamic Equivalence," "Creative Assimilation," and "Organic Progression." (See pp. 37-54.)

Ntsikana Gaga (c. 1780-1821) is an attractively mysterious figure in Xhosa history. A Cirha, and son of a councillor of the famous chief Ngqika, he was the first Xhosa Christian. It was probably as a herd-boy that he heard the preaching of the first missionary among the Xhosa, Dr. J. T. van der Kemp of the London Missionary Society, who worked in Ciskei from 1799 to 1801. The missionary, however, made no Xhosa converts; it was only years later, about 1815, that Ntsikana underwent a conversion experience without the presence of any missionary or white person.[51]

Ntsikana's vision was dramatic. It is usually told this way. He was standing outside his hut when he saw a strange light strike his ox, called Hulushe, as the sun rose. A boy nearby could not see this light. Later in the day he went to a celebration with his family and miraculous occurrences continued: "Three times, as he started to dance, a raging wind arose out of clear blue sky forcing all dancers to stop. Tradition has it that he now became aware that the Holy Spirit had entered him, but the people thought him bewitched. He promptly took his family home and they were amazed when on the way he washed the red ochre from his body in the Gqora river, as a sign of his entry into a new life."[52]

The effects of this revelation continued the next day as he prayed and chanted, using the words "elelele homna," which may have been a Xhosafication of "alleluia amen." Eventually he gathered a group of disciples and settled into a new life, teaching them his hymns. These hymns spoke of the theology of the Creator and one true God, the coming Messiah who suffered for all people, and reconciliation among opposing groups. The latter theme was particularly timely due to the increasing tension between the Xhosas and the white settlers during this time.

Ntsikana and his disciples lived as a separate band within the larger Xhosa community, gathering twice a day for prayer, which included the singing of his hymns. A virtually unique characteristic of this group was that they "had learned their Christianity not from any European missionary, but from a fellow Xhosa who had all but discovered Christianity for himself, and who had interpreted the teachings of Christianity in a thoroughly Xhosa way for his followers."[53] Chief among those disciples was a man named Soga, father of Rev. Tiyo Soga, a Xhosa who bridged the cultural gap between traditional tribal life and European culture. Tiyo Soga became the first Xhosa ordained

---

51. David Dargie, "The Music of Ntsikana," *South African Journal of Musicology*, ed. Christoph Stroux, 2 (1982): 7.

52. Janet Hodgson, "Ntsikana's 'Great Hymn,' a Xhosa Expression of Christianity in the Early Nineteenth Century Eastern Cape," *Communications* (University of Cape Town) 4 (1980): 4.

53. David Dargie, "A Song for Dukwana," *East London Daily Dispatch*, December 14, 1995.

to Christian ministry, studying in Scotland, taking a Scottish wife, and becoming a missionary to his own people.

Ntsikana practiced an ascetic lifestyle, sending one of his wives back home. As a messenger of reconciliation, he warned Chief Ngqika and Chief Ndlambe to seek peaceful resolutions to conflict and tension within the Xhosa nation between factions of Ndlambe and Ngqika, which Ntsikana saw as particularly dangerous. Ntsikana was correct, and both leaders later regretted that they did not heed his counsel. While Ntsikana was wary of the influence of the whites coming into Xhosa lands, he was opposed to the prophet Makanda Nxele, who predicted that the Xhosa would conquer the whites in war. When Nxele's prophecy was not fulfilled, Ntsikana became revered as a true prophet.

The first permanent mission station was established at Tyumi, near Alice, in 1820. Ntsikana had planned on joining the mission but died before he was able to follow through. His sons, Kobe and Dukwana, led his followers to live near the new London Missionary Society mission under the leadership of Presbyterian minister John Brownlee. With them they brought Ntsikana's hymns.

J. K. Bokwe, mentioned earlier, was a Xhosa Presbyterian minister. His grandparents had been among the disciples of Ntsikana, and he had been taught by William Kobe Ntsikana, Ntsikana's grandson. His transcription of the text of the "Great Hymn" of Ntsikana was published in *Isigidimi sama-Xhosa* (The Xhosa Messenger) in November 1876 and again in *Christian Express* in 1878/79. Its first publication in sol-fa may have been in the collection *Amaculo ase Lovedale* (Lovedale Music) in 1885. Bokwe used tonic sol-fa notation to preserve Ntsikana's hymns, a system not generally suited to the scales or rhythms of African music. Until this time — for over fifty years — Ntsikana's hymns had been preserved orally. Bokwe distinguished four hymns, first published in 1894:

1. "Intsimbi" (Bell)
2. "Dalibom" (Life-Creator)
3. "Ingoma enqukuva" (Round Hymn)
4. "Ulo Tixo mkulu" ("Thou Great God," the Great Hymn)[54]

54. Dargie, "The Music of Ntsikana," 8. Additional information in this section comes from a column in the *East London Daily Dispatch* entitled "Iingoma zesiXhosa: Encounters with Xhosa Music," including "The Great Song" (September 2, 1995), "A Song for Dukwana" (December 14, 1995), and "Chance to Ring the Bell" (September 9, 1995). The column was resumed two years later in the paper as "World in Tune." "In the Steps of the Prophet" (August 11, 1997) appeared in this series.

Two hymns of the four will be discussed here. The first is the refrain of "Ingoma enqukuva," or Round Hymn. The text, "Ahomna, homna," may be a Xhosa version of "Amen," or is more likely words of reverence used when greeting a king. Ntsikana is using them to address the great God of heaven. The first example is a transcription by Dargie of an *uhadi* bow version of this song performed for him in 1981. It has several characteristics of Xhosa traditional music.[55]

In the example on page 133, the lower of the two lines designated for the *uhadi* bow denotes a typical syncopated rhythm played on the two fundamental pitches (indicated here as the notes F and G). The descending melodic line is very characteristic of Xhosa traditional music. All parts play the additive rhythm of 3 + 3 + 2 in the style of Xhosa music. The number of harmonic parts increases with the number of singers. The example shows one cycle of the song. It would be repeated with several melodic and textual variants being added until the hymn had been sung in its entirety. The alternating parallel major chords, a whole tone apart (F and G major in this transcription), are a major feature of Xhosa musical style. These chords are the fundamental pitches of the *uhadi*. The choral-type arrangement is based on the natural overtones of the *uhadi* bow. The clapping pattern supports the additive 3 + 3 + 2 rhythm and provides a kinesthetic reinforcement to the singing. It is likely that traditional musicians would dance as well. The lead singer may add verses over the basic three-voice cycle. Following the second example are paraphrases of verses drawn from Ntsikana's Great Hymn for the lead singer.[56]

The second selection is the text of "Ulo Tixo mkulu," or the Great Hymn of Ntsikana. The text below appears in many sources, but usually in this sequence and structure with only minor variants. One can recognize the sources of the paraphrased text above in the fuller text that follows.

You are the Great God who dwells in the heavens.
You are the true shield.

55. Dargie, "The Music of Ntsikana," 12. The cassette *African Sunday II* contains the original recording by Nosinothi Dumiso and Nomountain Qadushe, with the *uhadi*, made near Lumko in 1981. Their version of the song contains a historical reference to the "war of Mlanjeni" (known to the British as the Eighth Frontier War), which commenced in this region in 1850 and lasted for twenty-seven months. During this war a combined force of British and Boers killed over two hundred local people in the Battle of Imvani, close to Mackay's Nek. The two older ladies who sang this song for Dargie had no knowledge of the war of Mlanjeni. More information is found in David Dargie, "Significance in Songs: A Look at Three Traditional Xhosa Songs," in *Papers Presented at the Symposium on Ethnomusicology 1996*, 14, ed. Andrew Tracey, International Library of African Music (Grahamstown: Rhodes University, 1997).

56. Original version from Dargie in *Sing an African Song*, 4.

Example 4.6. "Ahomna, homna," by Ntsikana[57]

Transcription of words and music copyright © 1981 David Dargie.
Administered by Choristers Guild. Used by permission.

57. From *Halle, Halle*, Teacher's Edition, 48. A recording of this selection with *uhadi* is on the *Halle, Halle* CD (no. 9).

You are the true fortress.
You are the true forest (of refuge).
It is you who dwells in the highest.

You created life, you created on high.
You are the creator who created the heavens.
You created the stars and the Pleiades.
A Star flashed forth, bringing us your message.
You created the blind — did you not create them for a purpose?

The trumpet has sounded, it has called for us.
You are the hunter who hunts souls.
You gather together flocks rejecting each other.
You are the Great Blanket with which we are clothed.

Your hands are wounded.
Your feet are wounded.
Your blood — why is it streaming?
Your blood was poured out for us.
Are we worthy of such a ransom?
Are we worthy to enter your homestead?[58]

While the text of this song undoubtedly has many variants and has experienced many modifications since it was conceived by Ntsikana following his vision, historical evidence suggests that its basic message and structure are intact. While some of the images are natural, e.g., the reference to the Pleiades, a constellation visible in the Southern Hemisphere, or the agrarian images of the "hunter" and the "Great Blanket," one cannot as easily account for the christological references in the final section. This is especially true as there had been little European-based Christianity in the Xhosa region since Dr. Vanderkemp's influence in 1799, at least fifteen years before Ntsikana conceived the song, and Joseph Williams's presence, between 1816 and 1818. In personal correspondence (May 7, 1999) Dargie notes that "it is possible that one or both of these missionaries may have tried to express Christian teaching in African terms, though full credit [goes] to Ntsikana for shaping a truly African

58. Dargie, *Sing an African Song*, 11. Another version is available in Desmond Tutu, *An African Prayer Book* (New York: Doubleday, 1995), 12. Dargie comments on Ntsikana's reference to the blind: "I believe this is an input of theology by Ntsikana to try to give reasons for a problem and cause of suffering among his people. Glaucoma is a common Eastern Cape problem. . . . Such blindness is often interpreted by diviners as a call by the ancestors for the sufferer to become a medium or diviner." Correspondence with the author, May 7, 1999.

theology." In African theology, however, it is not necessary to trace the sources and discover how this text came to be. This is a Western analytical process. From the African perspective one accepts the text as a gift of God through one of God's prophets. One cannot measure the authenticity of Ntsikana's life and hymns strictly in terms of their historicity, although there is considerable historical evidence. The authenticity of Ntsikana's hymns ultimately may be discerned only by their abiding influence on the spiritual life of the Xhosas, by their persistent presence as a living artifact of Xhosa cultural heritage, and therefore by the embodiment of hope for liberation for the Xhosa people. Indeed, the Christ, whose hands and feet were wounded, was present in the struggles of the Xhosa people when they were in an ongoing conflict with the white settlers for many decades during the nineteenth century and relegated to the "independent homelands" of Transkei and Ciskei in the twentieth century. Ntsikana's prophecy of the "Great God" who "gather[s] together [the] flocks rejecting each other" was being fulfilled in the minds of many in the election of Nelson Mandela, a Xhosa president, in 1994.

In 1809 Ntsikana was chosen over several past chiefs and heroes of the tribe as a national patron of the Xhosa people, and the Saint Ntsikana Memorial Association was founded. The work of Xhosa composer Benjamin Tyamzashe, mentioned earlier, assured that the music of Ntsikana was taught in the schools. For Dargie, the story of Ntsikana gathered momentum when he learned in 1978 through Janet Hodgson, a lecturer at Cape Town University, of a recording of Ntsikana's songs performed by John Bokwe's son, S. T. Bokwe. The recording (1957) was one of the many made by the pioneer ethnomusicologist from South Africa, Hugh Tracey.[59]

Yet the song lives on in oral tradition for many who do not read words or music. In his travels among Xhosa traditional musicians, Dargie has heard several versions of Ntsikana's hymns. Sometimes the singers recognize the music but do not know Ntsikana's tradition behind it. There is no question that Ntsikana's hymns are the transmitters of Xhosa heritage. In spite of conventional colonial views to the contrary, oral tradition can preserve history.[60]

---

59. This recording is available through the International Library of African Music on cassette tape, "Ntsikana's Bells and Ntsikana's Song," arr. J. Knox Bokwe, *Sound of Africa: Xhosa* (TR-26). The contents of this remarkable collection of recordings is catalogued in Hugh Tracey, *The Sound of Africa Series*, 2 vols. (Grahamstown, South Africa: ILAM, 1973). The arrangement by "J. Knox Bekwe [sic]" is performed by his son, Selborne T. Bokwe, in King Williamstown District, Cape Province, South Africa. Tracey's notes indicate that the "song was chanted by Ntsikana regularly at the dawn of day, standing at his hut door, summoning the people to morning prayer. As people gathered they joined in the strains, adding different parts" (2:49).

60. My experience is limited and anecdotal. It is interesting, however, to note that on five

The story of Ntsikana's life comes full circle for Dargie now. After leaving the priesthood in 1989, Dargie lived in Germany for several years, where he married. He conducted workshops in Germany on African music and facilitated the appearance of Xhosa traditional musicians in Europe on several occasions. In 1995 he returned to South Africa with his wife when he was appointed chair of the music department at Fort Hare University in Alice, one of the only universities opened to black South Africans under apartheid. During apartheid other universities were designated for "coloureds" or Indians only. At Fort Hare Dargie established a music major that put African music at the core of requirements for graduation. Fort Hare is not far from Tyume, the site where Ntsikana's followers joined the first permanent mission soon after his death in 1821. For Dargie, Nelson Mandela's election to the presidency of South Africa completes a cosmic circle that begins with Ntsikana. Mandela, a Thembu Xhosa who attended Fort Hare University, fulfills Ntsikana's prophecy for peace and liberation in South Africa. Dargie makes this link explicit in the following excerpt:

> Back in the bad days of the 1980s, I often heard young anti-apartheid activists say: "We don't want revenge, we don't want to chase anybody out of the country, we only want our own rights and our own place in our own land."
>
> Then Nelson Mandela emerged from jail and stunned the world with his proclamation of the policy of reconciliation. As president he has put this policy into practice, and has called on all peoples of our land to work together to build the future. Who could have foreseen such attitudes and such a policy? Yet they were foreshadowed long ago by the teaching and by the songs of Ntsikana the Prophet.[61]

In June 1997 the TRC, which was formed by Mandela, visited East London, Dargie's boyhood home. Archbishop Desmond Tutu was present. Dargie opened the session by playing Ntsikana's song on his *uhadi*,[62] a reminder to Tutu of the two Ntsikana hymns that had been played in 1984 at his installation as Anglican archbishop of Cape Town. This was one of many meetings

---

occasions in November 1998 I had the opportunity to inquire about Ntsikana's hymn with Xhosa churchpeople from a variety of denominations. While they did not all recognize Ntsikana as the composer, they all recognized the melody when I hummed it. As Christians, they seemed fascinated to discover the origins of this song. It would appear that oral tradition does indeed preserve cultural memory of the musical artifact and is a form of history.

61. Dargie, "The Great Song."

62. A photo of Dargie with the caption "Song Lines of Africa" appeared in the *East London Daily Dispatch*, June 19, 1997, 1.

held around the country that culminated in the presentation of the completed report to Mandela on October 29, 1998. During that event Archbishop Tutu cited one particular account of a black South African woman who wanted to know who had tortured and killed her husband. Tutu asked her, "Why do you need to know this? What purpose will it serve?" Her response stunned the TRC panel. "I must know who did these terrible things," she said, "so that I can forgive him." For David Dargie, Ntsikana's prophecy for peace is fulfilled in these words.

What Is Liberation Hymnody?

Given the preceding discussion, is it possible to propose an answer to the question, "What is liberation hymnody?" My response is based on insights provided by two South African priests, Albert Nolan and Richard Broderick. They conducted sessions for fellow priests on liberation theology in locations around South Africa in 1986 in the days immediately following the second emergency. An ecumenical group of churches had just published the controversial "Kairos Document" that sought to engage the church in opposing political oppression in South Africa. Nolan stated that "The Kairos Document comes straight out of the flames of our South African townships."[63] While South African liberation theology has roots in Latin America, the unique conditions of oppression and the church's role in South African society dictated a contextualized response. Drawing from Nolan's overview of South African liberation theology, *To Nourish Our Faith: The Theology of Liberation for Southern Africa*, I will attempt to answer the question, "What is liberation hymnody?"

1. Liberation theology attempts "to answer the faith questions of *oppressed peoples*."[64] Is it God's will that they should suffer? Should they accept suffering with patience and resignation and wait for rewards in heaven?

Deep in the spiritual roots of Xhosa theology derived from Ntsikana's Great Hymn, the prophet speaks of a Creator who not only "hunts souls" but

---

63. Albert Nolan and Richard Broderick, *To Nourish Our Faith: The Theology of Liberation for Southern Africa* (Hilton, South Africa: Cornerstone Book, 1987), 72. A more recent reflection on the significance of the Kairos Document is contained in a paper entitled "A Voice from South Africa: Charles Villa-Vicencio," interviewed by Patricia M. Markun, in *Woodstock Report*, no. 23 (October 1990): 3-5, produced by the Woodstock Theological Center. See www.georgetown.edu/centers/woodstock/report/r-fea23.htm for the complete text of the interview.

64. Nolan and Broderick, 6, italics in original.

seeks reconciliation by "gather[ing] together flocks rejecting each other." This Creator is a fortress on the one hand, yet is vulnerable and wounded on the other. This wounded One suffers in our pain and does not hide from us in places of splendor. The wounded One is a "Great Blanket with which we are clothed" to protect us. Inherent in the words of Ntsikana's Great Hymn are the seeds of a suffering God who cares deeply for each member of the "flock."

Intrinsic in the singing of African church music is also a sense of the coming kingdom as an existential reality. From Dargie's perspective, an African should not have to wait for heaven to sing and dance the gospel in ways that are culturally relevant. By clothing liturgy in the garb of African sounds, the hidden God of African traditional religion does not remain distant but speaks to us directly on our own terms.[65] The process of moving away from music shaped by the worldview of the colonial oppressors, toward a liturgical music shaped by the cultural perspective of the oppressed, is for Africans a potential act of incarnation. It transforms an African's relationship with God from the ethereal to the existential. It potentially alters one's response to pain and suffering from passive acceptance to dynamic engagement.

Nurturing the revelation of Ntsikana, whose hymns are icons of Xhosa spirituality and cultural heritage, and engaging the African people in creating their own songs for the liturgy are empowering ways of responding to the needs and questions of oppressed peoples now.

2. **All theology is contextual.** "While Christian faith remains the same at all times and in all circumstances, the theological attempt to answer questions about this faith will vary according to the different historical and social contexts that give rise to the questions."[66] Embedded within the presuppositions of the Second Vatican Council was the declaration that the "Church earnestly desires that all the faithful be led to that full, conscious, and active par-

---

65. According to S. A. Thorpe, *African Traditional Religions: An Introduction* (Pretoria: University of South Africa, 1991), many expressions of traditional African religion in southern Africa tend toward a "conception of the Supreme Being [who] is seemingly more in the nature of a creative force which set the world in action and then withdrew" (105). In *Primal World Views: Christian Dialogue with Traditional Thought Forms*, ed. John B. Taylor (Ibadan, Nigeria: Daystar Press, 1976), G. M. Setiloane alludes to the covert nature of God in his poem "I Am an African," when he says:

> He hid Himself, UVELINGQAKI,
> That none should reach His presence . . .
> Little gods bearing up the prayers and supplications
> Of their children to the Great God. . . . (57)

66. Nolan and Broderick, 11.

ticipation in liturgical celebrations called for by the very nature of the liturgy."[67] The faithful can enter into a "full, conscious, and active" liturgical celebration only if the liturgy is contextual — if it embodies (incarnates) the faith of a given cultural and historical context. Anscar Chupungco describes the relationship between liturgical and cultural context this way:

> Liturgical inculturation may be described as the process whereby the texts and rites used in worship by the local church are so inserted in the framework of culture, that they absorb its thought, language, and ritual patterns. Liturgical inculturation operates according to the dynamics of insertion in a given culture and interior assimilation of cultural elements. From a purely anthropological point of view we may say that inculturation allows the people to experience in liturgical celebrations a "cultural event" whose language and ritual forms they are able to identify as elements of their culture.[68]

Needless to say, singing the "Tantum ergo" in Latin to "My Darling Clementine," cited earlier, does not engage the kind of interaction needed to make liturgy a contextual event. One of the methods of Dargie's approach to liturgical inculturation was to invite the faithful to composition workshops, literally giving them a voice in the musical molding of the liturgy. In order to inspire creativity, Dargie often engaged indigenous musicians to perform at the composition workshops so that the participants could "capture the style of the music, by composing with the same scales, harmony, rhythms, even though using different melodies, arrangements, etc."[69] The speech-to-song technique he used, including biblical texts and liturgical ordinaries and acclamations, allowed these rites to take on a melodic character inherent to the tonal structure of the language.

The use of indigenous musical styles also encourages dance. Dargie notes that an abstract concept of music does not exist in African languages. African musical terms indicate active participation, e.g., to lead a song, to follow a song, to clap with a song, to dance with a song, etc. In an effort to remove any physical manifestations from the music, be it clapping, dancing, swaying, etc., Dargie notes that missionaries had attempted to change the meaning of one of the functional terms for singing in Xhosa from "sing little songs" to "sing while keeping still." A new vocabulary of abstract musical

---

67. "Constitution on the Sacred Liturgy," art. 14.

68. Anscar Chupungco, *Liturgies of the Future: The Process and Methods of Inculturation* (New York: Paulist, 1989), 29.

69. Dargie, *Workshops*, 23.

terms in Xhosa was devised by colonial missionaries to accommodate their concept of appropriate church music.[70]

Attempts to squeeze African rhythms and melodies into the Western tonic sol-fa system of notation also distort the basic character of the music. The subtleties of the Xhosa scale, for example, and the complexities of Xhosa traditional polyrhythms cannot be communicated easily in any Western-notated forms.[71]

To summarize, Dargie's approach to liturgy and the music that embraces it is highly contextual. He encouraged and facilitated situations in which the faithful could express the rites in their own musical style, using techniques that attempted to capture and transmit African music on its own terms — using recordings (versus written music), indigenous musicians, indigenous instruments, and dance — and eschewed Western melodies, conceptual terms, and notational systems that stripped African music of its essence and assimilated it into preexisting Western structures and worldviews. Nolan notes that "one of the biggest problems with Western theology is that it thought it was a universal theology."[72] Substitute "culture" for "theology" and repeat this sentence. Then substitute "music" for "theology" and repeat it again. As an ethnomusicologist who became bimusical, both as a Western and Xhosa musician, Dargie exemplifies an understanding of contextual church music, i.e., musical liberation for the African Christians.

3. **All theology is political.** Nolan notes that "culture, however, is not the only context that gives rise to the questions about faith. Much more urgent and demanding are the questions that arise out of different *political contexts.*"[73]

It is at this point that many Western liturgists and church musicians become increasingly uncomfortable. Within the general history of Western aesthetics, the philosophy of formalism values art that does not point beyond itself, i.e., that finds meaning only within a juxtaposition of internal artistic resources and organization.[74] Regardless of one's perspective about art within

70. Dargie, "Xhosa Church Music," 66.

71. Dargie refers to the tonic sol-fa system used by Bokwe, Tyamzashe, and other African church musicians as a "destructive method" that reduced African musical styles to pale imitations with elementary Western harmonies and simplified rhythms because "the regrettable sol-fa system . . . can only with great difficulty be used for transcribing any but the most simple music: diatonic music with little use of chromatic tones, and with the simplest rhythm (even as western music understands rhythm)." See "African Methods of Music Education — Some Reflections," *African Music* 7, no. 3 (1996): 37.

72. Nolan and Broderick, 14.

73. Nolan and Broderick, 15, italics in original.

74. For a concise discussion of formal versus referential meaning that takes into account Western aesthetics as well as non-Western perspectives, see Jean-Jacques Nattiez, *Music and Dis-*

a museum or secular music heard in concert halls, forms of art within liturgy point intrinsically to a cosmic reality beyond their existence and to a functional significance inherent in their structure. The notion that an artistic work lives in a cultural vacuum holding no accountability or influence beyond its own existence may be defensible in a broader Western aesthetic context. But it is heresy when applied to Christian liturgy where music sustains the flow of the liturgy, encourages the participation of the assembly, and provides a more holistic sense of community than aesthetic models based primarily on passive observation.

Given the penchant for formalism in Western aesthetics, some might assume that Christian liturgy somehow should be apolitical or free from those influences that would keep the worshiper from having a purely transcendent relationship with the Creator. While I would not deny the validity of transcendence in liturgy, to secure transcendence by not dealing with the world of political struggle and oppression is transcendence by default, i.e., self-delusion. The incarnational aspect of Christian theology demands that the structures and substance of liturgy intersect with reality in all its forms: personal, social, cultural, and political.

Following up on his assertion that "all theology is political," Nolan observes that the "only difference is between those who are aware of this and those who are not." By analogy I would suggest that all liturgy is political. The only difference is between those who are aware of this by necessity or intention and those who are not, either by ignorance, self-deception, or social arrogance.

African music functions in the life of the community from which it originates differently than music in the Western classical tradition. Ezekiel Mphahlele states that "African music should be looked at as part of [an] integrated community of things, of phenomena. It is looked at as an organically functional thing, it sets body movement into being and the mind is integrated with it, attitudes are integrated with it."[75] There are several qualities about African music that easily make it serve as a political vehicle: portability, flexibility, accessibility, and valence.[76]

---

course: Toward a Semiology of Music, trans. Carolyn Abbate (Princeton: Princeton University Press, [1987] 1990), 111-27.

75. Ezekiel Mphahlele, "African Humanistic Thought and Belief: Background to an Understanding of African Music," in *Papers Presented at the Third Symposium on Ethnomusicology,* ed. Andrew Tracey (Grahamstown: International Library of African Music, September 16-19, 1982), 18.

76. This particular list of characteristics, while my own, is the result of my experiences in African music and numerous authors' descriptions and analyses, especially the following: Kofi Agawu, *African Rhythm* (Cambridge: Cambridge University Press, 1995); Paul Berliner, *The Soul*

African music is portable. It demands few resources to produce. The most important one is the body, both as a conveyor of the human voice, as a percussion instrument, and as a dancer. African music can be performed anywhere. Any instrumental effects that are required usually can be carried by hand or simulated with whatever resources are readily available. It can be sung on the move or in the street as easily as in more formal spaces. In traditional African music, the communal space where people gather for the market, to conduct business, or to celebrate is usually out of doors. This arena also becomes the venue for musical performance and participation.

African music is flexible. Because of its cyclic structure and oral means of transmission, not only can African music be taken anyplace without the need for formal musical notation, it can be modified to meet the needs of the situation at hand. Texts can be created on the spot that make the song more relevant to the current situation. Because leadership can come from anyone within the group, all assembled may suggest additions and modifications to a song. In response, the gathered community either validates or ignores the suggestion; if validated the originator of the musical modification or addition is empowered, uniting the group behind the idea. The call-response pattern typical of many African styles allows for several leaders to emerge in sequence, offering a new "call" appropriate to the response that has been previously established.

African music is accessible. It is not always accessible to those who do not understand or perceive its principles of organization, but within the particular community out of which it emerges it is easily accessible. Furthermore, most African musical traditions have sufficient underlying principles of organization in common to allow varying tribal groups within Africa to participate in each other's music with very little effort. It is not uncommon for different groups to share songs among themselves. The cyclic organization of the musical experience allows those who perceive the recurring cycles to join in and, perhaps, improvise a part. The call-response patterns of African music allow for the community to respond with regularity and predictability once the pattern is perceived. While text can be extensive, it is often limited to the length of a cycle with cues by the leader when the text changes.

---

of Mbira (Chicago: University of Chicago Press, 1978); John Blacking, *How Musical Is Man?* (Seattle: University of Washington Press, 1973); John Miller Chernoff, *African Rhythm and African Sensibility: Aesthetics and Social Action in African Musical Idioms* (Chicago: University of Chicago Press, 1979); Yaya Diallo and Mitchell Hall, *The Healing Drum: African Wisdom Teachings* (Rochester, Vt.: Destiny Books, 1989); Samuel A. Flood, *The Power of Black Music* (New York: Oxford University Press, 1995); and J. H. Kwabena Nketia, *African Music in Ghana* (Evanston, Ill.: Northwestern University Press, 1963), as well as writings already cited by Dargie and Andrew Tracey.

African music has the quality of valence — that is, the quality to unite, interact, react, or merge with other aspects of the environment. It is perhaps this quality that prompted the following statement on sacred music in the "Constitution on the Sacred Liturgy": "The musical tradition of the universal Church is a treasure of inestimable value, greater even than that of any other art. The main reason for this preeminence is that, as sacred song closely bound to the text, it forms a necessary or integral part of the solemn liturgy."[77] "Valence" is a term primarily associated with chemistry. It refers to "the combining capacity of an atom or a radical determined by the number of electrons that it will lose, add, or share when it reacts with other atoms."[78] The "combining capacity" of African music allows it to draw together disparate environmental elements and transform not only events in the immediate sense but also occurrences in the past that influence and interact with the present. Africans have an abiding sense of their past. Community consists not only of the living but also the "living dead" who stand in solidarity with the living.[79] The quality of *anamnesis* pervades the African sensibility, reliving past experiences through song, integrating them with present struggles, and drawing strength from the "living dead" or communion of saints.

John Miller Chernoff notes that the "community dimension is perhaps the essential aspect of African music. . . . [Africans] do not want to distinguish the audience from the musicians at a musical event."[80] African musical practice solidifies those assembled into the *ecclesia* — those gathered bodily

77. "Constitution on the Sacred Liturgy," art. 112.

78. *The American Heritage Electronic Dictionary,* 3rd ed., version 3.0A (Wordstar International, 1993).

79. See John S. Mbiti, *Introduction to African Religion* (London: Heinemann Educational Books, 1975), 119-20, for a discussion of the "living dead." G. M. Setiloane provides an understanding of "living dead" in his poem "I Am an African," quoted in Taylor, ed., *Primal World Views:*

> Ah . . . yes . . . ! it is true.
> The dead are very present with us;
> They speak to me in the wind and the rain,
> Through fellow-man, and living creatures,
> Birds of the air, and reptiles gliding in the grass.
>
> The dead are not dead, they are ever near us:
> Approving or disapproving all our actions,
> They chide us when we go wrong;
> Bless us and sustain us for good deeds done,
> For kindness shown, and strangers made to feel at home;
> They increase our store, and punish our pride! (57)

80. Chernoff, 33.

for God's service in the world as well as the living dead in spirit. Let us turn to some examples of South African song that illustrate these qualities.

"Siyahamba"[81] is a well-known Zulu/Xhosa song that has been incorporated into several recent hymnals and has become widely sung in North America.[82] Dargie recalled that "Siyahamba" was a freedom song originating with Amadodana, a Methodist young men's group.[83] Usually translated "We are marching in the light of God," the simple text contains layers of meaning. "We" is a word of community, the community of those living and the community of the living dead. "Marching" is an action that unifies the community as they move physically and spiritually in the same direction. It is a physical, kinesthetic response to the Spirit, not a passive acquiescence. "The light of God" has meaning on several levels. While a symbol of creation and of Jesus Christ, "the light of the world," it is also a common refrain in songs of healing or *ngoma* throughout southern and central Africa. This refrain, "Let darkness be replaced with light," is coded language for "seeing clearly."[84] God is the source of clear sight in the midst of the struggle, i.e., the source of discernment and truth. As we march, we can see our way ahead. Our path is clear. Where there is light, there is hope.

When this message is combined with African music's natural valence, the words become embodied in the lives of the community that sings and dances it. The accessibility of the musical form draws all present into the song's cyclic structure immediately. Its portability allows the song to be taken to places of "darkness" where its message can illuminate evil in its myriad forms and offer the singer hope as he or she sees clearly the path ahead. Its flexibility allows for the performer/participants to add to the basic song a message that draws into it the existential reality of the situation. "We" grow in number as we "march," for there are those who join us literally on the way. The song accommodates and even facilitates a growing, evolving community of believers. "We are marching," knowing that the living dead are singing with us. If this song is taken into the liturgy as a processional or recessional, it

81. Portions of this section appeared in an earlier article, "Siyahamba, South African Freedom Song," *Chorister* 51, no. 6 (December 1999): 23-27. Dargie comments that the text is basically the same in Siswata (the Swazi people), Xhosa, and Zulu.

82. See n. 6 above for several hymnals that include a version of "Siyahamba."

83. In a visit to Dallas on March 21, 2000, Dargie mentioned this and another song in Nyberg's collection, *Freedom Is Coming*, "Singabahambayo" (p. 17). This song is translated "On earth an army is marching, we're going home. Our longing bears a song, so sing out strong. Sithi Halleluya."

84. John M. Janzen, *Ngoma: Discourses on Healing in Central and Southern Africa* (Berkeley: University of California Press, 1992), 111-18.

brings with it the struggle of the streets and sanctifies it in the Sanctus of the Eucharist. Liturgy is not hermetically sealed from daily life; rather it sanctifies daily struggle.

The story of "Sikhulule" by Thozama Dyani was told earlier. The text reads "Liberate us, Lord; in your love and mercy, set us free." This petition is a prayer of urgency growing out of a specific act of violence within a broader context of oppression. An act of violence led to a song that, in turn, led to a musical setting of the Mass. Freedom is joined to the love and mercy extended by Christ rather than to the hate and revenge that may result from encounters with oppression and violence. Singing this song within the liturgy allows those who know its story or who have experienced similar events to bring the violence before God whose own Son suffered a violent death. When the need arises for this song to be sung outside the formal liturgy, it brings with it the hope of Christ's wounded and resurrected body. The qualities of music and community mentioned earlier allow it to unite the political sphere of human activity with the liturgical realm of spiritual experience.

Other examples could be cited, but the principle remains. In apartheid South Africa, the priest who administered the sacraments on one day may have marched in the funeral of a slain child the next, hoping to ward off additional violence. Archbishop Oscar Romero's brutal death while administering the sacrament in El Salvador reminds us of the sacramental nature of all life whether placed within the official liturgy or in the context of resistance that confronts evil and brings it into the light.

4. **Liberation theology is self-conscious.** It does not assume that one size fits all, but identifies the situation of a particular group. The African experience, according to Nolan, "gives rise to faith questions about suffering, human dignity, poverty and most of all about liberation from oppression."[85] These are disturbing questions that interfere with the comfort of padded pews and an anemic spirituality insulated from reality. These are the questions of liberation in liturgy.

Dargie's ministry of musical liberation has at its roots the raising of consciousness among the African people. As the quotation at the beginning of this chapter indicates, having pride in one's heritage is a source of identity and the springboard to liberation. The training of an ethnomusicologist is one that engenders self-consciousness. Nothing heightens the delights, differences, and detriments of one's culture of origin more quickly than to live in and learn from another culture. Attempting to appreciate an alien culture raises one's level of self-consciousness.

85. Nolan and Broderick, 17.

Briefly stated, liberation hymnody draws upon the indigenous sounds, metaphors, and movements of those who are oppressed by unjust social, political, and economic systems as a way of creating community and expressing hope. Songs of liberation may be incorporated into a formal liturgy, serving both the musical needs of worship and expressing solidarity in the midst of political struggle. They also may be taken out of the context of established liturgy and sung in the streets — the liturgy of life — where the music serves as a proclamation of hope, a vehicle for community, and a solidifying force in the face of direct opposition.

The process of encouraging African Christians to find their musical roots and bring these into liturgy has been threatening to some. Dargie has been accused of *Verwoerdism*, or "pushing the people back into the bush."[86] *Verwoerdism* assumes that one culture is superior and that other perspectives pale in comparison. Embedded in *Verwoerdism* are classism, ethnocentrism, and elitism. For the musical liberator the question is not "Which culture is the superior?" The question is "How is the incarnation manifest through the symbols, rituals, and creative expressions of my culture?" Or, put another way, "What do the symbols, rituals, and creative expressions of my culture offer those seeking a fuller understanding of the God who dwells — tabernacles or pitches a tent — among us?" (John 1:14). Making the incarnation a vital reality for a particular cultural perspective, in this case that of the Xhosa people, is the work of liberation. Dargie notes: "This is something most important in the church — that people feel it is their church, that they are understood. As a white, one has to learn how to work under black leadership. And if black people are to lead with confidence, they must feel that their heritage and culture are understood and accepted by those whom they are to lead. It seems that this message reaches beyond the work of the church, in preparing the way for full liberation."[87]

Conclusion

In a discussion with Fr. Anselm Prior, O.F.M., director of the Lumko Institute and longtime friend of David Dargie, he said, "If there is one theme that ties together Dave's ministry, it is musical liberation."[88] Perhaps one of Dargie's

---

86. Dargie, "African Church Music," 9.
87. Dargie, "African Church Music," 12.
88. Interview with Fr. Anselm at Lumko Institute, Delmenville, South Africa, November 13, 1998.

former parishioners, now a member of the popular South African musical group Amampondo, put it best:

> Seems like it all began at St. Francis' Church down Cape Town way. Father Dave Dargie was another kind of Irish Roman Catholic missionary. Instead of the Virgin Mary, holy sperm and other sins, he preached: STICK TO YOUR ROOTS, enjoy and explore them.
>
> Dave Dargie had done some research in Transkei and Zimbabwe on indigenous instruments and song. He encouraged roots music not by pulpit-preaching but by showing his "congregation" how to make and play a large variety of traditional instruments.
>
> According to Amampondo's Simpiwe and Mandla, who were St. Francis churchites from youth on, he was the "guy who brought the light."[89]

---

89. Rose (an anonymous designation for the author), "Amampondo's Spiritual Roots," *Vula* 2 (1985): 7. Amampondo (the Mpondo People) is a musical group, most of whom learned to play marimbas from Dargie. The marimbas, produced by Brother Kurt Huwiler, who worked in Umtata for the Lumko Institute, were developed in 1979 and tuned to both Xhosa and Afro-diatonic scales. Among those who learned to play the instruments for the first marimba Mass were three who formed their own musical group and have gone on to produce their own CDs. This article discusses Dargie as a spiritual father to this popular South African musical group.

CHAPTER 5

The Spirit of Ngoma

Patrick Matsikenyiri and
Indigenous Song in Zimbabwe

If you can talk, you can sing. If you can walk, you can dance.

SHONA SAYING[1]

One way to know Patrick Matsikenyiri (b. 1937) is to journey with him to his tribal homeland. While Patrick has traveled abroad extensively for study and consultations on African music, he has rarely lived more than a few hours' drive from his homeland. Biriiri is a mountainous area approximately 120 kilometers south of Mutare, Zimbabwe, near the border of Mozambique. When he comes home to this land bestowed to his grandfather by the headman, a representative of the tribal chief who is the custodian of communal land,[2] the fullness of Patrick's life comes into perspective. It is a life very close to the land and to the extended family with whom he shares his tribal home.[3]

On this land Patrick has planted trees, raised animals, and made rela-

1. Quoted in Paul W. Chilcote, "A Singing and Dancing Church: Methodist Worship in Kenya and Zimbabwe," in *The Sunday Service of the Methodists,* ed. Karen B. Westerfield-Tucker (Nashville: Abingdon, 1996), 238.
2. Sebastian Bakare, *My Right to Land — in the Bible and in Zimbabwe: A Theology of Land* (Harare: Zimbabwe Council of Churches, 1993), 49.
3. Information for this section as well as many of the personal observations throughout this chapter come from conversations with Patrick Matsikenyiri in Mutare and Harare, Zimbabwe, between November 21 and December 14, 1998, including participation in the conference choir for the World Council of Churches Eighth Assembly in Harare, a choir prepared and directed by Patrick.

tionships, many of which are over six decades old. He has built his family home on the place where his father was born, a mountainside overlooking the valley where members of his extended family live, farm, and raise animals. Patrick's father bears the title Father of the Nation, Nyamazha, a person who advises the chief and is an intermediary between the chief and the people. The father of the tribe is the first to hear of the death of the chief and eventually installs the chief's successor. It is the position of tribal father that Patrick will assume upon his father's death.

In order to appreciate the songs Patrick writes and the context in which he shares them, it is helpful to have some background on the region of Africa now known as Zimbabwe.

Brief History of Zimbabwe

Patrick is a Shona, the major tribal group in Zimbabwe. The roots of the Shona empire can be traced to a region close to the center of modern Zimbabwe near Masvingo in the southeastern highlands where the ruins of the Great Zimbabwe remain. The Great Zimbabwe is a mountain of rock out of which a fortress was carved. By the time of the initial colonial insurgence in this area by the Portuguese in the early sixteenth century, the empire was already waning, well past its zenith (1250-1450). During the declining centuries of the Shona after 1450, conflict in this region between the Shona and other groups was caused by tribal migrations from the regions now called Mozambique and South Africa. The Ndebele, the other major tribal power in modern Zimbabwe, were Zulus who were driven north out of southern Africa by the bellicose Shaka's Zulus. During the nineteenth century the Portuguese influence centered in the coastal region of Mozambique on the Indian Ocean.

In the 1870s British adventurers and land speculators entered the region, possibly spurred on by rumors of gold from the Portuguese. England's economic interests intensified and the British South Africa Company was formed under the leadership of Cecil John Rhodes. By 1890 Rhodes and his "Pioneer Column" had marched to the future site of Salisbury, now Harare, and solidified control over the region. The settlers continued to look for gold. But when it was not to be found, they exchanged gold mining for farming, claiming vast tracts of productive land as their own. It was Rhodes's intent to divide the country among the pioneers: "There will probably be reserves for the natives, and the remainder will be what I might call public land, so that you [the British pioneers] will be the first entitled to select land. There will thus be native reserves, free grants to yourselves, and the balance of crown land, not to be sold under 3s. (shillings) per morgen."[4]

The colonials had staked out most of the arable land by the 1930s. The authority of the chiefs, who in precolonial days were the custodians of communal lands, was almost totally undermined. The 1930 Land Apportionment Act solidified the settlers' hold on the vast majority of land and consequently prevented African ownership of land. This act divided the country into six land zones: European Area, Native Reserve, Unassigned Area, Native Area, Forest Area, and Undetermined Area.[5] European control of the land was guaranteed in perpetuity as banks would make loans to "European descendants only." In a familiar pattern of colonization, natives were forcibly removed from lands and resettled in designated reserves.[6]

In spite of uprisings by the Africans, especially the *Chimurenga* (rebellion) of 1896, when white settlers and traders were killed, the British South Africa Company, supported by interests in England, maintained and tightened its control on Rhodesia. Threats of political domination by Afrikaners, longtime settlers of Dutch descent from South Africa, led to the formation of Southern Rhodesia in 1910. (Northern Rhodesia later became Zambia.) The formation and increasing influence of African political groups such as the African National Congress (ANC) in South Africa, the Zimbabwe African People's Union (ZAPU), and the Zimbabwe African National Union (ZANU) during the early 1960s contributed to a sense of empowerment to the African population. Incipient independence movements in West and East Africa, spreading south through Kenya (1963), Tanzania (1964), and Zambia (1964), led Prime Minister Ian Smith to announce a Unilateral Declaration of Independence from Britain in 1965. Smith maintained control of the African population by installing a council of chiefs, paid by the government, whom he insisted represented the native people.[7]

4. A 1919 quotation by Cecil John Rhodes cited in Bakare, *My Right to Land,* 41.

5. Bakare, *My Right to Land,* 41.

6. Thomas Sowell, *Conquests and Cultures: An International History* (New York: Basic Books, 1998), 82-87, notes how the British used two methods of establishing rule throughout their colonial empire in the nineteenth and twentieth centuries. One was the method of "indirect rule," making use of local leaders trained in British institutions and/or appointed by Britain to rule according to British law and economic interests. Such was the case in India and Nigeria. The second was the rule of white settlers who displaced local populations, herding them on to reserves, as was the case in Kenya, Rhodesia (now Zimbabwe), and South Africa. In the latter case, these lands were more desirable to the white settlers.

7. General information on the British South Africa Company of Cecil Rhodes, the movement toward independence in the southern region of Africa, and the Ian Smith years before majority rule was established by Africans in 1980 is readily available in many sources. See David

Smith's government faced hostility on two fronts: from the British government because Rhodesia had declared independence, and in the form of a second *chimurenga* on April 28, 1966, when ZANU guerrillas were killed after engaging Rhodesian troops. A pattern of hit-and-run attacks on white settlers by guerrillas followed with further reprisals by the Rhodesian government. But the guerrilla forces were not unified and were easily overwhelmed by the Rhodesian national army. Angola's and Mozambique's independence from Portugal in 1975 set the stage for intensified action by the guerrillas as liberation movements pushed farther south. The guerrillas were able to gather, train, and be supplied in neighboring countries which had gained independence, and to continue attacks on white farming areas. These attacks created a siege mentality among the settlers. The guerrillas often hit hotels and tourist locations while the government disrupted the lives of the people by arbitrarily closing missions and schools.

It was during this time that some of the worst slaughter took place on both sides of the conflict. Entire villages were accused, first by one side and then by the other, of either harboring and aiding guerrillas or holding allegiance to the Rhodesian government forces. The official policy of the Rhodesian government stated: "If villagers harbour terrorists, and terrorists are found running about in villages, naturally they will be bombed and destroyed in any manner which the commander on the spot considers desirable in the suitable prosecution of a successful campaign."[8] On the other hand, guerrillas often entered villages demanding allegiance to the independence movement by directing a person suspected of being a government sympathizer to execute a family member or fellow villager on the spot.[9]

Lamb, *The Africans* (New York: Vintage Books, 1983), 331-37. Roland Oliver and J. D. Fage provide a helpful overview of the road to independence throughout Africa and the early years following independence in many African countries in *A Short History of Africa* (New York: Penguin Books, [1962] 1988), 200-262. Ali A. Mazrui, *The Africans: A Triple Heritage* (Boston: Little, Brown, 1986), operating from the perspective of Islam, places the historical struggles for independence among African nations within the broader context of the evolution of African civilization, cultural characteristics, and evolving African identity that synthesizes traditional African culture with Islamic and Western influences. Sanford J. Unger examines events in postliberation Zimbabwe in his chapter "Zimbabwe: Shattered Hopes," in *Africa: The People and Politics of an Emerging Continent*, 3rd ed. (New York: Simon and Schuster, 1989), 321-40.

8. A 1977 Rhodesian government policy articulated by P. K. van der Byl, minister for information, quoted in Barbara McCrea and Tony Pinchuck, *Zimbabwe and Botswana: The Rough Guide* (New York: Penguin Books, 1996), 366.

9. This difficult and conflicting period of the struggle of independence has been the source for some of the most provocative literature by Zimbabwean writers. Rather than histories, novels and short stories capture the collision of values, the disruption of ways of living, the

In 1979 an election finally was held — an election, however, that excluded the popular ZAPU and ZANU parties. Bishop Muzorewa, the first African bishop in the United Methodist Church and a seemingly malleable candidate supported by Smith, was elected prime minister. The supposedly "liberated" country was called Zimbabwe-Rhodesia or, sarcastically by some, Rhobabwe. Smith continued, though, to control the army, police, judicial system, and civil service. No one was fooled, including newly elected prime minister of England, Margaret Thatcher. In spite of hopes by Smith that the conservative Thatcher would support this thinly veiled political scheme, she proved no more sympathetic to the white Rhodesians than had her more socialistic predecessors. Muzorewa and Smith alternated leadership of the government on a monthly basis. When Muzorewa unexpectedly and cleverly dissolved the government, he neutralized Smith's plans to maintain control, eventually sending the entire process into negotiations in Lancaster, England.[10] Finally, lacking support from abroad and pressured by the guerrillas, Smith was forced to hold open elections between ZAPU and ZANU on March 4, 1980. Robert Mugabe, representing ZANU, became prime minister, while Rev. Canaan Banana, a Methodist minister[11] and popular leader during the liberation struggle, became the first state president of a majority-ruled Zimbabwe.

The disaster predicted by Smith did not occur, and white Rhodesians who chose to remain did not find their standard of living slipping by any measurable degree.[12] The Mugabe government agreed to compensate the

---

impossible choices made in the hope of survival, and the utter disregard for individual rights that took place on both sides of the struggle. I recommend especially Chenjerai Hove, *Shadows* (Harare: Baobab Books, 1991), and two books by Yvonne Vera, a collection of short stories, *Why Don't You Carve Other Animals* (Toronto: TSAR Publications, 1992), and a novel, *Without a Name* (Harare: Baobab Books, 1994).

10. This interpretation of Bishop Muzorewa's role in securing an equal place in the negotiations for African rule in Lancaster, England, comes from Matsikenyiri, who was a close friend of the bishop. Internal struggles between Mugabe and Muzorewa for power usually have led to a different explanation that focused on the unjust election of Muzorewa because of the exclusion of ZAPU and ZANU. Most interpretations of events of this time assign Muzorewa a figurehead role as prime minister, serving as a pawn of Smith. Matsikenyiri disagrees with this prevailing view and sees Muzorewa as a clever strategist working under very difficult circumstances, because of pressures from both Smith and Mugabe. In spite of this, Muzorewa was able to overcome the seemingly insurmountable obstacles that allowed all parties to go to the bargaining table in Lancaster as equals.

11. Banana was a minister in the British-planted Methodist Church while Muzorewa was a bishop in the United States–planted United Methodist Church.

12. Events in Zimbabwe during 2000-2002 have, however, led to the government under Mugabe's rule seizing land from white Zimbabweans and the settling of white farmlands by

white settlers for land and attempted to steer a course between capitalism (like Kenya) and socialism (as in Mozambique). However, extended terms of office, common in many African countries, contribute to political corruption. Zimbabwe is no exception as Mugabe, to date the country's only prime minister since African rule was instituted in 1980, continues in power. Political corruption and conflict contribute to economic difficulties, exacerbated by famine and drought. Unemployment is on the rise. Inflation is high. The overwhelming majority of arable land remains in the control of white settlers. In an attempt to meet the long-delayed expectations of the African populace, the Mugabe government was forced to confiscate land at the end of the 1990s, much of it owned by absentee English landlords and administered on site by Boers, descendants of South Africa's Afrikaners. The high level of international debt threatens to unravel political structures as government services constantly are being cut.[13]

But the silent and potentially most pervasive threat to the Zimbabwean people and African culture in the future is the rising AIDS epidemic. Well over half the known AIDS cases in the world are found in southern Africa, especially Zimbabwe and South Africa, with some estimates running as high as 40 percent of the people having been infected with the HIV/AIDS virus.[14] These cultural roots and the struggles of the current context have shaped Matsikenyiri and provide a backdrop for his music.

Living in Old Mutare and Modern Mutare

Modern Mutare (the word means a "metal that looks like gold") was moved fourteen kilometers from its original site on the other side of Christmas Pass

---

black Zimbabweans against the will of the whites. This has led to the death of several white Zimbabweans.

13. Sebastian Bakare highlighted the problem of debt in Zimbabwe for the WCC Eighth Assembly in Harare, December 1998, in his book prepared for the assembly, *The Drumbeat of Life: Jubilee in an African Context* (Geneva: WCC Publications, 1997), 30-34.

14. See Bakare, *The Drumbeat of Life*, 34-36. Economic implications of AIDS are explored by Hugh McCullum, "You're in the Deadly Centre," *Jubilee* 3 (December 7, 1998), in which he states that "Zimbabwe has suddenly, in the past two years, turned into the deadly centre of the world's AIDS epidemic. It has the highest rate in the world, a rate which is getting out of control of health practitioners and, most of all, the society" (7). AIDS and its effect on traditional culture and values is also a common subject of literary works in Zimbabwe. For example, see Alexander Kanengoni, *Effortless Tears* (Harare: Baobab Books, 1993), 71-76. Sekai Nzenza-Shand explores this theme throughout her novel *Songs to an African Sunset: A Zimbabwean Story* (Oakland: Lonely Planet, 1997).

into a nearby valley almost one hundred years ago by colonial leader Cecil Rhodes in order to connect it to the train line between Mozambique and Harare (then Salisbury). The original site became the Old Umtali Mission — a pronunciation of "Mutare" by the Ndebele guides of the first settlers[15] — started in the 1890s by American Methodist bishop Joseph Crane Hartzell on land granted to him by Rhodes. It was at this mission, now called the Old Mutare Mission, that Patrick received his initial education.

As was often the case, the names of the Africans were not written down until the British registered them. It was common for African names to be mispronounced by the British and, therefore, misspelled. Such is the case with Patrick's name, Matsikenyiri. According to the way it is pronounced in Shona, it would be more accurately spelled "Mwatsi*keny*ere," with a rising inflection on the third syllable. Once the names were written down and entered into legal documents, however, it was impractical, if not impossible, to correct them. I heard the African pronunciation most often when fellow Zimbabweans called out to Patrick. The name has dual meanings, one militant — "you have stepped on a land mine and it will blow" — and one musical — "you whistle the horn of a *kudu* and it makes a sound." The first meaning is ironic, as the Mozambique border near Mutare was heavily mined by the Rhodesian government during the struggle for independence, and remains so to this day. The second meaning was a portent of a vocation that would lead him into church music.

After his education Matsikenyiri entered a double career in 1961 as a church leader and a headmaster. Within the Methodist church he served the Mutare District as a lay leader and district secretary, traveling up the mountains by motorcycle on the weekends and preaching at two or three services each Sunday. Since Mutare is on the border with Mozambique, these congregations were often mixed groups consisting of people from both countries. It was also during this time that his reputation as a musical leader grew.

Often asked to lead music at women's gatherings, he became the conference music director in 1968, a position he held until he left for study in the United States in 1990. Because of his reputation in church music and work as director of music in the Mutare District, Matsikenyiri was part of the team that revised the United Methodist hymnal, *Ngoma,* in 1964, and has continued to make corrections and revisions in succeeding editions.[16]

15. Andrew Tracey advised me that this kind of pronunciation discrepancy was quite common in Zimbabwe. Correspondence with the author, September 16, 1999.

16. *Ngoma: dze United Methodist Church Ye Zimbabwe* (Harare: Conference Board of Publications and Communications, [1964] 1995). L. G. Zhungu, chairman of the hymnal proj-

Robert Kauffman was the first missionary sent by the Board of Global Ministries of the United Methodist Church in the United States. Kauffman was a musicologist who made a study of African music, finally focusing his efforts on Zimbabwe, where he collected and analyzed traditional songs.[17] He was a guiding light for the 1964 publication of *Ngoma,* writing an extensive *Mavambo* (preface).

In 1968 Matsikenyiri met Olof Axelsson of the Church of Sweden Mission, and they became close friends. In December Patrick traveled to Bulawayo to teach music during the Christmas recess when he was freed of his duties as headmaster. It was Axelsson who, along with earlier work by Kauffman, encouraged Patrick to continue to develop an African approach to church music. Axelsson notes that Kauffman followed a three-step approach in developing African church music: (1) collect extensive recordings of traditional Shona music on tape and analyze the music for its salient features, techniques, and forms; (2) find Shona composers who had some theoretical musical training to compose music for the church; (3) modify the traditional musical styles and forms to some degree "in order to get away from the accusations of being too traditional . . . being diplomatic so that the new music wouldn't indicate too much of the traditional African worship."[18]

While similar to African compositional experiments among the Catholics conducted by Joseph Lenherr in Zimbabwe at the time, Kauffman's approach was more conservative. Lenherr preferred Shona musicians with no Western training and was less likely to manipulate traditional African musical forms.[19] In this way the Catholic Church responded more fully to the reforms of Vatican II (1963-65), while the Methodist church developed styles that modified African traditional music practices to some degree to fit the tastes of parishioners who may have been reticent to incorporate traditional music into worship. This moderate approach guided Kauffman in his work on

---

ect, acknowledges Matsikenyiri's contributions to the hymnal in the foreword, especially for "noting mistakes in some songs and missed lines and verses in some songs" (3).

17. Chilcote, 243-44.

18. Olof Axelsson, "The Development of African Church Music in Zimbabwe," in *Papers Presented at the Symposium on Ethnomusicology* (Grahamstown, South Africa: Rhodes University, September 24-26, 1981), 5.

19. Axelsson, 5. Kauffman later completed a dissertation and published several articles related to his experience with the Shonas. They include "Multi-Part Relationships in the Shona Music of Rhodesia" (Ph.D. diss., University of California at Los Angeles, 1970); "Shona Urban Music and the Problem of Acculturation," *International Folk Music Council* 4 (1973): 47-56; "African Rhythms: A Reassessment," *Ethnomusicology* 24 (1980): 393-416; "Multi-Part Relationship in Shona Vocal Music," *Selected Reports in Ethnomusicology* 5 (1984): 145-59.

Ngoma in 1964, sometimes fitting biblical texts to existing traditional tunes[20] or composing original church music in modified traditional styles.

The liberation movement began in 1964 in Zambia and Tanzania, built gradually, and continued in earnest in 1975 with the independence of Angola and Mozambique. At this point Mutare's position near the Mozambique border became strategic for both sides. Guerrilla forces slipped across the border for training and supplies, and Rhodesian government troops were intent in cutting them off as much as possible from reentering the country. The mountains along the border were heavily mined, and those who lived on the border were scrutinized by Rhodesian forces for possible assistance to the guerrillas. On the other hand, the guerrillas, fragmented and often undisciplined, desperately needed the support of as many villagers as possible in order to continue their struggle. It was in this crucible that Patrick found himself in 1976, partly because of the location of his homeland and partly because he was a prominent citizen of the Mutare area.

On one occasion guerrillas approached Patrick's home and demanded evidence of his allegiance to the cause of liberation. Stories of what could happen under these circumstances were well known.[21] For example, it was common knowledge that if someone had "sold out" to the government troops, the person who brought the charges against the "traitor" to the guerrillas could be required to beat and kill the accused. It was in this manner that a brother was asked to kill his father or another brother. The alleged "traitors" were rarely given the opportunity to defend themselves. When the guerrillas approached Patrick, he did not know if he was being accused or if someone in the community had falsely claimed he was cooperating with the Rhodesian government. Fortunately several of the younger men in the guerrilla group had attended music workshops conducted by Patrick in the past and vouched for him, and he was spared. Songs they had learned in his workshops were often sung in the guerrilla camps and on national broadcasts.

A much more difficult time of reckoning came when he was approached at home by Rhodesian government soldiers. Within full view of his family, Patrick was forcibly removed by the commanding officer from his home with the muzzle of a gun under his chin, made to sit on the ground in

---

20. Chilcote, 244, notes an example of how Kauffman took a traditional hunting song, "Baya wa baya," and encouraged participants in a church music workshop to fit a biblical text to it. The result was "Ngatikudze Musiki" (Let Us Praise the Creator), number 44 in *Ngoma*.

21. Alexander Kanengoni's collection of stories entitled *Effortless Tears* devotes several stories to the terrors perpetrated by some guerrillas in search of "sellouts" to the Rhodesian government. Several stories capture incidents in profound detail, including "The Men in the Middle," 51-56, "Things We'd Rather Not Talk About," 57-64, and "Circles," 89-94.

pouring rain for several hours without cover, and placed in the back of a truck to be driven to a detention center.[22] Only when some of the soldiers acknowledged knowing his father, a prominent Methodist layman, was he released. Being a religious leader, however, was no guarantee of safety from government troops. Churches suspected of harboring guerrillas could be bombed. In one such case the church was bombed and burned to the ground. The only surviving artifact was the pulpit Bible — a sign of hope to the people. Through these circumstances Matsikenyiri walked a tightrope between the guerrillas and the government, sensing at all times the providence of God in his life.

When the school where Patrick worked was closed by the government during the struggles for independence in 1977, he was hired by the Church of Sweden Mission to compose a passion play. In 1978 he completed *From Chaos to Life: Creation to Resurrection*, a work based on biblical foundations and, in light of the turmoil of the independence movement, with existential implications.

It is to Matsikenyiri's work as a headmaster and his personal struggles during the liberation struggle that we now turn. Matsikenyiri served as headmaster of Rowa Primary School between 1961 and 1977. A headmaster has the potential to be a force for developing relationships within the community as well as educating the children, a role that Patrick relished. He was often in the homes of the students. He organized the community to upgrade facilities, adding new buildings even when funds were limited. In addition, he focused on improving the faculty's teaching skills, moving away from corporal punishment of children to more positive behavioral motivators. Known for being able to bring order out of troubled and chaotic situations, Patrick worked for more positive approaches to discipline and motivation.

He met Rev. Canaan Banana in 1977. Banana was one of the major leaders of the liberation movement who later became Zimbabwe's first state president under majority rule in 1980. Patrick helped Banana fit a Ndebele text to a traditional wedding song that placed the liberation struggle within a spiritual

---

22. Detention was a common mode of dealing with suspected traitors during the many liberation struggles throughout Africa. A person in detention was held without formal charges, for an unspecified length of time, and with no personal rights, including the right of contact with one's family. Some detainees were beaten and died while incarcerated. Some classic African literature has been written out of the experience of detention by leading authors. Perhaps the best-known works are Wole Soyinka, *The Man Died: The Prison Notes of Wole Soyinka* (New York: Noonday Press, 1972), who was detained in Nigeria, and Ngugi wa Thiong'o, *Detained: A Writer's Prison Diary* (London: Heinemann, 1981), who was detained in Kenya and continues to live in exile.

context. Soon after composing this song, Banana went into exile in Botswana until the liberation. This song became a rallying cry for the guerrillas in Zimbabwe and beyond and remains popular today.[23]

In 1977 the government closed the Rowa Primary School where Patrick had been serving as headmaster. Out of work, he went to his homeland of Biriiri to be a headmaster. When this school also was closed, Patrick decided not to assume the role of headmaster again because his son and brother were in the guerrilla movement. Being a headmaster in a border area where guerrillas trained could place him in a situation where he would have to confront his own family. For a time he served as a clerk in Gweru. Given the treacherous nature of the war years, leaving one's family alone, even at home, was

---

23. In November 1998 Otto Nkululeko Ntshanyana, a Methodist minister in South Africa, told me how Banana's songs were translated into Xhosa and adapted to their struggle against minority white rule. Zimbabwe's struggle for independence inspired black South Africans in their opposition against apartheid. One used by the Xhosa Methodist ministers in their congregations is as follows. The first two stanzas appear in *Sibanye* (Queenstown District of the Methodist Church of South Africa, n.d.), 44. The third stanza was not in *Sibanye*, but is often added spontaneously in worship and other occasions. The translations have been provided by Xhosa Methodist minister Sipho Somngesi.

Thula sizwe ungabokala	Be still O nation, don't cry
U Jehova wakho	Your God
Uzosingobela	Will fight for you
Unkululeko, si so ithola	Freedom, we will get it
U Jehova wakho	Your God
Uzosingobela	Will fight for you
Thula sizwe ungabokhala	Be still O nation, don't cry
uMandela wethu	Mandela, our hero
uzosinqobela	is going to fight for us.

A second example of a song by Banana is a Xhosa/Zulu version of the wedding song that Banana composed with the assistance of Matsikenyiri. This song appears in a collection of Zulu songs gathered in workshops conducted by then Catholic priest David Dargie in the late 1970s and recorded in *New Church Music in Zulu* (Lady Frere, South Africa: Lumko Music Department, 1980), 31. The Bantu languages of Zulu and Ndebele are vitually the same in this instance.

Leader:	*Igazi lemVana* (Xhosa)	The blood of the Lamb
	Ebunzimeni (Xhosa)	We are experiencing hardship
People:	*He, he, a helele*	(an exclamation of hope and promised victory)
	linamandl' igazi lemVana.	The blood of the Lamb is powerful
Leader:	*Umzimba weNkosi* (Xhosa)	The body of the Lord
	Ekuthokozeni (Zulu)	We are experiencing hardship
People:	*He, he, a helele*	(an exclamation of hope and promised victory)
	unamandl' umzimba weNkosi.	The body of the Lord is powerful

most difficult. In 1978 he was hired by the Church of Sweden Mission and worked with his friend Olof Axelsson. A bishop in the United Methodist Church then recognized Patrick's long and devoted unremunerated service to the church as music director and lay leader, and secured a position for him at Hilltop School in 1979. After the liberation when the school at the Mutambare Mission reopened, he was appointed headmaster. The facilities and records were in shambles. He worked hard to improve buildings, establish a program in agriculture, set standards for writing and administration, and involve teachers in decision making or governance at the school. In an effort to expand the worldview of the students, he constructed a world map on the grounds and surrounded the continents with water and fish. Students could literally walk on the continents. Six inspectors selected the Mutambare Mission as the best school out of 760 schools in the region.

From Local Church Musician to Global *Animateur*

Matsikenyiri continued to serve until 1990 as conference director of music for the United Methodist Church in Zimbabwe, a position without remuneration. In spite of the turmoil of the independence struggle in the 1970s and the establishment of a new majority-rule government in the 1980s, he led many ecumenical workshops that developed the skills of local church musicians. As he was leaving this position, Patrick established a conference choir competition among United Methodist church choirs that continues to this day.

In 1979, just before the end of the war, Matsikenyiri's influence became global when he was invited to the World Council of Churches (WCC) in Geneva to plan music for a Mission and Evangelism Conference. The WCC had contributed to the freedom struggle in Zimbabwe and neighboring South Africa amid considerable criticism and opposition. It was an important symbol of hope for Zimbabwe for the WCC to invite Patrick to lead music in such a prominent arena. In 1980 he participated in the Mission and Evangelism Conference held in Melbourne. Continuing on the WCC Worship Committee in 1982, he served as an *animateur* (musical animator or leader) for the Sixth Assembly of the WCC in Vancouver. During the 1990s Patrick became a member of the Global Praise Working Group of the General Board of Global Ministries of the United Methodist Church in the United States. A series of conferences has been held throughout the United States and in London. In 1998 Patrick prepared the conference choir for the WCC Eighth Assembly held in Harare and served again as *animateur*.

In 1990 Patrick left his position at Mutambara Mission for formal music study at Shenandoah Conservatory of Music in the United States. Completing both the BME and MME degrees by 1993, he was contacted by Africa University, a new United Methodist institution begun in 1992.[24] Although Matsikenyiri had hoped to continue his education on the doctoral level at Boston University in educational administration, he returned home to prepare a choir for the inaugural of the vice-chancellor and opening of Africa University in 1993. He became a lecturer in music in the Faculty of Humanities of the university and developed a four-year music major beginning in 1996, the only program of its kind in Zimbabwe. His choir, starting out with ten students in 1993, grew to one hundred voices from over ten African countries by 1998. During the summers of 1998 and 1999 he toured the United States with twenty members of the choir. Plans for the choir include traveling annually to the United States to present concerts to all jurisdictions of the United Methodist Church. As providence would have it, Africa University is located across the road from the Old Mutare Mission where Patrick received his initial education, within easy driving distance of his tribal homeland. Once again Patrick and Aves Matsikenyiri are back home in southeastern Zimbabwe.

Music in African Culture and Worship

Although the focus of the material thus far has been historical, significant musical issues have also emerged. These tell us much about the way music functions in African culture and worship.

1. Musicianship is recognized by African society regardless of formal training in the Western sense; musical leadership is conferred by the community based upon their trust of the leader. Africans as a people generally consider themselves to be musical regardless of formal training. Furthermore, Africans understand themselves to be natural composers and possess the ability to perform complex cross-rhythms. As a Zimbabwean pastor noted, "only a few of us were born with weak

24. Complete details on Matsikenyiri's academic background and the start of Africa University are available in a collection prepared by Patrick for the Board of Global Ministries of the United Methodist Church, *Africa Praise Songbook: Songs from Africa,* ed. S T Kimbrough, Jr., and Carlton R. Young (New York: GBGMusik, 1998), inside back cover.

25. Blantyre Covenant, art. 17, "The Worshipping Church in Africa," *Black Sacred Music: A Journal of Theomusicology,* ed. John Michael Spencer, 7, no. 2 (fall 1993): 38.

beats."[25] From a Western perspective, musical literacy often seems to indicate the musicality of an individual. As anyone who has attempted to write down African music can tell you, the complexity of the music often defies traditional Western notational practice. Perhaps because of the stress on musical literacy in the West, Western concepts of music and musical pedagogy often run opposite to African ways of learning and making music. South African ethnomusicologist David Dargie notes that Western music education usually proceeds in a progression of (1) theory, (2) technique, and (3) music making, while African music education is the opposite: (1) music making, (2) technique, and (3) discourse on music (theory).[26] While Matsikenyiri received formal instruction in music at the Old Mutare Mission, his development as a musician and his use of music within the Methodist church was a vocation that was recognized by others because of his ability, not because of specific Western musical training. This "official" training came during his fifth decade of life.

2. Music making in African society focuses on singing *with* the people, i.e., helping the people find their song, rather than singing solos or performing *for* the people. John Miller Chernoff notes that "perhaps the most fundamental aesthetic in Africa [is that] without participation, there is no meaning. When you ask an African friend whether or not he 'understands' a certain type of music, he will say yes if he knows the dance that goes with it. The music of Africa invites us to participate in the making of a community."[27] Matsikenyiri's work in workshops throughout Zimbabwe and the world emphasizes the song of people who are fully engaged.

3. Music making shapes community in African culture. This aspect of music has not gone unnoticed by ethnomusicologists. The ability to forge an "enhanced group identity . . . as [people] together sense similar types of affect" is integral to music's nature to encourage unity.[28] John Blacking is more specific about the potential of music to unify disparate groups within a society: "Music can bridge the gulf between the true state of human being and the predicament of particular human beings in a given society, and especially the alienation that springs from the

26. David Dargie, "African Methods of Music Education — Some Reflections," *African Music* 7, no. 3 (1996): 30-37.

27. John Miller Chernoff, *African Rhythm and African Sensibility: Aesthetics and Social Action in African Musical Idioms* (Chicago: University of Chicago Press, 1979), 23.

28. John E. Kaemmer, *Music in Human Life: Anthropological Perspectives on Music* (Austin: University of Texas Press, 1993), 148.

class struggle and human exploitation."[29] The songs by Rev. Canaan Banana, including ones composed with the assistance of Matsikenyiri, as well as songs taught in Patrick's workshops became sources of cohesion and unity among the disparate guerrillas fighting for majority rule in Zimbabwe.

4. Texts in African cultures often may appear simple and direct, but they carry layers of meaning and significance. For example, the text of the collaborative song composed by Banana and Matsikenyiri draws from the symbols of the communion rite, the blood and body of Christ:

Leader: The blood of the Lamb
We are experiencing hardship

People: He, he, a helele (an exclamation of hope and promised victory)
The blood of the Lamb is powerful

Leader: The body of the Lord
We are experiencing hardship

People: He, he, a helele (an exclamation of hope and promised victory)
The body of the Lord is powerful

Placed within the context of the liberation struggle, this song became a source of strength for weary bodies. Even as human blood was spilled and human bodies were broken in civil war, the blood of the Lamb was already shed and the body of the Lord was already broken for humanity. Furthermore, the blood and body of Christ have the power to overcome the evil of oppression. The symbols of the Eucharist not only function within the liturgy, but sanctify the political struggle for independence.

5. There is a link between the struggle for political independence and the search for indigenous musical expression within the liturgy. While it may be difficult to prove a direct causal connection, the spirit of independence that swept south toward Zimbabwe in the 1960s and 1970s combined with the liturgical reforms of Vatican II in the early 1960s to produce a climate ripe for moving away from a dominance of Western musical idioms in African worship and toward indigenous musical styles. The rise of the field of ethnomusicology in the 1960s and 1970s paved the way for Western musicians like Olof Axelsson from the Lutheran Church of Sweden Mission, Joseph Lenherr from the Catholic

29. *Music, Culture, and Experience: Selected Papers of John Blacking,* ed. Reginald Byron (Chicago: University of Chicago Press, 1995), 171.

Church, and Robert Kauffman from the Methodist church to encourage Africans to compose their own music and develop indigenous expressions suitable for African liturgies.[30]

6. Any event that calls for celebration demands music, and its commemoration is enriched through music. As J. H. Kwabena Nketia, one of the leading African musicologists, notes, "A village that has no organized music or neglects community singing, drumming, or dancing is said to be dead."[31] When Africa University opened, it was natural to ask Matsikenyiri, as the former conference director of music, to come home and guide the musical part of the celebration for the installation of the vice-chancellor. Just as the investiture of a chief of a tribe is a high moment that demands elaborate musical preparation, so did the musical preparations for the leadership of the university. Furthermore, Matsikenyiri composed a song, "The Dream," that captured the spirit of the original vision of the founder of Old Mutare Mission, Bishop Hartzell, in the 1990s. In "The Dream" he thanks the General Conference of the United Methodist Church, expresses appreciation to President Mugabe of Zimbabwe, and commemorates the growth of the original dream over one hundred years later.[32] It would not have been a proper African celebration without music (singing, drumming, and dancing).

---

30. Joseph Kerman documents this development to some degree in *Contemplating Music: Challenges to Musicology* (Cambridge: Harvard University Press, 1985). See esp. chap. 5, "Ethnomusicology and 'Cultural Musicology,'" 155-81. The publication of several major general ethnomusicological works during the 1960s and early 1970s brought the field to maturity. Many of these were based on decades of previous research in specific cultural contexts. For example, see this selective but representative list of English-language publications in order of date of publication: Charles Seeger, "Semantic, Logical, and Political Considerations Bearing upon Research into Ethnomusicology," *Ethnomusicology* 5 (1961): 77-80; Curt Sachs, *The Wellsprings of Music* (New York: Da Capo Press, 1962); Alan P. Merriam, *The Anthropology of Music* (Evanston, Ill.: Northwestern University Press, 1964); Bruno Nettl, *Theory and Method in Ethnomusicology* (London: Collier-Macmillan, 1964); Alan Lomax, *Folksong Style and Culture,* publication no. 88 (Washington, D.C.: American Association for the Advancement of Science, 1968); Mantle Hood, *The Ethnomusicologist* (New York: McGraw-Hill, 1971); John Blacking, *How Musical Is Man?* (Seattle: University of Washington Press, 1973); J. H. Kwabena Nketia, *The Music of Africa* (New York: Norton, 1974).

31. J. H. Kwabena Nketia, "Music in African Cultures: A Review of the Meaning and Significance of Traditional African Music" (Institute of African Studies, University of Ghana, 1966, mimeographed), 20, quoted in Chernoff, 36.

32. For complete text and music, see "The Dream," composed by Patrick Matsikenyiri, in *Africa Praise Songbook,* 20.

Ngoma: An African Conceptual Framework for Music

Having made these observations, I wish to establish an understanding of *ngoma,* a word with layers of meaning. *Ngoma* is the title of the United Methodist hymnal in Zimbabwe. In this limited context *ngoma* refers to a "hymn," a later, somewhat abstract meaning probably coined as a result of contact with missionaries.[33] The dictionary meaning of *ngoma,* however, is "drum" — a method of making music, the experience of music itself.[34] David Dargie cautions that African terminology related to music does not refer to theoretical or aesthetic abstractions, but to concrete experience, i.e., "existentially perceived concepts."[35] *Ngoma* should be thought of as an active process of experiencing drumming, playing drums, or dancing to drums, as well as the name of the artifact.

John M. Janzen surfaces an additional dimension of *ngoma* in his book by that title. His research indicates that *ngoma* refers to a ritual healing throughout many parts of central and southern Africa.[36] For example, in Tanzania the "term *ngoma* is widely recognized as connoting performance, drumming, dancing, celebration, and ritual therapy. This understanding of ngoma means that performances are independent of healing functions, leading to a distinction between ngoma of entertainment and of healing."[37] Discussing traditional religious practices in South Africa among the Zulu and Xhosa tribes, Janzen demonstrates that *ngoma* rituals are often a synthesis of traditional and Christian religious perspectives, as well as multilingual mani-

---

33. D. Dale, *A Basic English-Shona Dictionary* (Harare: Mambo Press, 1975), 77, does not include *ngoma* as a term for "hymn." Matsikenyiri is the source for this meaning of the word. *Ngoma* is generally the term for "drum." Specific words for song include *rwiyo* (pl. *nziyo*) — a song, chant, or psalm; *rumbo* (pl. *dzimbo*) — song or hymn. According to Andrew Tracey, the differences between the last two are dialectical. Tracey does not recognize the use of *ngoma* as a generic term for "song." Therefore I am led to believe that this is a provincial use of the term — a specialized jargon — among Shona United Methodists in Zimbabwe.

34. D. Dale, *Duramazwi: A Shona-English Dictionary* (Harare: Mambo Press, [1981] 1983), 153.

35. David Dargie, *Xhosa Music: Its Techniques and Instruments with a Collection of Songs* (Cape Town: David Philip, 1988), 64.

36. Once again Andrew Tracey has cautioned me about ascribing broader meanings to the term *ngoma* specifically to the Shona, though broader meanings may be common in other parts of eastern Africa. Correspondence with the author, September 16, 1999. Therefore I am moving beyond a Shona use of the term and using it as a metaphor for a larger concept of healing and community.

37. John M. Janzen, *Ngoma: Discourses of Healing in Central and Southern Africa* (Berkeley: University of California Press, 1992), 21.

festations that, in his example, include English, Afrikaans, Xhosa, and Zulu languages.[38] He relates the practice of singing to suffering in a two-step process: "[W]ithin the complex symbol 'ngoma' there are at least two levels of narrative or performative understanding. The first is the importance of song-dance in defining and coming to terms with the suffering; the second is the importance of moving the sufferer toward a formulation of his or her own personal articulation of that condition."[39] It is also helpful to understand the African perception of health. Amandina Lihamba notes: "Health and disease are social phenomena with implications beyond the individual, the physical, and the present. Performances are often concerned with the maintenance of community and individual health, the prevention of ill health, and the restoration of health and with instilling survival knowledge."[40] Thus one finds that many African writers develop themes of cleansing society, restoration of the natural order (i.e., the cosmic equilibrium), and the entire society or community as sufferer.[41]

The role of singing in healing is prominent in traditional practices, e.g., among the Zulu people in South Africa. Those responsible for healing individuals and restoring wholeness to the community are the *izinyanga* (doctors) and *izangoma* (diviners). Distinctions between the two practitioners have become blurred in recent days as many *izinyanga* are also

38. Janzen describes and interprets a specific ritual on 110-18.

39. Janzen, 118.

40. Amandina Lihamba, "Health and the African Theatre," *Review of African Political Economy* 36 (September 1986): 35.

41. Janzen, 109, summarizes these themes from Wole Soyinka's work. One can point to many works in African literature that deal with one or more of these aspects of healing. See, e.g., Nigerian author Chinua Achebe, *Things Fall Apart* (New York: Anchor Books, [1959] 1994), as he explores how an African village copes with those among them who create a disequilibrium in everyday life and, finally, how traditional village society disintegrates in the clash between colonial oppression and traditional African values. A more recent novel by Achebe, *Anthills of the Savannah* (London: Heinemann, 1987), can be seen in the light of how Nigerian society struggles to restore a sense of cosmic equilibrium in the face of the suffering during the Biafran civil war. The winner of the 1985 Nobel Prize in literature, Nigerian Wole Soyinka, establishes a child's perspective of the cosmic equilibrium of African society in his autobiographical work *Aké: The Years of Childhood* (New York: Vintage Books, [1981] 1983). Kenyan author Ngugi wa Thiong'o seems to stress the issues of cleansing African society, especially of colonial influences, in *Petals of Blood* (London: Heinemann, 1977) and *Decolonizing the Mind: The Politics of Language in African Literature* (Nairobi: Heinemann Kenya, [1981] 1986). The theme of the suffering society comes through in the work of Zimbabwean Chenjerai Hove, *Bones* (Harare: Baobab Books, 1988). As these themes are a part of many African novels and plays, it would not be accurate to state that the above examples relate only or even primarily to the motif I ascribe to them. My analysis is admittedly subjective at this point.

izangoma.[42] The role of the *isangoma* (the singular form of *izangoma*) is distinct in that this person is a mediator between the living and the "living dead" (ancestors) — a manifestly religious role.[43] Music (singing, dancing, and drumming) is an integral part of the transformation that takes place in the process of healing. The role of the musician/healer is so important in traditional society that she or he must be available to the village at all hours to perform healing rituals. According to Yaya Diallo, "Technical versatility on the drum, while appreciated, is not considered as crucial as the musician's good will and willingness to serve."[44]

While this discussion of healing applies generally to most African cultures, the Shona of Zimbabwe have their own perspective on traditional healing. A *nganga* is responsible for uniting society, establishing solidarity among the people, and recommending treatment for illnesses.[45] Even in traditional society, the value of Western medicine is recognized among the people so that restoration of physical wholeness may be a combination of traditional herbal remedies and Western therapeutic measures.

Instruments have therapeutic value as well. Drums are an important part of traditional music making throughout most of Africa and are used in healing, invocation, and celebrations. Diallo, from Mali, West Africa, has called the drum "the psychiatrist of my culture."[46] Among other favorite Shona instruments is the *hosho*, a gourd rattle or a tin can with seeds or rice in it, widely used in traditional music and seemingly ubiquitous in Christian churches where it accompanies virtually all music except standard Western hymns that use keyboard accompaniment. The marimba is also popular among many groups. In recent days it is used more often by the Christian church than in traditional musical performance.[47]

Perhaps the most notable of all Shona traditional instruments is the

42. S. A. Thorpe, *African Traditional Religions* (Pretoria: University of South Africa, 1991), 43.

43. See John S. Mbiti, *Introduction to African Religion* (London: Heinemann Educational Books, 1975), 119-20, for a discussion of the "living dead."

44. Yaya Diallo and Mitchell Hall, *The Healing Drum: African Wisdom Teachings* (Rochester, Vt.: Destiny Books, 1989), 47.

45. Thorpe, 59.

46. Diallo and Hall, 199.

47. Paul F. Berliner, *The Soul of Mbira* (Chicago: University of Chicago Press, [1981] 1993), 23. The Shona marimbas proved so popular in churches that they have been adapted to other groups by ethnomusicologist David Dargie, who developed marimba Masses among the Xhosas of South Africa. An example of a marimba Mass can be found on the cassette *Africa Sunday II*, no. 126 (Delmenville, South Africa: Lumko Missiological Institute, 1990), complete with listener's guide.

mbira. Its most prominent religious association is with calling forth the ancestors. While the *hosho* and marimba can be found in Christian worship, the *mbira* is rarely used in this context. Reasons for this are both cultural and practical. In addition to the *mbira*'s associations with bringing out the ancestors in traditional rituals, it produces a gentle sonority with intricate cross-rhythms that would not effectively support congregational singing. While the *mbira* can be played in an ensemble, it often is used alone with the *mbira* player singing at the same time. A complex and versatile instrument, it can imitate the cross-rhythms of a drum ensemble, yet is said metaphorically to sound like a flute when played well.[48]

I suggest that even the form or structure of most African music lends itself to healing in at least three ways. First, African musical form is cyclic; it is based on a fundamental repetitive structure.[49] The cyclic patterns of African music provide a foundation over which the lead singer improvises, preparing and encouraging the community for their role. Each repetition of a cycle allows the participating singer-dancer to settle into the beat and structure. Since the kinesthetic component of the musical experience is primary, there is a natural cathartic response for the individual and a unifying dimension that solidifies the community as they both feel the beat and see others participating. The aural/oral element is part of a sensory fabric that makes up the totality of African music making. Repetition of the fundamental cyclic pattern actually frees the mind to pursue additional layers of experience as the participant settles into the recurring segment. Musical anthropologist John Blacking suggests that as the repetition "releas[es] the brain from the task of immediate attention to environmental stimuli, [the music] stimulates creative thinking by allowing the 'memory surface' of the brain to deal with information for its own sake."[50] Furthermore, "music itself may generate experiences and thoughts that transcend the extra-musical features of the situation."[51] To the Western observer it may appear that not much is happening and that the music goes on forever with no planned end in sight. To the African singer-dancer, this is exactly the point. The cycles create a predictable monotony — not to be confused with boredom — allowing the mind to transcend current struggles and seek divine answers in the midst of the commu-

48. Berliner, 23-24.

49. Andrew Tracey provides a helpful introduction to cyclic structures in African music in "Transcribing African Music in Pulse Notation," a monograph published by the International Library of African Music, Rhodes University, Grahamstown, South Africa, 1997, 3-11.

50. *Music, Culture, and Experience: Selected Papers of John Blacking*, 152.

51. *Music, Culture, and Experience: Selected Papers of John Blacking*, 153.

nity gathered for worship. Boredom leads to distraction and enervation, while monotony centers, relaxes, and ultimately refreshes.[52]

The second aspect of African musical form is call-response. Those entrusted to provide the "call" in this structure guide the experience by engaging the people as they sing the fundamental cycles of the song. The lead singer serves several functions. He or she begins the selection, setting the tempo and establishing the mood. As the responders join in, there is an affirmation of the lead singer's selection of song, both its appropriateness to the occasion and her or his authority to lead. This affirmation extends to the roles assumed — the relationship between leader and followers singing various parts of the song. After a cycle or two, the drums and *hoshos* enter, further solidifying the experience. Then the people establish a rhythmic participation that forges solidarity among the assembled.

Once the cycles are firmly established, the lead singer provides cues for word changes by anticipating the beginning of a cycle by a few pulses. She or he may also exhort the singer-dancers by soaring above their part and deviating from the established rhythm either by anticipating or delaying the pulse. The lead singer may also provide existential commentary, making the theme of the song relevant to the life of the community at that particular moment. In this way the lead singer is in partnership with the community as both fulfill their respective roles in the call-response form. At the same time, the lead

---

52. The distinction between boredom and monotony can be found in Ronald Grimes, *Beginnings in Ritual Studies* (Lanham, Md.: University Press of America, 1982), who notes that "Liturgy as a form of work does not surprise, though it may keep us open to serendipitous moment by its very monotony. . . . Liturgy is a full emptiness, a monotony without boredom, a reverent waiting without expectation" (44). Tom F. Driver further develops this idea in *The Magic of Ritual* (New York: HarperCollins, 1991), where he speaks of "ritual boredom" in which rituals "have lost touch with the actualities of people's lives and are thus simply arcane; or else the people have lost the ability to apprehend their very need of ritual, do not see what rituals are good for, and thus do not find them even potentially valuable" (7). While popular usage indicates that "boredom" is a synonym for "monotonous," in this context a monotonous activity, though repetitive, establishes the safe context in which an activity can take place or be performed and, by virtue of its repetitive, monotonous character, free the individual to move freely, both mentally and physically, within the rule of this safe environment, even to improvise. Monotony has a character of what Driver calls "ritual performance." He indicates that all ritual performances "require limits. . . . This delineation of what to do and not to do is rooted in ritualization's being, . . . a process of channeling and marking, of making pathways for behavior. In order to achieve definite form, ritualization encourages certain acts, *reinforcing them with repetition and slight variation,* while ruling others out. In short, ritual performance requires (and makes) rules of the game, *whether these be known from previous usage or come to be elaborated on the spot*" (100, italics mine). Thus, while boredom causes lack of interest and participation, i.e., ritual boredom, monotony facilitates freedom and safe space, i.e., ritual performance.

singer exhorts the people, drawing them into community. As an exegetical commentator, the lead singer develops the fundamental theme of the congregation's cycle. In addition, the lead singer provides a hermeneutical dimension by applying the text of the song to the joys and struggles that are existential to the assembly. If the lead singer carries out her or his role well, she or he is "doing *ngoma*" or playing a therapeutic role within the worship experience.[53] Furthermore, anyone in the congregation may become the lead singer either through designation by another leader or by individual assertion, giving evidence to the flexibility of the form, the mutuality of the experience, and the general assumption of those gathered that there are few "weak beats" in an African congregation.

Finally, leadership of call-response form does not stop with the lead singer but extends to any who would conduct prayer or preach. If the lead singer, the presider, or the preacher has made a worthy diagnosis of the community's concerns and hopes, the assembly will immediately respond in kind and the therapeutic process is under way.

Another way the structure and presentation of African music "performs *ngoma*" is through its highly oral nature, as opposed to dependence on literary materials. This is not to imply that Africans attending church do not read. Literacy remains an important issue, and most people in the African congregations I have attended do read. Neither is this to imply that materials requiring literacy are not used. While a written order of worship is rare, all who have the necessary financial means bring both Bibles and personal hymnbooks with them to church. Even though this is done by a much higher percentage of Africans than normative-culture North Americans, the narrative qualities of Scripture and preaching, and the use of many cyclic songs alongside Western hymns with sequential stanzas, render these written tools as aids to memory rather than primary literary resources.[54] Traditional African culture recognizes the power of the spoken word over the written word. Robert Kauffman notes that "in the Shona language . . . the verb *kunzwa* (to hear) also means to understand, to perceive, and to see."[55] In many places there remains a suspicion of the written word as compared to the spoken word.

53. Janzen, 110-29, discusses the nature of "doing *ngoma*" within a traditional healing ritual.

54. Mercy Amba Oduyoye offers a brief, but helpful, chapter on the interaction between oral tradition and written biblical narrative in "Expressions, Sources, and Variants of African Theology," in *Hearing and Knowing: Theological Expressions of Christianity in Africa* (Maryknoll: N.Y.: Orbis, 1986), 45-55.

55. Robert Kauffman, "Music Goes beyond Words," *WACC* (World Association for Christian Communication) *Journal* 26, no. 2 (1979): 7.

In spite of literacy and reading materials, there is an essential "hearing dominance" which is part of cultures with a high degree of oral tradition versus a "sight dominance" for literary cultures.[56] Furthermore, in the African oral tradition, dancing with music combines kinesthetic involvement with hearing dominance. This facilitates a therapeutic environment in several ways. Rather than looking down constantly at hymnals or printed orders of worship "to see where I am," the African worshiper is looking up at the community and the leaders, moving to the rhythm of the musical pulse, and listening to the music in order to fit in her or his part and hear how the lead singer is contextualizing the song. A combination of looking, moving, and listening orients the African worshiper in worship, rather than a dependency on the written page. Walter Ong identifies one of the characteristics of oral cultures as their ability to relate existential struggle to the gathered assembly. "Writing fosters abstractions that disengage knowledge from the arena where human beings struggle with one another. It separates the knower from the known. By keeping knowledge embedded in the human lifeworld, orality situates knowledge within a context of struggle."[57]

In summary, the cyclic structure of African music, the call-response pattern of interaction, and the essentially oral character of the experience produce an environment where *ngoma* (singing hymns, playing drums, and experiencing healing) can take place. Africans go to church primarily to be a part of a healing community. Mercy Oduyoye observes that for Africans, healing is both spiritual and physical, private and political; for the "human being is still an integrated person in Africa."[58] Singing is an integral part of establishing the spirit of *ngoma* in the liturgy. In worship and through music the disparate congregation becomes one in Christ. As John Miller Chernoff has noted, the "community dimension is perhaps the essential aspect of African music. . . . [Africans] do not want to distinguish the audience from the musicians at a musical event."[59] In liturgical terms *ngoma* is the responsibility of all assembled, not just the professional clergy or designated musicians.

56. Walter J. Ong, *Orality and Literacy: The Technologizing of the Word* (London: Routledge, 1982), 5.

57. Ong, 43-44.

58. Oduyoye, *Hearing and Knowing*, 101.

59. Chernoff, 33.

The Songs

Thus far we have focused on the historical, cultural, and musical ethos from which African music in a broader sense draws its power. Finally we move to an analysis of songs selected from the more than eighty compositions of Matsikenyiri in the hope of gaining at least a partial appreciation for them in their cultural and liturgical context. My intention is to provide the readers with tools helping them understand this music by being able to read culturally between the lines. The analysis I have undertaken is a thoroughly Western exercise, however. There is no substitute for listening to, dancing with, and singing African songs with Africans in worship. As helpful as I hope this analysis might be, armchair ethnomusicology is as incomplete as "virtual worship" — worship separated from a quality of knowing that can come only from being physically present with the assembly. Western culture finds it very valuable to engage in discourse about music. Most African cultures cannot separate knowledge of music from performance and find little need, if any, to verbally explain it. Furthermore, many musical behaviors stem from unconscious cultural motivations that may be very difficult to articulate verbally.[60] Therefore, as we conclude this chapter by analyzing selected songs composed by Patrick Matsikenyiri, readers must realize that they will not know this music until they hear *(kunzwa)* it through participation.[61]

Example 5.1 (p. 172) is one of Patrick's best-known songs. It is a gathering song that may be used by the choir during their processional into the sanctuary. As the choir proceeds down the aisle, the congregation joins in. It may also be used for gathering at the table for the Lord's Supper.

The basic cycle of the congregation's part is standard length for many traditional Shona songs.[62] Many singers, especially the lead singer, will anticipate the initial pulse of each phrase, diminishing the "squared-off" look the

---

60. Kaemmer, 14, distinguishes between "practical consciousness" and "discursive consciousness." Practical consciousness is "apparent when a musician can perform on his instrument but is unable to explain it to anyone else." Discursive consciousness "is that aspect of knowledge which a person is able to verbalize or explain." Both are distinct from "the unconscious aspects of life [that] seldom appear as discourse, but may be important motivations for musical behavior."

61. Dale, *Duramazwi*, notes that the verb stem -*nzwa* (to hear) also means to understand, to feel, or "to perceive by touch, sight, hearing, or tasting." Therefore, to hear and understand *(kunzwa)* music is to participate directly in the experience of music making.

62. Tracey, "Transcribing African Music," 4, describes the varying lengths of the cycles of different tribal groups.

Example 5.1. "Jesu tawa pano" (Jesus, We Are Here), Patrick Matsikenyiri[63]

song has in its notational form. When the melody descends, as with the initial descending third on the word *Jesu*, it is common for all to glide (slide) to the next pitch.[64] Oral versions of the song vary, causing the harmony to change from cycle to cycle and even to "clash" at times. John Bell noted a clash in harmony, according to Western classical harmonic practice, and called Patrick's attention to it. Patrick laughed at John's observation and said, "My dear John, if you know the history of our country, you would know that we have had so many clashes that a little difficulty in the harmony will cause us no problems."[65]

This song would be accompanied by *hoshos*, usually playing eighth-note patterns, and drums playing quarter-note and eighth-note patterns. The lead singer usually sings over or ties together the phrases, in this case after every

63. Matsikenyiri, comp. and arr., *Africa Praise Songbook*, 1. A CD and cassette of the songs in this collection are available. See *Africa Praise 1*, sung by the Africa University Choir.

64. These characteristics and others of Shona performance practice are described in the foreword of *Sing! Zimbabwe*, comp. Patrick Matsikenyiri and Maggie Hamilton (Harare: Ecumenical Arts Association, 1998), viii. This collection of thirty songs comes with a cassette and is also available from Counterpoint, Christian Aid Office, Carrs Lane Church Centre, Birmingham B4 7SX, UK.

65. John L. Bell, *Many and Great: Songs of the World Church* (Chicago: GIA Publications, [1990] 1992), 51.

four half-note pulses. This practice is not indicated in the score except in the case of the last phrase, "Mambo Jesu" (King Jesus). Matsikenyiri notes that "simple steps and arm movements accompany . . . these songs, the movement often being in a cross-rhythm, giving an additional sense of energy."[66] If several *hoshos* are played along with the physical movement, one gets a sensation of visual and aural cross-rhythms providing complexity and animation to what appears to be an uncomplicated song in written form.

Ethnomusicologist I-to Loh collected songs throughout Africa during the mid-1980s in conjunction with the WCC.[67] Loh's transcription of "Jesu tawa pano" can be found in example 5.2 (p. 174). This transcription reveals a more complex cross-rhythm of three against two (12/8 versus 4/4 meter in Western notation).[68] This points out that there is no one "right" way to perform African music, though there is a range of musical possibilities dictated by the performance practice within the tradition. These two transcriptions also indicate the fluidity of oral tradition.

The simplicity of the text, "Jesus, we are here for you," belies the complexity of all that is being said between the lines, especially to the Western observer. Oral tradition captures truth in shorter segments or proverbs. Alec Pongweni notes that "Shona oral traditions are classifiable into categories that serve a common purpose. There are proverbs, folktales and songs, for example, that exhort the folk directly or otherwise, to become assimilated into society through sharing and practising values, both moral and material, that make Shona society not only distinct, but also functional. Such values include generosity, recognition of consanguinity and all the responsibilities and privileges that it implies, the responsibilities of parenthood and so on."[69] To state the nature of proverbs in a proverbial form, "Proverbs are the daughters of experience" (Sierra Leone), and "A wise man who knows proverbs, reconciles difficulties" (Yoruba).[70] Proverbs speak

66. Matsikenyiri, *Sing! Zimbabwe*, viii.

67. The transcriptions of these songs were published as *African Songs of Worship*, ed. I-to Loh (Geneva: World Council of Churches, 1986). While "Jesu tawa pano" was not in this collection, it did appear in a later collection published in Taiwan as *Ban-bîn Siong-chàn* (literally, Ten Thousand People Praise, or Let All Nations Praise). This collection is analyzed in chap. 3.

68. I-to Loh taught this version in a Taiwanese music camp in Tainan during July 2001 as I played percussion. I recall his description and a bit of good-spirited frustration with Patrick as Loh attempted to transcribe the song over several days. Loh noted with a smile that Patrick made the process more difficult since he never sang it the same way twice.

69. Alec J. C. Pongweni, *Shona Praise Poetry as Role Negotiation: The Battles of the Clans and the Sexes* (Harare: Mambo Press, 1996), 18.

70. *African Proverbs*, comp. Charlotte and Wolf Leslau (New York: Peter Pauper Press, 1962), 5.

Example 5.2. "Jesu tawa pano," transcribed by I-to Loh (from *Ban-bîn Siong-chàn* [Let All Nations Praise] [Taiwan, 1996], 9)

Music copyright © Patrick Matsikenyiri.
Musical transcription © I-to Loh. Used by permission.

truth in general terms but leave the application to the individual who hears the proverb. The genius of proverbs lies in their general application or lack of specificity.

"Jesu tawa pano" has a proverbial quality to it. It is an expression that one hears at various places throughout a Shona Methodist worship experience, almost as an acclamation. It is an expression of community. A Western worshiper might have a tendency to say "Jesu ndiri pano" (Jesus, I am here). The plural "we" is an affirmation that the community has a role in the health and spiritual well-being of the individual worshiper. In modern Zimbabwe worshipers may arrive at church on foot because they do not have sufficient money for public transportation. They may arrive knowing that a family member or friend is in the final stages of AIDS. They may arrive having lost their job in an inflationary economic environment. They may not be able to purchase medicine for a sick child. They may be separated from their family or forced to work a great distance away from home, sending money home to the family each week. It literally is a miracle that many people "are here" in worship.

The congregation is here for Jesus, the one who understands their situation because he has suffered as they now suffer. In what ways do the Shona understand the nature of Jesus? Canaan Banana suggests that the understanding of Jesus as *n'anga,* or healer, is particularly strong among the Shona. He is a healer that can make the ultimate difference. "Jesus viewed his healings as a means of inaugurating the Kingdom of God. Curing the sick was a sign of a more fundamental restoration of health and wholeness, of forgiveness and reconciliation which characterizes God's reign."[71]

Furthermore, Christ's role as mediator between God and the people suggests Christ as their ancestor. "Ancestorship is characterized by five main elements: natural relationship, supernatural status, mediation, title to regular sacred communications with one's earthly relatives and [exemplarity]. There is a brother ancestorship that exists between a dead individual and his/her brothers or sisters in the nuclear family."[72] Christ is an ancestor to humanity as a brother through the line of Adam. As Christ is one with *Mwari* (God), he carries supernatural status and functions as an intercessor (mediator) for the African Christian. Through prayer we enter into dialogue with this most important of ancestors.[73] The lead singer may further define the nature of the re-

---

71. Canaan Banana, *Come and Share: An Introduction to Christian Theology* (Harare: Mambo Press, 1991), 63.

72. Banana, 65.

73. Mercy Amba Oduyoye framed her presentation to the Eighth Assembly of the WCC in the form of "A Letter to My Ancestors" (WCC Plenary Address, Harare, Zimbabwe, Decem-

lationship between the assembled and Jesus in subsequent cycles of the song: "Master, we are here," "Savior, we are here," etc. At the same time, the visual representation of the community is enacted in movement, and the song continues until the leader senses that the community is once again being shaped.

While it would be misleading to suggest that each worshiper brings with her or him all these meanings and more to "Jesu tawa pano," it is fair to say that both subconscious and conscious understandings are triggered by the experience of participating in this song as singer-dancer within the gathered Christian community. Those who sing "Jesu tawa pano" are also affirming that they are here with this worshiping community because they belong. As the Setswana (South Africa) proverb says: "Motho ke motho ka motho yo mongwe" — literally, "a person is a person through other people," i.e., a person becomes human through his or her interaction with other people.[74] The English equivalent might be, "No man is an island."

"Iropa"

This traditional song (see example 5.3, pp. 177-78) is based on a cyclic structure found often in traditional Shona music. In this song the dialogue between the lead singer and the congregation completes the idea. The cycle begins with the congregation singing "regwayana" (we are saved). The lead singer inserts "Iropa" (by the blood) before the congregation's statement, thereby completing the statement, "By the blood (of Christ) we are saved." Once again there is the community emphasis on "we" rather than the first-person singular of the North American gospel song, "I am saved by the blood of the Lamb." The second cycle states that the result of the first cycle is an act of "God's grace." The third cycle offers praise to God that "we have all been saved." Literally translated, the third cycle means "Ululate to the God *(Baba)* who saved us all." In African cultures women ululate (a high-pitched, warbling expression of joy) out of respect to a leader or person held in high esteem. This free expression of joy and praise takes place above the singing of the congregation.

Patrick noted that "I would not be here now if it were not for the blood of Christ." For him this song is reminiscent of his encounters with the guerrillas and the Rhodesian troops during the struggle for all-Africa rule. In addition, there is the connection with the song that Banana composed with Pat-

---

ber 11, 1998), Document AF 1, 7-12. In this "letter" she both acknowledged her debt to her ancestors as a Christian and expressed to them her fears for the future of the church in Africa.

74. Ellen K. Kuzwayo, *African Wisdom* (Cape Town, South Africa: Kwela Books, 1998), 29.

rick's assistance, "The Blood of the Lamb Is Powerful."[75] For Patrick and for many who sing this song, there is an underlying political reality that Christ was with them in their struggle for independence.

Example 5.3. "Iropa" (By the Blood), by Patrick Matsikenyiri[76]

75. Banana, 1.

76. From Patrick Matsikenyiri, *African Praise Songbook* (New York: GBGMusik, 1998), 6.

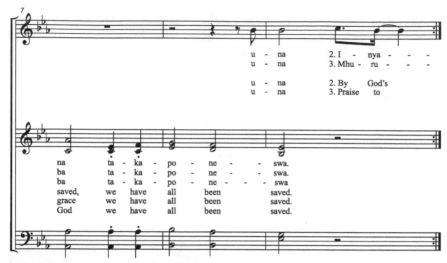

For some Western churchgoers, the mixing of politics with liturgy is an intrusion. However, Banana notes that in the African church "theologizing is time and place specific, [and] the church articulates its theological praxes from concrete contexts."[77] Liturgy is by necessity political if it is existential. Banana links salvation with the ecclesiology of the African church that includes the poor. "We have all been saved" includes the poor. Again Banana notes: "The ecclesiology of salvation has developed the image of a church of the poor, to be understood not only in the sense that it must be a poor church in order to fulfill its mission, nor mainly in the sense that the church must be preoccupied with the poor and be for the poor, but in the sense that it must understand itself and act from the poor."[78]

"Ndovimba naye"

Note in example 5.4 (pp. 179-80) how the soprano melody has a different rhythm than the lower three parts. On every fourth written measure the soprano part anticipates the three lower parts. This overlapping is characteristic of musical practice in southern Africa and is performed spontaneously by the lead singer or others who feel so inspired. The overlapping soprano part (in

77. Banana, 91.
78. Banana, 65.

Example 5.4. "Ndovimba naye" (I Trust in the Lord), by Patrick Matsikenyiri[79]

79. Matsikenyiri, *African Praise Songbook*, 9.

the written score) maintains the forward momentum of each cycle at the end of each phrase (every four pulses).

The text is a simple expression of trust inspired by the shepherd of Psalm 23 and images of the Good Shepherd in John (10:11). One should note that agrarian ways of life, including the raising of animals, are common in Africa, giving this song more relevance than it might have in urban contexts. It seems that almost everyone returns to their homeland in the country during holidays. Matsikenyiri notes that this "Is a song for everyday life. I trust Jesus.

I travel with him. I work and study with him. He is the purpose for whatever I do. The song expresses the fullness of our faith in Jesus."[80]

"Uyai mweya wakachena"

Examine the English translation provided below in poetic form.

Refrain: Come now, O Holy Spirit,
    come now with hope, O Holy Spirit.

1. The children you have given to us live in hope;
    let hope now fill our children.
  The heirs of old, heirs of your own Kingdom, lived with hope eternal.
  The heroes, heroes of the Holy Scripture did great things
      through hope eternal.
  The holy ones, holy ones on earth lived through faith,
      through faith enduring.

Refrain.

2. Holy Savior, grant to us your blessings that we find hope in living.
  O give us now your love, your love eternal join us as one forever.
  Inspire us, inspire us with a passion everywhere to spread your love.
  Be with us now and through all our trials. Grant us life
      with you forever.[81]

Refrain.

This song begins with an invocation to the Holy Spirit to bring hope. Stanza one recounts with joy the sources of hope — children, forebears (ancestors), the heroes of the Bible (both as saints and ancestors), and the holy ones on earth (including the freedom fighters for majority rule in Zimbabwe). Stanza two contains petitions (italicized in the following) to Jesus to "*grant* blessings" to sustain hope, "*give* us now your love" that joins us together as one body in Christ, "*inspire* us" to spread God's love, and "*be with us*" in all difficulties so that we might have "life with [Christ] forever."

80. Matsikenyiri, *African Praise Songbook,* vii.
81. Matsikenyiri, *African Praise Songbook,* 17. English adaptation by S T Kimbrough.

I find it interesting how this song follows the general structure of a Collect — (1) invoking God (or, in this case, the Holy Spirit); (2) recalling the witness of God (through children, heirs, heroes, and holy ones); (3) making a petition through Jesus ("grant," "give," "inspire," "be with us"); and (4) giving the reason for the petition (that we might have "life with you forever"). Even the petition to "grant us blessings" is offered within the framework of maintaining hope during difficult times.

There are aspects of this African Collect that bear analysis. The hope of the children and their future is entwined with the "living dead," as John Mbiti calls the ancestors. One is reminded of the famous chapter on faith, Hebrews 11 ("by faith Abel . . . , by faith Enoch . . . , by faith Noah . . . , by faith Abraham . . . ," etc.), as stanza one recounts those who lived in faith. The African sense of the extended family, including the children and forebears, is present. Furthermore, the "heroes" of the Bible join this great company of ancestors. The plea in stanza two to "give us your love" so that we may be "one forever" is an ancient prayer of the church. It echoes the *Epiclesis* of the Great Thanksgiving of Hippolytus (ca. 215 C.E.), who invoked the Holy Spirit to "Gather into one all those who share these sacred mysteries."[82] As Matsikenyiri discussed this section of the hymn, it was clear that this prayer for unity was not only eschatological but also was for political unity now in the face of splintered and ineffective governmental organizations and fractured societal and tribal structures. As has been stated earlier, "theologizing is place and time specific" in African life.

When Patrick thought of "heroes" and "holy ones," once again it was within the context of the struggle for majority rule in Zimbabwe. He recalled an incident where the guerrilla forces had called the people of a local village together. Gathering for worship was sometimes restricted by both sides during the struggle for African rule in Zimbabwe, especially in those areas suspected of either harboring government fugitives from guerrillas or holding allegiances to the Rhodesian government. Some members of this village continued to go to church, in spite of an order not to participate in worship. When asked "Who is going to church?" an old woman stood up and confessed, adding that she would continue to go to church no matter what the guerrilla commander ordered. The commander paused and said, "This is an honest woman. If all people were as truthful and brave as she, the country would be free." For Matsikenyiri this woman was a "holy one" in the midst of a freedom struggle with many unholy actions.

82. Great Thanksgiving from *The Apostolic Tradition* (ca. 215), ascribed to Hippolytus, the oldest text in existence that is undoubtedly a liturgy for Holy Communion.

Example 5.5. "Uyai mweya wakachna" (Come, Holy Spirit), by Patrick Matsikenyiri

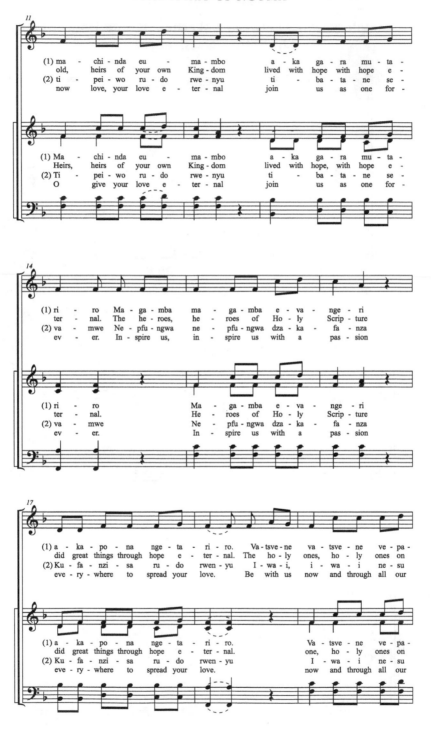

The musical structure of this hymn is a hybrid between African traditional music and Western musical syntax. Western hymnlike stanzas carry the sequential content of this Collect, but each stanza is framed with a refrain reminiscent of gospel song structure. The refrain functions theologically to "surround" all that is recalled and requested by an invocation of the Holy Spirit to be present now. The congregation's cycle is reminiscent of traditional African music. The music of the cycle remains virtually the same while the text changes when prompted by the lead singer. The refrain contains two cycles with identical text and music. The cyles of the stanzas are twice as long with virtually the same music, but with continual text changes more in keeping with Western hymn structures. Furthermore, the lead singer overlaps the ending of most phrases in a typical traditional African manner. It is in this way that the unity of African cyclic structure is accommodated to the sequential nature of a Collect prayer form.

"Chitsva-mubhebhura"

The text of an additional song sheds light on the connection between singing and the power of the Holy Spirit in the African church. Once the song is established, the people maintain the refrain "Sing a song and seek the Holy Spirit" while the leader offers examples of life circumstances that challenge the believer.

Chitsva-
Chiri mubhebhura gara ne Mweya Mutsvene
Chitsva-
Tarirai idi oh Mweya Mutsvene
Wanya tukwa-
Tamba ne rwiyo utsvake Mweya Mutsvene.
Wanya shushwa-
Tamba ne rwiyo utsvake Mweya Mutsvene.
Wanya rwawa-
Tamba ne rwiyo utsvake Mweya Mutsvene.
Wanya firwa-
Tamba ne rwiyo utsvake Mweya Mutsvene.

> The newness —
> In the Bible it says, abide in the Holy Spirit.
> The newness —
> Look, it is true, O Holy Spirit.
> Even if you are persecuted,
> Sing a song and seek the Holy Spirit.
> Even if you are abused,
> Sing a song and seek the Holy Spirit.
> Even in illness,
> Sing a song and seek the Holy Spirit.
> Even if your loved ones die,
> Sing a song and seek the Holy Spirit.

In May 1999 Patrick was preparing to take members of the Africa University Choir to the United States for a tour of United Methodist churches. Just as they were preparing to leave Harare, the choir was asked to sing for a nationally televised worship service in a Harare congregation. He chose one of his songs, "Zviro zvacho zvanyanya" (The Insurmountable Situation). In this song he cites specific problems that plague the everyday lives of Zimbabweans: the falling Zimbabwe dollar, rampant political corruption, divisions in society by color and tribe, and the increasing polarization between the haves and the have-nots. Following the worship service a reporter asked Patrick about the appropriateness of singing about political issues in church. He responded by saying, "The same people who go to church are the workers and consumers who suffer every day." In "Zviro zvacho" the cycle the choir sang states that prayer is the answer to insurmountable situations. Each cycle repeated the petition for the Holy Spirit to come and restore justice to this troubled land.

"Chitsva-mubhebhura" calls for a similar remedy to life's situations (persecution, abuse, illness, death) in a short cycle: sing a song and seek the Holy Spirit. It is reminiscent of a Pauline passage: "We are troubled on every side, yet not distressed; we are perplexed, but not in despair; persecuted, but not forsaken; cast down, but not destroyed" (2 Cor. 4:8-9 KJV). Though the conditions cited in "Chitsva" are less politically overt than in "Zviro zvacho," the political reality that contributes to the circumstances of persecution, abuse, illness, and death is no less evident to the singer.

The music suggests an overwhelming hope in the face of the maladies of human existence. The hope embodied in this song could move the liturgy from the safe space of monotony to a full-blown celebration. This celebration, in the context of suffering and in the presence of the Holy Spirit, is not a party. Ronald Grimes notes that "celebration is not to be identified with western optimism; it is not mere yes-saying. It is a mode of embracing the present which draws future and past into itself."[83] Fully cognizant of the living dead that have gone before and the power of the Holy Spirit to intervene in the present, the singer of "Chitsva" anticipates future celebrations when suffering will be relieved and hope for justice fulfilled.

Conclusion

This exposition on the life, cultural context, political history, and hymns of Patrick Matsikenyiri is a case study on how to "read between the lines" of African hymnody. Since this music comes to us primarily through oral tradition, dependence upon the artifact of the printed page does not indicate who sings these songs, how they are sung, the conditions under which they are sung, the conscious and subconscious cultural experiences the people bring to their singing, and the theological and liturgical roles these songs might play in worship. In short, the question is: How does the singing of these songs affect the piety of those who sing them, both individually and collectively?

It is difficult to draw the threads of these few songs and the stories behind them into any consistent and conclusive theological fabric. This would take a much more thorough analysis of a vast number of songs and the context in which they are used. Canaan Banana cautions us against searching for a Western-style systematic theology, as his "theology originates from the ghetto. It emanates from mundane situations of crisis, incertitude, an inchoate life and futility, all caused by individualism." Such theological experiences do not

83. Grimes, 47.

organize themselves systematically. "Is there systematic agony or systematic hunger?"[84] Mercy Oduyoye questions the "justification for demanding one uniform system of theology throughout the Christian community, but that theology reflects awareness of the horizon toward which all believers move."[85]

The search for a unified faith perspective signified by *ngoma* — hymn singing, drumming, healing — is a holistic fusion of living and liturgy that Africa offers world Christianity. African church music offers the world church a particular manifestation of what it meant for Jesus Christ to "tabernacle" among Africans (John 1:14). Singing and dancing African church music allows the world to experience the incarnation in fresh and vibrant ways.[86] It is a perspective that responds with the entire body. It is a perspective that seeks community amid division. It is a perspective that seeks hope for future generations in the wisdom of the ancestors. It is a perspective that unites physical and spiritual healing within the context of community. It is a perspective that addresses both personal struggle and political conflict within the context of liturgy. It is a perspective in which music — singing, dancing, playing drums — is both a metaphor for and means of *ngoma*.

84. Banana, xi.

85. Oduyoye, *Hearing and Knowing*, vii.

86. For an example of the integration of singing and dancing in the African understanding of music and the relationship between traditional dance and dance used in some liturgical settings, see the videotape by Thomas Kane, *The Dancing Church: Video Impressions of the Church in Africa* (Paulist, 1992).

CHAPTER 6

The Wild Goose Sings

John Bell and the Music of the Iona Community

The Three Who are over me,
The Three Who are below me,
The Three Who are above me here,
The Three Who are above me yonder,
The Three Who are in the earth,
The Three Who are in the air,
The Three Who are in the heaven,
The Three Who are in the great pouring sea.

A CELTIC PRAYER FOR PROTECTION[1]

It is the last Sunday evening of the month in Glasgow, Scotland. Over 150 people, from youth to senior adults, have gathered in the main hall of a local Church of Scotland. Students, professional people, working-class persons,

1. From *Carmina Gadelica: Hymns and Incantations* (Edinburgh: Floris Books, 1992), 217. *Carmina Gadelica* is a six-volume collection of Celtic spirituality in the form of ballads, incantations, prayers, and poetry (both pagan and Christian) gathered from oral tradition by Alexander Carmichael (1832-1912) over sixty years, primarily during the second half of the nineteenth century, in the highlands and islands of Scotland.

In addition to John Bell and Graham Maule, I am grateful for comments by Robert Batastini and John Thornburg on this paper. Their suggestions have only strengthened its content. Any deficiencies are solely my responsibility. A significantly shorter version of this chapter was published as C. Michael Hawn, "The Wild Goose Sings: Themes in the Worship and Music of the Iona Community," *Worship* 74, no. 6 (November 2000): 504-21.

and others from the greater Glasgow area have assembled for Last Night Out, an evening of singing, worship, and workshops sponsored by the Wild Goose Worship Group (WGWG). Taking its name from one of the ancient Celtic symbols for the Holy Spirit,[2] the WGWG is devoted to rejuvenating older patterns of participative worship and liturgy, exploring new liturgical forms, and disseminating new liturgical and musical materials. The music includes songs by John Bell and others used by the Iona Community, as well as congregational expressions from around the world.

This evening begins with worship on justice-related subjects. The structure of the liturgy is influenced by the Church of Scotland, but the manner of presentation feels very different from a usual Scottish Presbyterian service. The first thing one notices is that all people are expected to sing, not just an occasional hymn but throughout the service, during acts of praise, in preparation for intercessions, and in response to the Word. Those assembled (not an official "congregation") learn a variety of songs on the spot related to the theme. Members of the WGWG lead everyone in four-part singing, in many cases without written music. This is not the usual church fare with organ and Victorian hymns, but unaccompanied singing of folk songs from Scotland and Ireland and songs of the world church, along with newer tunes prepared by the WGWG.

Following the service the people divide into workshops for reflection on the theme of the day. These include a "magazine-type" format on the following topics: "Biblical Exploration" — a Bible-based exploration, often starting from people's experience; "News Headlines" — a current-affairs workshop, focusing on a recent issue of concern; "Personal Effects" — looking at the theme from a personal angle; "Perspective" — often an alternative or particularly provocative angle on the theme; "Art & Soul" — a creative hands-on workshop for those who prefer a less analytical and more artistic approach; "Re-Activate" — often taking a political or justice-oriented approach; and "Global Report" — a forum on international issues often led by someone from another country or a traveler recently returned from an international visit. All the workshops are highly interactive. After a time of coffee and tea, all return to worship where members of the WGWG share the leadership, drawing responses from the assembly. A homily is rarely offered and singing is central.

2. On August 13, 2001, I heard Brian Woodcock, warden of the Iona Community through August 2001, relate a story about the origins of the wild goose as a symbol of the Holy Spirit. Ron Ferguson, leader of the community, was asked by George MacLeod about the Celtic origins of the wild goose symbolism. Ferguson told MacLeod that he had borrowed the idea from MacLeod some years earlier. Ferguson then asked MacLeod if the wild goose was indeed a symbol of the Holy Spirit. MacLeod responded, "It is now."

Who attends this service? Some are regular church folk who are leaders in their local congregations. Some are members of the Church of Scotland or another denomination who have become disenchanted with or alienated from established ecclesiastical structures. Others may not attend church at all. They have heard that Last Night Out is a gathering where people can express their frustration and disappointment with organized religion, ask any questions of faith without fear of repudiation or indifference, and hear what Scripture has to say about the current struggles and social issues that affect them. And, they SING!

Last Night Out is not another denomination — nor indeed is the Iona Community — but they are alliances of people from around the world who support the activities of the WGWG. It is a ministry drawn from the wells of the vision of George MacLeod, founder of the modern Iona Community in 1938, and immersed in the ethos of Saint Columba, who landed on the island of Iona in western Scotland in 563 C.E. Before discussing the work of John Bell and the Wild Goose Worship and Resource Groups, it may be helpful to review the historical, cultural, and spiritual antecedents of the community.

The Iona of Saint Columba (521-97 C.E.)

> *Thursday of Columba benign,*
> *Day to send sheep on prosperity,*
> *Day to send cow on calf,*
> *Day to put the web in the warp.*
> *Day to put coracle on the brine,*
> *Day to place the staff to the flag,*
> *Day to bear, day to die,*
> *Day to hunt the heights.*
> *Day to put horses in harness,*
> *Day to send herds to pasture,*
> *Day to make prayer efficacious,*
> *Day of my beloved, the Thursday,*
> *Day of my beloved, the Thursday.*[3]

Saint Columba, a monk from a wealthy house in Ireland, came to the island of Iona on the western coast of Scotland in 563 in order to establish a monas-

---

3. From *Carmina Gadelica*, as found in *The Celtic Vision*, ed. Esther de Waal (London: Darton, Longman and Todd, 1988), 201. Esther de Waal notes that "St Columba was always remembered on a Thursday, and the day looked on as a lucky day for any enterprise" (190).

tery. Much of the information on the life of Columba has been subject to embellishment by early accounts that are more hagiographic than historical in nature. Current New Age distortions of Celtic spirituality threaten to pervert the heritage of Columba today.[4] In the interest of separating fact from fiction, the Iona Community recently commissioned Ian Bradley, a lecturer in church history at Aberdeen University and a minister in the Church of Scotland, to write a biography of Columba upon the fourteen hundredth anniversary of his death. The result of this commission, *Columba: Pilgrim and Penitent*,[5] is an attempt to discern the essence of Columba's life and message in light of the legends that surround the saint, such as taming the Loch Ness monster, performing an exorcism on a pail full of milk, floating stones in water, and healing. Bradley's book provides historical substance to Columba's ministry in the face of current popular Celtic distortions.[6] Because of the prominence of Celtic spirituality in many Christian circles and the unavoidable association of the Iona Community with its Celtic heritage, I offer selected contextual remarks about the Iona of Columba and some of the more lyrical connections between Columba's life and the ministry of the current Iona Community.

Bradley suggests that three primary features make up Columba's character: he was "part pilgrim, part penitent and part politician."[7] It is perhaps in these three areas of Columba's life that we can see both the foundation of his

---

4. I have noticed that recent bookseller catalogues often have a "Celtic" section. A friend gave me a CD of "Celtic music." Upon closer examination, this "Celtic music" turned out to be "Celtic stylings derived from our heritage" by a Scottish praise and worship group offering a Celtic "influence, as well as our testimonies." Many of the songs were not Celtic in origin but were arrangements of music using "Celtic sounds." It appears that the range of scholarship varies greatly, and that the word "Celtic" in the title of a book or on the label of a CD sells these days.

5. Ian Bradley, *Columba: Pilgrim and Penitent* (Glasgow: Wild Goose Publications, 1996). Bradley's earlier publication, *The Celtic Way* (London: Darton, Longman and Todd, 1993), provided a context for the more focused study on Columba.

6. Quoting from Bradley's earlier work, *The Celtic Way*, Gilbert Márkus notes in "The End of Celtic Christianity," *Epworth Review* 24, no. 3 (July 1997), that a romanticized view of Celtic Christianity is emerging espousing that "[r]acially or culturally 'Celtic' qualities combined with Christianity to produce a uniquely happy form of the faith" (45). Márkus, noting that the slaughter of innocent Celtic Christians is often mentioned along with the killing of aboriginal Australians and Native Americans, states that "'Celtic religion' is far more admired in England and California than it is by Gaelic speakers in Scotland, Catholic or Calvinist." He concludes that we deal with our guilt for what we have done to the "noble savage," as these groups represent, by "pretend[ing] that we are really Celtic, or American Indian, or whatever. . . . [Thus,] we can reinvent ourselves as innocents" (53).

7. Bradley, *Columba*, 23. During this section, page numbers from Bradley's text will be cited directly in the body of the text.

monastic life and continuity with the work of the Iona Community of the twentieth century. The tradition of the *peregrini,* or pilgrim, is not as common to spiritual life in North America. It finds biblical roots in the narrative of the people of Israel wandering in the wilderness, leaving their own country and family (Gen. 12:1). There is much speculation concerning the events that led to Columba's decision to migrate from Ireland to Scotland. Bradley is not entirely convinced, as is often alleged, that Columba was banished from Ireland for illegally copying a fine psalter belonging to Finian of Moville (52), especially since he "maintain[ed] close contact with his royal relations back in Ireland" (32). Nor is he totally persuaded that Columba's motive was exclusively missional, as has been suggested by others, since he seems to have spent much of his time as an ecclesiastical administrator (33-34).[8] Nor were Columba's missionary efforts the only ones of this time. Ninian also spawned a movement that brought Christianity to southern Scotland in the seventh century, indicating that Columba may not have been the "unchallenged apostle of Scotland and chief evangelist of the Picts" (38). Regardless of Columba's motive for coming to Scotland, the *peregrinatio* was a part of the religious ethos of the time and links Columba's Iona with the Iona of the twentieth century. This can be seen in the activities of the WGWG, which takes song and liturgy to the people of Glasgow and beyond. It is also manifest in the Iona pilgrims, many of whom come annually to this isolated island for retreat, Bible study, and worship. The spirit of the *peregrini* is also manifest in the global peregrinations of John Bell, the primary troubadour of the community.

Bradley and many others leave no doubt that Columba was a penitent. His existence was ascetic by any standard. In addition to observing the seven daily hours of the offices, during which all 150 psalms were chanted each week, early sources indicated that he would rise before sunrise, go down to the shore, and chant "the three fifties," or all 150 psalms, before sunrise (53). This relationship to the sea comes to light in a traditional acclamation, "Gloria," often introduced by Bell in sessions (see example 6.1, p. 194). He indicates that it may have been sung antiphonally between a group of monks on shore and another departing by sea on mission, continued until neither could hear the other.

Copying sacred manuscripts and participating in solitary retreats were other activities of the penitent monk. Bradley notes that the "ideal of

---

8. At this point Bradley's account offers a modest corrective to, or at least amplifies, some of the earlier information on Columba published by the Iona Community in *What Is the Iona Community?* (Glasgow: Wild Goose Publications, 1988). This publication focuses on Columba's missionary activity almost exclusively (5-6).

Example 6.1. "Iona Gloria" (traditional)

solemnly

Glo - ri - a,   Glo - ri - a,   Glo - ri - a,   in   ex - cel - sis   De - o.

peregrinatio involved a certain degree of exile, renunciation and searching for one's own desert place of resurrection" (25). As we shall see, the rule of the twentieth-century Iona Community, while not ascetic by the standards of Irish monastic life, encourages a kind of penitence and commitment that distinguishes its members from many in modern society.

Celtic monastic life was not entirely one of exile and hermitage, however. It was also one of active political engagement. Those parts of the island north of Hadrian's Wall (modern Scotland) and Ireland were virtually excluded from the unifying effects of the Pax Romana, leaving competitive and combative tribes.[9] Within many tribal factions that dominated the political landscape of Scotland during Columba's day, the monasteries were places of education, medicine, arts, and hospitality, as well as religious life. Bradley suggests that times of extended withdrawal and solitude were balanced with periods of intense administrative activity, including church planting (25). Indeed, the reputation of Columba was based in part on his ability to forge relationships with local kings and establish a *familia* of churches and monasteries amid warring, divided tribal loyalties. Bradley states that "it is impossible to ignore the considerable evidence . . . that both king making and church planting ranked high on Columba's own agenda" (28). Adomnan, Columba's early biographer, suggests that, as abbot, Columba consecrated kings, perhaps being the first in Europe to do so (31). As a man from an Irish family of considerable means, he may have presided on some occasions as a "Celtic chieftain rather than a humble monk" (32).

Perhaps most relevant for the Iona Community of today, Columba was a pilgrim, poet,[10] and pray-er of psalms who presided as abbot over a monas-

---

9. Thomas Sowell, *Conquests and Cultures: An International History* (New York: Basic Books, 1998), 22-67, offers helpful background on those areas of the current United Kingdom that were beyond Rome's cultural and political influence during the height of its era of conquest.

10. See David N. Power, "Affirmed from Under: Celtic Liturgy and Spirituality," *Studia Liturgica* 27, no. 1 (1997): 1-32, for an excellent scholarly treatment of Celtic hymnody and psalter prayers, as well as verse related to the Celtic affinity with nature, penance, martyr-

tic *familia,* offering hospitality to pilgrims and planting churches within the context of an alien culture. "Hospitality was sacred because Christ was in the stranger."[11] A *peregrini* must be willing to welcome other travelers. The modern Iona Community continues this practice.

Columba lived a disciplined life balanced by periods of intense solitude and active political engagement. Furthermore, Esther de Waal notes that the "Celtic peoples are peoples who know suffering, deprivation, exile, oppression. And yet they have learned through all of this to find the light in the darkness."[12] This equilibrium between solitude, political engagement, and identification with those who suffer and experience oppression may be the richest spiritual trust of the Celtic context to the vision and work of the Iona Community today. John Bell and Graham Maule confirm the significance of the legacy Columba left on the small island of Iona:

> The Iona Community has always attempted to marry the work of peace-making and political engagement with the practice of prayer.
>
> This has developed out of an understanding of the Incarnation which is rooted deep in Celtic spirituality. Celtic Christians believe that when the Word became flesh in Jesus, a new significance was given to the material order and to human affairs. Creation and the work of humans then became arenas in and through which God could be praised.[13]

---

ology, and devotion to saints and to Christ, with examples drawn primarily from the *Antiphonary of Bangor.*

11. Ronald Ferguson, *Chasing the Wild Goose: The Story of the Iona Community* (Glasgow: Wild Goose Publications, 1998), 25. Ferguson quotes the Gaelic Rune of Hospitality:

> I saw a stranger yestreen:
> I put food in the eating place,
> Drink in the drinking place,
> Music in the listening place:
> And in the sacred name of the Triune
> He blessed myself and my house,
> My cattle and my dear ones.
> And the lark said in her song
> Often, often, often
> Goes the Christ in the stranger's guise.
> Often, often, often
> Goes the Christ in the stranger's guise.

12. Esther de Waal, "The Celtic Way of Prayer," *Cistercian Studies Quarterly* 32, no. 3 (1997): 372.

13. John L. Bell and Graham Maule, *Love + Anger: Songs of Lively Faith and Social Justice* (Glasgow: Wild Goose Publications, 1997), 8.

As a tribute to the saint, the WGWG wrote a hymn, sung to the traditional Irish tune ST. COLUMBA:

> From Erin's shores Columba came
> To preach and teach and heal,
> And found a church which showed the world
> How God on earth was real.
>
> In greening grass and reckless wave,
> In cloud and ripening corn,
> The Celtic Christians traced the course
> Of grace through nature borne.
>
> In hosting strangers, healing pain,
> In tireless work for peace,
> They served the servant Christ their Lord
> And found their faith increase.
>
> In simple prayer and alien land,
> As summoned by the Son,
> They celebrated how God's call
> Made work and worship one.
>
> God grant that what Columba sowed
> May harvest yet more seed,
> As we engage both flesh and faith
> To marry word and deed.[14]

© 1989 GIA Publications, Inc. Used by permission.

The Iona of George MacLeod (1895-1991)

The legacy of Columba was paramount to George MacLeod, the founder of the modern Iona Community,[15] who commented on the distortions of the saint's ministry and its relevance today: "The island of St. Columba . . . ! How

14. John L. Bell and Graham Maule, *Love from Below: The Seasons of Life, the Call to Care, and the Celebrating Community* (Glasgow: Wild Goose Publications, 1989), 123.

15. This chapter omits a discussion of the establishment of the old Benedictine Abbey in the thirteenth century, repairs to the abbey in the fifteenth century, and the later decline of the abbey up to the time of MacLeod during the mid–twentieth century. See Ferguson, 40-45, for a brief description of these centuries of activity.

falsely men misread his work if they visualize his mission to the mainland as purely a 'religious' movement. True to his patron of Tours, his whole evangel was compact of every aspect of man's living. Agriculture, fishing, education, craftsmanship — these were the domains he insisted must be brought in thrall to the sovereign will of the All Highest. And in our day and generation is not this essentially the challenge we must face?"[16]

Much to the amazement of parishioners and clergy, MacLeod left a thriving parish ministry in industrial Clydeside, Govan, the dock area of Glasgow, to found the modern Iona Community in 1938. In spite of economic depression and high unemployment, worship at the Govan Old Parish Church was filled with people. He was admired for a pioneer ministry in a difficult area of Glasgow. MacLeod had serious doubts, however, about the ability of the established Church of Scotland to meet the needs of working-class people and young persons. He wanted to experiment with a new way of theological preparation that would bring together industrial workers and ministers in community.

At the crux of his concern was the way ministers were educated — separate from and ignorant of the working people that would undoubtedly be a part of their parishes. So he set off to a small island, distant from and nearly inaccessible to populated areas of Scotland, with twelve young ministers and artisans, equally divided, to rebuild the ruins of the old Iona Abbey established by the Benedictines in the thirteenth century. They built communal huts that would allow the small band to begin this experiment of community, from which they could eventually restore the ruins of the old Cistercian Abbey.[17] Commenting on this Cistercian connection, MacLeod noted:

> And in an Abbey built by the Cistercians! Certainly our purpose is not to be cloistered. But the "religious life" was not the only splendor of Rome! The Abbey in its day stood on the outposts of an idea that was of the essence of our Faith — and must be made the essence of our Faith again —

16. *The Coracle: Rebuilding the Common Life; Foundation Documents of the Iona Community* (Glasgow: Wild Goose Publications, [1938] 1988), October 1938, 4. Page numbers in the remainder of this section refer to the collection of the three initial issues of the *Coracle* found in this publication. Since this source contains facsimiles of these issues, the pages are not numbered consecutively throughout the book. Therefore, notes in the body of the text will refer to the date of each issue followed by a page number.

17. A word of explanation is appropriate here as there may be confusion between the Old Iona Abbey being called both Benedictine by Ronald Ferguson (see n. 15 above) and Cistercian by George MacLeod. Saint Bernard of Clairvaux (1090-1153) was one of the most effective reformers of the Order of Saint Benedict. The movement Bernard and his followers inspired has survived and thrives in two major autonomous branches, the Benedictines and Cistercians.

that there is but one Faith, One Lord, One Baptism, One God and Father of us all. . . . The background of all our thinking must be the sense of a Church that is worldwide, whose welcome is for all. Else the strivings for Community be partial, for we will not have been based upon the Word. (October 1938, 4)

As the plan evolved, the two groups learned from each other. The summer months were spent on the island in study, work, and worship. The winter months were spent in an industrial urban setting ministering in pairs in housing projects and experimenting in different ways of living in Christian community. It was not the intent of the founder to set up permanent residence on the remote island of Iona, but to use it as a place for training and an impetus for mission as it had been in the days of Columba.[18]

The first official newsletter from Iona, entitled the *Coracle* — the name refers to a small boat like the one used by Columba to travel from Ireland to Scotland — was published in October 1938. It helped to define the mission of the community for a broader audience. The rebirth of the Iona Community was a laboratory or "collective experiment" in community. This community was established within the Church of Scotland by volunteers, living in a common hut, sleeping, eating, working, and worshiping together. War was on the horizon. The twin threats of communism and fascism were existential realities. To the casual observer, the complete absurdity of this small group of ministers and artisans retreating to a remote island to worship twice a day, working under ascetic conditions, must have defied words. Some of the islanders soon accepted the invitation to join the community for daily worship at 8 A.M. and 10 P.M. Visitors from the mainland also came to observe and volunteer, joining the simple morning and evening prayer services that included a sung psalm, a hymn, Scripture, and prayer. The participation of the islanders and the visitors from the mainland provided spiritual support for this nascent community (October 1938, 5-13).

By the time the second *Coracle* was published in May 1939, the General Assembly of the Church of Scotland was "cordially commending the scheme" (May 1939, 1). More ministers and artisans had volunteered, and there was sufficient funding to see them through the summer. Nearly a thousand "Friends of Iona Community" had sent support. Twelve laypersons and nine ministers were "in full community" by the summer of 1939.

The second *Coracle* reinforced the spiritual link between Iona, founded by Saint Columba, and the Govan Old Parish Church, founded by Saint

18. For more information, see *What Is the Iona Community?*

Constantine, one of Columba's monks. Govan was also a mainland site for the preparation of ministers who lived among working-class people. This spiritual bond has been strengthened today by the location of the Pearce Institute, which houses Wild Goose Publications on Govan Road, adjacent to the Govan Church.

MacLeod defined the movement further by stating forthrightly that the Iona experiment was based on community, worship, and laity. The times of retreat to the island were to be balanced by ministry in the "housing schemes" of Govan. Later, in the second *Coracle*, MacLeod defines the community from a negative perspective (May 1939, 18):

1. The modern Iona Community was not a resurrection of a "dream of the past"; this was not a movement back to the good old days when Christianity was great. Above all, it was "not a return to Rome."
2. Iona was not a pacifist community. With war imminent and invasion possible, Iona supported persons who took positions ranging from conscientious objector to chaplain and even infantryman.
3. Iona was not a visionary movement, "seeking helplessly to play at being Franciscans." Poverty, celibacy, and banishment to a remote isle were not the ideals of the community. They would return to the mainland for the winter.
4. The revitalization of the modern Iona Community was more than the enterprise of one man.

The retirement of MacLeod in 1967 and the continued influence of the community since that time have proven this latter point.

The second *Coracle* also emphasized the loss of vision by the Church of Scotland. "The glory of the Church of Scotland used to be summed up in the phrase 'Kirk and Mart,'" MacLeod noted (May 1939, 16). Programs that once had been under the purview of the church — caring for the poor and providing education, physical fitness, and even social life for the people — had now been superseded by the state. It was MacLeod's hope to form a new community that would encourage the Church of Scotland to find a renewed identity.

The importance of change was an early theme of MacLeod's ministry and continues to be a primary motif in the work of the WGWG. The world is changing. Society is changing. Therefore the church and its worship must change. It was from MacLeod that John Bell draws on the theme of a church that today is recalcitrant about change. Bell traces this attitude in part to sentiments expressed in Victorian hymns like Henry Francis Lyte's "Abide with Me," which reads, in the third line of stanza two, "change and decay in all around I see."[19] Bell considers the nature of change in his reflection "Change-less and Changing," based on Hosea 2:14-23 and John 15:1-17:

> God is love and that love is constant and changeless. But when I say that God is changeless, I realize that I say not only a very comforting thing, but a very dangerous thing. Because it only takes a little thought or a little thoughtlessness to deduce that we should be changeless too. If from Scripture we learn that we are made in God's image, and we learn that God is changeless, we presume that we should be changeless too. But it doesn't work that way. The proof that we have been grasped by the changeless love of God is that we never remain the same, but are trans-formed, converted, turned upside down, inside out.[20]

When we look later at major themes in the hymns of the Iona Community, we will encounter the poetic embodiment of this spirit.

MacLeod challenged the church to recover the "essential grandeur" of Reformed worship. All life belongs to God. There is no schism between the sacred and the secular. The home and the family were at the heart of real wor-ship. The pace of civilization had negated their power. Corporate worship de-rived its influence from a diet of family prayer. Without regular family prayer, young people did not find meaning in traditional corporate worship. MacLeod observed that the family circle was no longer the center of people's lives. He proposed a liturgical strategy for adapting worship to this changing reality. The revitalization of worship would need to go beyond "ornamenting the preliminaries." "All life should be a Sacrament" became MacLeod's mes-sage to the church and the world (May 1939, 23-24). The church needed alter-native ways for presenting the Christian year and the life of Christ. MacLeod sounds like a church renewal prophet of the late twentieth century when he comments on a youth culture that is much more oriented to visual stimula-tion ("pictures," i.e., movies) than to reading books. Liturgical structures have meaning only when surrounded by a vital, living faith.

By the time of the third *Coracle* in November 1939, war was a reality. Ac-

---

19. See John Bell, "Reforming Worship: Change Is Not a Dirty Word," *Reformed Worship* 40 (June 1996): 5. Ian Bradley, *Abide with Me: The World of Victorian Hymns* (London: SCM Press, 1997), graciously notes that "John Bell, the leading contemporary Scottish hymn writer, has pointed to the damage done to the cause of reform and moving on in the life of churches by the deadening effect of [this line] from 'Abide with me'" (234). Later he adds that "it is good for [Victorian hymnody enthusiasts] to be confronted with the withering judgment of a leading contemporary hymn-writer like John Bell" (245).

20. John L. Bell, *Wrestle and Fight and Pray: Thoughts on Christianity and Conflict* (Edin-burgh: Saint Andrew Press, 1993), 5-6.

tivities in the housing projects were to some extent hampered by blackouts. In spite of this, 200 islanders (out of a total population of 450) gathered for worship. Friends of the community now numbered 2,000. The commitment to transfer the work of the community to the mainland during the winter months became strengthened through increased numbers and improved strategies. In addition to training men for working in the housing projects, men were also prepared for serving faithfully in the army.

Worship remained central to life on the island during the summer months. Worshiping twice daily, in the ancient abbey, the community used a form adapted from the daily prayer at the Govan Old Church in Glasgow.[21] Much of the community's time was spent in intercessory prayer, responding to requests sent to them. To a rigorous schedule of activities was added a choir rehearsal two nights a week under the leadership of a minister from Czechoslovakia. The choir was composed of the full members of the community, people who had not been chosen for their musical aptitude. "By the force of [the director's] enthusiasm he somehow welded us into a choir that was soon able to carry through the daily services — with some twenty-five items a week — without instrumental accompaniment" (November 1939, 16). Thus did the first three editions of the *Coracle* outline an experiment in community, nurtured by the Celtic spiritual legacy of Columba and evolving within the heritage of the Church of Scotland.

As the community survived World War II and settled into the mid-1950s, its mission became more global. Urban Scotland was no longer the topic of this enlarged vision; the focus was on peace, poverty, and injustice in the Two-Thirds World, and Africa, a continent just beginning to rid itself of colonial rule — a process that would continue through the end of the twentieth century.[22] Though holding at one time the position of moderator for the General Assembly of the Church of Scotland, MacLeod tested his denomination's patience to the limit on several occasions. Ronald Ferguson, a later leader of the community, noted that MacLeod was neither "patient, diplomatic nor tactful" at times, "and had he been, the Iona Abbey would probably still be in ruins today."[23]

By 1967 the restoration of the abbey was completed and the Very Reverend Lord MacLeod of Fuinary relinquished leadership of the Iona Community. In 1985 the original huts used to house the community, built in the late 1930s, had outlived their usefulness as summer housing for young peo-

21. Ferguson, 55.
22. Ferguson, 95.
23. Ferguson, 76.

ple. The MacLeod Center, just up the road from the abbey, replaced the old huts. This facility is devoted to reconciliation, designed for families, is fully handicap-accessible, and maintains the community's commitment to young people.

Full members of the Iona Community live by a fivefold rule of (1) praying and Bible study; (2) sharing and use of money, including the giving of a tithe (10 percent) of disposable income (after taxes, insurance, and pension); (3) sharing and the use of time, including adequate time for recreation, physical activity, and family; (4) meeting with fellow members, including three plenary sessions on the mainland and a week on the island of Iona each year; and (5) working for peace and justice, both locally and internationally.[24] While the majority of Iona's two hundred members are in Britain, the present Iona Community is a global, ecumenical "movement of . . . over 1,400 Associate Members and about 1,600 Friends"[25] from many denominational traditions in the United States, Africa, India, Australia, and New Zealand. Although rooted in the ethos of Saint Columba and the heritage of the Church of Scotland, the Community of Iona has captured the imagination of many who are searching for a new sense of community. Iona exists both on the island of Iona and in the ministry of the WGWG in urban centers on the mainland. Through pilgrimage to the island, common prayer, and a commitment to justice and peace, the influence of the Iona Community extends far beyond its Scottish roots.

MacLeod constructed prayers that are at once prophetic, grand, and bountiful. His prayers have the sense of poetry. Rather than describe MacLeod's vision of the church, I include a prayer that captures this vision in his own words:

> Lord Christ, Your church is a mystery:
>   It is not a human amalgamation of people trying to be loyal to You.
>   It is not an army of soldiers drilling together to achieve
>   the discipline to be brave.
>   It is not a human list of souls trying sincerely to be good.
> It is a mystery of Your own creating:
>   It is Your continuing body on earth:
>   It is flesh of Your flesh and bone of Your bone:
>   It is Your bride.

24. See *What Is the Iona Community?* 8-12, for a complete description and explanation of "The Rule and Concerns of the Iona Community."

25. Bell and Maule, *Love + Anger*, 78. Current information on the activities of the community may be found at http://www.iona.org.uk/.

So there just aren't a lot of churches: because You can't have
   a lot of bodies.

So we ask You to open our minds and our hearts next time
   we sit at the communion table
to see Baptists and Anglicans: Orthodox and Romans and
   Presbyterians all sitting at the same communion table
because that is how You see them:
one body now with You, Your bride, bone of Your bone and
   flesh of Your flesh.
Our prayer is that You enlarge our hearts
to serve all Christians with uncalculating love: without waiting:
even should they spurn us or turn from us.
We thank You for the present unity of the Church.
Help us to go right ahead in the light of it.

Let us pray for the less worthy members of the Church:
They are already limbs of Your mystical body:
forgetful You are already the head, and they the limbs.
Less worthy members who retain signs of their one-time earthiness:
with continuing prejudices:
all too ready to whisper the damaging libel about their neighbors:
especially when that libel is true.
All too eager to retell the nasty joke to gain popularity:
forgetting the weaker brethren.
All too tribal, as if Bethlehem were a Scottish village and Nazareth
   an English town:
or Capetown were Calvary itself:
when you really died for all men everywhere:
At a crossroads whose signpost had to be in Latin and Hebrew
   and Greek and Urdu and Russian and Afrikaans.
Yes, Lord, we pray for the less worthy members of the Church.
They are of course none other than ourselves.[26]

© 1985 GIA Publications, Inc. Used by permission.

26. *The Whole Earth Shall Cry Glory: Iona Prayers* by Rev. George F. MacLeod (Glasgow: Wild Goose Publications, 1985), 36-37.

John Bell and Graham Maule and the Formation
of the Wild Goose Worship Group[27]

John Bell (b. 1949) grew up in Kilmarnock, a small town south of Glasgow. He received degrees in music, English, and theology from the University of Glasgow. Upon graduation from Trinity College in 1974, he was ordained in the Church of Scotland and left for Amsterdam to work with English-speaking churches for two years. Rather than serve in more traditional parish work, he returned to Glasgow to do youth work for the Glasgow presbytery of the Church of Scotland. As an adolescent, his father, at times an agnostic, told Bell of his respect for George MacLeod. Bell was familiar with the Community House in Glasgow, run by the Community, "a city-centre cafe which served cheap but wholesome food to tramps and teachers, which advertised meetings for trade-unionists, anonymous gamblers, anti-apartheid activists, and which also held daily worship in the middle of the meeting place."[28] It was not until his ordination that Bell became aware of the ministry of the Community more fully. After organizing youth ministry for the presbytery for approximately five years, John became a member of the Iona Community in 1980. He was committed not because the Iona Community was a place for liturgical innovation but because it was "a place where the potentials of the socially marginalised as well as the socially successful would be attested."[29] Thus Bell developed a core of volunteers that planned end-of-the-month youth workshops, bringing together young people for fellowship, reflection, and worship. At the conclusion of the evening, all would prepare worship together. These monthly workshops, called Last of the Month, attracted four hundred to five hundred young people. The workshops and worship were designed around biblical themes relevant to the lives of the young people, e.g., the Ten Commandments, the Beatitudes, etc. Those attending were often on the fringe of the church, and their knowledge of the biblical tradition was negligible.

---

27. Much of the information for this section comes from a visit to the flat shared by John Bell and Graham Maule in Glasgow, August 18-20, 1997. As John was out of town during part of this visit, I am particularly grateful for the extended conversations with Graham Maule on this occasion and again in Indianapolis, Ind., April 17-19, 1998, where I had the opportunity to work with Graham as a "stand-in" for John at the Indianapolis Conference on Worship, Music, and Culture organized by Ted Gibboney. Other information comes from participating in conferences where John Bell has been leading, including the Hymn Society Annual Conferences in 1992, 1995, and 1998, as well as leadership at Perkins School of Theology, Southern Methodist University, in March 1996.

28. John Bell, "Flight of the Wild Goose," *Reformed Liturgy and Music* 34, no. 2 (2000): 15.

29. Bell, "Flight," 15.

"We will not take what is not ours," for example, is a song based on the eighth commandment — you shall not steal. Bell composed this song in order to share both biblical truth and the wider ethical and social ramifications of current ecological awareness. The text is set to a driving, syncopated rhythm.

We will not take what is not ours;
The freedom of a separate place,
The future of a different race,
The unrestrictiveness of space.
WE WILL NOT TAKE WHAT IS NOT OURS.

We will not take what is not ours
Nor ravage, exploit or pollute
Till nature mourns her barren state
And justice limps both blind and mute.
WE WILL NOT TAKE WHAT IS NOT OURS.

We will not take what is not ours
And offer then to heaven the dross
Of poverty caused by our greed
To win despite our neighbor's loss.
WE WILL NOT TAKE WHAT IS NOT OURS.[30]

© 1989 GIA Publications, Inc. Used by permission.

In 1983 Bell and Maule, one of those early volunteers and a student of architecture, brought together eight of the volunteers to reflect on the worship needs of the young people participating in Last of the Month. Bell and Maule were employed in 1984 to coordinate the Iona Community's youth ministry, whose events to this time had been mostly educational in nature. There was a need for worship materials that could speak to the experience of a younger generation and bring the liturgical dimension of Last of the Month into focus. Though the Iona Community originated within the Church of Scotland, the faith heritage of these eight people was more ecumenical in nature, including persons from Baptist and Church of Wales traditions. After six weeks of reflection the WGWG was formed and expanded to sixteen people. Until 2000, the group continued to meet weekly in Bell and Maule's Glasgow flat to sing, reflect on the theological gaps in the sung repertoire of the liturgy, and critique the songs that had been written, usually by Bell. The WGWG

30. Bell and Maule, *Love from Below,* 75, stanzas 1, 3, 4.

were volunteers who were a mixture of students and professional and working-class people. While the group began primarily as a student group, its participants have changed over the years, many leaving to become effective parish ministers or follow other paths of service. Last of the Month events continued until 1986 when the energies of Bell and Maule became more focused on raising funds for the development of the MacLeod Center on Iona.

In 1984 the activities of the WGWG began in earnest and, by 1986, their first recording, *A Touching Place,* was released. Early print resources included a collection of MacLeod's prayers, *The Whole Earth Shall Cry Glory, The Iona Community Worship Book,* and *Heaven Shall Not Wait: Songs of Creation, the Incarnation, and the Life of Jesus.* In October 1986 Wild Goose Publications was formed as the entity responsible for producing and publishing materials for the Iona Community. The Wild Goose Resource Group (WGRG) was set up to develop and promote new forms of worship. Publishing interests evolved organically out of the need to revitalize worship.

The inclusion of world songs developed naturally out of the desire to be in solidarity with the poor and the oppressed around the globe. Early materials were drawn from the Swedish collection of South African songs entitled *Freedom Is Coming* (1984), edited by Anders Nyberg;[31] songs from the 1984 World Council of Churches Assembly in Vancouver; and a few songs from Malawi and neighboring countries arranged by Tom Colvin, a long-standing member of the Community. Formal publications of world song began when *Many and Great: Songs of the World Church,* volume 1, appeared in 1990 in the UK and 1992 in the United States. This was soon followed by *Sent by the Lord: Songs of the World Church,* volume 2, in 1991 abroad and 1992 in the United States. Many of these songs first surfaced as an addendum of "World Church Songs" in a text-only format in the back of a book of liturgies entitled *A Wee Worship Book* (1989), published only abroad. These collections provide world song to a broader audience and have become staple resources for accessible global materials since that time.

While publications have been a major thrust of the Wild Goose Worship and Resource Groups since the early 1990s,[32] they continue to work in other

---

31. According to Graham Maule, "We originally started importing *Freedom Is Coming* from Sweden around 1984. However it was becoming increasingly costly to maintain such a supply (and the books were getting damaged in transit), so we negotiated to begin publishing it in 1990. However, this was in the UK only." Correspondence with Graham Maule, October 3, 2000.

32. The following is a representative list of publications by the WGWG, many of which are available from GIA Publications in the United States: *Psalms of Patience, Protest, and Praise* (1993); *Come All You People: Shorter Songs for Worship* (1994); companion volumes *Innkeepers and Light Sleepers: Seventeen Songs for Christmas* (1992); *The Courage to Say No: Twenty-Three*

venues to develop the experience of singing as well. In 1991 Last Night Out was formed. This monthly event, described at the beginning of this chapter, is more ecumenical and intergenerational than the earlier Last of the Month encounters for youth. Attendance is usually between 150 and 200 persons, who meet at Renfield Saint Stephen's Church, a Church of Scotland parish.

In 1994 four members of the Worship Group were employed full time as enablers of the activities of the Resource Group — John Bell, Graham Maule, Alison Adam, and Mairi Munro. They are supported in part through a year-to-year grant from the Church of Scotland and from the royalties received from publications produced by the WGRG. The larger Worship Group continued to meet and try out new songs in worship, usually prepared in advance by John, until it disbanded in 2000. These songs drew their inspiration not only from the rule of the Iona Community but also from the needs of the poor and working-class people in Glasgow, perceived gaps in the ministry of established churches, and the inability of the church to reach many disenfranchised people.

In 1996 the Worship Group established the Big Sing, a nonliturgical event aimed at providing people with the experience of group singing. Perhaps even to a greater degree than in the United States, Scotland specifically and Britain in general have moved away from singing as a communal expression. In Scotland group singing is limited to the church, a forum that reaches relatively few persons, and football (soccer) matches. Bell finds that he must make a case for congregational singing in a culture largely void of such experiences.[33] The Big Sing helped people explore their voices as part of a community experience in a nonthreatening environment. These occasional gatherings drew as many as 250 people in the Glasgow area and other sites, including Ireland. Much of the singing was done without any written music. With the assistance of the members of the Worship Group, the Resource Group tried out newer songs. While John usually presided at these events,

---

Songs for Lent and Easter (1996); *Love + Anger: Songs of Lively Faith and Social Justice* (1997); *When Grief Is Raw: Songs for Times of Sorrow and Bereavement* (1997). *God Never Sleeps, The Last Journey: Songs for the Time of Grieving* (1996), and *Psalms of David, Songs of Mary* (1998) provide choral materials. Text-only books published by the WGRG have not been generally available in the United States. These include *The Iona Community Worship Book,* rev. ed. (1991), John Bell's *He Was in the World: Meditations for Public Worship* (1995), and *The Pattern of Our Days: Liturgies and Resources for Worship,* ed. Kathy Galloway (1996). *The Last Journey* (1996) is published separately as a book of meditations with accompanying recording. For virtually all these collections there are cassette tapes and CDs available. For a current listing of Wild Goose publications, see http://www.iona.org.uk/wgp/index.htm.

33. John L. Bell, *The Singing Thing: A Case for Congregational Singing* (Glasgow: Wild Goose Publications, 2000), explores this topic in depth.

members of the Worship Group shared the leadership of songs. By 2002 the four members of the WGRG reorganized, with several members pursuing other interests. This group had been together for nearly fifteen years. Bell remains employed full time, continuing an extensive travel schedule around the world.

Themes of Iona Liturgy and Music

Having provided some contextual information concerning the Columban legacy, the renewal movement of George MacLeod, and the development of the Wild Goose Worship and Resource Groups, I turn to themes of the community. My analysis will include the following areas: (1) the group creative process developed by the WGWG, (2) the underlying sense of oral tradition that informs both the literature and the process, (3) songs of the world church, and (4) the biblical foundation and hermeneutic of the songs within liturgy. By examining these areas we should be able to draw some conclusions concerning the nature of liturgical contextualization practiced by the Iona Community and the WGWG.

Group Creative Process of the Wild Goose Worship Group

"The songs from Iona are not composed in solitude on the beach of the tiny island off the western coast of Scotland with the waves lapping at the shore," John will tell you. Many compositions originated in the context of urban Glasgow in a flat behind a nineteenth-century church, next door to a tenement, in a working-class neighborhood, or during one of the many trips Bell takes to lead sessions or gather new materials. The songs of the WGWG are "the product of ongoing argument, experiment, study, discussion, questioning and listening to the conversation of ordinary people. They are also the product of being stunned by the unquestionable relevance of the Word of God, which eyes, blinded by bias, presumption, or cynicism, had long avoided."[34] The WGWG develops the songs as a part of a group creative process:

– Someone has an insight or an idea which excites others and informs or challenges faith;

34. John L. Bell and Graham Maule, *Heaven Shall Not Wait: Songs of Creation, the Incarnation, and the Life of Jesus* (Chicago: GIA Publications, [1987] 1989), 8.

- John picks over it and drafts a rough copy of a song;
- Graham scrutinizes, corrects, and amends it;
- somehow a tune emerges from a folk tradition or from midair;
- the tune is either left alone, given accompaniment, or harmonized;
- the Worship Group sings it through and comments on it;
- the song, now in its third version, is sung at public worship;
- a final revision is made.[35]

Rather than a solitary act of composition, musical creation is a community activity.[36] One might draw an analogy between the compositional process followed by the WGWG and the Bible study of the Latin American Base Community. In this highly participatory process of Bible study, the needs and context of the lay participants shape the hermeneutic of the selected Scripture.[37] Bell notes, in a recent collection, that few of the songs originating with the WGWG "are contemporary with the publication of the book. The vast majority have been sung, scrutinized and amended several times in the past five or six years and have proven their worth in places far from a printing press."[38] Although Bell appears as the author/composer of the vast majority of songs published in the early volumes of the Iona Community, in many cases he served as a facilitator of the group creative process or a scribe who artistically shaped the inspirations, conceptions, and convictions of the WGWG into a final printed form.

---

35. Bell and Maule, *Heaven Shall Not Wait*, 8.

36. The WGWG follows a process similar to that used by other religious communities. For example, much of the music of the Taizé Community was published under the name of Jacques Berthier (1923-94), a longtime friend of Taizé. In reality, Berthier usually worked with selected brothers in the Community to refine these sung prayers. The songs were tested in the daily prayer of the Community and, based upon this experience, modified. Since Berthier's death, this process continues with the brothers, especially with the ostinato forms. Father Joseph Gelineau, a friend of the Community in the early days after World War II, assisted in the development of congregational psalms and mass settings since Berthier's death. Brother Jean Marie coordinates much of the musical composition and publications. Since Berthier worked in a group creative process with the brothers for many years, it is natural for several of the brothers to continue this approach following his death. See Brother Jean Marie, "Prayer and Song in Taizé: Opening the Doors to an Inner Life," *Ecumenism* 31, no. 124 (December 1996): 16-18, for recent developments in Taizé song, and the videocassette *Praying with the Songs of Taizé* (Chicago: GIA Publishers, 1996).

37. See Ernesto Cardenal, *The Gospel according to Solentiname*, vol. 1 (Maryknoll, N.Y.: Orbis, 1976), for a prototype of exegesis done in a Latin American base community.

38. John L. Bell and Graham Maule, *The Courage to Say No: Twenty-Three Songs for Lent and Easter* (Chicago: GIA Publications, 1996), 4.

The Influences of Oral Tradition in the Music of the Iona Community

I propose that the music and pedagogical process for transmitting the music reflect an understanding of oral tradition and a balance between oral practice and literate product. In both the creative process and the transmission of songs to an assembly, the WGWG demonstrates a high degree of "secondary orality," a term used by Walter Ong. Creative process and transmission of songs are crucial to establishing the kind of liturgical environment that draws persons disenchanted with the church into the gatherings hosted by the WGWG. "Primary orality," a culture without a written language, rarely exists today. Even highly technological cultures and subcultures, however, "preserve much of the mind-set of primary orality," according to Ong.[39] Secondary orality is sustained by television, radio, telephone, and other electronic media. Ong outlines several aspects of orality that are relevant to this discussion and shed light on the work of the WGWG.

First of all, the Scottish, Irish, and English folk songs used as vehicles for many of the texts written by the WGWG draw from the wells of oral tradition. Ong indicates that folk songs from the British Isles "developed on the edge of orality"[40] in both oral and written forms. As conveyors of story songs, these ballads kept alive many of the myths of their communities of origin and were the mode for transmitting basic cultural stories from generation to generation as well as to other groups. Their modal sounds have been picked up not only by singers but also by popular dance groups and instrumental ensembles, adding to the resurgence of Celtic tradition both within the British Isles and beyond those shores. Bell and Maule recognized this when they noted: "We live in a country which has a glorious heritage of folk music, of fiddle and pipe tunes, of vocal melodies all in danger of disappearing into oblivion. But where are the spiritual songs which have clothed themselves in this musical richness? Why is it that Africans, Asians, and Central Americans have allowed the Gospel to take root in their folk music, but we in Britain have, by and large, avoided such an association as if Christ had never joyed to see children piping and dancing in the street?"[41]

In the three larger volumes of song published by the Iona Community, *Heaven Shall Not Wait* (1987), *Enemy of Apathy* (1988), and *Love from Below* (1989), there were 150 songs with stanzas, plus 33 shorter chants and re-

---

39. Walter J. Ong, *Orality and Literacy: The Technologizing of the Word* (New York: Routledge, 1982, 1988), 11.

40. Ong, 159.

41. Bell and Maule, *Heaven Shall Not Wait*, 7.

sponses.[42] Forty-six, or nearly one-third, of the songs with stanzas have their roots in the folk song legacy of the British Isles: 23 Scottish, 9 Irish, 11 English, and 3 Gaelic. Many of these songs draw upon the oral reservoir of Celtic culture that continues to be transmitted by musical groups and through electronic means today.

The method of transmission of these songs to an assembly demonstrates a significant awareness of secondary orality spawned by TV, CD, and radio culture. These songs are often taught "by ear," without the aid of instrumental accompaniment, in as many as four parts, with little or no reference to the printed score. Members of the WGWG position themselves among the people in order to facilitate congregational participation. In "minimizing the spoken (or preached) word and maximizing music, color, movement, and symbols,"[43] the WGWG differentiates its liturgy from that of many established congregations. Quoting Lévi-Strauss, Ong notes that the oral mind "totalizes" rather than analyzes an experience.[44] The gestalt that results from the use of a variety of symbolic media integrates more completely with the participant than a liturgy dominated by more didactic linear analysis — the stuff of words only, especially many traditional sermons. By depending less on the spoken word and more on a variety of symbols, media, and participatory forms of music and movement, the liturgies of the WGWG encourage a higher degree of secondary orality, balancing sequential analysis with the "totalizing" effect of the experiential. While printed liturgies and songs are usually available, they are designed to be cues for participation in a liturgical drama rather than a thorough cognitive analysis of the "theme for the day." I

---

42. A note on the shorter songs is in order. Many persons assume that these are along the lines of Taizé ostinati and meant for continual repetition. Kenneth Hull has a helpful article on Iona music, "A Decade of Wild Goose Songs," *Reformed Liturgy and Music* 34, no. 2 (2000): 20-34. I believe that he is mistaken, however, in his analysis of two volumes of "shorter songs for worship" (*Come All You People*, 1994, and *There Is One among Us*, 1998), when he says they "explore a genre that has been associated primarily with the Taizé Community: brief one-stanza songs that can be repeated indefinitely, whose texts are based on scripture." Bell cautions against Taizé-like repetition of these songs explicitly in the Preface of *Come All You People* (11). While correct about the use of Scripture, Mr. Hull gives a false impression here or does not appreciate the inherent difference between Taizé prayer and the more overtly justice-centered incarnational liturgies of Iona. It is one of the dangers of looking at the music of either Taizé or Iona separate from the liturgies that incorporate the music. Maule notes in this regard that "The 'wee' songs are in fact closer to the Roman Catholic genre of acclamations, etc." Correspondence on October 3, 2000.

43. John L. Bell and Graham Maule, *Enemy of Apathy: Songs of the Passion and Resurrection of Jesus, and the Coming of the Holy Spirit* (Chicago: GIA Publications, 1988, rev. 1990), 7.

44. Ong, 39.

believe it is this balance between symbolic experience and verbal analysis that accounts for the effectiveness of worship for many people who are liturgically resistant. This balance is achieved through encounters that use a high degree of secondary orality.

The use of many songs with refrains, shorter forms — chants, responses, and ostinati — composed by the WGWG, and world song also contributes to a sense of orality in the liturgy. The inclusion of shorter forms frees people from following a "schedule of liturgical activities" and allows them to enter into a fuller participation of ritual mystery. Ritual music (music that enhances ritual movement) is used extensively within the liturgies of the Iona Community and is extremely lyrical in approach, emphasizing metaphor and mystery over fact and dogma.[45] This is not to imply that catechesis and biblical content are not important to the WGRG. They are. It is a recognition, however, that persons who are alienated from the traditional forms of liturgy may be in search of mystery and community more than doctrine. It is also an understanding that liturgy that includes prayer, songs, ritual, stories, and symbols shapes faith more than liturgy dominated by analytical sermons or inflexible exegeses. It is a hermeneutic of participation that draws those assembled into a potentially transformative experience. According to Bradley, the Celtic legacy of "the Columban Church [held] that faith should be sung as well as spoken, expressed in poetry rather than prose and communicated through symbol, image and metaphor as much as through concept, reason and argument."[46] The WGWG maintains the essence of their Columban legacy.

Unaccompanied singing contributes to a sense of secondary orality. A cappella singing demands both a strong commitment to the process by each singer and a carefully prepared leader. Bell often notes what he considers to be the negative effect of the organ on congregational singing. "Human beings find it easier to imitate another human being than to copy a 12-string guitar, grand piano, or pipe organ. They also pick up the pitch and the rhythm of notes when they are signed in the air [chironomy] much more easily than when they are merely sung."[47] Bell prepares people unaccustomed to singing a cappella by having a brief congregational rehearsal before the beginning of the formal liturgy. "The best time to teach is before anything happens, while people are still settling down. If they learn a new song then, they will recognize it as a familiar friend when used later in the service. *Never* antagonize a

---

45. I am referring to a quality of liturgy discussed by Edward Foley in *Ritual Music: Studies in Liturgical Musicology* (Beltsville, Md.: Pastoral Press, 1995), 135-36.

46. Bradley, *Columba*, 99.

47. Bell and Maule, *Heaven Shall Not Wait*, 124.

congregation by teaching a new song the minute before it is to be used."[48] It is this approach to music making that takes advantage of a characteristic of orality noted by Ong: "Oral communication unites people into groups."[49] The act of rehearsal, singing unaccompanied in parts, following the simple chironomy of the leader, and weaving the music into a liturgical tapestry rich in metaphor, symbol, and ritual enables liturgically disenchanted and cynical individuals to find *communitas.*

Songs of the World Church

Victor Turner uses *communitas* to indicate the solidarity of a community who experiences liminality or moments "in and out of time," the blending of "lowliness and sacredness," and "homogeneity and comradeship."[50] *Communitas* is natural to a Celtic perspective that blends the sacred and secular and views the incarnation as an act of redemption for all the material world. The inclusion of materials from the world church reinforces a Christian sense of *communitas* — the sense of being in solidarity with those who struggle. Liminality may result from praying, singing, and moving to songs that symbolize the struggle of those who suffer personal abuse, cultural stereotyping, political oppression, economic deprivation, and religious persecution. Humanity does not have to be physically present in all its diversity for us to pray for it. If we are open, singing songs of the world church brings the praise and petitions of the world to us. The sounds, texts, and movements of these global gifts may be unsettling to us, disrupting the order of things as we have perceived them. As Bell notes, such worship "engages our thoughts, prayers and protestations."[51]

The WGWG has made an immeasurable wealth of global sung prayers available to the Euro–North American church through the publication of the collections *Many and Great* (1990) and *Sent by the Lord* (1991). Many of the songs are transcriptions from their countries of origin. Others have been arranged by Bell. A brief note about the origins and/or use of each song follows the score. Original languages (or transliterations in the case of Asian

---

48. Bell and Maule, *Heaven Shall Not Wait,* 124. For a more complete list of suggested teaching techniques, see "Ten Golden Rules for Enabling the Least Confident of People to Teach New Songs for the Most Cynical of Congregations," in *Heaven Shall Not Wait,* 124-35.

49. Ong, 69.

50. Victor Turner, *The Ritual Process: Structure and Anti-Structure* (Ithaca, N.Y.: Cornell Paperbacks, 1969), 96.

51. Bell and Maule, *Love + Anger,* 8.

songs) are often included along with English-language singing translations. It did not escape Bell that these two books would appear in time for the 500th anniversary of the commemoration of the "discovery" of America by Christopher Columbus. Bell noted that "For many people in Central and South America, this is not a time for joy, but a time for deep regret as that occasion calls to mind the succession of waves of colonial, religious, and financial imperialism which has beleaguered many of the countries of the region right to the present day."[52] As Scotsmen, Bell and Maule participate in the paradox of having been victims of imperialism as well as having perpetrated oppression upon others. The Scottish experience with England has often resulted in the former, while Scottish immigrants to the United States have participated in the latter.[53]

No volumes devoted entirely to world songs are planned because the WGRG now consciously sees these materials as an integrated and complementary part of their musical vocabulary. However, more recent publications include world songs as a matter of course along with folk songs from North America, the United Kingdom, and Europe and materials written by Bell. While the theme song from *Come All You People: Shorter Songs for Worship* (1994) comes from Zimbabwe, the practice of including world song among all publications began in earnest with *The Courage to Say No: Twenty-Three Songs for Lent and Easter* (1996), and continues with *Love + Anger: Songs of Lively Faith and Social Justice* (1997), which includes material from Rwanda, Pakistan, South Africa, India, and South America along with Western folk materials and original melodies. Bell and Maule feel that it is time to integrate world songs within the body of Western song as a symbol of Christian unity rather than in special global collections. A publication strategy that segregates international hymnody from Western congregational song might indicate that world song is optional for Westerners. A more extensive example of this approach is a hymnal edited by John Bell, *Common Ground: A Song Book for All the Churches* (1998). The diversity of sung resources is one of the major strengths of the liturgical life of the Iona Community and the work of the WGRG. This diversity opens the door to liminality by weaving songs from Scotland's Celtic roots, songs of fresh insight created in a communal process, and songs of the world church into the fabric of liturgy.

---

52. John L. Bell, ed., *Sent by the Lord: Songs of the World Church*, vol. 2 (Chicago: GIA Publications, [1991] 1992), 7.

53. Sowell, 68-82, discusses both the contributions of the Scots in various areas of life and the migration of Scots-Irish, sometimes referred to as the "Celtic fringe," to the southern United States and their role as oppressors of slaves in the Civil War.

The Biblical Foundation and Hermeneutic of Iona Community Liturgy

Bell describes the songs of the WGWG in three ways: they are Scottish, incarnational, and biblical. "By Scottish we mean that [our worldview] is rooted very firmly in the culture we are part of. . . . By incarnational we mean that the text speaks of a Gospel that is wedded to time, place and people. . . . By biblical we imply that while not all our materials directly quote scripture, it is the revelation of God through scripture and the breadth of human emotions offered to God in the psalms which guide our thinking."[54] Communicating the truth contained in Scripture is central to the aims of the Iona Community and the work of the WGWG. As a renewal movement within the Church of Scotland, it is consonant with these roots for the Iona Community to place Scripture at the center of liturgical life. Therefore it is a sine qua non in the creative process of the WGWG. There are many ways in which this is evident.

Celtic tradition is often noted for its trinitarian way of being. This is illustrated beautifully in an old Irish poem attributed to Columba, the incipit of which is provided here:

> The path I walk, Christ walks it.
> May the land in which I am be without sorrow.
> May the Trinity protect me wherever I stay,
> Father, Son and Holy Spirit.[55]

Another poem attributed to Columba begins,

> The High Creator, Ancient of Days and Unbegotten
> was without origin of beginning and without end;
> He is and shall be to infinite ages of ages
> with Whom is Christ the only begotten and the Holy Spirit,
> coeternal in the everlasting glory of the Godhead.
> We set forth not three gods,
> but we say there is One God,
> saving our faith in three most glorious persons.[56]

The three larger collections mentioned earlier, *Heaven Shall Not Wait, Enemy of Apathy,* and *Love from Below,* find their overarching shape in the structure of the Trinity. The first volume contains "Songs of Creation, the Incarnation,

54. Bell, "Flight," 18.

55. Oliver Davies and Fiona Bowie, *Celtic Christian Spirituality: An Anthology of Medieval and Modern Sources* (London: SPCK, 1995), 38.

56. Quoted in Bradley, *Columba,* 57, from *The Irish Liber Hymnorum,* ed. J. H. Bernard and R. Atkinson, vol. 2 (London: Henry Bradshaw Society, 1898), 150.

and the Life of Jesus;" the second "Songs of the Passion and Resurrection of Jesus, and the Coming of the Holy Spirit." These two volumes focus on a "retelling of the events of the gospels," while the third volume includes "songs which deal more with the life of Christ's disciples" and "the celebration of our experience of faith."[57]

The WGWG brings the biblical narrative into its songs in a variety of ways. One common approach is through the style of a ballad that draws the singer into the story:

> A pregnant girl none will ignore:
> Her husband knocks a guest-house door.
>   Who is the girl?
>   Why knock the door?
> Thus starts a tale of which there's more.[58]

© 1989 GIA Publications, Inc. Used by permission.

Sometimes the use of the first-person perspective, such as in "The Beggar," draws the singer into the song, though not without a certain amount of irony and, perhaps, discomfort:

> I sit outside the rich world's gate,
> I rake the rich world's dross
> And marvel that my poverty
> Is what you call my cross.
>
> I am the beggar called your Lord,
> The squatter called your King;
> I am the Saviour of the world,
> A torn and tattered thing.
>
> Chorus: O who has ears to hear my Cry?
>   And who has eyes to see?
>   And who will lift my heavy load?
>   And who will set me free?[59]

© 1989 GIA Publications, Inc. Used by permission.

The Celtic sense of the presence of Christ in all of life's activities and encounters is a theme that runs throughout many songs. "We Met You, God" has

57. Bell and Maule, *Love from Below*, 6.
58. "The Carol of the Nativity," stanza 1, in Bell and Maule, *Heaven Shall Not Wait*, 46.
59. "The Beggar," stanzas 1 and 5, and the refrain, in Bell and Maule, *Love from Below*, 61.

seven stanzas, one for each day of the week.[60] It is shaped by the creation narrative of Genesis 1, but each stanza ends with a different but distinctly christological quote: "I am the way," "I am the truth," "I am the life," "I've chosen you," "Come, follow me," "You are my friend," etc. "Today I Awake" draws directly from Celtic trinitarian prayer, the four successive stanzas beginning:

> Today I awake
> And God is before me. . . .
> Today I arise
> And Christ is beside me. . . .
> Today I affirm
> The Spirit within me. . . .
> Today I enjoy
> The Trinity round me. . . .[61]

When encountering the life of Christ, the WGWG is not content to allow us the comfort of viewing the incarnation solely as a historical event. They focus on the parts of Christ's life particularly ignored by the church. Maule notes that the church "deals with [Christ's] birth and his death (along with his invisible, inaccessible, gloriously, triumphant cosmicness) at great length. We're more interested in the (more offensive, contended) three years of [Christ's] ministry in everyday, culturally conditioned, politically occupied Israel."[62] Some songs place us in the middle of the drama as a character, such as "Easter Evening," based on one postresurrection encounter with Christ, sung to the beautiful Scottish tune SILKIE:

> As we walked home at close of day,
> A stranger joined us on the way.
> He heard us speak of one who'd gone
> And when we stopped, he carried on.
>
> "Why wander further without light?
> Please stay with us this troubled night.
> We've shared the truth of how we feel
> And now would like to share a meal."[63]

© 1988 GIA Publications, Inc. Used by permission.

---

60. "We Met You, God," in Bell and Maule, *Heaven Shall Not Wait*, 12-13.
61. "Today I Awake," in Bell and Maule, *Love from Below*, 13.
62. Correspondence with Graham Maule, March 10, 1999.
63. "Easter Evening," stanzas 1 and 2, in Bell and Maule, *Enemy of Apathy*, 68-69.

Setting the Psalms calls for flexibility of musical style and perspective depending on the emotional context of the psalm. Some are contemporary paraphrases such as "Happy Is the One," based on Psalm 1:

> Happy is the one
> who does not take bad advice for a guide,
> nor walks the path on which sinners have trod,
> nor sits where the cynics mock.[64]

© 1993 GIA Publications, Inc. Used by permission.

Another example is a paraphrase of Psalm 130, employing the classic Psalter tune SOUTHWELL, commonly associated with the text from the Greek by Synesius of Cyrene, "Lord Jesus, think on me." This direct language is much more traditional than many texts by the WGWG, even reminiscent of the English-language Psalters of earlier centuries:

> Out of the direst depths
> I make my deepest plea.
> O graciously bow down your ear
> and listen, Lord, for me.
>
> If you kept note of sins,
> before you who could stand?
> But since forgiveness is your right,
> our reverence your command.[65]

© 1993 GIA Publications, Inc. Used by permission.

Perhaps it is the incarnation, drawn from biblical accounts and steeped in Celtic spirituality, that is most central to the work of the WGWG. Bell responds to the tendency to romanticize the birth of Christ in a characteristically candid commentary:

> To say that there is nothing wrong with traditional Christmas carols is to be less than discerning. Some — perhaps the majority — are good. But there are some which tell patent lies about the Nativity or about Jesus himself.
>
> There is no biblical evidence to support the theory that "snow had fallen,

64. "Happy Is the One," stanza 1, in John L. Bell, *Psalms of Patience, Protest, and Praise* (Chicago: GIA Publications, 1993), 4.
65. Bell, "Out of the direst depths," *Psalms*, stanzas 1 and 2, pp. 48-49.

snow on snow," but there is substantial evidence to suggest that Jesus did not "honor and obey" throughout all his wondrous childhood. What about him running away from his family when returning from Jerusalem?

There is also the temptation to depict the characters in the Nativity story as less than full-blooded. Mary tends to be portrayed as anemic, docile, and constantly doting, not the kind of woman who could cope with a pile of dirty nappies. Joseph is sometimes depicted as spineless, and the shepherds and wise men, perhaps too closely modeled on their Sunday-school Nativity play stereotypes, lack either humor or surprise.[66]

The allusions above to Christina Rossetti's interpretation of the weather at the time of Christ's birth in her well-known poem, "In the Bleak Mid-Winter," and Cecil Frances Alexander's viewpoint on Jesus' childhood in her equally venerable hymn, "Once in Royal David's City," illustrate nineteenth-century notions of the incarnation — a perspective that Bell considers "the verbal equivalent of Victorian stained glass."[67] Neither does Bell mince words concerning the damage he feels that Victorian-era hymnody has done to the Christian faith: "The Victorians dumped on us a legacy of forced piety, sentimentalism and deceptive images of God in their hymns. Their tunes, with mushy harmonies or pedantic melodies, were little better."[68] One might be tempted to dismiss Bell's comments as a personal "soapbox" or diatribe based on individual taste. I believe, however, that the hymnody of the Victorian era represents for Bell and Maule a time in British society when classism elevated a few at the expense of many, and the arrogance of the waning British Empire affected the Anglican Church at its core. This sentiment manifests itself in a hymnody that lacks realism not only about the radical nature of the incarnation, but also about the poor and oppressed whose "estate" in life had been "ordered" by God, according to Cecil Frances Alexander in her hymn "All Things Bright and Beautiful."[69]

---

66. John L. Bell, *Innkeepers and Light Sleepers: Seventeen New Songs for Christmas* (Chicago: GIA Publications, 1992), 7.

67. Bell, *Innkeepers and Light Sleepers*, 7.

68. Quoted in Bradley, *Abide with Me*, 245.

69. The entire infamous stanza reads,

> The rich man in his castle,
> The poor man at his gate,
> God made them, high or lowly,
> And ordered their estate.

Lionel Adey, *Hymns and the Christian "Myth"* (Vancouver: University of British Columbia Press, 1986), referring to this stanza, notes, "Idolatry comes in when a system that reflects the

According to the dogma of nineteenth-century classism, the best one might hope for was an attitude of noblesse oblige if one came from the lower classes.

It is for this reason that the theology of the incarnation and the narrative of the life of Christ are so central to the hymns of the WGWG. Compare the nativity scene set by Rossetti and Alexander to "Justice in the Womb" by the WGWG:

Not the foremost of her gender,
Not the finest of her race;
Favored now in reputation,
Flound'ring then in deep disgrace.

Refrain: Though for her no rights or room,
There is promise in the woman:
There is justice in the womb.

Cowed and occupied her country,
Dented was her people's pride:
Such a girl, in such a nation,
Could have been a soldier's bride.

Forced to make a tiresome journey,
Flanked by her redundant groom;
All the brightness in her body
Longs to end the godless gloom.

All the power of heaven contracted,
Gathers in this mother's pain:
God, confounding expectations,
Sows her seed against the grain.[70]

© 1992 GIA Publications, Inc. Used by permission.

One discovers in this text and others a rare combination of poetic realism and awe-filled mystery. The result is disturbing, discomforting, and disquieting. For the WGWG will not allow you to relegate the incarnation to a historical

---

economic and power structure of a given time and place is treated as divinely ordained and immutable. For long periods before the scientific and industrial revolutions, the divine will and the social structure were easily confounded" (12).

70. "Justice in the Womb," in Bell, *Innkeepers and Light Sleepers,* 20-21.

observance or romantic recollection. Based on Bell's experience with the empty sanctuaries and largely ineffective traditional religious structures of his homeland, he understands that the cynics who would rarely or never enter these places — especially some young people, working-class folk, students, poor — are looking for authenticity. The songs and liturgy of the WGWG are not designed to prompt a sentimental moment of togetherness or a sensational surge of stimulation. The point is not to "feel good" but to feel again — feel a sense of the holy and an experience of community that potentially awakens in the most recalcitrant skeptic an awareness of the incarnation and how this mystery, in the richest sense of Celtic spirituality, pervades all of our existence.

Conclusion

After this analysis, with what are we left? We are left with more than collections of music, potential anthems, and a few liturgical innovations. I suggest that we are left with an approach for liturgical renewal that is needed among mainline churches on both sides of the Atlantic.[71] I offer the following as a summary of this renewal movement:

- Restore singing to the people.
- Allow singing to build and sustain the worshiping community by using as little accompaniment as possible.

71. Concerning the appearance of songs from the Iona Community in recent hymnals in the United States and Canada, the impact of these hymns did not take hold until the middle of the 1990s. The following hymnals list hymns by Bell and/or the Iona Community: *Chalice Hymnal* (1995), 6 hymns; *The New Century Hymnal* (1995), 6 hymns; *The Covenant Hymnal: A Worshipbook* (1996), 3 hymns; *Voices United* (1996), 8 hymns; *The Book of Praise* (1998), 21 hymns. This does not include all the world songs that were made available through Iona collections. Robert Batastini, an editor for GIA who publishes Iona Community materials in the United States, comments on their influence in America: "I'm not sure I can say much with certainty about the use of Iona material in the parishes. I sense that the world music is getting a bit more play than John [Bell]'s original material. For certain, I can tell you that John Bell as a speaker and clinician is in ever growing demand in the States, and it crosses all sorts of denominational lines. People like what he does and what he has to say. He addresses sophisticated audiences (clergy, music professionals, etc.) as well as ordinary folks, and is received equally well across the spectrum." Personal correspondence with the author, February 16, 1999. For comments on the Iona Community's materials in one recent hymnal, see C. Michael Hawn, "Ecumenical and Global Congregational Song in the Late Twentieth Century," in *The New Century Hymnal Companion*, ed. Kristen L. Forman (Cleveland: Pilgrim Press, 1998), 204-5.

- Explore the folk song resources of your region and acquaint yourself with them. These contain the essence of your culture.
- Explore the songs of the world church. These are the prayers of others, and by singing them we sing in solidarity with all of God's people.
- Shape the flow of the liturgy in the manner of your heritage, not only its recent manifestations. Maule reminds us that "tradition is consonant with adaptive change and extends further than the earliest memories (or prejudices) of the oldest living member."[72] One does not have to re-invent the shape of the liturgy, just breathe new life into old bones.
- Be knowledgeable about your spiritual heritage, including hymns. For "if we are not familiar with the great hymns which have shaped Christian life and faith through centuries, we have little by which to judge modern writing."[73]
- Look at biblical content in light of contemporary need. Don't settle for conventional responses to existential dilemmas. Give those assembled an opportunity to tell you what they think the Scripture is saying.
- Balance prophetic insight with liturgical comfort. The security and comfort of liturgy must be authenticated by an awareness of those who experience insecurity, discomfort, and injustice in its many manifestations — political oppression, racial discrimination, economic deprivation, gender exclusion, class struggles, etc.
- Preparing liturgy needs to be a community experience, not a solitary act by the minister or musician at the computer.
- Enliven the liturgy with metaphor — symbols, rituals, movement, poetry, drama, song, narrative — minimizing the one-way medium of the sermon and spoken word.

Finally, be open to the spirit of the wild goose in liturgy which may alight at any time in unexpected and disturbing ways. Norman Shanks, the current leader of the Iona Community, noted that a North American told him that the wild goose might be an effective Celtic symbol in Scotland, but that it would not work in the USA because there the "wild goose is a pest and people want to shoot it." Later Shanks thought, "I realized that if ever there was a good reason for the wild goose being a symbol of the Holy Spirit it was because it is a pest and people want to shoot it!"[74]

Sydney Carter captured the spirit of the wild goose in his hymn "Bird of

72. Correspondence with Maule, March 10, 1999.
73. Introduction, in Bell and Maule, *Heaven Shall Not Wait*, 7.
74. Ferguson, 184.

Heaven." It is quoted in the preface to Ferguson's history of the Iona Community, *Chasing the Wild Goose:*

> Catch the bird of heaven,
> Lock him in a cage of gold;
> Look again tomorrow,
> And he will be gone.
>
> *Ah! the bird of heaven!*
> *Follow where the bird has gone;*
> *Ah! the bird of heaven!*
> *Keep on travelling on.*
>
> Lock him in religion,
> Gold and frankincense and myrrh
> Carry to his prison,
> But he will be gone.
>
> Bell and book and candle
> Cannot hold him any more,
> For the bird is flying
> As he did before.[75]

75. Sydney Carter, *Green Print for Song* (London: Stainer & Bell, [1969] 1974), 24-25. Stanzas 1, 2, 4, and refrain.

CHAPTER 7

Form and Ritual

Sequential and Cyclic Musical Structures and Their Use in Liturgy

Throughout this book the reader is introduced to a variety of musical forms from world song. While musical styles may vary from culture to culture, one may find continuity among world musics in the underlying structures. The purpose of this chapter is to distinguish between the role of congregational musical styles and musical structures within liturgy. Understanding the relationship between musical structure and the rites and rituals of faith communities may assist musical presiders in understanding their task more thoroughly. It is essential for leaders of global music to understand not only the style of the music but also how the specific structure of the music undergirds the successful presentation of a given selection.

Both style and structure have their role in enabling congregational participation in worship. It has been my experience, however, that those who prepare worship make practical decisions about the choice of congregational music in liturgy primarily on the basis of accessibility of musical style and appropriateness of text. While these are important criteria, the role of a congregational song's musical structure and how it may inform liturgy is less likely to be taken into consideration. Musical form is a significant factor in determining the effectiveness of the congregation's involvement in the ritual. As a

An earlier version of this chapter appeared in article form as "Form and Ritual: A Comparison between Sequential and Cyclic Musical Structures and Their Use in Liturgy," in *Anál Dé: The Breath of God. Music, Ritual, and Spirituality,* ed. Helen Phelan (Dublin: Veritas Publications, 2001), 37-54.

way of exploring the role of musical structures in shaping ritual behavior, I will focus on the fundamental characteristics and ritual uses of sequential and cyclic musical structures with reference to hybrid forms derived from these.

Characteristics of Sequential Musical Structures

As is the case with many Protestants, I was nurtured in worship through the singing of hymns. By hymns I am referring to metered poetry set in stanzas. The sequential structure of classic Western hymnody is usually evident in the development of a theological theme over several stanzas. A basic theological concept or scriptural pericope usually comes to light in stanza one. Stanza two develops this theme or continues the scriptural paraphrase, and so on, until the hymn climaxes in a concluding stanza that draws all the points together into a whole. A doxological formula, an eschatological reference, a cosmic allusion, a petition, or a strong hermeneutical application may strengthen the climax of a hymn. A hymn tune sustains the sequential progression of the poetry by being recycled for each stanza. Skillful organists provide a musical interpretation of the text by careful phrasing and varied articulations of the melody and by choosing appropriate registration and dynamic levels for each stanza according to the text. An exceptional organist may modify the harmonies discreetly from stanza to stanza in hope of furnishing the text with a more interesting musical foundation.

Organists, hoping to realize both a poetic and a musical climax, may employ a variety of musical strategies, especially on the final stanza. These may include an increased fullness in organ registration, the use of an alternate harmonization (implying that the congregation should sing in unison), or a change in tonal center, usually ascending through a modulation following the penultimate stanza to a key a semitone or tone higher than the previous stanzas.

Given the sequential nature of the text, its teleological character is inherent to its performance: a classic Western hymn text is going somewhere. One must note where the text begins and follow carefully the progression of thought through to its conclusion, a process that may take place in as few as two or three stanzas or as many as seven, eight, or more in some of the classic ballad hymns. A strophic musical structure, repeating in its entirety with each stanza, masks the inherently sequential nature of the text.

How does the singer know when the text has reached a climax? While an organist may provide specific external cues for recognizing the apex of the poem, literary clues internal to the text also may assist the careful singer. In addition to following the content of the text carefully, the singer can see the end of the hymn coming on the printed page, e.g., only two stanzas to go. Since it is a literary structure, the singer should encounter an ultimate thought beyond which any further material would be anticlimactic. For example, consider the final stanza of Isaac Watts's famous hymn, "When I Survey the Wondrous Cross":

> Were the whole Realm of Nature mine,
> That were a Present far too small;
> Love so amazing, so divine,
> Demands my Soul, my Life, my All.[1]

In previous stanzas Watts led the singer through the agony of the crucifixion complete with an invitation to visualize Christ, from top to bottom, on the cross. In the final stanza the singer shifts away from a posture at the foot of the cross to a cosmic perspective focusing on the meaning of Christ's sacrifice. There is nothing more that can be said. The hymn is complete.[2]

Charles Wesley often used an eschatological reference at the culmination of a text.[3] Such is the case in his well-known "Love Divine, All Loves Excelling":

> Finish then thy new creation,
>   Pure and spotless let us be;
> Let us see thy great salvation
>   Perfectly restored in thee;
> Changed from glory into glory,
>   Till in heaven we take our place,
> Till we cast our crowns before thee,
>   Lost in wonder, love and praise.[4]

---

1. Selma L. Bishop, *Isaac Watts: Hymns and Spiritual Songs, 1707-1748* (London: Faith Press, 1962), 353.

2. A stanza not usually included in modern hymnals, "His dying Crimson like a robe . . . ," adds to the device of hypotyposis employed by Watts. Watts placed it as the penultimate stanza, however, not as the final one.

3. The eschatological character of Charles Wesley texts has recently been highlighted in Teresa Berger, *Theology in Hymns?* trans. Timothy E. Kimbrough (Nashville: Kingswood Books, [1989] 1995), 137ff.

4. "A Collection of Hymns for the Use of the People Called Methodists," in *The Works of John Wesley,* ed. Franz Hildebrandt and Oliver Beckerlegge, vol. 7 (Nashville: Abingdon, 1983), 547.

If one is truly "lost in wonder, love and praise" in heaven, then there are no further stanzas to sing.

A reference to the triune God is a classic way to bring a hymn to its conclusion. This may be seen as an extension of the practice of Christianizing the psalms by adding a Gloria Patri at the conclusion of the psalm. Edward Plumptre applies this formula to the concluding stanza of his processional hymn "Rejoice, Ye Pure in Heart":

> Then on, ye pure in heart!
>> Rejoice, give thanks, and sing;
> Your festal banner wave on high.
>> The Cross of Christ your King.
> Praise him who reigns on high,
>> The Lord, whom we adore,
> The Father, Son, and Holy Ghost,
>> One God for evermore.[5]

Over the centuries a doxological formula expressing the triune God has become a resting place for prayer, sung or spoken.

The skilled poet employs many other literary techniques to achieve a sense of climax and conclusion in strophic hymnody. As there are too many possibilities to list here, one final approach must suffice. In addition to those given above, a way of concluding a sequentially structured hymn text is to end with a petition. Concluding petitions, found throughout the history of Christian song, call to mind the inherent relationship between singing and praying. This is a relationship that is organically connected to the roots of the Judeo-Christian heritage, though not, of course, limited to Christian tradition.[6]

---

5. In *Hymns Ancient and Modern Revised* (London: Hymns Ancient and Modern, Ltd., 1972), 875.

6. The Jewish heritage of prayer stresses the unity of prayer and song. Music in the early synagogue functioned in three ways, according to Eliyahu Schleifer: "psalmody, cantillation of Scripture, and the liturgical chant in which the statutory prayers were recited by a local worship leader." See Eliyahu Schleifer, "From Bible to Hasidism," in *Sacred Sound and Social Change: Liturgical Music in Jewish and Christian Experience,* ed. Lawrence A. Hoffman and Janet R. Walton (Notre Dame, Ind.: University of Notre Dame Press, 1992), 24. Although Christianity has its musical roots in this Jewish ethos, evidence suggests that early Christians developed new songs and forms for their embryonic worship. Unlike much of our worship today, Edward Foley suggests, their worship maintained "no sharp distinction between the sung and the spoken, no clear division between what we might call the musical and the non-musical, nor any denial of the fundamental lyricism of Christian worship." See Edward Foley, *Foundations of Christian Music: The Music of Pre-Constantinian Christianity* (Washington, D.C.: Pastoral Press, 1992), 84. Liturgical scholar Paul Bradshaw states that "It is often . . . difficult to determine when the New

Latin verse often ends with a doxological confession. But consider briefly the classic petitions found at the close of many Latin poems. These examples, taken from the sequences approved during the Council of Trent, have served as models for hymnic petitions for many centuries since their conception.

In the final stanza of the "Veni sancte Spiritus" (attributed to Stephen Langton, d. 1228), sometimes called the golden sequence, the imperative form of the Latin verb *dare* (to give or grant) begins four of the final six lines. The metrical translation by John Mason Neale (1852), though indicating three petitions (see italics), obscures the incessant power of the Latin imperative *da*.

Da tuis fidelibus	*Fill* thy faithful, who confide
in te confidentibus	in thy power to guard and guide
sacrum sepentarium;	with thy sevenfold mystery:
da virtutis meritum;	here thy grace and virtue *send;*
da salutis exitum,	*grant* salvation to the end,
da perenne gaudium.	and in heaven felicity.[7]

The "Dies Irae" (attributed to Thomas of Celano, fl. 1215) concludes with an implied Kyrie Eleison and the familiar *dona eis requiem*. The metrical translation is by W. J. Irons (1848) as found in the *English Hymnal* (1906):

Lacrymosa dies illa,	Ah! that day of tears and mourning!
quae resurget ex favilla	from the dust of earth returning
iudicandum homo reus,	man for judgement must prepare him;
huis ergo *parce* deus.	*spare*, O God, in mercy *spare* him!
Pie Jesu Domine,	Lord, all-pitying, Jesu blest,
dona eis requiem.	*grant* them thine eternal rest.[8]

In both cases the petitions are of such gravity that the hymn must end and wait in eschatological hope for a response.

Sequential structures are inherently literary in form. Unless they have a

---

Testament authors are citing topical prayer-forms with which they are familiar and when they are not, *or even to separate hymns from prayers, since both may employ a similar construction."* See Paul Bradshaw, *The Search for the Origins of Christian Worship* (New York: Oxford University Press, 1992), 43, italics mine.

7. From Erik Routley, *A Panorama of Christian Hymnody* (Collegeville, Minn.: Liturgical Press, 1979), 65.

8. Routley, 65. Routley notes that the English versification is at best a noble attempt that allows the singer the opportunity to sing the gist of the text with the original melody. His literal translation is as follows: "Oh, what a day of tears and lamentation, when man, waiting for judgment, rises from earth's ashes: spare him in that day! Kind Lord Jesus, give them rest!" (66).

refrain or are sung repeatedly so that they are committed to memory, these forms depend on the eye for participation. Poetic devices in the Euro–North American cultural context, having evolved over the centuries from Greek and Latin poetry, are often dependent upon visual media.[9] This literary quality has many benefits for ritual. Songs suitable for a given liturgical tradition may be gathered into a single collection. Collections may be organized around the performance of the liturgy and specific rites that constitute a valid enactment of the rituals central to that liturgy. Many collections may have a domestic as well as a corporate life, deepening the personal piety of the participant and enabling a more complete corporate involvement.[10] While the Roman Catholic tradition also had service books that supported its rites such as the *Liber Usualis* and the Sacramentary, the complexity of these books limited their use only to highly trained and literate professional musicians and clergy.[11] The

9. For a brief reference tool of poetic devices, see Austin C. Lovelance, *The Anatomy of Hymnody* (Chicago: GIA Publications, 1965), 91-102. For a much more extensive understanding of the literate hymn tradition, see J. R. Watson, *The English Hymn: A Critical and Historical Study* (Oxford: Clarendon, 1997).

10. Among Protestants, inexpensive collections by eighteenth-century hymn writers like Isaac Watts and Charles and John Wesley set the trend in this regard. The Wesleys were particularly concerned that their collections were affordable to the poor. Since these collections were individually owned, they were used at the Society meetings in corporate contexts and in domestic settings as well. These brief collections were theologically or seasonally organized. See the following facsimile reprints by the Charles Wesley Society: *Hymns on the Lord's Supper* (Bristol, 1745); *Hymns for Our Lord's Resurrection* (London, 1746); *Hymns for Ascension-Day and Hymns for Whitsunday* (Bristol, 1746); *Hymns for the Nativity of Our Lord* (London, 1745). *The Book of Common Prayer* serves a dual domestic/corporate use for many Anglicans as well. Many faithful Anglicans bring their own copy to worship and refer only minimally to it because of the intimate familiarity with the book. In the Reformed tradition, John D. Witvliet notes the roles of the Genevan Psalter in shaping both domestic and corporate spirituality. See "The Spirituality of the Psalter: Metrical Psalms in Liturgy and Life in Calvin's Geneva," *Calvin Theological Journal* 32, no. 2 (November 1997): 273-97, for a thorough explanation of the dynamic of the Genevan Psalter between home and church.

11. Jack Goody points out in *The Power of Written Tradition* (Washington, D.C.: Smithsonian Institution Press, 2000) that written works such as these serve several purposes. They provide the possibility of canonization of a body of material, something impossible in oral cultures where there "is no evidence of a fixed utterance existing over long periods of time. . . . In other words, canonization is virtually impossible" (126). While this allows written works, especially of a religious nature, to "establish relatively stable internal norms over large areas" (44), written works can also inhibit diversity of opinion and possess a "hegemonic force" that promotes a dominant perspective. Of course, other writings can in time destabilize such forces for "countercultural, revolutionary, or critical purposes" (130). The fact that the *Liber Usualis* was controlled by an educated male clergy within a largely illiterate social context made destabilization much less likely.

people did not sing from them, so they had no domestic use. Though the Book of Hours was available for private devotions, it was not a formal part of the Mass.[12] Since Vatican II an array of hymnals have become one option for facilitating the rituals of Catholic liturgy.[13]

Sequential structures use many words. Although recent hymn writers vary from classic metrical patterns somewhat, they continue to organize the many words into stanzas structured by a metrical construction and a rhyme scheme. Though guided by the eye on the page, meter and rhyme provide sonorous organizational patterns that aid memory and allow for more cohesive corporate participation. While mnemonic devices are helpful, sequential written forms lend themselves to analysis and a copious use of words.[14] Because of the visual dimension, the singer is clearly aware of the beginning and may anticipate the conclusion of the hymn by seeing how many stanzas remain. The written text and musical form combine to energize the singer toward the culmination of the hymn. In this sense it is a relatively closed structure — more or less predictable in length and quality of experience — not likely open to significant textual or musical variation or improvisation. Furthermore, both the music and the text, as contained on the page, may be kept and reread for further reflection or analysis following the singing of the hymn.

Characteristics of Cyclic Musical Structures

It was during my first visit to the Taizé Community in southeastern France that I became aware of the power of cyclic forms.[15] The music that facilitated

12. For more detailed information on pre–Vatican II rites and music, see John Harper, *The Forms and Orders of Western Liturgy from the Tenth to the Eighteenth Century* (Oxford: Clarendon, 1991).

13. Other options include seasonal missalettes that usually remain at the church and are not used at home. Recent Catholic hymnals in the United States range from *Worship*, 3rd ed. (GIA, 1986) and *Gather* (GIA, 1988) for traditional Anglo congregations to *Lead Me Guide Me* (GIA, 1987) for African American congregations and *Flor y Canto* (Oregon Catholic Press, 1989) for Spanish-speaking congregations. *Hymnal for the Hours* (GIA, 1989) is for use with daily offices, and *By Flowing Waters* (Liturgical Press, 1999) uses only plainsong style for the liturgy. *Ritual Song* (GIA, 1996) combines aspects of several of the English-language hymnals. This sampling, while not complete, explores the various genres of Roman Catholic hymnals available in the United States.

14. I am referring here to work done by Walter J. Ong in *Orality and Literacy: The Technologizing of the Word* (New York: Routledge, [1982] 1988), 38ff.

15. There are many sources that speak of Taizé prayer. For a concise introduction, see

the corporate prayer used a very different structure than the hymns of my tradition. Brief texts were sustained by concise musical statements — ostinato, canon, litany, refrain, or response. At first the repetitions seemed like sheer redundancy, but after a time I sensed that repetition was not an accurate description of this musical experience. While on the surface those gathered for corporate prayer might seem to be repeating the same musical mantra over and over again, I discerned that theme and variation was a more apt description of the musical and liturgical experience. A brief song, usually eight to twelve measures in length, consisted of a short theme that shaped one cycle. Each time the theme returned there were variations: a worshiper might become gradually aware of a deeper centering or relaxation of the body after several cycles; a cantor might sing various scriptural or devotional texts above the primary theme on successive cycles; an instrument might provide a variation on the theme; the singer/pray-er might focus on an icon, or hum or sing harmony or become aware of another's harmony. Rather than redundancy, the experience was replete with variation as the main theme or cycle returned again and again.

Teaching in Africa broadened my experience with this form of theme and variation. Once again I participated in shorter musical forms with a brief text. In this case the musical styles differed radically from the generally meditative sung prayers of Taizé. Though repetition is present, there are also significant modifications: the leader(s) varies the text in a call-response manner; percussion instruments provide subtle variations; dancers interact with the percussion and singing; the intensity seems to gather with each recurrence of the theme. As mentioned in chapter 4, it was not until I spent some time with ethnomusicologist Andrew Tracey in South Africa that I began to understand the broader implications of what he calls cyclic musical structures.[16]

Cyclic musical structures embrace a variety of musical styles.[17] Regardless of style, the effective presentation of a cyclic structure or the performance of a ritual in liturgy depends upon establishing a clear distinction between what Ronald Grimes calls boredom and monotony. "Liturgy as a form of

Brother Jean Marie, "Prayer and Song in Taizé: Opening the Doors to an Inner Life," *Ecumenism* 31, no. 124 (December 1996): 16-18. A visit to the Taizé website, http://www.taize.fr/en/en_index.htm, also provides additional background.

16. Tracey discusses the nature of cyclic musical structure in "Transcribing African Music in Pulse Notation," a monograph published by the International Library of African Music, Rhodes University, Grahamstown, South Africa, 1997.

17. For example, the praise and worship phenomenon in the United States, highly influenced by charismatic worship practices, makes extensive use of cyclic structures or variants thereof.

work does not surprise, though it may keep us open to a serendipitous moment by its very monotony. . . . Liturgy is a full emptiness, a monotony without boredom, a reverent waiting without expectation."[18] Tom F. Driver provides further perspective in his discussion of "ritual boredom" in which rituals "have lost touch with the actualities of people's lives and are thus simply arcane; or else the people have lost the ability to apprehend their very need of ritual, do not see what rituals are good for, and thus do not find them even potentially valuable."[19] While popular usage equates "boredom" with "monotony," in this context a monotonous activity, though repetitive, establishes the safe environment in which a ritual may take place or be performed. By virtue of its repetitive, monotonous character, a ritual may enable the individual to move freely, both cognitively and kinesthetically, within the rule of this safe environment, even to improvise. Monotony has a character of what Driver calls "ritual performance." He indicates that all ritual performances "require limits. . . . This delineation of what to do and not to do is rooted in ritualization's being, . . . a process of channeling and marking, of making pathways for behavior. In order to achieve definite form, ritualization encourages certain acts, *reinforcing them with repetition and slight variation,* while ruling others out. In short, ritual performance requires (and makes) rules of the game, *whether these be known from previous usage or come to be elaborated on the spot.*"[20] Ritual boredom is enervating, causing lack of interest and participation, while monotony facilitates freedom and safe space, i.e., ritual performance. Cyclic structures offer a repetitive ground over which numerous variations may take place. Without these variations the repetition is subject to boredom. Skillfully performed musical variations provide enough difference to avoid boredom, but not so much difference to disturb the benefits of monotony.

Other characteristics of cyclic musical structure include this form's essentially oral/aural nature and the effects that this has on kinesthetic response. Books are not necessary for the performance of cyclic structures in the same way that they facilitate sequential musical forms. In fact, books may impede the embodiment of cyclic song. Songs either may be learned orally or, in the case of Taizé chants, may be acquired initially from a score, which is set aside once the short cycle has been internalized. In the case of African music, movement is essential to the performance of the song. Meditative cyclic

---

18. Ronald Grimes, *Beginnings in Ritual Studies* (Lanham, Md.: University Press of America, 1982), 44.

19. Tom F. Driver, *The Magic of Ritual* (New York: HarperCollins, 1991), 7.

20. Driver, 100, italics mine.

structures such as Taizé chants also have a kinesthetic dimension as the singer assumes more relaxed postures that encourage centering. Closing one's eyes or focusing on an icon is a traditional way of praying in this manner; holding a book, however, may inhibit the worshiper's ability to achieve a centered state of being. Regardless of mood, cyclic structures encourage a physical response, either toward the ecstatic or toward the meditative, and the use of books ultimately hampers the successful performance of these songs.[21]

In addition to our discussion of "Orality and Community" in chapter 2, using Walter Ong as a source for analyzing Pablo Sosa's compositional approach, Jack Goody also offers insights in his more recent study, *The Power of Written Tradition.* Learning through oral means is more intergenerational:

> Oral learning entails a greater amount of showing, of participation. Hence the world of childhood is less segregated from that of adults. Children sit or play around when discussions and performances are taking place, absorbing at least the general atmosphere of these activities and occasionally, if they listen attentively, some of their content as well. Much more learning depends upon the voice, upon face-to-face interaction. Whereas in literate cultures an individual can go off by himself with a book, in oral cultures a partner is needed as narrator or instructor.[22]

The ramifications of this insight for liturgy are significant. Liturgies that are word-centered and literate-based may tend to segregate communities by age and, in the case of visual impairment, disability. If story, narrative, movement, and visual means of stimulation, e.g., symbols, banners, icons, etc., are absent, large portions of a community may be alienated from full participation. Cyclic musical structures offer some relief from extremely literate liturgies at this point as they allow for easier participation in the liturgy and a minimum use of the written word, if at all.

Musical anthropologist John Blacking brings together our discussion of cyclic structure and the value of monotony in ritual. He suggests that "by releasing the brain from the task of immediate attention to environmental stimuli, [music] stimulates creative thinking by allowing the 'memory sur-

---

21. The charismatic-influenced songs of the contemporary praise and worship style often project the text onto an overhead screen, freeing the hands to clap or the body to sway. In practice, even this projection becomes unnecessary as the cycles repeat and the song is internalized. The oral (versus literate) nature of these songs is further evident in that they are often learned by means of CDs or cassette tapes rather than through musical scores. Compact discs have become the electronic prayer books for Pentecostal and charismatic groups.

22. Goody, 24.

face' of the brain to deal with information for its own sake."[23] Furthermore, "music itself may generate experiences and thoughts that transcend the extra-musical features of the situation."[24] It is perhaps at this point that the mantralike ostinati of the Taizé Community place the singer in a state that allows "creative thinking" or, in this case, prayer to emerge. Through the unity of prayer and song, cyclic structures free the participant from the teleological imperative that dominates much of the Western perspective and engages the worshiper in a more timeless experience that transcends the tedium of the situation. The introduction to the United States edition of Taizé music states that the songs "express a basic reality of faith that can quickly be grasped by the intellect, and that gradually penetrates the heart and the whole being."[25] I believe that Ong, Goody, Grimes, Driver, Blacking, and the Taizé prayer are tied together by a single thread. Music with a cyclic structure most often draws upon orality more than literacy, and a sense of monotony, ritual performance, creative thinking, and centered prayer.

Figure 7.1 (on p. 235) attempts to summarize a comparison between the basic characteristics of sequential and cyclic musical structures. The refrain form, a hybrid musical form combining sequential strophic stanzas with a recurring cycle, comes in many variations. Together this spectrum of congregational song forms encompasses the diversity of musical structures that have been encountered in this book. All have important roles in Western worship. I propose that sequential structures are primarily content-oriented while cyclic structures are central in forging community.

Musical Structures and Ritual

At the heart of this proposal is the need for worship planners not only to choose appropriate musical styles and textual themes, but to find the most appropriate musical structure that supports particular rites and rituals in a given faith community. Consider for a moment a spectrum of congregational musical forms for use with ritual. At one end is a sequential structure that makes primary use of literate traditions with a focus on textual content. At the opposite end is a cyclic structure that is inherently oral/aural (though text and/or music may be written down at times) and focuses on the shaping of

---

23. *Music, Culture, and Experience: Selected Papers of John Blacking*, ed. Reginald Byron (Chicago: University of Chicago Press, 1995), 152.

24. *Music, Culture, and Experience: Selected Papers of John Blacking*, 153.

25. *Songs and Prayers from Taizé* (Chicago: GIA Publications, 1991), 29.

Figure 7.1. Spectrum of Congregational Song Structures: Comparison between Sequential and Cyclic Musical Structures

Refrain Forms

Response
Antiphon
Litany
Epimone

Sequential Structures ←	→ Cyclic Structures
Strophic	Theme and variation
Textual orientation	Movement orientation
Eye oriented	Ear oriented
Literate tradition	Oral tradition
Predictable performance time	Open-ended performance time
Linear in structure	Episodic in experience
Verbose	Concise
Comments on ritual activity	Participates in ritual activity
Content oriented	Community oriented
Moves toward climax in content	Moves toward total participation and integration of participants

Musical Considerations for Sequential Song

- Includes strophic hymns where the same music is repeated in successive stanzas
- Includes through-composed music and texts where there is no repetition of the music
- May include texts with brief textual repetition (usually on the last line) or epimone
- The essence of the text is essentially monochronic (teleological)
- Harmonic variations, varying instrumentations, and descants may provide musical variety from stanza to stanza

Musical Considerations for Cyclic Song

- Maintains a steady beat once the song begins
- Each repetition of a cycle needs some small variation
- Often uses a soloist (cantor) to sing over the cycle
- Improvisations by soloist over ends of phrases
- Often accompanied by physical response
- Integration of choir and congregation as a unit
- Polychronic (vs. monochronic) sense of time
- Textual improvisations to fit ritual context

community rather than the communication of content. Refrain and responsorial forms may combine aspects of both.

There are some caveats to such an approach. First, this model proposes
a spectrum of possible musical structures rather than a dichotomy between
two distinct poles of musical experience. Both sequential and cyclic structures may play a role in most liturgies rather than either one or the other.[26]
While I have associated building community primarily as a function of cyclic
forms, sequential musical structures may also bind an assembly together, especially through increased musical familiarity. Likewise, cyclic structures always have content, even if they usually use fewer words and more repetitive
oral/aural devices. In specific faith traditions a sequential hymn may, through
extensive use, become so familiar that it assumes a cyclic status. In this situation most participants would not need to use books and would be freer to
look up and enjoy a visual as well as aural sense of the gathered community.
Goody refers to the process of going back and forth between oral and literate
modes as "changing the communicative channel."[27] I propose that communicative channel switching in worship at appropriate points in the ritual offers
the possibility of increased variety and potentially includes more persons in
the ritual experience. U.S. congregations that rely solely on literate or oral
forms may not be reaching as diverse a group of participants nor communicating as effectively as they otherwise might.

At the heart of this proposal is the need to use diverse musical/textual
structures in liturgy: sequential, refrain/responsorial forms, cyclic structures,
and the many variants in between. This is not a treatise that proposes using
one form over another. Those who want to throw out either organs in favor of
guitars or drums in favor of the organ are anachronistic. This proposal is
about singing and praying more broadly and deeply than any one cultural
perspective is able to offer. Each structure and style engages the participant in
a different way. Figure 7.1 places each form on a spectrum. This implies that
no characteristic on one side of the spectrum is absent at another point in the
spectrum. It is a matter of degree. John Thornburg, a pastor/musician, says
this well: "Cyclic forms engage our being and thinking about community in
the moment. Sequential forms engage our being and thinking about community over time. In cyclic forms, we begin to be 'lost in wonder, love and praise.'
In sequential forms, we say that the Christian can be lost in wonder, love, and

26. Daily prayer offices often benefit by a unified musical style and structure due to their
brevity. Fuller services of word and table, by contrast, usually benefit from a diversity of musical
styles and structures due to the greater length of the liturgy and the complexity and variety of
ritual actions needed to sustain the liturgy.

27. Goody, 57.

praise in the hope that, one day, he or she will be able to feel that the creed has been internalized."[28]

As in any spectrum, there are countless variations between the two poles. For example, refrain forms combine aspects of both sequential and cyclic structures. The stanzas of a hymn with a refrain may provide a sequential component to the experience while the refrain itself functions in a cyclic manner. It is no accident that Roman Catholics focused on refrain and responsorial structures in their efforts to establish congregational singing after the reforms of the Second Vatican Council. Responsorial psalmody blends the structures by chanting the psalm text in its entirety and by either interspersing the text with an antiphon from time to time or concluding with a Gloria Patri. A sung litany provides another responsorial form that falls in between the sequential/cyclic perspectives on the proposed spectrum. Responses, e.g., *"Kyrie eleison,"* "Lord, hear our prayer," or "Thanks be to God," inserted between appropriate petitions or expressions of thanksgiving add a lyrical quality to the prayers that cannot be achieved by speaking alone. While litanies with brief responses may be written, they may be performed in an aural/oral manner that contributes a fuller sense of praying for the world in the midst of the community rather than offering individual intercessions and petitions.

The liturgical link between sequential and cyclic musical structures is the prayerful quality of the sung word. By prayerful quality I am not referring to Albrecht Dürer's "praying hands." This early sixteenth-century image suggests a private devotional approach to prayer rather than the prayers of the gathered corporate community. Dürer's print has become an icon for the act of praying that has obscured for many the differences between private and public prayer. Paul Bradshaw notes that much that passes as common or cathedral prayer in corporate worship is actually individual or monastic prayer. The intercessions of common prayer "should be focused not primarily upon ourselves and our own needs, nor even merely on those of other Christians but rather upon the needs of the whole world for which Christ died and which he desires to be saved. . . . Instead of this global vision of their vocation, Christians easily lapse into prayer that concentrates upon themselves and those near and dear to them."[29] The incorporation of music as a vehicle for prayer adds several dimensions to the ritual experience. Singing unifies the body as those gathered integrate their voices and bodies in unified rhythms, melodies, and harmonies. Singing a prayer adds an element of intentionality to the rite over speaking. By intentionality I mean that the act of singing takes

---

28. Correspondence with John Thornburg, March 22, 2002.
29. Paul F. Bradshaw, *Two Ways of Praying* (Nashville: Abingdon, 1995), 65.

more physical effort than speaking. Furthermore, singing together requires an intentional awareness of the gathered body more than does speaking, leading potentially to a greater sense of unity.[30] Singing also adds diversity to the soundscape of the liturgical experience. Sung responses may come from various communities in the history of the church or places around the world. The culturally specific quality of various musical styles links the prayers of an individual community to worshipers of every place and time. Singing also increases the emotional range of prayer. Rather than being limited to comfortable and predictable emotional responses, the affective aspects of prayer may range from the subtlety of centered prayer in all its serenity to more ecstatic dimensions of fully embodied prayer sustained by singing and dancing. The affective power of sung prayer has been addressed by Don Saliers: "At the heart of our vocation as church musicians and liturgical leaders is the question of how we enable the Church to 'pray well' — to sing and dance faithfully and with integrity. . . . When we are engaged in sung prayer, we are not simply dressing out words in sound; rather, we are engaged in forming and expressing those emotions which constitute the very Christian life itself."[31] Thus the prayerful quality of singing, regardless of musical structure, has an ethical dimension. Singing has the power to change faith communities. As Miriam Therese Winter states, "Who we are is how we pray, and how we pray is who we are becoming. . . . This is essentially why we sing: to express who we are and are becoming."[32]

In conclusion I will suggest some basic ways that sequential and cyclic musical structures may interact with specific parts of a rite in order to effectively enhance the congregation's participation. This understanding of the integral relationship between musical structure and ritual form is essential for incorporating global song into liturgy with integrity. In general I propose two principles for choosing between sequential and cyclic musical structures. While each faith community has its own traditions that may modify these principles, they may offer some guidance in a variety of ecumenical settings. Sequential musical structures generally work better when sung following a ritual action. Employing the long-established educational prescript of mystagogical catechesis — doing should precede explaining[33] — it follows

---

30. In the preface of this book I include several examples from the writings of the early church that use congregational singing as a metaphor for Christian unity.

31. Don Saliers, "The Integrity of Sung Prayer," *Worship* 55, no. 4 (July 1981): 291-92, 293.

32. Miriam Therese Winter, "Catholic Prophetic Sound," in *Sacred Sound and Social Change,* 153.

33. For example, in the early Christian church catechumens did not receive an explanation for the ritual of baptism before they participated in its mysteries. Mystagogical catechesis

that the significance of ritual actions, e.g., procession of the Word, sacramental actions, etc., is reinforced and intensified with a sequential hymn following the action. Sequential hymns offer a lyrical theological explanation for what has been observed and experienced by those assembled. *In general, sequential structures forge unity in the community through singing a common understanding of a ritual following a ritual action.*

In contrast, cyclic musical structures unite organically with ritual actions themselves as they are taking place. One practical reason for this is the fact that the assembly is not as dependent upon holding books or reading texts when participating in cyclic structures. Worshipers may observe and join in through singing and, when appropriate, dancing as the ritual transpires. For example, in many faith communities it is the practice during Eucharist to move forward toward stations or kneel at a communion rail to accept the bread and wine. Singing by the community enhances this ritual action in many ways. However, it has been my experience that singing lesser-known sequential hymns frustrates those assembled in that they must hold books in their hands if they are to sing effectively. Without the use of books, the quality of the singing diminishes considerably. Furthermore, taking a book forward inhibits the reception of the communion elements. What does one do with a hymnbook or order of worship while taking communion? The singing generally is less effective since a high percentage of those participating cannot sing as they move forward. Perhaps even more important to the experience is that a congregation, when singing a less familiar sequential form during a ritual action, may be denied the benefits of becoming more fully aware of both aural and visual representations of community. In this setting it is important to change the communicative channel from written script to total embodiment. *In general, cyclic structures forge unity in the community by embodying the ritual itself through singing, praying, and moving together.*

Cyclic structures allow all present the opportunity to participate more wholly through singing, whether in the pews or moving forward. Since cyclic songs are primarily transmitted through oral means (even if initially read from a page as an aid to memory), the assembly may look up and sense their participation in the totality of the ritual. Specific styles of music drawn from other cultures (both historical and contemporary) remind the community that the Lord's Supper is set at a table that transcends all times and places. Cy-

---

employed the concept of entering first into the baptismal act, followed by a detailed explanation. Examples of mystagogical catechesis may be found in Saint Cyril's (ca. 348) writings as well as others. See "St. Cyril of Jerusalem's Lectures on the Christian Sacraments," trans. R. W. Church, in James F. White, *Documents of Christian Worship* (Louisville: Westminster John Knox, 1992), 158ff., for representative examples by Cyril, Ambrose of Milan, and John Chrysostom.

clic musical structures emphasize the corporate nature of this ritual rather than individual piety. To draw from an earlier discussion in chapter 4, the oral character and kinesthetic potential inherent in cyclic music have a quality of *valence* — that is, the quality to unite, interact, react, or merge with other aspects of the environment. It is perhaps this quality that prompted the following statement on sacred music in the "Constitution on the Sacred Liturgy": "The musical tradition of the universal Church is a treasure of inestimable value, greater even than that of any other art. The main reason for this preeminence is that, as sacred song closely bound to the text, it forms a necessary or integral part of the solemn liturgy."[34] It is the quality of valency that allows those assembled, in the language of the Second Vatican Council, to become "full, conscious and active" participants in the drama suggested by the ritual rather than observers.

In summary, a focus on musical styles rather than structures disguises the underlying function and foundation that congregational singing provides within liturgy. Musical style at its best is an aural representation of how the people in varying places and times have responded to the established texts (biblical and traditional) and cultural circumstances of their congregations. Variations in musical style remind us of the myriad ways that the incarnation has been made manifest among us and of the diversity through which the Holy Spirit moves throughout the church. Congregational musical structures, however, may be embodied in a wide range of musical styles. An appropriate use of musical structures speaks to the inherent quality of valence in liturgy — how music relates organically to the established rites and rituals of the faith community. An understanding of the role of musical structure and how it interacts with liturgical ritual is essential for those who serve as musical presiders. I shall refer to these as enliveners of worship in the next chapter.

34. "Constitution on the Sacred Liturgy" (1963), in *The Liturgy Documents: A Parish Resource*, 3rd ed. (Chicago: Liturgy Training Publications, 1991), art. 112.

CHAPTER 8

The Church Musician as Enlivener

Even a cursory glance at hymnals and hymnal supplements produced in North America since circa 1985 provides evidence of unprecedented diversity of world song. The most obvious indications of cultural diversity include the number of bilingual hymns in many denominational hymnals — most commonly Spanish and English and Korean transliterations and English.[1] If one looks more closely at North American hymnals compiled for primarily Anglo congregations,[2] other evidence of diversity appears, e.g., litanies, prayers, creeds, and confessions from sources beyond the Euro–North American context; authors, translators, composers, and arrangers listed in appropriate indexes who come from Africa, Asia, or Latin America; hymn tune names in non-Euro–North American languages. An even closer examination will often reveal hymnal committees that are much more ethnically and racially diverse. The inclusion of more cyclic forms in a variety of musical styles — including those of the Taizé and Iona communities, African and Asian sources, and contemporary Christian music — provides evidence of diversity. These songs look different on the page than Western traditional sequential/strophic hymns. They also increase the length of the listings of irregular meters in the metrical indexes. The astute hymnal user may notice that many hymnals have attempted an even deeper level of mu-

---

1. Specific denominational traditions may include French, German, or Dutch bilingual hymns depending on the ethnic origins of the group. Occasional African and Native American languages may also appear, and even a transliterated Japanese hymn, "Here, O Lord, Your Servants Gather," may be found in a few hymnals.

2. I have explored this topic in "The Tie That Binds: A List of Ecumenical Hymns in English Language Hymnals," *Hymn* 48, no. 3 (1997): 25-37.

sical diversity by attempting to provide arrangements that are faithful to the musical style of the melody rather than supplying a kind of generic neo-Victorian harmonization. Arrangements sensitive to the original musical idiom may provide percussion parts from time to time in the hymnal and further suggestions in hymnal companions, keyboard accompaniment volumes, or supplementary texts.[3]

The cultural diversity of musical and worship sources and the appropriate integration of these materials into liturgy demand a fresh perspective on the role of the musical presider. This person guides the assembly in responding to each musical style with respect for the original context of the song (the sending culture) and sensitivity for those who attempt to bridge a cultural chasm to praise and pray with these songs (the receiving culture). I have chosen the term "enlivener" to refer to this person and the liturgical office he or she holds. I am indebted to Roman Catholic educator Michael Warren for this basic concept.[4] He distinguishes between the enlivener and the bureaucrat. The enlivener embodies the traditions of a faith community and attempts to explore its fullness by sharing its faith heritage in poetry, songs, rituals, and artifacts. The bureaucrat reduces the richness of a tradition to programs, ideas, and logical categories of thought. This disembodied form of transmission is cut off from the heritage that spawned it, "distort[ing] the tradition rather than disclosing it."[5] For the remainder of this chapter I will elaborate on the role of the enlivener as presented by Warren within the liturgical context as one who guides a congregation in praying for the world.[6] The

3. See, e.g., *Leading the Church's Song*, ed. Robert Buckley Farlee (Minneapolis: Augsburg Fortress, 1998). Excellent for ecumenical use, this work provides detailed supplementary stylistic assistance for Lutheran church musicians, including chapters on northern European, North American, African American, contemporary, Latino, African, and Asian musical styles. This text is bound with a CD so that the written word is supported with the aural presentations.

4. The term "enlivener" comes from Michael Warren, *Faith, Culture, and the Worshiping Community: Shaping the Practice of the Local Church*, rev. ed. (Washington, D.C.: Pastoral Press, 1993), 40ff.

5. Warren, 39.

6. The term "cantor" has a long history in Western liturgy. Paul Westermeyer ably presents the role of the cantor in *The Church Musician*, rev. ed. (Minneapolis: Augsburg Fortress, 1997). Edward Foley presents a complementary view of music in liturgy and musical leadership in *Ritual Music: Studies in Liturgical Musicology* (Beltsville, Md.: Pastoral Press, 1995). Though these excellent presentations encourage a fuller reclamation of the meaning of the role of the cantor, it is not usually the term of choice for global gatherings. Many ecumenical global meetings prefer *animateur* or its closest English equivalent, "animator." This term has its advantages as it implies that the leader is "one that provides or imparts life, interest, spirit, or vitality" to a gathering (according to *The American Heritage Electronic Dictionary*, 3rd ed., ver. 3.0A [Hough-

first section will outline the musical and liturgical context in which the enlivener functions — mapping the liturgical and musical field of the enlivener. The following section presents a more detailed examination of the office of the enlivener. The concluding section offers a brief description of a person that I believe embodies the work of the enlivener within a North American context, Mary Oyer.

Mapping the Liturgical and Musical Field of the Enlivener: Living in Liminality

Musical anthropologist John Blacking recognized the potential for music to unify disparate groups within a society. "Music," he wrote, "can bridge the gulf between the true state of human being and the predicament of particular human beings in a given society, and especially the alienation that springs from the class struggle and human exploitation."[7] Thus Blacking speaks of living not "*for* culture" but "*beyond* culture."[8] Taking Blacking's cue, I, who am a part of a specific cultural experience, must live both within the normative culture of the United States (*for* culture) and at the same time beyond the stereotypes that the normative culture imposes on anyone different from itself (*beyond* culture). This "beyondness" is a state of liminality or the threshold experience between two worldviews. Liminality is a state of continuity and discontinuity at the same time, a kind of bicultural identity. It is, according to Victor Turner, "the character of being neither here nor there but 'in between.'"[9] Those who choose to function in a deceptive "un-

---

ton Mifflin Company, 1993]). In local settings in the United States, however, neither *animateur* nor "animator" communicates well. The inability to use either "cantor" or *animateur* widely in the United States has caused me to consider yet another nomenclature.

7. *Music, Culture, and Experience: Selected Papers of John Blacking*, ed. Reginald Byron (Chicago: University of Chicago Press, 1995), 171.

8. John Blacking, *How Musical Is Man?* (Seattle: University of Washington Press, 1973), 7, italics in original. The theme of living beyond culture was very important to Blacking and was reiterated later in *Music, Culture, and Experience: Selected Papers of John Blacking*, where he says, "If the artist who expresses personal experience may in the end reach universal experience, it is because he or she has been able to live beyond culture, and not for culture" (240).

9. In Tom Driver, *The Magic of Ritual: Our Need for Liberating Rites That Transform Our Lives and Our Communities* (San Francisco: HarperCollins, 1991), 159. Driver is referring to Victor Turner, *The Anthropology of Performance* (New York: Performing Arts Journal Publications, 1986), in this quote. Turner's classic discussion of liminality, "Liminality and Communitas" (1969), can be found in *Readings in Ritual Studies*, ed. Ronald L. Grimes (Upper Saddle River, N.J.: Prentice-Hall, 1996), 511-19.

raced"[10] world may rarely experience such beyondness or liminality. For this is a normative worldview where the voiceless rarely come into earshot and the invisible seldom come into view. Liminality is disconcerting and unsettling — a state of being that may be intolerable in the normative culture where comfort, control, and security are valued above all else. Aspects of liminality are common, however, to many minority persons within the United States who function on a bicultural basis daily.

Liminality also describes the theological paradox of the relationship between the Creator and the creature. The Creator embraced continuity with the creature through the incarnation. Experiencing this continuity with the Creator requires a degree of separateness from ordinary life, however. It is to this paradox that Don Saliers refers when he states that to "address our lives in wholeness to God demands a discontinuity with ordinary life as well as a continuity."[11] The pull of the normative culture is so strong for those drawn to its comforts, security, and privilege that many may never choose to leave its grasp for the richer, but more disturbing, unpredictable realms of liminality. Liturgy is a time set aside in Christian experience for the potential convergence of the ordinary and the extraordinary, i.e., liminality.

A cross-cultural liturgical environment provides potential for liminality. Here the songs and prayers of another's experience, those of the strangers and aliens (Eph. 2:17-20), can be juxtaposed with those from one's culture of origin, illuminating both. In facilitating cross-cultural worship among those predominately in the normative mainline church culture, I have found that for some it is so disturbing that they choose to retreat to the secure places of their normative cultural experience. For others it is an opportunity to explore a new liturgical realm quite different, yet vibrantly alive. For the latter there is the possibility of liminality. It is necessary to sustain cross-cultural exploration over time so that worshipers in the normative culture may learn to pray and sing with and for the world. It is to this singing and praying that I now turn.

10. John Michael Spencer, *Sing a New Song: Liberating Black Hymnody* (Minneapolis: Fortress, 1995), vi-vii. Spencer borrows the term "unraced" from novelist Toni Morrison as a reference to those who "suppress a specific cultural ethnicity in favor of assimilation" and thus "view themselves as universal and, illusionally, as the world's majority."

11. Don E. Saliers, *Worship and Spirituality,* 2nd ed. (Akron, Ohio: OSL Publications, [1984] 1996), 23.

Mapping the Musical Field of the Enlivener:
The Axis of Musical Perception

I propose to map the cross-cultural musical/liturgical experience by using two intersecting axes.[12] One axis is musical perception; the other is prayer for the world. Along the continuum of the axis of musical perception are poles of musical experience ranging from musical authenticity in the sending culture to musical accessibility in the receiving culture.

Figure 8.1. Axis of Musical Perception

Musical Authenticity (Sending Culture)	Range of Musical Perception	Musical Accessibility (Receiving Culture)

The melodic and rhythmic aspects of a given musical style have been formed to a large degree by the complex interaction between sounds in the natural environment and human speech.[13] The syntax and inflections of our language(s) of origin shape musical perception from an early age. Musical learning is part of a larger complex process that molds our cultural preferences. Anthropologists call this process "enculturation." Enculturation is "the cultural learning process of the individual, the process by which a person is inserted into his or her culture."[14] While enculturation is largely informal and happens at a subconscious level, it also takes place in formal teaching and learning environments. From an anthropological perspective, enculturation is the process by which a person learns the rules of society through its symbol systems (language, music, arts, etc.). This process, according to Ronald Grimes, is how we are "programmed" or biologically "mapped."[15]

In any cross-cultural musical experience there will be a gap between the musical authenticity of the sending culture and the accessibility of the receiving culture. Stepping into this gap can cause a sense of instability and insecurity, even, in extreme cases where persons have few cultural reference points,

12. I am borrowing the concept of "mapping the field" from Ronald Grimes, *Beginnings in Ritual Studies* (Lanham, Md.: University Press of America, 1982), chap. 2, "Mapping the Field of Ritual."

13. I choose not to enter into the discussion of whether music preceded speech or speech was derived from music. Anthony Storr outlines the views on this subject in chap. 1, "Origins and Collective Functions," of *Music and the Mind* (New York: Ballantine Books, 1992), 1-23.

14. Aylward Shorter, *Toward a Theology of Inculturation* (Maryknoll, N.Y.: Orbis, 1988), 5. Shorter's quote refers to the anthropological term "*enculturation.*" The book as a whole is about the relationship between liturgy and culture, a process that he calls "*inculturation.*"

15. Grimes, 37.

utter chaos. It is into this gap that the enlivener leads others, for here one may discover the nature of liminality — attempting to exist in two worlds.

When encountering liminal experiences, there are two points of tension at work. At one extreme, it is natural for the receiving culture to reshape the experience of the sending culture into its own image, eliminating or "correcting" all aspects of the alien encounter that do not fit into previously learned symbol systems. This is a kind of ethnocentrism — in the sense that it is a tendency of the human condition to understand new experiences in a provincial way, a way based on previous experience. At the other extreme, a new encounter with the sending culture may reshape or reconstitute the experience of the receiving culture. This opens up the possibility that individuals in the receiving culture could modify previously learned habits in the face of new information and experiences. In this case one must expand existing perceptions, modify provincial musical tastes and behaviors, and move toward an understanding of musical authenticity from the perspective of the sending culture.[16] It is at this point that one enters the realm of liminality.

Liminality may result when an equilibrium is established between the authentic experience of the sending culture and the social/psychological structures of the receiving culture. It is rare for an individual to develop total intercultural empathy. This would require one to perceive the symbol systems of the sending culture in the same way as persons enculturated from birth in that context. However, experiences of cross-cultural liminality assume that one can move in the direction of intercultural empathy, especially if these experiences are repeated or ritually reinforced. Repeating ritual experiences decreases the possibility that an encounter with the sending culture will be reduced to musical novelty, sensationalism, or cultural stereotyping. It is the role of the enlivener to facilitate cross-cultural experiences so that a deeper, fuller equilibrium between the sending and receiving cultures may take place. Liturgy is a forum where such potentially transformative experiences can and should happen. Music is a primary medium for creating, sustaining, and nurturing this transformation. Liminal experiences have the potential to change our overall perspective. While liminal experiences in worship may at first appear as glimpses of a better way of relating to our neighbor, a broader or even cosmic worldview, or a faint hope for the realm of God on earth now, they

---

16. Leonard Meyer has demonstrated in *Emotion and Meaning in Music* (Chicago: University of Chicago Press, 1956) that our minds naturally attempt to fit new musical experiences into existing patterns of thought. See esp. chap. 5, "Principles of Pattern Perception: The Weakening of Shape."

may over time change our ethical perspective as we relate to those around us and take our worship into the world.

There are three additional aspects of the axis of musical perception that need elaboration. First, we must ask, what exactly is musical authenticity? This is especially difficult when the receiving culture learns music primarily through written means, e.g., a hymnal, and the sending culture transmits music primarily through an oral/aural process. Even recognized authorities in a given musical tradition will often disagree over the specifics of an "authentic" presentation. The range of cultural factors that determine musical authenticity in any attempted cross-cultural exchange is staggering. The Euro–North American classical tradition, for example, usually values musical performances that adhere to some degree to a written score. Musicians trained in Western culture receive music as much through the eye as they do through the ear. The eye may even shape the creation of the score to a significant extent, affecting the sound.[17] Audience participation tends to be passive in the literate tradition, widening the gulf between the performer and the audience. Musical presentations often take place in specialized venues designed specifically for that purpose, e.g., symphony hall, performing arts center, dance theater.

Oral musical traditions, on the other hand, are also concerned with the presentation and transmission of musical style. In the African context music may be so complex that it is difficult to render in written form using Western notation. Because of the tendency of oral tradition to adapt to a particular setting through improvisation, a written score tends to stifle creativity. Music presented in the context of oral tradition in Africa, for example, often depends upon an intricate interaction between drummers, singers, and dancers. The dancers often take the lead in an African ensemble, while the drummers respond to their complex choreography.[18] Presentations of African music may take place in social spaces that are multipurpose rather than designated for concert use. An "authentic" African musical experience will be participatory, eliminating the distance between the "congregation and the choir." Musical intensity increases through repetition or cyclic form.[19] While there are other examples, literate and oral cultures usually have significantly different understandings of the nature of an "authentic" musical experience.

The second issue related to the axis of musical perception is the role of

17. Walter Ong discusses the effect of print on the shaping of content in *Orality and Literacy: The Technologizing of the Word* (New York: Routledge, [1982] 1988). See chap. 4, "Writing Restructures Consciousness," and chap. 5, "Print, Space and Closure."

18. Yaya Diallo and Mitchell Hall, *The Healing Drum: African Wisdom Teachings* (Rochester, Vt.: Destiny Books, 1989), 98, describe this in detail.

19. Cyclic structures have been discussed in detail in chap. 7.

oppression of cocultures. There have been times when the music of one culture has been imposed upon another culture through political oppression, religious proselytization, or cultural hegemony. The musical result of this coercion depends on the duration and intensity of the oppression, proselytization, and/or hegemony of the normative culture, and the population size, cultural stability, and musical resilience of the oppressed culture. In the oppression, proselytization, and hegemony that took place between the various African tribal groups brought to the United States and their oppressors, there is evidence that the Africans maintained aspects of their musical traditions and eventually transformed the music of their oppressors into a new style.[20] The enlivener cannot force a cross-cultural equilibrium through the use of cultural hegemony. Cultural hegemony within liturgy does not lead to cross-cultural awareness but is blatant ethnocentrism. Oppressive ethnocentrism is not compatible with liturgical liminality.

There is a third dynamic in the continuum between musical authenticity and accessibility. This is the effect of technology and normative popular culture from the United States on virtually the entire planet. At first my sense of this phenomenon was only anecdotal, based on travels and study outside of Euro–North American contexts and sporadic observations of the role of North American popular culture on the economic and social life of these societies. The power of the media in the United States, especially movies, television, and music, to shape the values of young people in other countries, and the prevalence of U.S. fast-food chains and Western technology, carries a price that has both economic and cultural ramifications. The success of an emerging global market from the perspective of the United States may relate inversely to the influence of traditional cultural values and art forms in other cultures. My anecdotal experience gained broader verification, however, when I read on July 1, 1998, the following front-page article, "Panel to Preserve Culture: Countries Fear U.S. Hegemony":

> OTTAWA — Officials from 19 countries reacting to fears that the world is engulfed in a rising tide of U.S.-produced movies, television, music and other entertainment, took the first tentative steps Tuesday toward forming a protective international cultural alliance.
>
> Government ministers from Europe, Latin America and Africa met

---

20. My observations in other places where Africans have encountered oppression and cultural hegemony would bear this thesis out, specifically in Cuba, Haiti, and Brazil. The music that results from the singular mix of Africans with these normative European cultural contexts — Spain, France, and Portugal respectively — is unique to each manifestation of the African diaspora, but nevertheless, distinctly African.

here at the invitation of Canada's top cultural official, Heritage Minister Shelia Copps, and agreed to form a working group aimed at giving cultural issues greater prominence in foreign policy, trade and investment negotiations.[21]

I suggest that the power of the popular media in the United States is so strong, both within its borders and in many places beyond, that persons enculturated in the normative society of this country may experience little more than stereotypical manifestations of cocultures within the United States. In some countries the influence of media and technology from the United States is so prevalent that local traditions die out altogether or can only be preserved in a "museum" context supported by the tourist industry. It is at this point that the enlivener should offer a countercultural critique within liturgy.[22] To deny a congregation a fuller range of cross-cultural musical expression within liturgy limits the potential for liminality and increases the possibility of ethnocentrism. Liturgical ethnocentrism shapes God de facto into a provincial image that reflects the values of the normative culture. Singing a fuller range of song within liturgy offers the worshiper the potential of experiencing a deeper richness of God's creative diversity and a more abundant image of God made flesh *(imago Dei)* in the person of Jesus Christ. The theological mandate of the enlivener is to explore the diversity of creation and the breadth of the incarnation.

Mapping the Liturgical Field of the Enlivener:
The Axis of Prayer for the World

A second axis is prayer for the world. At one end of this axis, one asks the meaning of prayer in the sending culture. At the other end one determines the significance of the gift of this prayer to the receiving culture.[23]

21. Craig Turner, "Panel to Preserve Culture: Countries Fear U.S. Hegemony," *Albuquerque Journal,* July 1, 1998, A1.

22. See S. Anita Stauffer, "Worship: Ecumenical Core and Cultural Context," in *Christian Worship: Unity in Cultural Diversity,* ed. S. Anita Stauffer (Geneva: Lutheran World Federation, 1996), 14-19. Stauffer discusses the intersection of worship and culture as having *transcultural* elements and local *contextual* possibilities, and needing a *countercultural* critique. In another article, "Worship and Culture: Five Theses," *Studia Liturgica* 26, no. 2 (1996): 323-32, Stauffer adds a *cross-cultural* dimension, but with little explanation.

23. Rebecca Slough helpfully pointed out to me a distinction between praying "for" and "with" the world. I am suggesting that one prays with the world in the singing of songs from places where oppression dominates and hope may be on the wane. I can see a distinction between "with" and "for" on one level, though these two prepositions seem to merge in the experience of liturgy. Correspondence, January 18, 2002.

Figure 8.2. The Axis of Prayer for the World

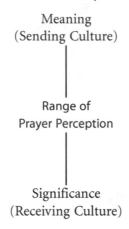

Meaning
(Sending Culture)

Range of
Prayer Perception

Significance
(Receiving Culture)

This axis clarifies an assumption implied throughout this book — that singing in worship is a form of prayer.[24] Reestablishing the inherent unity of prayer and song is essential to a liminal liturgy. My experience in cultures outside the Euro–North American normative context often indicates that this essential unity has not been lost. Furthermore, artistic symbol systems such as singing and dancing are unified in many cultures.[25] The relationship between prayer, song, and movement opens up the possibility for liminality to an even greater extent, especially in normative Western settings.[26]

The same possibilities for ethnocentrism or liminality exist along the axis of prayer for the world as along the axis of musical perception. However, if the normative culture reclaims the unity of singing and praying, the potential for liminality where the two axes meet in the center is enhanced. From the perspective of the enlivener, we are not just learning to sing new songs from other places. We are learning to pray in new ways, and in solidarity with others who embody these sung prayers. At one end of the axis of prayer for the world we ask questions of meaning[27] in the sending culture:

24. See chap. 7, n. 6, for a further clarification.

25. Jean-Jacques Nattiez, *Music and Discourse: Toward a Semiology of Music,* trans. Carolyn Abbate (Princeton: Princeton University Press, 1990), 54.

26. James L. Empereur, S.J., calls us to move beyond liturgical Cartesianism, i.e., "I think, therefore I worship," in "The Physicality of Worship," in *Bodies of Worship: Explorations in Theory and Practice,* ed. Bruce T. Morrill (Collegeville, Minn.: Liturgical Press, 1999), 137. Furthermore, the kinesthetic sense may be viewed as a sixth sense — a way to access the wisdom of the body (144).

27. I have adapted the idea of meaning and significance from Russell M. Yee, "Shared Meaning and Significance in Congregational Song," *Hymn* 48, no. 2 (April 1997): 7-11.

- Who prays this prayer?
- Under what conditions is it offered?
- How is this prayer used within the liturgy of the sending culture?
- What response does the pray-er expect?

At the opposite end of the axis the receiving culture asks hermeneutical questions:

- What is the significance of this prayer for me?
- How can my liturgy receive most graciously the gift of prayer from another culture?
- In what ways does this prayer reprioritize the praise that I render and the petitions that I offer?
- How might I pray in solidarity with the "strangers and aliens" outside my culture?

The critical juncture between the two axes has potential for a deeper liminality. Borrowing from David Augsburger, I call the search for a bridge between the sending and receiving cultures within liturgy a process of liturgical "interpathy."[28] Liturgical interpathy is the effort to span the breach with others who may not share one's values, cultural assumptions, or worldviews. It is the role of the enlivener to facilitate liturgical interpathy at the crossroads of the axes of music and prayer.

As figure 8.3, "The Liturgical and Musical Field of the Enlivener," indicates, a purpose of the enlivener is to guide the assembly from an essentially ethnocentric worship experience based solely on cultural accessibility and personal significance toward liminality and an openness to liturgical interpathy. Liturgy that moves in the direction of liturgical interpathy incorporates song and prayer from other worldviews in the hope that praying for the world may be more fully realized and embodied. The goal is not to imitate or become like Christians who embrace other worldviews. The purpose is to sing and pray beyond our zones of comfort, struggling with the instability, insecurity, and dis-ease of living for a moment partially *beyond* our culture(s) of origin in the threshold of time and space beyond our own. Liminality may open the worshiper to prayers from the depth of the Christian experience (the inherited tradition) and the breadth of current Christian experience (singing and praying globally). Both situations encourage liturgical plurality,

---

28. The term "interpathy" has been coined by David Augsburger in *Pastoral Counseling across Cultures* (Philadelphia: Westminster, 1986), 41.

Figure 8.3. The Liturgical and Musical Field of the Enlivener

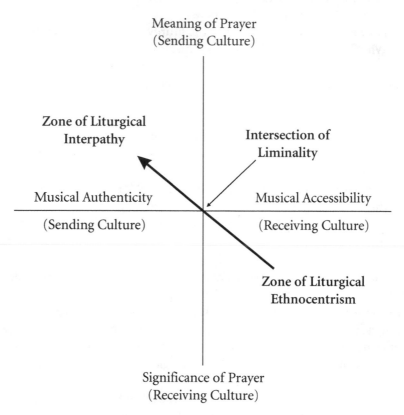

moving those gathered beyond the immediacy of a single point in space and time to the possibility of praying with Christians in all places and times.

The Office of the Enlivener

The enlivener exists within a dynamic liturgical environment that ranges between priestly and prophetic functions within liturgy.[29] The priestly role supports the movement of liturgy through sung prayer. The underlying structure of priestly music is one of ritual monotony, a very important and essential function in liturgy. While never resorting to boredom, it offers the worshiper

29. Tom Driver has influenced some of what follows, especially in his distinction between the priestly and the shamanic (see chap. 4, "Priest and Shaman: Two Pathways of Religious Ritual," in his *The Magic of Ritual,* 52-75). I have chosen to subsume many of Driver's shamanistic features under the rubric of the prophetic nature of the enlivener.

a safe space in which to pray. The prophetic role offers a critique of the culture, especially those aspects of culture that are most familiar to the worshiping community, by moving the assembly toward liminality — a threshold between those physically present and the needs and concerns of the church universal and a suffering world.

Each congregation offers fresh possibilities within the priestly/prophetic continuum. The priestly dimension of the enlivener may emphasize the security of forms and styles of music that are most accessible to the primary culture of the congregation. This music reinforces the cultural, theological, and liturgical identity of the congregation. The prophetic dimension of the enlivener selects music that, if not all of the time, often reflects a coculture within the congregation or the community, or a culture beyond the experience of most persons in the congregation. This music is prophetic because it originates beyond the primary culture of the congregation. Music that serves a prophetic dimension relates the ministry of the local congregation to the broader mission of the church in its depth (historically) and in its breadth (globally).

The cultural, ecclesiological, socioeconomic, and missional context of each congregation determines what music and rituals are priestly or prophetic. Prophetic music fosters a sense of suspense that may encourage a response ranging from expectation and anticipation to apprehension and anxiety, or even anger. Within a given liturgy, musical experiences may cover the entire range of the priestly-prophetic continuum for various members of the congregation. It is even possible for the same person to experience a wide range of responses within a single service. The potential for myriad artistic preferences and expressive diversity, especially within mainline Protestant congregations,[30] may overwhelm the enlivener. Within these cultural crosscurrents, what principles ground the work of the enlivener?

---

30. John E. Kaemmer, *Music in Human Life* (Austin: University of Texas Press, 1993), mentions the work of Herbert Gans, who identifies five types of societies (34-35). Each society has distinct expressive cultures, for which Gans uses the term "taste culture." Each taste culture emphasizes specific values and choices through expressive, artistic means. In Gans's 1974 study, *Popular Culture and High Culture* (New York: Basic Books), high culture refers to artistic expressions that support the taste culture of the powerful, wealthy, and well-educated segments of society. Popular artistic expressions conversely are the voice of the masses who may have less wealth, power, and education. While this analysis may be true in more traditional societies, it seems to be increasingly simplistic and irrelevant for the cultural complexity and crosscurrents found in the United States. I recommend Mark Slobin, *Subcultural Sounds: Micromusics of the West* (Hanover, N.H.: University Press of New England, 1993), for a more dynamic view on how music from different cocultures interacts. Jacques Attali presents an even more integrated and complex analysis of the relationship between music and society in *Noise: The Political Economy of Music*, trans. Brian Massumi (Minneapolis: University of Minnesota Press, 1985).

The enlivener seeks to stand in the dynamic center of the priestly and prophetic continuum. Music is more than a vehicle for personal expression, a channel for text, a common interest around which avowed musicians gather, a way to be in touch with one's feelings, or a vehicle for evangelism. While these may be by-products of music making, the enlivener is aware of deeper meanings and possibilities within the life of the community. Music making becomes a way of shaping prayer. It is a way of enabling the corporate church to pray more effectively and completely. Music making, indeed artistic expression in general, becomes the relational currency between the enlivener and the congregation on the one hand, and the congregation and the Christian tradition — past, present, and future — on the other. This is not a new office, but finds its roots in early Christian experience where, according to Michael Warren, leaders "were recognized as possessing the ability to keep the community in lively touch with its traditions and with the meanings embedded in those traditions."[31] It is also an office that calls the assembly to pray for the world. Liturgical theologians remind us that praying for the world is one of the essential actions of the *ecclesia,* those gathered as Christ's body in the world. Gordon Lathrop states that the primary "mission [of the church as assembly] may well be to maintain strong and healthy communal symbols of the truth about God and to do so for the sake of the well-being of the world."[32] Praying for the world is an essential link between a local congregation and the universal church. Praying for the world offers a defense against liturgical ethnocentrism — the shaping of God in the image of a particular worldview — and liturgical narcissism — liturgy in love with itself.[33]

What are the musical traits that are part of our shared Christian experience? I will suggest some that are both relevant to this study and embodied in the five global mentors included in this book:

- the unity of singing and praying in the support of corporate worship
- the diminishing of the expressive distance between the congregation and choir
- the embodiment of song more fully through dance

31. Warren, 40. Warren draws upon the work of Edward Schillebeeckx in his book *Ministry: Leadership in the Community of Jesus Christ* (New York: Crossroad, 1981) for this point.

32. Gordon Lathrop, *Holy People: A Liturgical Ecclesiology* (Minneapolis: Fortress, 1999), 13.

33. "Liturgical narcissism" is a term from Bernhard Lang, *Sacred Games: A History of Christian Worship* (New Haven: Yale University Press, 1997), 134. Liturgical narcissism means placing prayer for divine blessing and spiritual goods (forgiveness and illumination) over prayer for divine intervention.

- the balance between music as a bearer of content and shaper of community
- the "full, conscious and active participation" of the assembly
- the essential eschatological character of sung prayer, including expectant waiting and foretastes of the realm of God to come
- the belief in the essential goodness of God's creation and the power of the Holy Spirit to transform expressive cultural media into vehicles for the holy
- the cosmic awareness that when any local body of Christ gathers, the church of all places and times is present
- the witness in an individual congregation that Christ's saving work is present throughout the world in ways that stagger the imagination, even through the songs that reflect his incarnation among all the people[34]

These traditions provide guides to the quality and nature of the enlivener's work. The enlivener

- exists squarely within the community's life.
- points out the community's significance as a kind of living text (gospel).
- urges members to greater fidelity to the tradition ("living faith of the dead").[35]
- is not a bureaucratic functionary or a manager of doctrine.
- passes living tradition on through festivity and live interaction of the community engaged in celebrating its own life story — a process beyond words, a process so vital that it "must be danced, sung, shouted, pondered in silence around symbols that whisper."[36]
- does not pass living tradition on in a disembodied form of abstract theological ideas distilled from the tradition, but enables the people to embody the Word.
- is a catechist (catalyst) that cares for the fullness of the community.
- is the *delegado de la palabra* (representative of the Word).[37]

---

34. I am grateful to Rebecca Slough for bringing this to my attention.

35. Jaroslav Pelikan reminds us that traditionalism is "the dead faith of the living" while the historic liturgical traditions of the church are "the living faith of the dead" in *The Vindication of Tradition* (New Haven: Yale University Press, 1984), 65. Traditionalism might well be equated with the mentality of the bureaucrat mentioned earlier by Michael Warren.

36. Warren, 40.

37. Warren, 55-56. Warren reminds us that a *delegado de la palabra* is a dangerous person

- understands the festive nature of liturgy and incorporates the congregation into a timeless celebration with equanimity and equality.[38]
- recognizes that music not only reflects culture, but also is part of the formation of culture (glue of culture) as a system and as an individual response within the system.[39]
- inspires the congregation to live more faithfully within the tradition and to add new stanzas to the great song of the tradition.[40]
- is an invoker of the Spirit (prophetic role), not just a mediator (priestly role).[41]
- is not hired, but called. As in other offices within the church, the enlivener's position is not a job, but a vocation.

Skills of the Enlivener

It is the practice of much academic scholarship related to the church to present solid theological or philosophical groundings for a given topic, but to stop short of the pedagogical requirements that are necessary to achieve or at least begin to move toward the embodiment of the proposal being offered. It is at this point that I suggest skills that could lead toward the fulfillment of the office of the enlivener.

The enlivener should diminish the distance between the choir and the congregation. Both the established choir and the congregational choir have their roles in worship. In the global church the congregation is clearly the first and most important choir. The established choir is often evaluated on its ability to help the congregation sing better.[42]

---

in many countries, one who threatens the status quo and oppressors. The prophetic dimension of representing the Word comes again to the forefront.

38. Ronald Grimes reminds us that celebration "is not to be identified with Western optimism; it is not mere yes-saying. It is a mode of embracing the present which draws future and past into itself." See *Beginnings in Ritual Studies,* 49. This is reminiscent of Pablo Sosa's definition of fiesta in chap. 2.

39. John Blacking notes in *Music and Cultural Experience* that music is "not only reflexive; it is also generative, both as a cultural system and as human capability" (223).

40. I heard Bishop Joel Martínez of the United Methodist Church (USA) first use this metaphor in a sermon at Perkins School of Theology in October 1996.

41. Driver, 75. Specifically, Driver says, "The shaman invokes; the priest represents. . . . Revitalization of religious ritual in Westernized societies today would require overcoming the dominance of the priestly type by moving again toward the shamanic."

42. For many years I have been quoting Erik Routley on this point. As I recall, Routley says the first and most important choir is the congregation, and that the primary role of the es-

The enlivener should distinguish between a gesture that encourages the nuance appropriate to choral singing and a gesture that motivates persons, many of whom may not consider themselves musicians, to join in corporate song. For example, indicating relative pitch of a melody with the hand when teaching a song may be much more helpful than keeping the beat with a standard conducting pattern used in choral music.

The enlivener should use the voice as the primary medium for teaching. This does not mean he or she needs to be a highly trained singer. Western operatic quality would be detrimental in engaging others to sing. The voice needs to be clear, sure, and reasonably pleasant. It is more important that the musicianship of the enlivener be secure and not dependent on a keyboard to make music.[43]

The enlivener should be able to function in a variety of media: dance, song, instruments, including percussion, as well as voice. Recall that the meaning of music in many African languages is to sing, dance, and play drums.

The enlivener should be proficient in leading from both oral and written traditions. Such proficiency requires the ability to perform in a variety of ways and styles appropriate to the source of the song.[44]

The enlivener should be skilled in interpreting the sociological and cultural context of the community in song. Since song is a cultural artifact, the enlivener should be able to relate both the cultural and musical meanings embedded in the written texts and oral experiences.

The enlivener should be able to draw all into the celebration — chil-

---

tablished choir is to help the congregation sing better and then to sing on behalf of the congregation what it cannot sing for itself. As with several powerful statements by Routley, I cannot recall if I heard him say this in person or read it in one of his many books. I am confident of the source and the nature of the statement but cannot locate the reference.

43. John Bell's "Ten Golden Rules for Improving Singing in the Most Recalcitrant of Congregations" and "Ten Golden Rules for Enabling the Least Confident of People to Teach New Songs to the Most Cynical of Congregations" provide specific assistance in teaching songs to congregations. These are available in a variety of the Wild Goose publications referred to in chap. 6. More recently Bell has explored this area further in *The Singing Thing: A Case for Congregational Song* (Glasgow: Wild Goose Publications, 2000).

44. By performance I am referring to the skill of leading ritual performance as outlined by Tom Driver in *The Magic of Ritual*, especially as discussed in chap. 10, "Christian Sacraments as the Performance of Freedom." Many persons who lead Christian rituals are uncomfortable with using the word "performance" to describe the quality of their leadership. Yet skillful performers are needed to embody the office of the enlivener for the sake of the community that is being shaped by the ritual. Driver's "Fifteen Maxims for the Planning of Christian Rituals" (p. 212) is excellent practical advice for an enlivener.

dren, young people, adults; musical and less musical; majority and minority cultures. Festive occasions in the worshiping community are inter-generational at their best. They do not distinguish between the musical and so-called unmusical. They incorporate the diversity of the church present and the church in all times and places. The enlivener leads the assembly in song for those who cannot sing for themselves.

The enlivener should understand the tradition of the church in its biblical, liturgical, and musical manifestation and help the congregation both critique and embody this tradition in its sung prayer. Alice Parker links the historical role of the cantor with its Jewish origins: "The rabbi is teacher; the cantor, master of prayer."[45] Parker cites Rabbi Abraham Joshua Heschel and draws her approach from his interpretation of the cantor in Jewish practice:

> The right Hebrew word for cantor is *ba'al tefillah,* master of prayer. The mission of the cantor is to lead in prayer. [The cantor] does not stand before the Ark as an artist in isolation, trying to demonstrate his skill or to display vocal feats. [The cantor] stands before the Ark not as an individual but with a congregation. [The cantor] must identify . . . with the congregation. [The cantor's] task is to represent as well as inspire a community. Within the synagogue music is not an end in itself but a means of religious experience. Its function is to help us live through a moment of confrontation with the presence of God: to expose ourselves to him in praise, in self-scrutiny and hope.[46]

This is a daunting task at first glance. Achieving the skills needed to be an effective enlivener demands an intentional effort. In a given community, however, there are usually those who possess the instincts and experiences that may allow them to claim a vocation as an enlivener. Their gifts may need to be recognized and developed. Their instincts for sensing the nature and mission of the Christian community are authentic and promising. In some cases classically trained Western musicians may not recognize the gifts of enliveners. Potential enliveners have often already demonstrated their faithfulness to their faith community, a spirit that appreciates the uniqueness of others within the community, an understanding of the tradition, an inquisitive mind rooted in biblical truth, and an openness to fresh winds of the Holy Spirit. They may even be acknowledged to some degree as wisdom figures within the congregation. What potential enliveners often lack is clarity of vo-

45. Alice Parker, *Melodious Accord: Good Singing in Church* (Chicago: Liturgy Training Publications, 1991), 80.
46. Heschel, quoted in Parker, 80.

cation and an understanding that the office of the enlivener is a valid one. They may need the development of specific skills, but already have the intuitions that are hard to acquire through formal instruction. Nascent enliveners are often not the best bureaucrats. They usually resist being boxed into traditional positions and are always expanding the role that is assigned them.[47]

Potential enliveners not only bring expertise to a community, but they embody a spirit that acts as a magnet that pulls the community in new directions. The enlivener calls forth the gifts of others and moves offstage as often as possible. The priestly role of a mediator is the center of the ritual between the people and the Holy Spirit. The enlivener often works behind the scenes to create the conditions through which others are given a voice. Priestly functions are regular and predictable. The work of the enlivener is transformative and experimental.[48] While this work is demanding and draining, an enlivener will recruit others to this office and use them in ways that assure that a variety of gifts are manifest in the community. This not only relieves a single person from the impossible task of meeting the demands and having the expertise to fulfill this office, but it encourages the gifts of others. A bureaucratic approach will focus the leadership of a congregation's sung prayer only in one person in a clear hierarchy of accountability. While administratively clear, ritual boredom may often be the result. The enlivener helps the worshiping community understand themselves and bring their gifts to the transformative experience of liturgy.[49]

---

47. Tom Driver notes that shamans are relatively uncentered in comparison to the priest. This uncentered quality may relate to the fact that shamans (and by extension, enliveners) often move in liminal space and effect transformations of persons and communities rather than building up existing structures. This uncentered quality, however, does not refer to the shaman's (or enlivener's) style of leadership. Indeed, facilitating a ritual experience is a very focused endeavor. The uncenteredness of the shaman refers to the shaman's unwillingness to be totally bound by the status quo (a role that Michael Warren would assign to the bureaucrat), but also to her or his almost intuitive ability to see connections between the community's existential life and its heritage and the needs of the world. See Driver, 69-75, for a context for this discussion.

48. See Driver, 72, for the parallel statement between the priest and the shaman. Driver notes that the "shaman flits all over, . . . cueing others to their tasks, directing music, playing music, dancing, becoming possessed, disappearing and reappearing, greeting people, admonishing people, manipulating the scene, not representing the spirits but creating the conditions through which they come here and now and connect" (73-74).

49. It must be noted here that enliveners may also be dangerous people in the life of the community. Their charismatic nature and attunedness to others make them candidates for unhealthy manipulation of a community. This is why it is necessary for enliveners to be deeply rooted in the biblical witness of the church and invested in the needs of the world.

A North American Enlivener: Mary Oyer

The scene is the 1999 gathering of the Hymn Society in the United States and Canada in Vancouver, British Columbia. Over three hundred church musicians, pastors, and laity have assembled to share in a week of global congregational song led by three of the persons featured in this book: I-to Loh, Patrick Matsikenyiri, and Pablo Sosa. Each brought his own style of leadership to the sessions, drawing musical sounds, languages, and movements not thought possible from the largely Anglo, North American group. Completing the global list of presenters was Mary Oyer, who guided the group through morning prayer each day. Oyer (b. 1923) is also a veteran of global gatherings, having planned and guided worship at the Mennonite World Conference Assemblies. Since our heads were swirling with the sounds of Africa, Asia, and Latin America, Mary led morning prayer primarily from North American musical traditions. Her leadership of the prayer embodied the attributes of the enlivener that have been discussed above.

Mary guided each day's prayer with a sure voice, definitive gesture, and crisp instructions. She achieved variety in the unaccompanied singing by instructing the various vocal parts to sing in differing combinations on each stanza. After offering a brief contextual statement about a selection, she gave the pitches of each part, unaided by any instrument, and pulled the group into the spirit of the song with a strong gesture. Those assembled were quite willing followers. If they hesitated for a moment to enter into the tempo or style of the chosen selection, she drew them into her vision of the hymn through assertive but never dominating leadership and shaped a choir out of the individual members of this ad hoc congregation. There was nothing flashy in her leadership on these mornings. We were drawn together by a combination of Mary's knowledge of the craft of hymn singing, intuitive understanding of the relationship between singing and worship, and the authenticity of her identity as a leader of the people's song. On what basis would I place Mary Oyer alongside the others in this volume as an enlivener of global congregational song? Mary embodies capable musicianship, a global perspective, a love for the voice as the primary instrument of the church, and an understanding of the reciprocal energy between congregational singing and faith.

Biographical Background

Though Goshen, Indiana, has served as a home base for Mary Oyer virtually all of her life, she is a citizen of the world.[50] Her father was the dean of Goshen College. Following graduation from Goshen High School and Goshen College, with a major in music and a minor in art, Mary pursued graduate work at the University of Michigan in 1945. Concurrent with her study, she began teaching in the music department of Goshen College, completing her master of music degree in music literature in 1948. She developed a basic course on music, visual arts, and architecture that became a hallmark of her course offerings at Goshen College for decades to follow. Summers were devoted to travel and study in art, architecture, and her primary performing instrument, the cello. She began work on her doctor of musical arts (DMA) degree during the summer of 1953 and completed the degree following a yearlong sabbatical in 1958 in the areas of cello performance, art history, and medieval and cultural history of Europe. All of her DMA recitals consisted of works by Beethoven for cello. Upon the completion of her doctoral studies in 1958, she was appointed head of the music department at Goshen College.

Though Oyer continued her studies in the humanities, she began work in 1962 on the *Mennonite Hymnal* as executive secretary of the Joint Hymnal Committee, a project that included both the (Old) Mennonite Church and the General Conference Mennonite Church. As the only woman on the committee in a significant decision-making role, Mary endured a degree of discrimination when her expertise was not fully recognized.[51] The title of executive secretary belies the significant editorial work she contributed to the *Mennonite Hymnal*, published in 1969.

She studied hymnody with Erik Routley in Scotland during the 1963-64 academic year. He made her aware of the value of reading an entire hymn text rather than only the abridged versions that tended to be published in hymnals. "If you had the whole text, it changed the nature of the hymn." By the

---

50. Much of the information in this section comes from a two-day visit with Mary Oyer in Goshen during January 1999. Uncited quotations are from the interviews conducted during this time.

51. Mary Oyer has reflected on the difficulties of being a woman in her work as a hymnal editor and in worship in "An Interview with Mary Oyer," *Hymn* 45, no. 1 (January 1994): 14-17. Her student Ken Nafziger confirms that "Mary Oyer did an enormous amount of the work on the 1969 hymnal, but has not been, in my opinion, adequately credited for her efforts." Another bias against Oyer cited by Nafziger was that she was trained as an instrumental musician (cello), and instruments were forbidden in the Mennonite Church.

time she came to work on the next Mennonite hymnal, *Hymnal: A Worship Book* (1992), Oyer noted that there seemed to be a lack of interest in original texts brought on in large part by issues in inclusive language. Because of her musicological interest in representing the original music and text in an authentic form, this was a disturbing trend to her.[52] As a result of her study with Routley, she became a collector of complete original texts and tunes. The carefulness with which she alters existing texts is explained in her thorough introduction to the *Mennonite Hymnal* (1969).[53]

The committee recognized the arrogance of many of the mission hymns inherited from the nineteenth and early twentieth centuries with their implied Euro–North American superiority and their unidirectional focus of bringing the gospel to the lost. These hymns did not express the sense of partnership in mission that is a part of Mennonite missions around the world. As a result, hymns like Reginald Heber's "From Greenland's Icy Mountains" (1819) and H. Ernest Nichols's "We've a Story to Tell to the Nations" (1896), so prominent in many other hymnals to this point, were not present in this collection. Samuel Wolcott's "Christ for the World We Sing" (1869) and Mary Ann Thomson's "O Zion Haste" (1868) are hymns of missionary zeal, but they avoid the denigrating language directed to the lost and tend to replace a unidirectional approach to missions with a more cosmic view of one world needing Christ. Faced with a paucity of theologically appropriate Western mission hymns, the committee decided to join the global church in songs "that make sense to them." Six Asian examples[54] were included in the *Mennonite Hymnal* primarily for Women's Missionary meetings. Four of the six hymns are set in unison, stylistically appropriate for much Asian music, reflecting a nascent sensitivity to musical performance practice. These hymns are but a glimmer of global hymns that would appear in *Hymnal: A Worship Book* (1992).

In 1968 Oyer received a grant from the U.S. Health, Education, and Welfare Department to pursue African studies at UCLA. This proved to be the beginning of many summers and sabbatical years of study spent in Africa over the coming decades. A Fulbright Fellowship allowed Oyer to continue

---

52. "Interview with Mary Oyer," 16. This issue is discussed in more depth here.

53. "Introduction," *The Mennonite Hymnal*, ed. Mary Oyer (Scottdale, Pa.: Herald; Newton, Kans.: Faith and Life Press, 1969). Ken Nafziger noted that Oyer "carried all the notes from the 1969 *Mennonite Hymnal* around in her head without notes or cards. Between 1963 and 1969 she lived and breathed hymnody."

54. "God, the Lord Omnipotent" (55) from Taiwan, "May the Holy Spirit's Sword" (209) from China, "Jesus Merciful" (339) from China, "Heart and Mind, Possessions, Lord" (362) from India, "Here, O Lord, Your Servants Gather" (377) from Japan, and "Praise Our Father for This Sunday" (498) from China.

her African music study during the summer of 1969 in Senegal, Gambia, Ghana, Kenya, Uganda, Tanzania, and Zambia. By 1978 Mary was sharing the wealth of her summers of African music study with the Mennonite World Conference in Wichita, Kansas. A two-year leave from Goshen College between 1979 and 1981, during which Oyer worked in the National Archives of Kenya and studied Kikuyu music at Kenyatta University, sealed her love of African music. Though she found that her expertise as a cellist provided an entrée with the expatriate community in Africa, she immersed herself in the study of Swahili and African traditional music in order to gain an African perspective on the life and thought patterns of the people. Oyer notes that "one learns about another culture's music by trying to teach Western music to its musicians" as well as by studying the music of the culture.[55]

Ken Nafziger, professor of music at Eastern Mennonite University, is a protégé of Oyer, studying with her in the early 1960s. He observed significant changes in her approach to music in the decade of the 1960s. "I was in awe of Mary. She did things with a high degree of excellence. Her focus at this time was quite narrow — classical music only, no gospel songs or folk hymnody. After her experience in Africa, she struck terror into the hearts of her former students when she changed her views." According to Nafziger, Mary Oyer moved from a position of "greater exclusivity based on her classical music education to a greater inclusivity for a wider variety of hymnody and world song. The 1969 hymnal, with its inclusion of so many early American folk hymns, and her experiences in the study of African music changed her worldview."[56]

Oyer's African studies brought her into contact with such notable scholars as John Blacking, the Irish anthropologist and ethnomusicologist who conducted field research primarily in parts of southern Africa, and J. H. Kwabena Nketia, whose book *The Music of Africa* (1974) has become a standard source for this field. Once again she immersed herself in the study of African culture through *mbira* and one-stringed fiddle lessons. Nketia, who according to Oyer was "generous with whites studying African music," recommended African musicians for her instrumental study from the Institute of African Studies in Ghana. Out of these experiences she developed an approach to her study which involved getting into the actual thought processes of the people as much as possible. "You can like African music at a distance," says Oyer, "but this is a condescending approach. Most people in other

55. Correspondence with Mary Oyer, February 27, 2002.

56. Interview with Ken Nafziger, Eastern Mennonite University, Harrisonburg, Va., March 26, 1999.

cultures are pleased to see you try, even if you fail." Humility — described by Oyer as "the ability to fail" or "choosing the vulnerable position" — is the key for the North American wishing to learn about another culture's music.

Mary Oyer was involved significantly in the committee process for *Hymnal: A Worship Book* (1992). She was the chair of the Hymnal Project from 1984 to 1986 and was the representative of the Mennonite Church (the hymnal committee also included representatives from the Church of the Brethren and the General Conference Mennonite Church) for the preparation of this hymnal. Her work on the project concluded with the editing of the 150-selection *Hymnal Sampler* (1989) published in anticipation of *Hymnal: A Worship Book*.[57] This hymnal contains over sixty non-Western and cross-cultural hymns, compared to six in the 1969 hymnal. The cross-cultural contributions are as significant in many ways as the totally non-Western selections. For example, this book includes a South African musical setting for Isaac Watts's famous text, "When I Survey the Wondrous Cross" (260). The music, "Senzeni na?" (What have we done?), brings a new dimension to the singing of this familiar English-language hymn. "The music may at first seem too buoyant to sing with a text about suffering and loss. Yet this style can teach us to sing with energy, even through heartache and pain."[58] Oyer's contributions to *Hymnal: A Worship Book* set new standards for the inclusion of non-Western and cross-cultural song in North American hymnals. Ken Nafziger notes that "through the contributions of Mary Oyer, every hymn looks on the page like the style that it represents. In many hymnals all hymns look the same regardless of the musical style. Mary's goal was to make the page look like what the music sounds like." In *Hymnal: A Worship Book*, this is as true of plainsong hymns and Reformation chorales as it is of Native American and African hymns.

In her article "Hymnody in the Context of World Mission," Oyer presents a clear strategy for those who wish to engage in music making with other cultures.[59] In this article she addresses specifically sub-Saharan African

57. "Mary K. Oyer," in *Hymnal Companion*, comp. Joan A. Fyock (Elgin, Ill.: Brethren Press; Newton, Kans.: Faith and Life Press; Scottdale, Pa.: Mennonite Publishing House, 1996), 624.

58. *Hymnal Companion*, 375. Because of the similarity of the African tune with the chant melody for "Abide with Me" found in Joseph Funk's *Harmonia Sacra* (12th ed., 1867), Oyer speculates that "the tune may have gone to Africa with a missionary and has now returned to North America" (p. 375).

59. Mary K. Oyer, "Hymnody in the Context of World Mission," in *The International Hymnology Annual*, ed. Vernon Wicker, vol. 1 (Berrien Springs, Mich.: Vande Vere Publishing, 1991), 52-75. The following points are a summary from pp. 52-53. This article was originally an address presented in Lund, Sweden, in 1987 at a meeting of the Internationale Arbeitsgemeinschaft für Hymnologie (IAH), an international hymnology society, and published in the *IAH-Bulletin* 16 (June 1988): 53-74.

music, but I have found her approach to be helpful in other regions of the world as well. Her fourfold approach goes to the heart of moving beyond ethnocentric perspectives to a broader worldview:

1. *Participate in music making* by studying a traditional instrument with a teacher from the culture. This could also include joining a choir of African musicians, for example. It is important to experience the learning processes of another culture as well as its musical repertoire and to fit one's voice and body into the ensemble and rhythms of another culture's music.

2. *Engage a person from another culture in a discussion of common musical and hymnological interests.* This involves learning to listen as well as ask the right questions. This kind of discussion can be particularly helpful in gaining insight into how a person from outside your cultural perspective views musical and liturgical practices. Why are some rituals meaningful across cultures while others are not?

3. *Read literature written by poets, playwrights, and authors from the region of the world you are engaging.* A Western mind-set might suggest that one start with histories or cultural guides as a way of gaining insight into a given cultural context. Oyer directs the inquirer encountering a new cultural situation toward literature from the region. First of all, this is a more engaging and interesting way to learn. Second, one begins to discern common struggles and themes after reading just a few sources. Rather than being summarized by an intermediary source, literature expresses the conflicts and capabilities of a people through their own thought processes, cultural ways of interacting, and metaphors. Third, reading literature from a new cultural context opens up communication with those from that culture. For example, I, like Oyer, have found an immediate rapport with Nigerian students when I express my appreciation of Wole Soyinka's plays and political works or Chinua Achebe's classic novel, *Things Fall Apart.*

4. *Read the observations and insights of anthropologists, ethnomusicologists, linguists, and theologians.* A Western sensibility might suggest starting here first. Oyer stresses, however, that those who seek musical cross-cultural understanding begin with music, people, and the creative, artistic endeavors of the culture under consideration. There is a role for the observations of experts, but critical commentary needs to be based upon some empirical interaction with the culture. Given the degree of cultural diversity available to most persons in the United States, especially though not exclusively in urban situations, the student of a new

culture need not travel far to gain contact with those who have been nurtured in another worldview. Universities, civic groups, cultural festivals, and liturgical settings all offer possible points of convergence for those who would risk being the stranger in a new setting and a learner of new ways.

Through this approach to cultural learning and regular travel to the African continent, Oyer has developed expertise in playing African instruments and knowledge of African ways of conceiving music.[60] The significance of oral musical traditions, the relationship between melody and language, the role of rhythm in creating musical tension, African conceptions of harmony, and the role of African music and movement in the shaping of community are but a few of the many insights that she has learned from her experiences. Oyer also relates African musical practices to African ways of understanding their environment. The African sense of community, the relationship of the body to its surrounding situation, cyclical views of time, and dialogical patterns in culture all have their corollaries in musical experience. Drawing on the witness of the Xhosa Christian leader Ntsikana, Oyer puts a distinctive African face on Christian song and its contribution to Christian witness.[61] Ntsikana's story becomes part of the "cloud of witnesses" that nurtures a broader understanding of God's revelation.

Oyer believes that music itself, not just the texts, provides a key to culture. Cyclic forms (Oyer also uses the term "circular") provide a clue to a sense of time. Music continues until it has completed its work with the community that sings it. Compared to sequential structures that stop when a predetermined end has been reached, cyclic music "stops when the leader wants to or is tired." The actual shape of the music tells us "how a people perceive beginnings and middles and ends. . . . [I]s there a kind of ongoing circular movement that can be halted at any time?"[62] A cyclic understanding of time is sometimes referred to as *polychronic* time rather than *monochronic* or linear time (Western time).[63] Oyer observes this same quality in African American

60. Her study of the *mbira*, a favorite instrument of the Shona people in Zimbabwe and the Bukoba of Uganda, taught her a lot about the African musical process.

61. Aspects of the story of Ntsikana appear in at least two articles written by Oyer: "Hymnody," 68-70, and "Global Music for the Churches," in *Music in Worship: A Mennonite Perspective,* ed. Bernie Neufeld (Scottdale, Pa.: Herald, 1998), 69-70. See chap. 4 of this book for an in-depth discussion of Ntsikana's hymns and life.

62. "Interview with Mary Oyer," 17.

63. Edward T. Hall, *Understanding Cultural Differences* (Yarmouth, Maine: Intercultural Press, 1990), 43-50, elaborates on this distinction.

music where "Black Gospel goes on and on as long as the spirit moves, as long as it feels right to do so."[64] An Aristotelian view of drama, by contrast, is monochronic — a distinct beginning, middle, and end — with a climax. It is natural that musical structures and artistic forms should reflect the sense of time in given cultural settings.

The cyclic nature of African music and life has had an increasing effect on Oyer. The cyclic quality stresses the "organic wholeness" of the experience of hymn singing rather than focusing on a strong climax. The relative sameness of cyclic structures with smaller variations mirrors the cycles of the seasons and of life. According to Oyer, a life based on a cyclic perception of time has a smoothness to it that is similar to a person sitting on a riverbank watching the river pass by. Western culture values uniqueness and individuality while Africans value sameness and community. The musical structures that emanate from these cultures reflect these patterns of life.[65]

Oyer has led music at two Mennonite World Conferences. These events have been major occasions for the dissemination of world song. Conference songbooks have allowed those attending to take the songs back to local congregations. The *International Songbook* for the 1978 Tenth Assembly in Wichita, Kansas, is exemplary of the range of literature with sections on Africa (13 songs), Asia (14 songs), Central and South America (13 songs), Europe (11 songs), and North America (12 songs).[66] Each song is in English, German, Spanish, and French as well as in the original language if it is not one of these. European and North American songs also have occasional Dutch translations available. Percussion parts are suggested on some of the African songs, and accompaniments attempt to reflect the style of the originating musical context.

During my conversations with Oyer she posed and answered an important question: What do we (the North American church) have to gain by singing global songs? I paraphrase her response. Global songs have some characteristics that are quite different from the "rules" of Western music. These songs challenge our ideas of what is acceptable. The cyclic character and oral transmission of these songs cause us to listen carefully, more carefully perhaps than when we rely primarily on the visual transmission of the music through a musical score. The percussive aspect of much global music offers another mode of worship that is not so cerebral — more physical in response.

---

64. "Interview with Mary Oyer," 17.

65. Chap. 7 goes into greater detail on the characteristics and possibilities of cyclic musical structures in worship.

66. *International Songbook*, ed. Rosemary Wyse and Clarence Hiebert (Lombard, Ill.: Mennonite World Conference, 1978).

Songs from the world church provide a way of reaching out in mission that is not condescending or arrogant. "The western world has done so much that has wronged other parts of the world. We are caught up in the syndrome of being number one. Many global songs call us to penitential values that we don't have — a way of making amends."

Mary Oyer continues to contribute to world song. In addition to leading singing experiences in hundreds of local congregations, she has recently completed teaching for almost three years in the Master of Church Music program at Tainan Theological College and Seminary in Taiwan with I-to Loh. She even attempted to study Mandarin Chinese in her mid-seventies to prepare for this experience. Courses in Tainan included music bibliography, arts in the church, music history, and private cello instruction. Oyer embodies the concept of a North American enlivener. She notes, "music reveals what the culture is, and it reveals who the people are and what they value. It is a key to understanding people."[67] Enliveners of congregational song in local congregations may not have the professional education and experiences of Mary Oyer, but they can appreciate the relationship between singing and people in the service of liturgy.

Mary Oyer as Enlivener

I have chosen Mary Oyer as a primary example of a North American enlivener. The qualities she brings to her leadership of song provide a model for any who would aspire to this office. After talking with her, reading her writings, and observing her lead others, I offer a brief summary of those characteristics that reflect her skills as an enlivener.

- For Mary Oyer, the primary tool for communicating to the congregation is the voice in its simplicity, unadorned by instruments as much as possible. Though an instrumentalist in background, she has found her voice and uses it well to invite others to sing with her.
- Mary Oyer has attempted to experience the Christian witness in its depth and breadth. Her study of congregational song includes the range of classic Western hymnody and the breadth of the church's song throughout the world.
- Mary Oyer has become a citizen of the world in her perspective. Though proud of her Mennonite heritage, she is also aware of its limita-

67. "Interview with Mary Oyer," 17.

tions. She has made every effort to learn the processes of music making that are found in other cultural perspectives and to make music on the terms of others, not just on those of the Western world.

– Mary Oyer places her song within the context of worship. One of the joys of singing with her in Vancouver was to see her lead morning prayer with an Anglican priest. She used the shape of the classic Anglican liturgy as a vehicle to integrate songs from a variety of traditions, each chosen appropriately for its place in the liturgy of the day.

– Mary Oyer knows the cultural and theological context of each song she introduces. While she wants those gathered to pray and praise with the song, she wants them to understand the witness that a song brings with it from its original (authentic) setting. As much as possible Mary wants congregations in North America to experience the prayers of Christians from around the world on their own terms rather than to be assimilated into the ethos of the singer in the United States.

– Mary Oyer guides the people's sung prayer without dominating it. She knows how much to say (which is as little as possible) and when to move out of the spotlight. She has developed a conducting gesture that brings unity to the congregation's singing, but never dominates the song.

– Mary Oyer recognizes the congregation as the first and most important choir and prepares diligently for the task of leading the people's song. I have observed her practicing and preparing for a congregational singing event with as much insight and rehearsal as an orchestra conductor brings to her/his setting. Because the people's song is so important, it deserves careful preparation and honing of musical and communicative skills. When every word, gesture, and sung instruction counts, the level of preparation must be very high.

The office of the enlivener is rewarding and one of sacred responsibility. It is an office that creates space for sung prayer. Mary Oyer embodies this office with skill, grace, and humility. The question may arise, however: "Can I be an enlivener? I could never travel to Africa and Asia and spend the time it takes to acquire the skills that Mary Oyer has." To those who express this concern I would suggest two things: Any vocation worth following takes preparation and self-awareness. I am suggesting that the traditional role of the Western church musician needs to be expanded in order to enliven worship in the twenty-first century. There will be skills to learn, and they will take practice.

On the other hand, I would like to suggest that there may be more enliveners among us than have heretofore been acknowledged. These are people who have some training in music but, equally important, have a vision for how liturgy can more effectively involve the people, i.e., teach them to pray more broadly and deeply as they sing. These enliveners already have a sense of the vocation, but need the support of local congregations to hone their skills and the opportunities to guide congregations in sung prayer. Their vocation and graces need a name and identity — enlivener.

I shall close this chapter with an example of this kind of enlivener. I visited a congregation in the countryside outside of Tainan, Taiwan, one Sunday. This was during my first trip to Asia. I was feeling particularly disoriented after getting lost on two occasions earlier in the week and was totally dependent upon my hosts since I could not speak the language. While I had been to many services conducted in languages I did not understand, I was not particularly looking forward to worshiping in Taiwanese on this day. After I sat down, a man in this Presbyterian congregation came forward and began the service with fifteen minutes of singing. He had a strong natural voice and a radiant face. In fifteen minutes he took the congregation around the world with songs from Africa, Asia, and the Caribbean. Though the songs were sung in Taiwanese, I knew many of them and was able to join in. He taught the people these new songs effectively by oral means even though this congregation had a strong heritage of singing hymns from the hymnal. He used neither accompaniment nor assisting musicians. The entire congregation was his choir. I was immediately at home.

I thought he was a trained musician but found that he was quite proficient in traditional Taiwanese music and musical instruments but had never received formal musical instruction except as a member of the church choir. He received his vision for leading congregational song from a workshop with I-to Loh and was a more effective enlivener than the musically trained choir director at the church. His position in the church as an elder, his relationship with the people, his sure and clear voice, his understanding of how to teach a congregation a song, and his vision of singing world song in a rural Taiwanese congregation made him one of the most effective enliveners I have ever seen.

CHAPTER 9

Polyrhythmic Worship

The coherence of the conflicting rhythms is thus based upon a kind of tension which gives the music its dynamic power. The accents of a singer or a master drummer will engage and highlight various rhythms in order to increase the effect. Most significantly, then, once you are playing the music properly, it becomes extremely difficult to play your part unless the whole ensemble is playing; you depend on the other rhythms for your time.

JOHN MILLER CHERNOFF[1]

It should be noted that rhythm possesses two characteristic attributes. On the one hand it represents order and structure; on the other hand it can induce trance and ecstasy.

OTTO KAROLYI[2]

I recall an "aha!" moment during a talking drum lesson in Ogbomosho, Nigeria, in 1989. One of my duties as a visiting music professor at the Baptist seminary was to play piano for the required chapel services at 8 A.M. each weekday morning before classes began. Sitting near me on the front pew was

1. John Miller Chernoff, *African Rhythm and African Sensibility: Aesthetics and Social Action in African Musical Idioms* (Chicago: University of Chicago Press, 1979), 53.
2. Otto Karolyi, *Traditional African and Oriental Music* (New York: Penguin Books, 1998), 16.

a West African drum ensemble, usually consisting of five drummers. Because there were so many drummers among the seminary students, there was a different ensemble for each morning. The experience of playing hymns on an out-of-tune piano (pianos do not usually fare well in a tropical climate) accompanied by West African polyrhythms was a cross-cultural experience for both of us.

In one conversation with my drum instructor, Michael Olanjiwaru, a student at the seminary, I asked a question that seemed so logical to me: "Michael, who do you think is the best drummer in the seminary?" Michael was silent for some time. At first I thought he was being modest, because he could easily have been the best drummer. It turned out that I had not asked the right question. After some further exchange, Michael helped me understand that the question was not "who is the best drummer?" but "which is the best drum ensemble?" As Michael patiently explained to me, an individual drummer cannot be evaluated in isolation, but only in the context of an ensemble — a community of drummers. This was an entirely different philosophy from the one in which I had been trained. In my conservatory education I was judged by my ability as an individual performer, not as an ensemble musician.

This experience has caused a kind of Copernican revolution in my thought and practice as a liturgical enlivener. As a young church musician I was energized by the congregation's response to a solo I sang, an offertory I played, or a choral selection I conducted. Congregational song was important, but it was not of the same significance as the choir's finely honed anthems. Something happened to my worldview during the fall of 1989 as I participated in African worship experiences from the perspective of both the presider's chair and the pew. Worship was much more powerful when the presiding musicians made music with the people, not just for the people. The experience of liturgy did not revolve around me or my efforts to provide meaningful worship for those in the congregation. Worship revolved around the ritual shaping of those individuals gathered into a community in praise of God and in prayer for the world. As an enlivener in this experience, it was my role not to draw attention to my abilities but to become a prompter in a process of becoming one body in Christ.

I have searched for a musical metaphor that most nearly expresses this quality of liturgical experience. "Unison singing," "harmonic blending," or "contrapuntal complexity" all have metaphorical potential. These are essentially Western terms that describe the priorities of Euro–North American musical traditions. While descriptive to some degree of music in other parts of the world, "polyrhythmic music making" communicates a sonic tapestry that is usually the province of world music. As a liturgical metaphor it suggests an energy of competing rhythms that come together in an aural mosaic. Each tile of a mosaic has its own brilliance and character, yet it contributes to a larger picture. Each rhythm of a polyrhythmic collaboration has its distinct pattern, yet it combines with other rhythms to produce larger aural experience. This is not the experience of musical assimilation — a kind of musical-cultural hegemony where distinct rhythms merge in a melting pot of unified sonority. It is a mosaic where uniqueness is valued and the energy of each perspective contributes to the wholeness of the entire community.[3]

What might polyrhythmic liturgy look like? How might one recognize those diverse elements that, when placed in juxtaposition with each other, create a dynamic community or "kin-dom," as Kathy Black describes the diverse assembly in worship, where each individual has a place in God's family?[4] For the remainder of this chapter I will suggest some of the cross-rhythms that make up the polyrhythmic matrix of worship that celebrates the diversity of God's created order.

Polyrhythmic worship sings with the saints who have shaped us and the saints of the present age. In response to the Eucharist liturgy, polyrhythmic worship is not stuck in the past nor fixated on current fads, but sings with the faithful of every place and time. It avoids both liturgical amnesia and ephemeral cultural cults. Enliveners with polyrhythmic sensibilities do not forget the faith that has shaped us nor dwell only in the past. They do not embrace a current popular musical style exclusively while forgetting that Christians around the world are also praying at that same moment in myriad tongues and ways. Polyrhythmic worship embodies both the depth and heritage of liturgical tradition and the breadth of diverse ways of praying with the world church and fresh movements of the spirit.

Polyrhythmic worship incorporates the ordinary and the other. Ordinary refers to those rituals of any group that reflect their usual cultural currency — ways of being together and communicating, i.e., being in commu-

---

3. After settling on this metaphor, I discovered a complementary approach in Mark Taylor, "Polyrhythm in Worship: Caribbean Keys to an Effective Word of God," in *Making Room at the Table: An Invitation to Multicultural Worship*, ed. Brian K. Blount and Leonora Tubbs Tisdale (Louisville: Westminster John Knox, 2001), 108-28.

4. "Kin-dom" (vs. "kingdom") is the term cited by Kathy Black in *Culturally-Conscious Worship* (St. Louis: Chalice Press, 2000), 35. Originating with Ada Maria Isasi-Diaz, "kin-dom" is preferred by Black because it "does not have the hierarchical implications, class divisions, and connotations of dominance and power associated with 'kingdom.' It also serves as a reminder that we are all kin-members of the family of God."

nity. These ways offer security within a corporate liturgy. Ordinary may also refer to those parts of worship that are repeated each week, e.g., Offering, Creed, Doxology, etc. The "other" reflects those rituals, persons, and experiences that come from beyond the normative context of the worshiping community. These balance the security of the ordinary with the suspense of the other. Balancing the comfortable with the unsettling in worship[5] sets up a polyrhythmic dynamic that respects the ordinary of any cultural context while challenging the community with the prophetic witness of the "other" beyond our cultural expectations.

Polyrhythmic worship will celebrate the perspectives that come from differences in gender, vocation (laity versus clergy), generations, socioeconomic position, and cultural orientation. The bright voices of children and changing timbres of young persons should be just as common as the softer voices of senior adults. Presiders should come from all walks of life. Polyrhythmic worship will by nature be more democratic with as much equal access as possible to the various presiding offices that influence the preparation and presentation of worship.[6] This does not negate the significance of the vocation of ordination, but stresses the equality in vocation of all baptized Christians.

Polyrhythmic worship will balance concerns for the local community with prayers for the world. A congregation worshiping with a polyrhythmic sensitivity will avoid the provincial tendency to pray only for those who are near and dear. This worship will also raise the awareness of the assembly to those places and persons where God is at work in the world church. Polyrhythmic worship will not avoid mentioning places of suffering, alienation, and oppression. When global events provide reason to rejoice, the polyrhythmic community of faith will join in the celebration. In many circumstances global suffering and celebration will have local significance for cocultural groups in a given community. Polyrhythmic worship brings the near and far together in their prayers.

The soundscape of polyrhythmic worship will reflect the diversity of the community and their global concerns. Polyrhythmic worship will be open to the sounds of other languages and accents. The Scripture might be heard in at least one additional language each week. A stanza of a hymn or the refrain of a song might be sung in the original language or even in translation, if

5. Black, 107.

6. This would reflect what Eric H. F. Law calls "low power distance" rather than "high power distance," the latter indicating a preference for hierarchy and "an order of inequality in the world." See *The Wolf Shall Dwell with the Lamb* (St. Louis: Chalice Press, 1993), 19-22, for further discussion of this.

other than English. A witness or testimony might be shared bilingually or in translation. The Lord's Prayer might be prayed in several languages simultaneously. This spirit of Pentecost might also pervade the range of musical styles used in worship and the instruments that add color to the musical ensemble. Just as Isaiah 11 hopes for a time when the "wolf shall live with the lamb, the leopard shall lie down with the kid, the calf and the lion and the fatling together . . . ," perhaps worship wars will give way to a time when percussion from various regions of the world will share the space with a pipe organ, guitars with violins, a *khlui* (bamboo flute) from Thailand with a Western oboe, and a Sundanese *angklung* from Indonesia with the piano. Drawing from the intergenerational discussion above, the vocal timbres of all ages will shape the chorus of the faithful. Silence will also have a place in the soundscape of polyrhythmic worship. The range of aural expression will be diverse and vibrant.

Polyrhythmic worship is fully embodied worship. Cultures that have not been as aware of the kinesthetic possibilities will develop an appreciation for this sixth sense and the wisdom that comes from bodily awareness.[7] The role of dance in worship carries a troubled history.[8] Though some North African Coptic Christians danced, their behavior was not normative for the broader church. Paul Westermeyer notes that Ethiopian and Coptic Christians "were able to ground their rhythm and ecstasy in the word the way that the rest of the church could not, but their practice was exceptional and only later would become more normative for other orthodox Christians."[9] As we become aware of the Christian church in its myriad global manifestations, however, we encounter cultures that are much more comfortable with their bodies and use their bodies effectively in worship.[10] Carlton Young has noted that "Western thought tends to divorce emotion and the mind, and singing and dancing, while other cultures, including most in Africa, are not put together that way." He cites a conversation with Patrick

7. See James L. Empereur, S.J., "The Physicality of Worship," in *Bodies of Worship: Explorations in Theory and Practice,* ed. Bruce T. Morrill (Collegeville, Minn.: Liturgical Press, 1999), 144, for the idea of the kinesthetic sixth sense.

8. James McKinnon, *Music in Early Christian Literature* (Cambridge: Cambridge University Press, 1987), cites a significant number of references to dance.

9. Paul Westermeyer, *Te Deum: The Church and Music* (Minneapolis: Augsburg Fortress, 1998), 75.

10. See three videocassettes prepared by Thomas A. Cane that highlight the integral role of dance in worship from a global perspective: *The Dancing Church: Video Impressions of the Church in Africa* (n.d.), *The Dancing Church of the South Pacific* (1998), and *¡Fiesta! Celebrations at San Fernando* (1999), all published by Paulist Press.

Matsikenyiri (the subject of chap. 5) about the sensual quality of life among his people, the Shona:

> A child lives in the mother's womb for nine months, then for one and a half years is carried on the mother's back as she walks everywhere — her arms and legs transmit the rhythm of walking, the rhythm of physical labor such as hoeing in the garden or picking up branches to burn in the stove, playing with her and others' children, cooking, singing, and dancing. Children with nearly three years of rhythmic contact with another human, when they are young persons or young adults do not easily put these attributes aside in order to be Christians — that for many means to be converted into a non-feeling, non-dancing person.[11]

The natural use of the body in worship may be seen not only beyond the boundaries of the United States. In addition to immigrants and descendants of dancing peoples from around the world among us, young people in the United States have grown up in a culture where they have learned to move and express themselves with their bodies as well as their voices. Contemporary praise and worship gatherings often include persons swaying, clapping, and lifting their hands in the *orans* position of the early church as a part of their worship. Prayer may not only be said or sung, it may also be enacted. Many worship traditions, even among Protestants, have distinctive postures for prayer. A fuller use of the body may enhance ways of praying. All who participate in polyrhythmic worship must become vulnerable in areas of inexperience. Perhaps dance is as threatening as any for many Anglo North Americans. James Clifford invites those who come in contact with rituals that are new to them to become participant observers. Participant observers must be willing to be self-conscious and culturally displaced.[12] For many persons in the world "worship cannot take place, cannot be meaningful, without dance."[13] Polyrhythmic worshipers will not only hear a diverse community sing and speak as one, they will also see in dance the body of Christ.[14] As Bernard Cooke suggests, "The

---

11. Correspondence with Carlton Young, December 12, 2001. This quotation is from an unpublished paper delivered at Southern Baptist Theological Seminary, Louisville, Ky., October 2001.

12. James Clifford, *The Predicament of Culture* (Cambridge: Harvard University Press, 1988), 24.

13. Barbara Browning, *Samba: Resistance in Motion* (Bloomington: Indiana University Press, 1995), xiv. Browning is speaking specifically of Brazil in this quotation, but the same can be said of any African-influenced culture and many Asian contexts.

14. Pedrito U. Maynard-Reid makes an impassioned and articulate plea for holistic wor-

Word becoming flesh is not confined to the human Jesus of Nazareth, but is meant to find expression in the ecclesial body of the risen Christ."[15]

Polyrhythmic worship will seek to resist oppression in whatever form it manifests itself. By its nature it cannot tolerate the dominance of a single cultural perspective over another. Neither will it tolerate a romantic or exotic view of less familiar cultures. Romanticism does not provide a critique of accepted practices and rituals that demean, silence, or stereotype individuals or groups of cocultures within a larger cultural context.

Polyrhythmic worship is challenging and difficult. It is also visionary and rewarding. It includes not only the security and predictability of metrical binary rhythms but also enters into the uncomfortable marginality of less predictable polyrhythms. It avoids using only the lockstep uniformity of musical meters and employs the creativity, energy, and vitality of polyrhythmic complexity.[16] It rejects the security of the cultural clique for the adventure of being a bridge to those who live in the margins.[17]

Imagine with me the venerable hymn tune OLD 100TH with its roots in Calvin's *Genevan Psalter*. Rather than being limited only to the stately accompaniment of the pipe organ and Thomas Ken's doxology, "Praise God from whom all blessings flow," imagine a West African drum ensemble supporting the following text by Ruth Duck while singing this tune:

> Diverse in culture, nation, race,
> we come together by your grace.
> God, let us be a meeting ground
> where hope and healing love are found.
>
> God, let us be a bridge of care
> connecting people ev'rywhere.
> Help us confront all fear and hate
> and lust for power that separate.
>
> When chasms widen, storms arise,
> O Holy Spirit, make us wise.
> Let our resolve, like steel, be strong
> to stand with those who suffer wrong.

---

ship that achieves a balance between the "rational and physical" in *Diverse Worship: African-American, Caribbean, and Hispanic Perspectives* (Downers Grove, Ill.: InterVarsity, 2000), 203-13.

15. Bernard J. Cooke, "Body and Mystical Body: The Church as Communio," in *Bodies of Worship*, 50.

16. Taylor, 120, mentions similar ideas.

17. Black, 61.

God, let us be a table spread
with gifts of love and broken bread,
where all find welcome, grace attends,
and enemies arise as friends.[18]

© 1992 GIA Publications, Inc. Used by permission.

The polyrhythmic church has room for drums, organs, and much more.

---

18. Ruth Duck, *Dancing in the Universe: Hymns and Songs* (Chicago: GIA Publications, 1992), 26.

Bibliography

Achebe, Chinua. *Anthills of the Savannah.* London: Heinemann, 1987.

———. *Things Fall Apart.* New York: Anchor Books, [1959] 1994.

Adey, Lionel. *Class and Idol in the English Hymn.* Vancouver: University of British Columbia Press, 1988.

———. *Hymns and the Christian "Myth."* Vancouver: University of British Columbia Press, 1986.

Agawu, Kofi. *African Rhythm.* Cambridge: Cambridge University Press, 1995.

Alstott, Owen, ed. *Flor y Canto.* Portland, OR: OCP Publications, 1989.

Andrews, Edward Deming. *The Gift to Be Simple: Songs, Dances and Rituals of the American Shakers.* New York: Dover Publications, 1940.

Anselm, Fr. Interview. Lumko Institute, Delmenville, South Africa, November 13, 1998.

Aretz, Isabel. "Argentina." In *The New Grove Dictionary of Music and Musicians,* edited by Stanley Sadie, vol. 1, pp. 564-571. New York: Macmillan Publishers Limited, 1980.

Attali, Jacques. *Noise: The Political Economy of Music,* translated by Brian Massumi. Minneapolis: University of Minnesota Press, [1977] 1985.

Augsburger, David. *Pastoral Counseling Across Cultures.* Philadelphia: Westminster Press, 1986.

Axelsson, Olof. "The Development of African Church Music in Zimbabwe." In *Papers Presented at the Symposium on Ethnomusicology,* pp. 2-7. Grahamstown, South Africa: Rhodes University, September 24-26, 1981.

Bailey, John. *The Gospel in Hymns.* New York: Charles Scribner's Sons, 1950.

Bakare, Sebastian. *My Right to Land—in the Bible and in Zimbabwe: A Theology of Land.* Harare: Zimbabwe Council of Churches, 1993.

———. *The Drumbeat of Life: Jubilee in an African Context.* Geneva: WCC Publications, 1997.

Bal, Mieke. *On Meaning-Making: Essays in Semiotics.* Sonoma, CA: Polebridge Press, 1994.

Banana, Canaan. *Come and Share: An Introduction to Christian Theology.* Harare: Mambo Press, 1991.

Band, Edward. *Barclay of Formosa.* Ginza, Tokyo: Christian Literature Society, 1936.

Bangert, Mark P. "Dynamics of Liturgy and World Musics: A Methodology for Evaluation." In *Worship and Culture in Dialogue,* edited by S. Anita Stauffer, pp. 183-203. Geneva: The Lutheran World Federation, 1994.

————. "How Does One Go about Multicultural Worship?" In *What Does "Multicultural" Worship Look Like?* edited by Gordon Lathrop, pp. 24-33. Minneapolis: Augsburg Fortress, 1996.

————. "Liturgical Music, Culturally Tuned." In *Liturgy and Music: Lifetime Learning,* edited by Robin A. Leaver and Joyce Ann Zimmerman, pp. 360-383. Collegeville, MN: The Liturgical Press, 1998.

————. "Welcoming the Ethnic into Our Church Musical Diet." *Cross Accent: Journal of the Association of Lutheran Church Musicians* 5 (January 1995): 4-7.

Beeby, H. Dan. "Memories of the College in Memory of Shoki," *Theology and the Church* 21:2 (June 1996): 23-40.

Béhague, Gerard. "Tango." In *The New Grove Dictionary of Music and Musicians,* edited by Stanley Sadie, vol. 18, pp. 563-565. New York: Macmillan Publishers Limited, 1980.

Bell, Brian, ed. *Argentina.* Boston: Houghton Mifflin, 1997.

Bell, John L., and Graham Maule. *Enemy of Apathy: Songs of the Passion and Resurrection of Jesus, and the Coming of the Holy Spirit.* Chicago: G.I.A. Publications, 1988, rev. 1990.

————. "Flight of the Wild Goose." *Reformed Liturgy and Music* 34:2 (2000): 15-18.

————. *Heaven Shall Not Wait: Songs of Creation, the Incarnation, and the Life of Jesus.* Chicago: G.I.A. Publications, Inc., [1987] 1989.

————. *Love + Anger: Songs of Lively Faith and Social Justice.* Glasgow: Wild Goose Publications, 1997.

————. *Love from Below: The Seasons of Life, the Call to Care, and the Celebrating Community.* Glasgow: Wild Goose Publications, 1989.

————. *The Courage to Say No: Twenty-three Songs for Lent and Easter.* Chicago: G.I.A. Publications, 1996.

Bell, John L. "Hymns Are Heterogeneous." *Reformed Liturgy and Music* 31:1 (1997): 66-67.

————. *Innkeepers and Light Sleepers: Seventeen New Songs for Christmas.* Chicago: G.I.A. Publications, 1992.

————. *Many and Great: Songs of the World Church.* Chicago: G.I.A. Publications, [1990] 1992.

————. *Psalms of Patience, Protest and Praise.* Chicago: G.I.A. Publications, 1993.

————. "Reforming Worship: Change Is Not a Dirty Word." *Reformed Worship* 40 (June 1996): 5-11.

———. *Sent by the Lord: Songs of the World Church*, vol. 2. Chicago: G.I.A. Publications, [1991] 1992.

———. *The Singing Thing: A Case for Congregational Singing.* Glasgow: Wild Goose Publications, 2000.

———. *Wrestle and Fight and Pray: Thoughts on Christianity and Conflict.* Edinburgh: St. Andrew Press, 1993.

Belloc, Hilaire. *Europe and the Faith.* New York: Paulist Press, 1920.

Benedetti, Héctor Ángel. *Letras de Tangos: Antología de Tangos.* Buenos Aires: Macla, 1997.

Berger, Teresa. *Theology in Hymns?* translated by Timothy E. Kimbrough. Nashville: Kingswood Books, [1989] 1995.

Berliner, Paul F. *The Soul of Mbira.* Chicago: The University of Chicago Press, [1981] 1993.

Bevans, Stephan B. *Models of Contextual Theology.* Maryknoll, NY: Orbis Books, 1992.

Bigalke, Erich. "An Historical Overview of Southern Nguni Musical Behaviour." In *Papers Presented at the 4th Symposium on Ethnomusicology,* edited by Andrew Tracey, pp. 38-47. Grahamstown, South Africa: ILAM, Rhodes University, October 7-8, 1983.

Bishop, Selma L. *Isaac Watts: Hymns and Spiritual Songs 1707-1748.* London: The Faith Press, 1962.

Black, Kathy. *Culturally-Conscious Worship.* St. Louis: Chalice Press, 2000.

Blacking, John. *How Musical Is Man?* Seattle: University of Washington Press, 1973.

———. "Music Is Multimedia Communication." *WACC [World Association for Christian Communication] Journal* 26:2 (1979): 3-6.

———. *Music, Culture and Experience: Selected Papers of John Blacking,* edited by Reginald Byron. Chicago: University of Chicago Press, 1995.

Blackwell, Albert L. *The Sacred in Music.* Louisville: Westminster John Knox Press, 1999.

Bohlman, Philip V. "Representation and Cultural Critique in the History of Ethnomusicology." In *Comparative Musicology and Anthropology of Music: Essays on the History of Ethnomusicology,* edited by Bruno Nettl and Philip V. Bohlman, pp. 131-151. Chicago: University of Chicago Press, 1991.

Book of Common Worship. Louisville: Westminster/John Knox Press, 1993.

Boyer, Horace Clarence, ed. *Lift Every Voice and Sing II: An African American Hymnal.* New York: The Church Pension Fund, 1993.

Bradley, Ian. *Abide with Me: The World of Victorian Hymns.* London: SCM Press, 1997.

———. *Columba: Pilgrim and Penitent.* Glasgow: Wild Goose Publications, 1996.

———. *The Celtic Way.* London: Darton, Longman and Todd, Ltd., 1993.

Bradshaw, Paul F. "The Homogenization of Christian Liturgy—Ancient and Modern: Presidential Address," *Studia Liturgica* 26:1 (1996): 1-15.

———. *The Search for the Origins of Christian Worship.* New York: Oxford University Press, 1992.

———. *Two Ways of Praying.* Nashville: Abingdon Press, 1995.

Braley, Bernard. *Hymnwriters I, II, III*. London: Stainer & Bell, 1987, 1989, 1991.

Bria, Ion, and Dagmar Heller, eds. *Ecumenical Pilgrims: Profiles of Pioneers in Christian Reconciliation*. Geneva: WCC Publications, 1995.

Brother Jean Marie. "Prayer and Song in Taizé: Opening the Doors to an Inner Life." *Ecumenism* 31:124 (December 1996): 16-18.

Browning, Barbara. *Samba: Resistance in Motion*. Bloomington: Indiana University Press, 1995.

Bugallo, Rubén Pérez. *Catálogo Ilustrado de Instrumentos Musicales Argentinos*. Buenos Aires: Biblioteca de Cultura Popular, Ediciones del Sol, 1993.

Cane, Thomas A. *¡Fiesta! Celebrations at San Fernando*. New York: Paulist Press, 1999.

————. *The Dancing Church of the South Pacific*. New York: Paulist Press, 1998.

————. *The Dancing Church: Video Impressions of the Church in Africa*. New York: Paulist Press, n.d.

Cardenal, Ernesto. *The Gospel According to Solentiname*, vol. 1. Maryknoll, NY: Orbis Books, 1976.

Carmichael, Alexander. *Carmina Gadelica: Hymns and Incantations*. Edinburgh: Floris Books, 1992.

Carter, Sydney. *Green Print for Song*. London: Stainer & Bell, [1969] 1974.

Cartford, Gerhard, ed. *Libro de Liturgia y Cántico*. Minneapolis: Augsburg Fortress, 1998.

Cedeño, Rafel, ed. *Cantos de Vida, Amor y Libertad*. Buenos Aires: Madres de Plaza de Mayo, 1985.

Chandler, Paul-Gordon. *God's Global Mosaic: What We Can Learn from Christians Around the World*. Downers Grove, IL: InterVarsity Press, 1997.

Chenoweth, Vida. *Melodic Perception and Analysis*. Ukarumpa, Papua New Guinea: Summer Institute of Linguistics, 1972.

Chernoff, John Miller. *African Rhythm and African Sensibility: Aesthetics and Social Action in African Musical Idioms*. Chicago: University of Chicago Press, 1979.

Chilcote, Paul W. "A Singing and Dancing Church: Methodist Worship in Kenya and Zimbabwe." In *The Sunday Service of the Methodists*, edited by Karen B. Westerfield-Tucker, pp. 227-253. Nashville: Abingdon Press, 1996.

Christensen, Dieter. "Erich M. von Hornbostel, Carl Stumpf, and the Institutionalization of Comparative Musicology." In *Comparative Musicology and Anthropology of Music: Essays on the History of Ethnomusicology*, edited by Bruno Nettl and Philip V. Bohlman, pp. 201-209. Chicago: University of Chicago Press, 1991.

Chupungco, Anscar J. *Cultural Adaptation of the Liturgy*. New York: Paulist Press, 1982.

————. "Eucharist in the Early Church and Its Cultural Settings." In *Worship and Culture in Dialogue*, edited by S. Anita Stauffer, pp. 83-102. Geneva: Lutheran World Federation, 1994.

————. "Liturgy and the Components of Culture." In *Worship and Culture in Dialogue*, edited by S. Anita Stauffer, pp. 153-165. Geneva: Lutheran World Federation, 1994.

————. *Liturgical Inculturation: Sacramentals, Religiosity, and Catechesis.* New York: Paulist Press, 1992.

————. *Liturgies of the Future: The Process and Methods of Inculturation.* New York: Paulist Press, 1989.

————. *Worship: Progress and Tradition.* Beltsville, MD: The Pastoral Press, 1995.

Clifford, James. *The Predicament of Culture.* Cambridge: Harvard University Press, 1988.

Cobb, Jr., Buell E. *The Sacred Harp: A Tradition and Its Music.* Athens: University of Georgia Press, [1978] 1989.

Coe, Shoki. "Contextualization as the Way Toward Reform." *Theological Education* 9:4 (Summer 1973): 233-243.

————. *Recollections and Reflections.* 2nd ed. New York: The Rev. Dr. Shoki Coe Memorial Fund, and Tainan: Formosan Christians for Self-Determination, 1993.

Constitution on the Sacred Liturgy. Collegeville, MN: Liturgical Press, 1963.

Cooke, Bernard J. "Body and Mystical Body: The Church as Communio." In *Bodies of Worship: Explorations in Theory and Practice,* edited by Bruce T. Morrill, pp. 39-50. Collegeville, MN: The Liturgical Press, 1999.

Cooke, Deryck. *The Language of Music.* London: Oxford University Press, 1959.

Coplan, David B. *In Township Tonight! South African's Black City Music and Theatre.* New York: Longman, 1985.

Costas, Orlando E. *Christ Outside the Gate: Mission Beyond Christendom.* Maryknoll, N.Y.: Orbis Books, 1982.

Costen, Melva Wilson. *African American Christian Worship.* Nashville: Abingdon Press, 1993.

————. "Published Hymnals in the Afro-American Tradition." *The Hymn* 40:1 (January 1989): 7-13.

Dale, D. *A Basic English-Shona Dictionary.* Harare: Mambo Press, 1975.

————. *Duramazwi: A Shona-English Dictionary.* Harare: Mambo Press, [1981] 1983.

Dargie, David. "A Framework for Theory of African Music." Unpublished paper, ca. 1988.

————. "African Church Music, Old and New." *WACC [World Association for Christian Communication] Journal* 26:2 (1979): 18-21.

————. "African Sunday II Listener's Guide." *African Sunday II.* Delmenville, South Africa: Lumko Institute, 1988.

————. "Africa Sunday II," no. 126. Delmenville, South Africa: Lumko Missiological Institute, 1990.

————. "African Church Music and Liberation." In *Papers Presented at the 3rd Symposium on Ethnomusicology,* edited by Andrew Tracey, pp. 9-14. Durban: University of Natal, September 16-19, 1982.

————. "African Methods of Music Education—Some Reflections." *African Music* 7:3 (1996): 30-43.

————. "A New Kind of Missionary." Unpublished paper, 1979.

————. "A Song for Dukwana." *East London Daily Dispatch* (December 14, 1995).

———. "Group Composition and Church Music." In *Papers Presented at the Symposium on Ethnomusicology* (Grahamstown: Rhodes University, October 10-11, 1980), pp. 10-13.

———. *Lumko Hymnbook: African Hymns for the Eucharist.* Delmenville, South Africa: Lumko Institute, 1991.

———. *Make and Play Your Own Musical Bow.* Hogsback, South Africa, 1995.

———. "Methods of Teaching African Music: A Report on Some Experiments." *Symposium on Ethnomusicology* 13. University of Zululand, ca. 1996, pp. 1-8.

———. "Musical Bows in Southern Africa." *Africa Insight* 16:1 (1986): 42-52.

———, coll. *New Church Music in Zulu.* Lady Frere, South Africa: Lumko Music Department, 1980.

———. Personal communication. March 21, 2000.

———. Personal communication. November 1-8, 1998.

———. Personal correspondence. May 7, 1999.

———, ed. *Sesotho Church Music Collection.* Lady Frere, South Africa: Lumko Music Department, 1978.

———. "Significance in Songs: A Look at Three Traditional Xhosa Songs." *Symposium on Ethnomusicology* 14. Rhodes University, ca. 1997.

———. *Sing an African Song.* Hogsback, South Africa, 1994.

———. "Thank God for Music of uMdengentonga." *East London Daily Dispatch* (July 11, 1997).

———. "The Beloved B ka T: Benjamin Peter John Tyamzashe." *East London Daily Dispatch* (May 30, 1997).

———. "The Great Song." *East London Daily Dispatch* (September 2, 1995).

———. "The Music of Ntsikana." *South African Journal of Musicology* 2 (1982): 7-26.

———. "Thinking Back to Tiyo Soga." *East London Daily Dispatch* (June 13, 1997).

———. *Umngokolo.* Hogsback, South Africa, ca. 1993.

———. "Woman with the Baby on Her Back." *East London Daily Dispatch* (November 30, 1995).

———. *Workshops for Composing Local Church Music: Methods for Conducting Music Workshops in Local Congregations,* no. 40. Delmenville, South Africa: Lumko Missiological Institute, 1983.

———. "Xhosa Church Music." *Music and the Experience of God,* edited by David Power, Mary Collins, and Mellonee Burnim, pp. 62-69. Edinburgh: T. & T. Clark Ltd., 1989.

———, ed. *Xhosa Church Music Collection.* Lady Frere, South Africa: Lumko Music Department, 1978.

———. *Xhosa Music: Its Techniques and Instruments with a Collection of Songs.* Cape Town: David Philip, 1988.

———. "Xhosa Music: The Most Natural Music in the World." *The Talking Drum: Southern African Music Educators' Society Newsletter* 7 (May 1997): 10-12.

———. *Xhosa Zionist Church Music.* University of Zululand, 1987.

Davies, Oliver, and Fiona Bowie. *Celtic Christian Spirituality: An Anthology of Medieval and Modern Sources.* London: SPCK, 1995.

Dawn, Marva L. *Reaching Out without Dumbing Down: A Theology of Worship for This Urgent Time.* Grand Rapids: Eerdmans Publishing Company, 1995.

de Waal, Esther. "The Celtic Way of Prayer." *Cistercian Studies Quarterly* 32:3 (1997): 367-377.

————, ed. *The Celtic Vision.* London: Darton, Longman and Todd, 1988.

Delgado, Conchita, ed. *Cáliz de Bendiciones: Himnario Discipulos de Cristo.* St. Louis: Christian Board of Publications, 1996.

Dewey, John. *Art as Experience.* New York: Capricorn Books, 1934.

Diallo, Yaya, and Mitchell Hall. *The Healing Drum: African Wisdom Teachings.* Rochester, VT: Destiny Books, 1989.

Dix, Dom Gregory. *The Shape of Liturgy.* Westminster: Dacre Press, 1945.

Driver, Tom. *The Magic of Ritual: Our Need for Liberating Rites That Transform Our Lives and Our Communities.* San Francisco: HarperCollins Publishers, 1991.

Duck, Ruth. *Dancing in the Universe: Hymns and Songs.* Chicago: GIA Publications, 1992.

Echeverría, Esteban. "The Slaughterhouse." In *The Borzoi Anthology of Latin American Literature from the Time of Columbus to the Twentieth Century,* vol. 1, translated by Angel Flores and edited by Emir Rodríguez Monegal, pp. 209-222. New York: Alfred A. Knopf, 1992.

Empereur, James L. "The Physicality of Worship." In *Bodies of Worship: Explorations in Theory and Practice,* edited by Bruce T. Morrill, pp. 137-155. Collegeville, MN: The Liturgical Press, 1999.

England, John C. "Early Asian Christian Writings, 5th-12th Centuries: An Appreciation." *The Asia Journal of Theology* 11:1 (April 1997): 154-171.

England, John C., and Archie C. C. Lee, eds. *Doing Theology with Asian Resources: Ten Years in the Formation of Living Theology in Asia.* Auckland, New Zealand: The Programme for Theology and Culture in Asia, 1993.

Eskew, Harry, and Hugh McElrath. *Sing with Understanding.* 2nd ed. Nashville: Church Street Press, [1980] 1995.

Farlee, Robert Buckley, ed. *Leading the Church's Song.* Minneapolis: Augsburg Fortress, 1998.

Fassler, Margot, and Peter Jeffrey. "Christian Liturgical Music from the Bible to the Renaissance." In *Sacred Sound and Social Change: Liturgical Music in Jewish and Christian Experience,* edited by Lawrence A. Hoffman and Janet R. Walton, pp. 84-123. Notre Dame: University of Notre Dame Press, 1992.

Ferguson, Ronald. *Chasing the Wild Goose: The Story of the Iona Community.* Glasgow: Wild Goose Publications, 1998.

Flood, Samuel A. *The Power of Black Music.* New York: Oxford University Press, 1995.

Flor y Canto. Oregon Catholic Press, 1989.

Foley, Edward. *Foundations of Christian Music: The Music of Pre-Constantinian Christianity.* Washington, D.C.: The Pastoral Press, 1992.

————. *Ritual Music: Studies in Liturgical Musicology.* Beltsville, MD: The Pastoral Press, 1995.

Ford, Paul. *By Flowing Waters: Chant for the Liturgy.* Collegeville, MN: Liturgical Press, 1999.

Forman, Kristen, ed. *New Century Hymnal Companion: A Guide to the Hymns.* Cleveland: The Pilgrim Press, 1998.

Francis, Mark R. "Liturgical Inculturation in the United States and the Call to Justice." In *Living No Longer for Ourselves: Liturgy and Justice in the Nineties,* edited by Kathleen Hughes and Mark R. Francis, pp. 84-101. Collegeville, MN: The Liturgical Press, 1991.

————. *Liturgy in a Multicultural Community.* Collegeville, MN: Liturgical Press, 1991.

Fyock, Joan A., comp. "Mary K. Oyer." *Hymnal Companion.* Elgin, IL: Brethren Press; Newton, KS: Faith and Life Press; Scottdale, PA: Mennonite Publishing House, 1996.

Gans, Herbert. *Popular Culture and High Culture.* New York: Basic Books, 1974.

Gardner, Howard. *Frames of Mind: The Theory of Multiple Intelligences.* New York: Basic Books, 1983.

Gaston, E. Thayer. *Music in Therapy.* New York: The Macmillan Company, 1968.

Gather. Chicago: G.I.A. Publications, 1988.

Geertz, Clifford. *The Interpretation of Cultures.* New York: Basic Books, 1975.

González, Justo L. *Mañana: Christian Theology from a Hispanic Perspective.* Nashville: Abingdon Press, 1990.

————. *Santa Biblia: The Bible Through Hispanic Eyes.* Nashville: Abingdon Press, 1996.

Goody, Jack. *The Domestication of the Savage Mind.* New York: The Cambridge University Press, 1977.

————. *The Power of Written Tradition.* Washington: The Smithsonian Institution Press, 2000.

Gordon, Edwin E. *Sequence and Patterns in Music.* Rev. ed. Chicago: G.I.A. Publications, [1976] 1977.

————. *The Psychology of Music Teaching.* Englewood Cliffs, NJ: Prentice-Hall, 1971.

Grimes, Ronald. *Beginnings in Ritual Studies.* Lanham, MD: University Press of America, 1982.

Gutiérrez-Achón, Raquel, ed. *Himnario y Libro de Adoración.* Geneva Press and Westminster John Knox Press, 1999.

Hall, Edward T. *Understanding Cultural Differences.* Yarmouth, ME: Intercultural Press, 1990.

Hanslick, Eduard. *The Beautiful in Music,* trans. J. Cohen. New York: Liberal Arts Press, [1891] 1957.

Harling, Per. Personal conversation. August 22, 1998, Buenos Aires, Argentina.

Harper, John. *The Forms and Orders of Western Liturgy from the Tenth to the Eighteenth Century.* Oxford: Clarendon Press, 1991.

Hawn, C. Michael. "Ecumenical and Global Congregational Song in the Late Twentieth Century." In *Companion to the New Century Hymnal: A Guide to the Hymn*,
edited by Kristen Forman, pp. 199-207. Cleveland: The Pilgrim Press, 1998.

———. "Form and Ritual: A Comparison between Sequential and Cyclic Musical
Structures and Their Use in Liturgy." In *Anál Dé: The Breath of God: Music, Ritual and Spirituality*, edited by Helen Phelan, pp. 37-54. Dublin: Veritas Publications, 2001.

———. "From Center to Spectrum: Singing with the Faithful of Every Time and
Place." *The Hymn* 51:1 (January 2000): 28-35.

———. *Halle, Halle: We Sing the World Round.* Garland, TX: Choristers Guild, 1999.

———. "Music, Global." In *Encyclopedia of Protestantism*, edited by Hans J.
Hillerbrand. New York, NY: Routledge, forthcoming 2003.

———. "Praying for the World: Exploring Asian Hymnody." *Reformed Worship* 52
(1999): 28-33.

———. "Praying for the World: Global Singing in Worship." *Liturgy: Assembly Song*
17:2 (2002): 19-30.

———. "Singing with the Faithful of Every Time and Place: A Proposal for Liturgical
Plurality." *Reformed Liturgy and Music* 32:1 (January 1998): 15-21.

———. "Siyahamba, South African Freedom Song." *The Chorister* 51:6 (December
1999): 23-27.

———. "Sounds of Bamboo: I-to Loh and the Development of Asian Hymns." *The
Hymn* 49:2 (April 1998): 12-24.

———. "Taizé: That Little Springtime!" *Worship Arts* 45:4 (March-April 2000): 3-5.

———. "The Consultation on Ecumenical Hymnody: An Evaluation of Its Influence
in Selected English Language Hymnals Published in the United States and Canada since 1976." *The Hymn* 47:2 (April 1996): 26-37.

———. "The Fiesta of the Faithful: Pablo Sosa and the Contextualization of Latin
American Hymnody." *The Hymn* 50:4 (October 1999): 32-45.

———. "The Fiesta of the Faithful: Praising God in Spanish." *The Chorister* 49:7 (January 1998): 11-13, 24, 25.

———. "The Rhythm of Community: Worship Songs from Africa." *Reformed Worship* 51 (1999): 33-37.

———. "The Tie That Binds: A List of Ecumenical Hymns in English Language
Hymnals Published in Canada and the United States since 1976." *The Hymn* 48:3
(July 1997): 25-37.

———. "The Wild Goose Sings: Themes in the Worship and Music of the Iona Community." *Worship* 74:6 (November 2000): 504-521.

———. "Theological Trends in Twentieth-Century Hymns in the United States." In
Companion to the New Century Hymnal: A Guide to the Hymn, edited by
Kristen Forman, pp. 177-187. Cleveland: The Pilgrim Press, 1998.

———. "Unifying the Body: World Song in Worship." *Church Music Workshop* 10:2
(May-August 2000): 4-7, 41.

————. "Vox Populi: Developing Global Song in the Northern World." *The Hymn* 46:4 (October 1995): 28-37.

————. "Worship That Transforms: A Cross-Cultural Proposal." *Journal of the Interdenominational Theological Center* 27:1/2 (Fall 1999/Spring 2000): 111-133.

————. "Worshiping with Hospitalidad: Hispanic Worship Songs from around the World." *Reformed Worship* 50 (1998), 27-33.

Hernández, José. *El Gaucho Martín Fierro*. Buenos Aires: Distribuidora Basilico S.R.L., 1997.

Himnos de Vida y Luz. Independence, MO: Herald Publishing House, 1990.

Hintze, Otto, and Carlos Puig, eds. *¡Cantad al Señor!* St. Louis: Concordia, 1991.

Hobbs, June Hadden. *"I Sing for I Cannot Be Silent": The Feminization of American Hymnody, 1870-1920*. Pittsburgh: University of Pittsburgh Press, 1997.

Hodgson, Janet. "Ntsikana's 'Great Hymn': A Xhosa Expression of Christianity in the Early 19th Century Eastern Cape." *Communications* 4 (University of Cape Town, 1980): 4.

Hoffman, Lawrence A., and Janet R. Walton, eds. *Sacred Sound and Social Change: Liturgical Music in Jewish and Christian Experience*. Notre Dame: University of Notre Dame Press, 1992.

Hofstra, Marilyn M., ed. *Voices: Native American Hymns and Worship Resources*. Nashville: Discipleship Resources, 1992.

Hood, Mantle. *The Ethnomusicologist*. New York: McGraw-Hill Book Co., 1971.

hooks, bell. *Teaching to Transgress: Education as the Practice of Freedom*. New York: Routledge, 1994.

Hornbostel, E. M., and Curt Sachs. "Systematik der Musikinstrumente." *Zeitschrift für Ethnologie* 46 (1914): 553-590.

Hove, Chenjerai. *Bones*. Harare: Baobab Books, 1988.

————. *Shadows*. Harare: Baobab Books, 1991.

Hull, Kenneth. "A Decade of Wild Goose Songs." *Reformed Liturgy and Music* 34:2 (2000): 20-34.

Hunt, T. W. *Music in Missions: Discipling through Music*. Nashville: Broadman Press, 1987.

Hustad, Donald P. *True Worship: Reclaiming the Wonder and Majesty*. Wheaton, IL: Harold Shaw Publishers and Carol Stream, IL: Hope Publishing Company, 1998.

Hymnal for the Hours. Chicago: G.I.A. Publications, 1989.

Hymns Ancient and Modern Revised. London: Hymns Ancient and Modern, Ltd., 1972.

Jackson, George Pullen. *Spiritual Folk-Songs of Early America*. New York: Dover Publications, [1937] 1964.

Janzen, John M. *Ngoma: Discourses on Healing in Central and Southern Africa*. Berkeley: University of California Press, 1992.

Julian, John. *Dictionary of Hymnology*. London: John Murray, 1892.

Kaemmer, John E. *Music in Human Life: Anthropological Perspectives on Music*. Austin: University of Texas Press, 1993.

Kane, Thomas. *The Dancing Church: Video Impressions of the Church in Africa.* New York: Paulist Press, 1992.

Kanengoni, Alexander. *Effortless Tears.* Harare: Baobab Books, 1993.

Karolyi, Otto. *Traditional African and Oriental Music.* New York: Penguin Books, 1998.

Kauffman, Robert. "African Rhythms: A Reassessment." *Ethnomusicology* 24 (1980): 393-416.

———. "Multi-part Relationships in the Shona Music of Rhodesia." Unpublished Ph.D. dissertation, University of California at Los Angeles, 1970.

———. "Multi-part Relationship in Shona Vocal Music." *Selected Reports in Ethnomusicology* 5 (1984): 145-159.

———. "Music Goes Beyond Words." *WACC [World Association for Christian Communication] Journal* 26:2 (1979): 7-9.

———. "Shona Urban Music and the Problem of Acculturation." *International Folk Music Council* 4 (1973): 47-56.

Kay, S. *Travel and Research in Caffraria.* Oxford: Oxford University Press, 1833.

Kerman, Joseph. "Ethnomusicology and 'Cultural Musicology.'" In *Contemplating Music: Challenges to Musicology*, pp. 155-181. Cambridge, MA: Harvard University Press, 1985.

Kimbrough, Jr., S T, and Carlton R. Young, eds. *Global Praise 1.* New York: GBGMusik, 1996, rev. 1997.

Kraft, Charles H. *Christianity in Culture: A Study in Dynamic Biblical Theologizing in Cross-cultural Perspective.* Maryknoll, NY: Orbis Books, 1979.

Kuzwayo, Ellen K. *African Wisdom.* Cape Town: Kwela Books, 1998.

Lamb, David. *The Africans.* New York: Vintage Books, 1983.

Lang, Bernhard. *Sacred Games: A History of Christian Worship.* New Haven, CT: Yale University Press, 1997.

Langer, Susanne. *Feeling and Form.* New York: Charles Scribner's Sons, 1953.

———. *Mind: An Essay on Human Feeling*, vol. 1. Baltimore: Johns Hopkins Press, 1967.

Langford, Andy. *Transitions in Worship: Moving from Traditional to Contemporary.* Nashville: Abingdon, 1999.

Lathrop, Gordon. *Holy People: A Liturgical Ecclesiology.* Minneapolis: Fortress Press, 1999.

Law, Eric H. F. *The Wolf Shall Dwell with the Lamb: A Spirituality for Leadership in a Multicultural Community.* St. Louis: Chalice Press, 1993.

Leaver, Robin. "Theological Dimensions of Mission Hymnody: The Counterpoint of Cult and Culture." In *The Hymnology Annual*, vol. 1, edited by Vernon Wicker, pp. 37-50. Berrien Springs, MI: Vande Vere Publishing Ltd., 1991.

Leslau, Charlotte, and Wolf Leslau, comp. *African Proverbs.* New York: Peter Pauper Press, 1962.

Liesch, Barry. *The New Worship.* Grand Rapids: Baker Books, 1996.

Lihamba, Amandina. "Health and the African Theatre." *Review of African Political Economy* 36 (September 1986).

Lim, Swee Hong. "A Brief Survey of Asian Indigenous Hymnody." In *Companion to the New Century Hymnal: A Guide to the Hymn*, edited by Kristen Forman, pp. 146-153. Cleveland: The Pilgrim Press, 1998.

Loh, I-to, ed. *African Songs of Worship*. Geneva: World Council of Churches, 1986.

————. "Asian Worship." In *The Complete Library of Christian Worship*, vol. 7: *The Ministries of Christian Worship*, edited by Robert Webber, pp. 217-221. Nashville: Star Song Publishing Group, 1994.

————, ed. *Ban-bîn Siong-chàn*. Tainan, Taiwan: Department of Church Music, Tainan Theological Seminary, 1995.

————. "Contemporary Issues in Inculturation, Arts and Liturgy: Music." In *The Hymnology Annual: An International Forum on the Hymn and Worship*, edited by Vernon Wicker, vol. 3, pp. 47-56. Berrien Springs, MI: Vande Vere Publishing Ltd., 1993.

————. Personal communication. June 15-21, 1996, and April, 1999.

————. Personal conversation. June 20, 1996.

————. Personal correspondence. December 19, 2001.

————. Personal correspondence. November 22, 1996.

————. *Sound the Bamboo*. Christian Conference of Asia, [1990] 2000.

————. "'Sound the Bamboo'—The CCA Hymnal: A Survey of its Texts and Musical Styles." *Asian Journal of Theology* 11:2 (1997): 293-307.

————. "Taiwan." In *The New Grove Dictionary of Music and Musicians*, edited by Stanley Sadie, vol. 18, pp. 529-533. London: Macmillan Publishers Limited, 1980.

————. "Toward Contextualization of Church Music in Asia." In *The Hymnology Annual: An International Forum on the Hymn and Worship*, edited by Vernon Wicker, vol. 1, pp. 89-114. Berrien Springs, MI: Vande Vere Publishing Ltd., 1991.

————. "Transmitting Cultural Traditions in Hymnody." *Church Music Workshop* 4:3 (September-December 1994): 1-11.

————. "Tribal Music of Taiwan: With Special Reference to the Ami and Puyuma Styles." Unpublished Ph.D. dissertation, University of California, Los Angeles, 1982.

Loh, Sian-chhun, ed. *Sèng-Si*. Tainan, Taiwan: Presbyterian Church of Taiwan, 1964.

Lomax, Alan. *Folksong Style and Culture*. Washington, D.C.: American Association for the Advancement of Science, Publication No. 88, 1968.

————. *The Folksongs of North America*. New York: Dolphin Books, [1960] 1975.

Lorenz, Ellen Jane. *Glory, Hallelujah! The Story of the Campmeeting Spiritual*. Nashville: Abingdon Press, 1980.

Lovelance, Austin C. *The Anatomy of Hymnody*. Chicago: G.I.A. Publications, 1965.

Lyke, James P., ed. *Lead Me, Guide Me: The African American Catholic Hymnal*. Chicago: GIA Pub., 1987.

MacLeod, George F. *The Whole Earth Shall Cry Glory: Iona Prayers by Rev. George F. MacLeod*. Glasgow: Wild Goose Publications, 1985.

Malm, William P. *Music Cultures of the Pacific, the Near East and Asia*. Englewood Cliffs, NJ: Prentice-Hall, 1967.

Mandela, Nelson. *Long Walk to Freedom.* Boston: Little & Brown, 1994.

Markun, Patricia M. "A Voice from South Africa: Charles Villa-Vicencio." *Woodstock Report* 23 (October 1990): 3-5.

Márkus, Gilbert. "The End of Celtic Christianity." *Epworth Review* 24:3 (July 1997): 45-55.

Marshall, Madeleine Forell. *Common Hymnsense.* Chicago: GIA Publications, 1995.

Martínez, Raquel Mora. *Mil Voces para Celebrar: Himnario Metodista.* Nashville: United Methodist Publishing House, 1996.

Mathabane, Mark. *Kaffir Boy.* New York: Collier Books, 1986.

Matsikenyiri, Patrick, comp. and arr. *Africa Praise Songbook: Songs from Africa,* edited by S T Kimbrough, Jr., and Carlton R. Young. New York: GBGMusik, 1998.

Matsikenyiri, Patrick, and Maggie Hamilton, comp. *Sing! Zimbabwe.* Harare: Ecumenical Arts Association, 1998).

Maule, Graham. Personal correspondence, March 10, 1999.

————. Personal correspondence, October 3, 2000.

Maynard-Reid, Pedrito U. *Diverse Worship: African-American, Caribbean and Hispanic Perspectives.* Downers Grove, IL: InterVarsity Press, 2000.

Mazrui, Ali A. *The Africans: A Triple Heritage.* Boston: Little, Brown, and Company, 1986.

Mbiti, John S. *Introduction to African Religion.* London: Heinemann Educational Books, 1975.

McAllester, David P. "Some Thoughts on 'Universals' in World Music." *Ethnomusicology* 15:3 (September 1971): 379-380.

McClain, William. *Come Sunday: The Liturgy of Zion.* Nashville: Abingdon Press, 1990.

McCrea, Barbara, and Tony Pinchuck. *Zimbabwe & Botswana: The Rough Guide.* New York: Penguin Books, 1996.

McCullum, Hugh. "You're in the Deadly Centre." *Jubilee* 3 (December 7, 1998): 7.

McKinnon, James. *Music in Early Christian Literature.* Cambridge: Cambridge University Press, 1987.

Merriam, Alan P. *The Anthropology of Music.* Evanston, IL: Northwestern University Press, 1964.

Meyer, Leonard. *Emotion and Meaning in Music.* Chicago: University of Chicago Press, 1956.

Moody, Kathleen. "Sing and Make Music in Your Heart to the Lord." *Theology and the Church* 21:2 (June 1996): 66-68.

Mostert, Noël. *Frontiers: The Epic of South Africa's Creation and the Tragedy of the Xhosa People.* Johannesburg: Pimlico, 1992.

Mphahlele, Ezekiel. "African Humanistic Thought and Belief: Background to an Understanding of African Music." In *Papers Presented at the 3rd Symposium on Ethnomusicology,* edited by Andrew Tracey, pp. 15-19. Grahamstown: International Library of African Music, September 16-19, 1982.

————. *Down Second Avenue.* London: Faber & Faber, 1959.

Murray, Erena. *In Every Corner Sing: The Hymns of Shirley Erena Murray.* Carol Stream, IL: Hope Publishing Co., 1992.

Mursell, James. *The Psychology of Music.* New York: W. W. Norton, 1937.

Nafziger, Ken. Interview. Eastern Mennonite University, Harrisonburg, Virginia, March 26, 1999.

"Nairobi Statement on Worship and Culture: Contemporary Challenges and Opportunities." In *Christian Worship: Unity in Cultural Diversity,* edited by S. Anita Stauffer, pp. 25-28. Geneva: Lutheran World Federation, 1996.

Nattiez, Jean-Jacques. *Music and Discourse: Toward a Semiology of Music,* translated by Carolyn Abbate. Princeton: Princeton University Press, [1987] 1990.

Nettl, Bruno. *Folk and Traditional Music of the Western Continents.* 2nd ed. Englewood Cliffs, NJ: Prentice-Hall, 1965.

———. *The Study of Ethnomusicology.* Chicago: University of Illinois Press, 1983.

———. *Theory and Method in Ethnomusicology.* New York: The Free Press of Glencoe, 1964.

Ngoma: dze United Methodist Church Ye Zimbabwe. Harare: Conference Board of Publications and Communications, [1964] 1995.

Niebuhr, H. Richard. *Christ and Culture.* New York: Harper & Row, Publishers, 1951.

Nketia, J. H. Kwabena. *African Music in Ghana.* Evanston: Northwestern University Press, 1963.

———. "Music in African Cultures: A Review of the Meaning and Significance of Traditional African Music." Mimeographed. Legon, Accra, Ghana: Institute of African Studies, University of Ghana, 1966.

———. *The Music of Africa.* New York: W. W. Norton, 1974.

Nolan, Albert, and Richard Broderick. *To Nourish Our Faith: The Theology of Liberation for Southern Africa.* Hilton, South Africa: A Cornerstone Book, 1987.

Nyberg, Anders, ed. *Freedom Is Coming: Songs of Protest and Praise from South Africa.* Chapel Hill, NC: Walton Music Corporation, 1984.

Nzenza-Shand, Sekai. *Songs to an African Sunset: A Zimbabwean Story.* Oakland, CA: Lonely Planet Publications, 1997.

Oduyoye, Mercy Amba. "A Letter to My Ancestors." WCC Plenary Address, Harare, Zimbabwe, December 11, 1998, Document AF 1, 7-12.

———. *Hearing and Knowing: Theological Expressions of Christianity in Africa.* Maryknoll, NY: Orbis Books, 1986.

Oliver, Roland, and J. D. Fage. *A Short History of Africa.* New York: Penguin Books, [1962] 1988.

Olsson, David L. *Church Leaders Handbook: Willow Creek Community Church.* 2nd ed. South Barrington, IL: Willow Creek Community Church, 1991, 1993.

Ong, Walter J. *Orality and Literacy: The Technologizing of the Word.* New York: Routledge, [1982] 1988.

Oyer, Mary K. "An Interview with Mary Oyer." *The Hymn* 45:1 (January 1994): 14-17.

———. "Global Music for the Churches." In *Music in Worship: A Mennonite Perspective,* edited by Bernie Neufeld, pp. 67-82. Scottsdale, PA: Herald Press, 1998.

————. "Hymnody in the Context of World Mission." In *The International Hymnology Annual*, edited by Vernon Wicker, vol. 1, pp. 51-75. Berrien Springs, MI: Vande Vere Publishing, Ltd., 1991.

————. "Introduction." *The Mennonite Hymnal*, edited by Mary Oyer, no page numbers given. Scottsdale, PA: Herald Press and Newton, KS: Faith and Life Press, 1969.

————. Personal communication, January, 1999.

————. Personal correspondence, February 27, 2002.

Parker, Alice. *Melodious Accord: Good Singing in Church.* Chicago: Liturgy Training Publications, 1991.

Paton, Alan. *Cry, the Beloved Country.* New York: Charles Scribner's Sons, 1948.

Patrologiae cursus completus, series graeca (Paris: 1857-66), *Music in Early Christian Literature*, translated by James McKinnon and edited by J.-P. Migne. New York: Cambridge University Press, 1987.

Pelikan, Jaroslav. *The Vindication of Tradition.* New Haven: Yale University Press, 1984.

Plaatje, Sol T. *Native Life in South Africa.* Randburg, South Africa: Ravan Press, [1916] 1982.

Pongweni, Alec J. C. *Shona Praise Poetry as Role Negotiation: The Battles of the Clans and the Sexes.* Harare: Mambo Press, 1996.

Porter, James. "Muddying the Crystal Spring: From Idealism and Realism to Marxism in the Study of English and American Folk Song." In *Comparative Musicology and Anthropology of Music: Essays on the History of Ethnomusicology*, edited by Bruno Nettl and Philip V. Bohlman, pp. 113-130. Chicago: University of Chicago Press, 1991.

Power, David N. "Affirmed from Under: Celtic Liturgy and Spirituality." *Studia Liturgica* 27:1 (1997): 1-32.

Praying with the Songs of Taizé. Chicago: G.I.A. Publishers, 1996.

Procter-Smith, Marjorie. *In Her Own Rite: Constructing Feminist Liturgical Traditions.* Nashville: Abingdon Press, 1989.

Prudentius. *Hymns of Prudentius.* Translated by David R. Slavitt. Baltimore: The Johns Hopkins University Press, 1996.

Public Statements. 3rd ed. Taipei, Taiwan: The General Assembly of the Presbyterian Church in Taiwan, 1995.

Quasten, Johannes. *Music in Pagan and Christian Antiquity*, translated by Boniface Ramsey. Washington, D.C.: National Association of Pastoral Musicians, 1983.

Reagon, Bernice Johnson. *We'll Understand It Better By and By: Pioneering African American Gospel Composers.* Washington: Smithsonian Institution Press, 1992.

Reid, George. *The Afro-Argentines of Buenos Aires: 1800-1900.* Madison: University of Wisconsin, 1980.

Reve, Richard. *Emergency.* Capetown: David Philip, 1964.

————. *Emergency Continued.* Cape Town: David Philip, 1990.

Ricoeur, Paul. "The Model of the Text: Meaningful Action Considered as a Text." *Social Research* 38 (Autumn 1971).

Ringer, Alexander L. "One World or None? Untimely Reflections on a Timely Musico-logical Question." In *Comparative Musicology and Anthropology of Music*, edited by Bruno Nettl and Philip V. Bohlman, pp. 187-198. Chicago: University of Chicago Press, 1991.

Ritual Song. Chicago: G.I.A. Publications, 1996.

Rojas, Juan, ed. *Celebremos su Gloria*. Miami: Libros Internacional, 1994.

Romero, Oscar. "The Church's Mission amid the National Crisis." In *Voice of the Voiceless*, translated by Michael J. Walsh, pp. 114-161. Maryknoll, NY: Orbis Books, 1985.

Rose, C. *Four Years in Southern Africa*. London: Colburn & Bentley, 1829.

Rose. "Amampondo's Spiritual Roots." *Vula* 2 (1985): 7.

Routley, Erik. *A Panorama of Christian Hymnody*. Collegeville, MN: The Liturgical Press, 1979.

―――. *The Music of Christian Hymns*. Chicago: G.I.A. Publishers, 1981.

―――, ed. *Cantante Domino: An Ecumenical Hymnbook*. Melody Edition, 4th ed. London: Bärenreiter, 1974. Full Music Edition, 1980..

Sachs, Curt. *The Wellsprings of Music*, edited by Jaap Kunst. New York: McGraw-Hill, [1961] 1965.

Saliers, Don E. *Worship and Spirituality*. 2nd ed. Akron, OH: OSL Publications, [1984] 1996.

―――. "The Integrity of Sung Prayer." *Worship* 55:4 (July 1981): 290-303.

Samovar, Larry A., Richard E. Porter, and Lisa A Stefani. *Communicating Between Cultures*. 3rd ed. Belmont, CA: Wadsworth Publishing Company, 1998.

Schattauer, Thomas, Karen Ward, and Mark Bangert. *What Does "Multicultural" Worship Look Like?* edited by Gordon Lathrop. Minneapolis: Augsburg Fortress, 1996.

Schillebeeckx, Edward. *Ministry: Leadership in the Community of Jesus Christ*. New York: Crossroad, 1981.

Schleifer, Eliyahu. "Jewish Liturgical Music from the Bible to Hasidism." In *Sacred Sound and Social Change: Liturgical Music in Jewish and Christian Experience*, edited by Lawrence A. Hoffman and Janet R. Walton, pp. 13-58. Notre Dame: University of Notre Dame Press, 1992.

Schreiter, Robert J. *Constructing Local Theologies*. Maryknoll, NY: Orbis Books, 1985.

Searle, Mark. "Private Religion, Individualistic Society, Common Worship." In *Liturgy and Spirituality in Context: Perspectives on Prayer and Culture*, edited by Eleanor Bernstein, C.S.J., pp. 27-46. Collegeville, MN: The Liturgical Press, 1990.

Seashore, Carl E. *Psychology of Music*. New York: Dover Publications, [1938] 1967.

Seeger, Charles. "Semantic, Logical, and Political Considerations Bearing upon Research into Ethnomusicology." *Ethnomusicology* 5 (1961): 77-80.

Setiloane, G. M. *Primal World Views: Christian Dialogue with Traditional Thought Forms*, edited by John B. Taylor. Ibadan, Nigeria: Daystar Press, 1976.

Sharp, Cecil J. *English Folk-Songs from the Southern Appalachians*, edited by Maud Karpeles. New York: Oxford University Press, [1932] 1973.

Shaw, William. *The Story of My Mission in South Eastern Africa.* London: Hamilton Adams, 1860.

Shorter, Aylward. *Toward a Theology of Inculturation.* Maryknoll, NY: Orbis Books, 1988.

Slobin, Mark. *Subcultural Sounds: Micromusics of the West.* Hanover, NH: University Press of New England, 1993.

Sloboda, John A. *The Musical Mind: The Cognitive Psychology of Music.* Oxford: Clarendon Press, 1985.

Slough, Rebecca J. "'Let Every Tongue, by Art Refined, Mingle Its Softest Notes with Mine': An Exploration of Hymn-Singing Events and Dimensions of Knowing." In *Religious and Social Ritual: Interdisciplinary Explorations,* edited by Michael B. Aune and Valerie DeMarinis, pp. 175-206. Albany: State University of New York Press, 1996.

————. Personal correspondence, January 18, 2002.

Soga, J. H. *The Ama-Xosa: Life and Customs.* Lovedale: Mission Press, 1931.

Song, C. S. *Tell Us Our Names: Story Theology from and Asian Perspective.* Maryknoll, NY: Orbis Books, 1984.

————. *Theology from the Womb of Asia.* Maryknoll, NY: Orbis Books, 1986.

Songs & Prayers from Taizé. Chicago: GIA Publications, 1991.

Sosa, Pablo. "Anticoncerts: An Experiment in Breaking the Music Barrier." *WACC [World Association for Christian Communication] Journal* 26:2 (1979): 32-34.

————, ed. *Cancionero Abierto,* vols. 1-5. Buenos Aires: ISEDET, 1994.

————, ed. *Cantico Nuevo.* Buenos Aires: Methopress Editorial y Grafica, 1962.

————, ed. *Todas Las Voces: Taller de Música y Liturgia en América Latina.* Costa Rica: Ediciones SEBILA, 1988.

————. "Lo Latinoamericano Nuestra Música Liturgica." In *Todas Las Voces,* edited by Pablo Sosa, pp. 71-83. San José, Costa Rica: CLAI, 1988.

————. "On Singing 'Gloria' (World Premiere in Heaven)." In *Global Praise 1: Program and Resource Book,* edited by S T Kimbrough, Jr., pp. 81-84. New York: GBGMusik, 1997.

————. Personal communication, August 17-31, 1998.

————. "Pagura ... The Singer." In *Por Eso Es Que Tenemos Esperanza: Homenaje al Obispo Federico J. Pagura,* translated by M. Aaron Hawn. Quito: CLAI, 1995.

————. "Spanish American Hymnody: A Global Perspective." In *Hymnology Annual,* edited by Vernon Wicker, vol. 3, pp. 57-70. Berrien Springs, MI: Vande Vere Publishing Ltd., 1993.

Sowell, Thomas. *Conquests and Cultures: An International History.* New York: Basic Books, 1998.

Soyinka, Wole. *The Man Died: The Prison Notes of Wole Soyinka.* New York: The Noonday Press, 1972.

————. *Aké: The Years of Childhood.* New York: Vintage Books, [1981] 1983.

Spencer, John Michael. *Black Hymnody: A Hymnological History of the African-American Church.* Knoxville: The University of Tennessee Press, 1992.

————. *Sing a New Song: Liberating Black Hymnody.* Minneapolis: Fortress Press, 1995.

————, ed. *Black Sacred Music: A Journal of Theomusicology* 7:2 (Fall 1993).

Stauffer, S. Anita. "Worship and Culture: Five Theses." *Studia Liturgica* 26:2 (1996): 323-332.

————. "Worship: Ecumenical Core and Cultural Context." In *Christian Worship: Unity in Cultural Diversity,* edited by S. Anita Stauffer, pp. 7-22. Geneva: Lutheran World Federation, 1996.

Steedman, A. *Wanderings and Adventures in the Interior of Southern Africa,* vol. 1. London: Longman, 1835.

Stillman, Amy Lu'uleialoha. "Beyond Bibliography: Interpreting Hawaiian-Language Protestant Hymn Imprints." *Ethnomusicology* 40:3 (Fall 1996): 469-488.

Storr, Anthony. *Music and the Mind.* New York: Ballantine Books, 1992.

Taylor, Mark. "Polyrhythm in Worship: Caribbean Keys to an Effective Word of God." In *Making Room at the Table: An Invitation to Multicultural Worship,* edited by Brian K. Blount and Leonora Tubbs Tisdale, pp. 108-128. Louisville: Westminster John Knox, 2001.

Taylor, Mark Kline. *Remembering Esperanza: A Cultural-Political Theology for North American Praxis.* Maryknoll, NY: Orbis Books, 1990.

Termperley, Nicholas, ed. *The Hymn Tune Index,* 4 vols. New York: Oxford University Press, 1998.

The American Heritage Electronic Dictionary. 3rd ed., version 3.0A. Houghton Mifflin Company, 1993.

The Iona Community. *The Coracle: Rebuilding the Common Life; Foundation Documents of the Iona Community.* Glasgow: Wild Goose Publications, [1938] 1988.

The Iona Community. *What Is the Iona Community?* Glasgow: Wild Goose Publications, 1988.

The Liturgy Documents: A Parish Resource. 3rd ed. Chicago: Liturgy Training Publications, 1991.

Thielen, Martin. *Ancient Modern Worship: A Practical Guide to Blending Worship Styles.* Nashville: Abingdon, 2000.

Thiong'o, Ngugi wa. *Decolonizing the Mind: The Politics of Language in African Literature.* Nairobi: Heinemann Kenya, [1981] 1986.

————. *Detained: A Writer's Prison Diary.* London: Heinemann, 1981.

————. *Petals of Blood.* London: Heinemann, 1977.

This Far by Faith: An African American Resource for Worship. Minneapolis: Augsburg Fortress, 1999.

Thornburg, John. Personal correspondence, March 22, 2002.

Thorpe, S. A. *African Traditional Religions: An Introduction.* Pretoria: University of South Africa, 1991.

Tracey, Andrew. "African Values in Music." International Library of African Music. Paper submitted for Gerhard Kubik Festschrift (1994).

————. Personal correspondence, September 16, 1999.

————. "The System of the Mbira." In *Seventh Symposium of Ethnomusicology*, pp. 43-55. Grahamstown, South Africa: International Library of African Music, 1988.

————. "Transcribing African Music in Pulse Notation." In *The International Library of African Music*, pp. 1-20. Rhodes University, Grahamstown, South Africa, 1997.

Tracey, Andrew, and Heather Tracey. Personal communication, October 31 and November 1, 1998.

Tracey, Hugh. *The Sound of Africa Series*, 2 vols. Grahamstown, South Africa: International Library of African Music, 1973.

Turner, Craig. "Panel to Preserve Culture: Countries Fear U.S. Hegemony." *Albuquerque Journal* (July 1, 1998): A 1.

Turner, Victor. "Liminality and Communitas." In *Readings in Ritual Studies*, edited by Ronald L. Grimes, pp. 511-519. Upper Saddle River, NJ: Prentice-Hall, 1996.

————. *The Anthropology of Performance*. New York: Performing Arts Journal Publications, 1986.

————. *The Ritual Process: Structure and Anti-Structure*. Ithaca, NY: Cornell Paperbacks, 1969.

Tutu, Desmond. *An African Prayer Book*. New York: Doubleday, 1995.

Unger, Sanford J. *Africa: The People and Politics of an Emerging Continent*. 3rd ed. New York: Simon and Schuster, 1989.

Vegh, Michael, ed. *Praise Hymns and Choruses: Classic Songbook*. Expanded 4th ed. Maranatha Music, 1997.

Vera, Yvonne. *Why Don't You Carve Other Animals*. Toronto: TSAR Publications, 1992.

————. *Without a Name*. Harare: Baobab Books, 1994.

Vigil, José María, and Angel Torrellas, eds. *Misas Centro Americana*. Managua: CAV-CEBES, 1988, with cassette.

Wainwright, Geoffrey. *Doxology*. New York: Oxford University Press, 1980.

Walker, Wyatt Tee. *"Somebody's Calling My Name": Black Sacred Music and Social Change*. Valley Forge, PA: Judson Press, 1979.

Warren, Michael. *Faith, Culture, and the Worshiping Community: Shaping the Practice of the Local Church*. Rev. ed. Washington, D.C.: Pastoral Press, 1993.

Watson, J. R. *The English Hymn: A Critical and Historical Study*. Oxford: Clarendon Press, 1997.

Webber, Robert. *Blended Worship: Achieving Substance and Relevance in Worship*. Peabody, MA: Hendrickson Publishers, [1994] 1996.

————. *Planning Blended Worship: The Creative Mixture of Old and New*. Nashville: Abingdon Press, 1998.

————. *Renew: Songs and Hymns for Blended Worship*. Carol Stream, IL: Hope Publishing Company, 1995.

Weber, Max. *The Rational and Social Foundations of Music*. Southern Illinois University Press, 1958.

Wesley, Charles. *Hymns for Ascension-Day and Hymns for Whitsunday*. Bristol, 1746.

————. *Hymns for Our Lord's Resurrection*. London, 1746.

————. *Hymns for the Nativity of Our Lord*. London, 1745.

————. *Hymns on the Lord's Supper.* Bristol, 1745.

Wesley, John. "A Collection of Hymns for the Use of the People Called Methodists." In *The Works of John Wesley,* vol. 7, edited by Franz Hildebrandt and Oliver Beckerlegge. Nashville: Abingdon Press, 1983.

Westermeyer, Paul. *Te Deum: The Church and Music.* Minneapolis: Augsburg Fortress Press, 1998.

————. *The Church Musician.* Rev. ed. Minneapolis: Augsburg Fortress, 1997.

White, James F. "St. Cyril of Jerusalem's Lectures on the Christian Sacraments," translated by R. W. Church. In *Documents of Christian Worship.* Louisville, KY: Westminster/John Knox Press, 1992.

Winter, Miriam Therese. "Catholic Prophetic Sound after Vatican II." In *Sacred Sound and Social Change: Liturgical Music in Jewish and Christian Experience,* edited by Lawrence A. Hoffman and Janet R. Walton, pp. 150-173. Notre Dame: University of Notre Dame Press, 1992.

Witvliet, John D. "The Spirituality of the Psalter: Metrical Psalms in Liturgy and Life in Calvin's Geneva." *Calvin Theological Journal* 32:2 (November 1997): 273-297.

————. "Theological and Conceptual Models for Liturgy and Culture." *Liturgy Digest* 3:2 (1996): 5-46.

Worship. 3rd ed. Chicago: G.I.A. Publications, 1986.

Wright, Timothy. *A Community of Joy: How to Create Contemporary Worship.* Nashville: Abingdon Press, 1994.

Wyse, Rosemary, and Clarence Hiebert, eds. *International Songbook.* Lombard, IL: Mennonite World Conference, 1978.

Yee, Russell M. "Shared Meaning and Significance in Congregational Song." *The Hymn* 48:2 (April 1997): 7-11.

Young, Carlton R. "Ethnic Minority Hymns in United States Mainline Protestant Hymnals 1940-1995: Some Qualitative Considerations." *The Hymn* 49:3 (July 1998), 17-27.

————. Personal correspondence, December 12, 2001.

————, ed. *The United Methodist Hymnal.* Nashville: United Methodist Publishing House, 1989.

Zindi, Fred. *Music Ye Zimbabwe: Zimbabwe Versus the World.* Gueru, Zimbabwe: Mambo Press, [1985] 1997.

Index of Names

Index of Subjects

Aesthetics, musical, 22-23
Africa: African National Congress. *See* ANC;
  Coptic Church in, 275; culture and music
  in, 160-63, 247, 271-72; cyclic nature of music in, 267; dance in, 275n.10; definition of
  music in, 257; diaspora of African culture
  in Americas, 248n.20, 276n.13; oral musical
  tradition in, 108-9, 116-17, 119-21, 131, 135,
  142, 167, 169-70, 172-73, 187, 247; struggles
  for independence in, 104-6, 150-56, 158, 162,
  177; Truth and Reconciliation Commission.
  See TRC; Western views of traditional music in, 112-13
African Music, 115
AIDS: in southern Africa, 153, 175
AILM (Asian Institute for Liturgy and Music), 79-80
Anamnesis, 14, 143
ANC (African National Congress), 106, 150
Animateur, 68, 100-101, 159, 242n.6. *See also*
  Cantor; Enlivener
Apartheid. *See* South Africa
Argentina: *cabecitas negras*, 35; demographics
  of, 35-36; *desaparecidos*, 39, 49, 50;
  descamisados, 38; *Madres de Plaza de Mayo*,
  39, 40, 69; politics of, 37-39; popular poetry
  of, 40; *porteños*, 35, 64
Asian Institute for Liturgy and Music. *See*
  AILM

Bias versus prejudice. *See* Culture;
  Ethnocentrism

Cabecitas negras. See Argentina
Cancionero Abierto, 60, 66-67
Cántico Nuevo, 53, 61-62
Cantor, 231, 235, 242n.6, 258. *See also*
  Animateur; Enlivener
CCA (Christian Conference of Asia), 1, 79, 80
Celtic Christianity, 189n.1, 190-96, 213-21
Christian Conference of Asia. *See* CCA
CLAI (Consejo Latinoamericano de Iglesias),
  65, 68
Cocultures. *See* Culture: cocultures
*Common Ground: A Song Book for All
  Churches*, 214
Communitas (Turner), 213
Community: and orality, 233. *See also* Music:
  and community
Composition, communal: and David Dargie,
  118-20; and John Bell, 208-9; and Pablo
  Sosa, 66; and Taizé Community, 209n.36
Consejo Latinoamericano de Iglesias. *See*
  CLAI
Contextualization: of Pablo Sosa, 60-61, 69-71;
  of Shoki Coe, 77, 79n.18
Culture: and African music, 160-63; bias versus prejudice in, 7-9; bicultural perspective,
  7; center versus periphery dichotomy in, 2-
  6; cocultures versus subcultures, 4, 7, 9, 15,
  19, 21, 49n.19, 248, 249, 253, 253n.30, 277;
  definition of (Geertz), 15; dominant, 3n.4;
  emic versus etic perspective of, 28, 29n.96;
  living beyond (Blacking), xvii, 6, 243,
  243n.8, 244, 249, 251, 274; majority, 3n.4;

Index of Hymns, Hymn Tunes, and Musical Works

CPSIA information can be obtained
at www.ICGtesting.com
Printed in the USA
LVHW110348011221
704789LV00008B/90